Arizona Heart Institute Foundation Cookbook

A Renaissance in Good Eating

Arizona Heart Institute Foundation

Phoenix, Arizona

On the Cover—see pages 31–35 for description and recipes
  James Todd Rash, Art Director
  Spencer Phippen, Artist
  Vincent Guerithault, Chef

Arizona Heart Institute Foundation, 2632 North 20th Street, Phoenix, Arizona 85006, 602–266–2200 or 1–800–835–2920.

Table of Contents

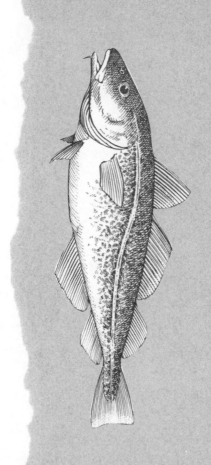

Medical Director
Edward B. Diethrich, MD

Registered Dietitian
Margaret Zukas, MS, RD

Writer
Patricia Arnold

Art Director
James Todd Rash

Illustrators
Spencer Phippen
Craig Foster

Cover Design Team
James Todd Rash, Art Director
Spencer Phippen, Artist
Vincent Guerithault, Chef

Production Team
Becky Bowman
Amy Butcher
Sue Carroll
Joyce Day
Doug Fuller
Shawn Furgason
Amii Hale
Tish Houser
Ruth Kaspar
Cassie Kemp
Tim Lindvig
Carol Ann Mesquita
Donna LaMay Newman
Traci Todaro
Donna Marie Watts
Richard Williams

Consultants
Diana Dalsass
Vincent Guerithault
Sally Rubens Kenler, MS, RD
Marilyn Majchrzak, MS, RD

reface

The Arizona Heart Institute & Foundation began setting national standards for innovative patient care with its founding in 1971. Prevention of cardiovascular disease has always been a primary objective. In the early 1970s, very few cardiologists and almost no cardiovascular surgeons made any real effort to modify the destructive factors of atherosclerosis in their patients. The Arizona Heart Institute & Foundation was an early pioneer in the treatment of heart disease through diet and exercise. The concepts developed at the Institute more than two decades ago are now practiced worldwide.

Educational programs directed at the prevention of heart disease empower people to make positive and lasting lifestyle changes. When people learn how to take charge of their lifestyles and get good medical care, heart disease can be prevented, slowed, or even reversed. Most people can improve their health just by making the commitment to take care of themselves. Programs for preventive care offered at the Arizona Heart Institute & Foundation include weight management, nutrition counseling, psychology services, stress management, smoking cessation, and behavior and lifestyle modification.

The Arizona Heart Institute Foundation Cookbook: A Renaissance in Good Eating is part of the preventive care program. Understanding the relationship between diet and health is the first step in making appropriate lifestyle changes. This cookbook teaches the principles of a heart-healthy diet and includes many recipes that prove good nutrition does not have to be boring or unpalatable—in fact, more than 100 recipes were contributed by professional chefs who believe that fine cuisine and good health are compatible goals.

The Arizona Heart Institute & Foundation believes that everyone should follow a heart-healthy diet; it should not be thought of as a restrictive list of foods that is only followed—often unhappily—by sick people. Most Americans are accustomed to a modern diet that focuses on speed and convenience, often relying on fast foods and packaged products; a heart-healthy diet primarily requires a return to more natural foods, such as whole grains and fresh fruits and vegetables (see *Food & Society* on page 1). The greatest challenge—and the greatest benefits—may be in simply reducing the amount of fat in the diet and eating more vegetables and grains. This book includes many practical, easy-to-follow tips for achieving these goals. Advice about nutrition, weight loss, exercise, cardiovascular disease, and other health topics is printed in the margins throughout the book.

Unlike many cookbooks that focus on a specific health problem, *The Arizona Heart Institute Foundation Cookbook* is also a good basic family cookbook (again, a heart-healthy diet should be the standard diet). A wealth of information about more than 100 foods and other ingredients, cooking techniques, and other culinary topics is included, making this book a valuable resource for any cook. Inexperienced cooks will find basic instructions and easy recipes; amateur chefs will enjoy trying a variety of challenging and unusual recipes, many of which were contributed by professional chefs. The wide variety of recipes forms a collection

that offers something for all tastes. Every member of the family should find new favorites, making a heart-healthy diet easy and enjoyable to follow.

The Arizona Heart Institute & Foundation is a strong advocate for children's health education, and this cookbook was designed with their needs in mind. It includes a wide variety of recipes that are easy for children to prepare and that they will enjoy eating (see "Children's recipes" in the Index). Because heart disease begins in childhood, heart-healthy habits that will help prevent cardiovascular disease should be acquired early in life. Letting children help in the kitchen encourages them to take an interest in food and how it is prepared; most children enjoy eating meals they have helped plan, cook, and serve. Cooking with a child also gives the parent many opportunities, in a companionable environment, to teach and reinforce the principles of a healthy diet.

Recipes in this book that are not attributed to chefs were contributed by Arizona Heart Institute & Foundation employees, who submitted their family favorites or developed new recipes specifically for this heart-healthy cookbook. All of these contributions were modified to some degree and then retested in home kitchens. Each of these recipes was enjoyed by the test cooks and their families.

Margo Malouf
Carol Ann Mesquita
Judy Milas, RD
Nanci Montgomery
Judy Neumueller
Donna LaMay Newman
Jayne Newmark, RD
Erica O'Boyle
Patti Olson
Reggie Ponder
Yvonne Prah
Edna Reyes
Patrice Roberts
Erika Scott
Rosita Skeete
Cathy Smith
Angela Szczublewski
Cindy Thompson
Traci Todaro
Eddie Trayler, RN
Catherine Trier
Mary Vaught, RN
Diana Washington
Paula Wasylenko, RCVT
Marcia Watson
Sue Welch, RN
Meredith Williams

Nutrition Analysis

Computer analysis by the
staff from The Christ Hospital
Cardiovascular Research Center,
2350 Auburn Avenue, Cincinnati, Ohio 45219.

Sharon Ames, RD, LD
Nutrition Data Coordinator

Suzanne Hopper, MEd, RD
Chief Nutritionist

June Minnery
Diet Technician

Alan Leach
*Data Management/
Analysis Consultant*

Continuing a Tradition

The Arizona Heart Institute Foundation Cookbook is the latest entry in a series of books and other services provided by the Arizona Heart Institute Foundation in response to widespread public demand for more information about the prevention or treatment of heart disease. Several of these publications are quoted in the margins throughout this cookbook.

Women and Heart Disease. In the past, women were often excluded from research studies on heart disease, largely because it was believed that heart disease primarily affected men and only rarely occurred in women. Recent evidence shows that once they have passed menopause, women are as susceptible to atherosclerotic disease as men. Now that the truth about women and heart disease is beginning to be understood, much research into the diagnosis and treatment of coronary artery disease and hypertension in women is underway. A nationwide effort to promote better understanding of the incidence and progress of cardiovascular diseases in women is also being made.

Recognizing the need for current information, Edward B. Diethrich, MD, the founder and medical director of the Arizona Heart Insitute & Foundation, has written *Women and Heart Disease.* This book gives proper perspective to the differences men and women experience when afflicted with heart disease, and it points out the difficulties in correctly diagnosing heart disease in women. Actual patient cases help personalize the information. A specially designed Heart Test for women is also included. *Women and Heart Disease* is available in bookstores or through the Arizona Heart Institute Foundation (1–800–345–4278).

Heart Test. When ABC's "20/20" program broadcast the "Great American Heart Test" in 1981, using the self-assessment Heart Test developed by the Arizona Heart Institute & Foundation, over a quarter of a million people sent their results to the Foundation. This landmark program inspired Dr. Diethrich's book *Heart Test,* which includes the test and the complete program for prevention of heart disease.

Heart-Healthy Lessons for Children. The Arizona Heart Institute & Foundation is a nationally recognized leader in the development of nutrition guidelines for reducing heart disease risk in adults. Now, these principles are being taught to elementary school children so they can adopt life-long healthful eating habits at an early age. *Heart-Healthy Lessons for Children* is a five-lesson course that provides basic information about the heart and blood vessels, a description of heart disease and its consequences, the risk factors for heart disease, and the principles of sound nutrition. It also discusses the importance of exercise and explains why smoking is dangerous. *Heart-Healthy Lessons for Children* has been featured on CNN news and in several major publications.

Toll-Free Hotline. New treatments and diagnostic capabilities are developing so rapidly that many people are unsure about their options for cardiac care. The Arizona Heart Institute Foundation fills this knowledge gap with a national toll-free hotline. The cardiovascular nurses who staff this hotline can answer your questions about a healthy heart or about the diagnosis and treatment of heart disease. Articles and videotapes on a variety of topics can be mailed to you at no charge. Call 1–800–345–4278 for free information, to purchase any of our publications or clay animation videos, or to schedule an appointment.

Mr. Heart Adventure Series. The Arizona Heart Institute Foundation's clay-animated videos for children and adults explain the importance of good nutrition, exercise, and heart-healthy lifestyle choices. The series includes the award-winning *Smart Heart, Couch Potato,* and *Don't Be A Spud,* starring NBA superstar Charles Barkley. These videos are shown in classrooms, often in conjunction with a touring stage show. The videos are also broadcast as public service announcements on national television.

Diagnosis & Treatment

The Arizona Heart Institute & Foundation offers the most advanced techniques available for the prompt, accurate diagnosis and treatment of cardiovascular disease. Nearly all diagnostic tests are performed on an outpatient basis, a concept pioneered by the Arizona Heart Institute & Foundation. Hospital admissions are required only for patients who have acute conditions.

Whenever possible, nonsurgical methods for treating heart disease are used. Alternatives to surgery include balloon angioplasty, intravascular stents, atherectomy, and laser procedures (for free information about these techniques, please call the toll-free hotline).

Surgical patients are admitted to the Institute's primary care partner, the Cardiovascular Center of Excellence at Healthwest Regional Medical Center. The Center contains the most modern equipment available for treating cardiovascular disease; it is continually upgraded with new technology, ensuring that patients receive state-of-the-art care.

The Arizona Heart Institute & Foundation's leadership role in developing new technologies for treating cardiovascular diseases has carried its reputation far beyond the United States. Physicians come to Phoenix from around the world to learn the techniques pioneered at this institution. Patients also represent many nationalities.

Putting You First

Above everything else, the Arizona Heart Institute & Foundation always puts patients first. Services provided for your convenience include:

- The hospitality of a private outpatient clinic
- All tests and treaments performed in one central location, usually in one day
- Acceptance of Medicare assignment
- Assistance in filing insurance claims
- Free transportation within Maricopa County
- Airport pickup—just five minutes away
- RV hook-ups
- Nearby low-cost accommodations

When I restored the 1797 Depuy Canal House 25 years ago, I didn't depend on cooking in the old stone fireplaces or on using an icebox for storage, as romantic as that might sound. Rather, I built on a modern kitchen with materials recycled from local urban renewal projects.

Similarly, traditional foods, like quinoa and amaranth grains, can be seasoned and served in unique combinations with other foods to satisfy today's adventurous eye and palate. Nouvelle cuisine creatively combined the foods of the world. However, it was often wasteful. Today restaurants seldom buy lobsters just for the tails and discard the rest. At the Depuy Canal House, we find a use for almost everything.

By using more fruits, vegetables, whole grains, and legumes, we eat healthier foods that are easier for both the individual and the environment to digest.

John Novi
Depuy Canal House

Food & Society

Utopia refers to a place of social and political perfection. Their discovery of the New World offered Europeans an unprecedented opportunity to make their utopian ideal a reality. While they fell short of this impossible goal, they did construct a social and political system that was far better than most. Over the years, Americans have continued to pursue the elusive utopian society that brought the earliest settlers to these shores—and that still attracts current-day immigrants.

As a society, our attitudes about the ideal and our expectations for the future have changed dramatically over the past 250 years. Distinct and markedly different utopian concepts have, each in turn, directed us toward new social and economic paths. These utopian and futuristic views also affected daily living, including our attitudes about food and nutrition. How we went from a diet of wholesome natural foods to highly processed foods—and where we are headed next—might be explained in terms of society's changing utopian ideals.

Spiritual Utopia

In the mid-1800s, interest in utopia was at its height. Everyone talked about it, and many people joined societies that were committed to making the utopian life a reality. During this period, the utopian concept focused on spiritual, agrarian, or communitarian values.

The Shakers founded the earliest and most successful religious communities, starting in 1787. The movement was at its peak from 1825 to the 1840s, when 6,000 members lived in 18 Shaker villages in eight states. To make their communities a Heaven on earth, they sought superiority in all things, achieving a standard of living that was well above average. Because they stressed thrift and did not tolerate waste, they invented many time- and labor-saving devices and developed methods that increased the productivity of their herds and crops. Their contributions to American life were far greater than would be expected from such a small group. The Shakers are still respected for their farsighted achievements in diet, agriculture, architecture, furniture-making, and marketing.

Their healthful diet and lifestyle enabled the Shakers to set records for long life. Plain, wholesome food eaten in moderation, emphasizing fresh vegetables and fruits, was central to the Shaker faith. Zestful eating glorified God, but waste was, of course, abhorred (outside the Shaker communities, New England parents commonly told their children to "Shaker your plate," meaning clean your plate.) The Shakers also insisted on using whole grains to make flour for bread. They were among the first to criticize millers for removing the germ from the wheat kernel before grinding it into flour.

The Reverend Sylvester Graham was another early religious advocate for whole grains. He preached against the mistreatment of the body with bad food and other evils, including salt, condiments, white bread, hot mince pie, and feather beds. Invoking a spiritual argument in support of whole grains, he taught that to remove part

of the wheat kernel was "to put asunder what God had joined together." During the 1830s, thousands of his followers formed Grahamite societies; they shopped at grocery stores that sold the foods he recommended and stayed in Grahamite hotels, which had very strict dining rooms. Graham flour (coarsely ground whole-wheat flour) was used to make graham crackers, which are still called *digestive biscuits* in England. The prototype of cold breakfast cereals, Granula, was introduced during this period by Dr. James Caleb Jackson, a Grahamite.

Up until the end of the 19th century, Americans often ate porridge, fried potatoes, steak and pie, or other greasy foods for breakfast. In the late 1890s, Dr. John Harvey Kellogg revolutionized the way Americans eat breakfast by inventing a new kind of meal. In 1865, Ellen White, a leading Seventh Day Adventist, had founded the Western Health Reform Institute, a sanitarium for church members. She gave a medical school scholarship to Kellogg and, after graduation, he returned to the sanitarium in Battle Creek, Michigan, with the intention of developing a healthier diet for his patients. As a medical student with limited funds and kitchen facilities, Kellogg had found it difficult to cook cereals (his daily breakfast consisted of seven graham crackers and an apple). As a practicing physician, he was

Health Food

The 1880s saw a national preoccupation with food and health, and the term *health food* first entered the language during this period. The expression originally referred to fad foods thought to help one toward good health, like the cold breakfast cereal revolution.

Wilbur O. Atwater, of the U.S. Department of Agriculture, was the first government official to offer dietary advice. In 1894, he observed, "How much harm is done to health by our one-sided and excessive diet no one can say. Physicians tell us that it is very great." He warned Americans against high-fat, high-sugar foods and recommended a low-fat, moderate-protein, high-complex-carbohydrate diet.

Atwater's 1895 food guide omitted fruits and vegetables, however, because they have a low calorie count. Vitamins had not been discovered, so no one knew about the nutritional value of these two food groups. Nevertheless, the benefits of some fruits and vegetables were recognized. The English navy carried limes on sea voyages as they knew (without knowing why) that citrus could prevent scurvy.

The first vitamin, A, was isolated in 1913. (Its discoverer, Elmer McCollum, also originated the idea of health-protective foods.) Scientists continued marching through the alphabet, reaching vitamin K in 1934 and niacin (one of the many B vitamins) in 1937.

Vitamin pills became popular in the 1940s. By this time, the term *health food* had been redefined to describe foods that were high in specific vitamins, minerals, protein, and other nutrients. In one of life's great ironies, these advances in nutrition knowledge were immediately followed by the technological changes and advertising campaigns that made bad diets the national norm for several decades.

determined to develop a ready-to-eat cereal. Kellogg became the owner of the institute in the mid-1870s, renaming it the Battle Creek Sanitarium; thousands of patients and health food faddists flocked to his doors. Kellogg advocated large doses of bran and developed his own line of nearly 60 health foods, beginning with Granola. Kellogg's is still a leading name in breakfast cereals.

The cereal-based health-food movement had a huge following. By 1898, for example, Ralston's Health Club boasted 800,000 members. Dr. Ralston gave his endorsement and name to many health-food products, including Purina Wheat. Dozens of ready-to-eat cold breakfast cereals, including Shredded Wheat, Grape-Nuts, Wheaties, and Cornflakes, flooded the market during this period. This health-food movement fostered a major food industry that is still thriving, although its dedication to good nutrition has been largely compromised.

Technological Utopia

In the 1880s, Edward Bellamy wrote the influential novel *Looking Backward,* which described a utopian Boston in the year 2000. One of the most widely read novels in American history, this book was directly responsible for a period of unprecedented growth in the book publishing industry. More than 200 other utopian works were published by the

turn of the century, making the utopian novel the national literary form.

During this period, the concept of utopia changed from a spiritual or communitarian basis to one of technology and science. New discoveries and new theories in every scientific field proliferated. Technological progress was confidently expected to eliminate social problems and create a perfect society. Visionaries also tried to predict the coming effects of technology on daily life—a work-free home was often a central theme.

Technological advances quickly revolutionized the food supply and home-cooking practices in America. From the 1830s to the 1930s, most Americans had iceboxes (*leftovers* became a new practice and word in the 1890s, largely because iceboxes extended food storage periods). Electric refrigerators were first sold in 1916, priced at about $900. They did not become affordable for most people until about 1930. In fact, a significant number of American homes did not have modern kitchens or even electricity in the 1930s and '40s. Electrification, including home refrigerators, was almost universal by the 1950s.

Refrigerated railroad cars were able to transport perishable foods over long distances. Local availability of fresh fruits and vegetables was no longer limited by the seasons and weather. Fresh fruits and berries were shipped from the south to the north in winter, and garden-fresh vegetables traveled from California across thousands of miles to the East. Fresh produce and meat were available year-round wherever railroad tracks were laid. By 1930, produce traveled an average of 1500 miles to market.

After 1917, Clarence Birdseye perfected an artificial fast-freezing technique for preserving produce, meat, and fish, imitating a natural food preservation practice he had learned from the Eskimos. This invention led to the creation of the vast frozen-food industry, beginning in the 1920s. During World War II, frozen foods were shipped to servicemen around the world. By the 1950s, they were in common use.

These advances in transportation and food storage led to profound changes in American diets. Previously, local food sources dictated the cooking styles of a community—giving rise to the distinctive ethnic and national cuisines of the world. Technology now made out-of-season and exotic foods (like bananas) available to the masses; they were no longer luxury items. Commercially frozen and canned foods saved housewives countless hours of work. Americans accepted greater variety in food choices and time-saving convenience foods as the clear benefits of modern science and technology. They naturally embraced these changes, and

more to follow, without question or skepticism. (The society that accepted the atom bomb as a positive image in advertising and named a bathing suit, the bikini, after an atomic test site certainly felt little reason to be concerned about mere packaged foods.)

Food manufacturers worked hard to create a national mass market for their products. Aggressive marketing through national women's magazines helped solidify the acceptance of factory-prepared, ready-to-eat foods. Americans began to accept this as a standardized national diet, designed by modern industry. Quality, freshness, and flavor were becoming less important to consumers than convenience and modernity.

Following World War II, America went through an unprecedented period of economic growth. Technological advances in manufacturing created new, high-paying jobs, enabling many factory workers to move up to the middle-class. Material goods were in abundant supply, and ordinary people had more discretionary money to spend than ever before in history. Thanks to a low birth rate during the Depression and slow population growth during the war, there were also fewer people to share in this abundance. Income distribution was fair—the middle class made up 35% of the population and earned 42% of the nation's income. Because the economy was booming and the workforce was shrinking, the changes in manufacturing and business demanded by new technology and international politics were virtually painless. Americans of that era knew that science and technology had the unquestionable power to guarantee a prosperous future.

Once people had bought all the things they had missed during the war years, advertisers had to develop new sales pitches to keep people spending. Taking advantage of the widespread conviction that technology would lead to perfection in the future, advertisers began to equate futurism with consumerism. People were encouraged to buy things not because they needed them, but because they wanted them. You could buy a better future, and Americans purchased 75% of all the cars and appliances on earth to secure that dream.

Advertisers exploited the public fascination with technology, science, and the future. Kitchen appliances, architecture, fashion, even lipstick, revealed a preoccupation with space travel and speed—exaggerated tailfins on automobiles symbolized the times. Food choices also reflected the modern life. Thousands of American children guzzled Tang—an orange-flavored instant drink—because it was promoted as the drink the astronauts took into outer space.

Swanson's introduced the first precooked frozen food, *Chicken Pot Pie,* in 1951. The first complete frozen meal on an aluminum tray, Swanson's heat-and-serve turkey dinner, debuted in 1953, just about the time that televisions became widely available. Taking advantage of the new American craze for eating in front of the TV, the C.A. Swanson company obtained the trademark name *TV Dinner* for its frozen meals. These convenience foods, served on TV trays, met the needs of modern families as television became the center of the household. Children became an economic force—for the first time in history—when advertisers began targeting them with television commercials for toys, snacks, and breakfast foods.

The percentage of income Americans spent on food increased in the 1950s. Packaged convenience foods—including canned goods, frozen dinners, box mixes, instant soups and drinks, and snacks—accounted for the largest part of this increase. These manufactured foods commanded much higher prices than their ingredients warranted. Because of their profitability, the food industry became the most aggressive marketing force of the time. A tremendous range of ready-to-eat and convenience foods entered the market. Products with names like *cheeze* and *froot* were accepted as real foods. Nutrition had little or no importance in the food choices Americans made. Americans loved back-of-the-box recipes, instant mixes, and fast-food restaurants. They wanted something modern, easy, and fun to eat.

Food attitudes began changing in the 1960s. Economic prosperity enabled many ordinary people to travel abroad, and thousands had lived in other countries while in the military. These Americans were exposed to real food and delicious ethnic dishes. Julia Child's cooking show on television brought haute cuisine to the masses and created an enormous popular interest in gourmet cooking. *She cooked from scratch!* She didn't need canned goods or box mixes, and she gave thousands of people the desire and confidence to learn how to cook with real food for themselves.

Freshness, flavor, and quality became important again. Nutrition was still poorly understood, however. Butter, eggs, cream, red meat, and other high-fat foods held a large place in the new culinary scene. For the most part, only hippies on communes and "health-food nuts" were interested in whole grains, fresh produce, and vegetarian diets—they were outside mainstream America.

The New Utopia

By the 1970s, technology had begun to lose its appeal. It was clear that, far from guaranteeing social gain, technology was more likely to kill us. The threat of nuclear war and global destruction was ever-present. Industrial pollutants had damaged land, sea, and air. Science fiction literature and films—gloriously and positively optimistic in earlier years—now envisioned a dark and bleak future. Mutant monsters, scientists run amok, and last-man-and-woman-on-earth themes became common. In real life, thalidomide babies, Love Canal, and a succession of other nasty shocks made Americans increasingly unwilling to accept high-tech "advances" without question or skepticism.

Jerome Rodale introduced the term *organic food* in 1948 to describe food grown without chemical fertilizers and insecticides, in an early campaign to discourage their use. Rachel Carson's best-selling book *Silent Spring* brought the chilling consequences of pesticide use to the attention of the general public in 1962. Mercury in seafood, red dye #2, and other problems also heightened concerns about the quality, safety, and availability of food. Americans have begun to reject growing and food processing techniques that use pesticides, growth hormones, preservatives, and other chemicals. Following recent reports about Alar and cancer, they refused to buy apples treated with this chemical, causing enormous financial losses for apple growers. They now question the sale of unlabeled genetically engineered foods.

The future isn't what it used to be.

Arthur C. Clarke

Pure Food

I founded the Coalition because I wanted to be sure food is as safe to eat as it is tasty. It is not for me to hold up the future of biotechnological food sciences or to stand in the way of progress. It is for me to fulfill my obligations and meet my own responsibilities. As a chef, I am responsible for every plate of food that is served to every one of my patrons, and I want to know what's on it. I am committed to this obligation to my customers, who put their dietetic, allergic, and religious confidence in my hands.

Because federal policy does not require safety testing of all genetically engineered foods and will not require them to be labeled, I am not being permitted to fulfill that obligation. How can I be sure that a tomato's gene pool does not contain a food that someone has a concern about? A label that lists all of the food genes in the new tomato would eliminate that risk.

I must trust that all consumables served to my customers are safe, pure, nutritious, and of the best quality available to me. I know and understand what Mother Nature has intended with regard to foods, and I trust in that. I am not yet convinced that bioengineered foods deserve that same trust. Until I am, I would like to be able to choose not to serve them.

Rick Moonen
Chef's Coalition for
Pure Food Campaign

The new utopian ideal will apparently be based on environmental issues, with food safety and availability an important objective. Humanitarian considerations will also be emphasized—for example, the people have demanded laws that require fishermen to use dolphin-safe methods for harvesting tuna. Much work, and tremendous expense, will be needed to restore the environment and the fruits of the earth to their former, safer state.

The food preferences Americans acquired in this century probably kill 300,000 to 400,000 people a year. Eight of the ten leading causes of death are associated with poor diet. Heart disease, cancer, stroke, diabetes, and atherosclerosis account for more than two-thirds of all deaths in America. Overconsumption of fat is thought to be one of the chief culprits. High-fat, high-sodium, high-cholesterol, and highly refined and processed foods are now recognized as injurious to health. Consumers are beginning to reject these choices in favor of whole grains and fresh produce, and they are reducing the amount of fatty red meat, butter, cream, eggs, and other fats in their diets.

Highly processed foods are not likely to disappear from American grocery stores. In response to consumer demand for fresh, wholesome, healthful foods, however, most food manufacturers now include so-called all-natural, low-sodium, low-fat, high-fiber, low-cholesterol, or low-calorie items in their product lines (there's even a claim for a "healthier" Twinkie). Packaging boldly, sometimes misleadingly, proclaims these new attributes. Fast-food restaurants aggressively compete for customers who want low-fat, low-sodium meals. In the 1950s, none of these issues interested the average consumer at all.

Nutritionally acceptable frozen, canned, and other convenience foods have commanded a significant, and growing, amount of shelf space in supermarkets. Many foods that were not seen in neighborhood stores of the 1950s are now widely available. Exotic fruits and vegetables like star fruit, kiwis, arugula, and radicchio are commonplace. Nutritious grains like amaranth, quinoa, couscous, bulgar wheat, and barley are growing in popularity. The demand for organically grown produce and free-range poultry is increasing. Many foods and ingredients previously stocked only in health-food stores are readily available in ordinary supermarkets.

A Renaissance in Good Eating

Better understanding of the relationship between diet and health has led to sweeping revision of the dietary recommendations made by nutritionists as well as the federal government. The United States Department of Agriculture's new Food Guide Pyramid (see *Food & Health* on page 12) emphasizes whole grains, vegetables, and fruits while minimizing fats and animal proteins. This new approach to meal planning is actually a return to the way most people ate before technology intervened. Statistics often show that the incidence of certain diseases, including heart disease, is generally higher in industrialized nations; the lower rates in some other countries are often attributed to their traditional diets (minimally processed foods that are low in fat) and less stressful lifestyles. America's renewed interest in age-old food choices (such as quinoa, the staple food of the Incas) is expected to reap significant health benefits in the years to come.

The Arizona Heart Institute Foundation Cookbook celebrates this renaissance in good eating. Naturally seasoned fresh ingredients are the basis for these recipes. Many newly available exotic foods (commonplace ingredients in far-away countries and long-ago societies) are featured. Unfashionable but nutritious foods like rutabagas and parsnips are given a starring role in delicious new ways. Helpful information about how to select, store, and serve these ingredients for maximum flavor and nutritional benefit is included. The true flavors of real foods dominate the final dishes because fat, salt, and artificial ingredients are downplayed. Creative seasonings with herbs, spices, and other natural flavorings that complement the food are emphasized.

Next to brandy, lard is the greatest curse civilized man has brought to the Indian.

Carl Lumholtz
New Trails in Mexico
1912

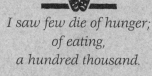

Food & Health

Eight of the ten leading causes of death in the United States are linked to improper diet, including heart disease, cancer, stroke, diabetes, and atherosclerosis. About half of all deaths in the United States are the result of cardiovascular disease, which affects more than 68,000,000 Americans in one form or another, including high blood pressure, coronary heart disease, and stroke. Many cancers are also related to diet—40% of all cancers in men and nearly 60% in women. About one-third of all deaths from breast, colon, and prostate cancer may be attributed to high-fat and low-fiber diets.

Health-care costs are driven up by lifestyle choices that promote disease and injury. On average, it costs $30,000 to treat a patient who has heart disease, which can usually be prevented by appropriate diet and exercise. Treating a smoker for lung disease costs $29,000. The effects of alcoholism cost $250,000 per patient, and drug abuse costs $66,000 per patient. All of these problems are avoidable, yet only 3% of America's health-care dollars is spent on preventing disease. At a time when Americans are gravely worried about the ever-increasing costs of health care, it makes sense to adopt no-cost preventive measures—including diet, exercise, smoking cessation, and limited alcohol consumption—that can save billions of dollars in medical care.

A nutritious diet promotes overall good health and can help reduce the risk of developing chronic disease. The dietary guidelines of the Arizona Heart Institute & Foundation are designed to help you achieve these objectives.

Cardiovascular Risk Factors

Cardiovascular risk factors are conditions that increase the chance that a person will develop heart disease. The three greatest risk factors for cardiovascular disease that can be controlled are cigarette smoking, high blood pressure, and high blood cholesterol. Most other risk factors can also be managed (obesity, lack of exercise, diabetes, and stress), but a few are beyond your control (age, sex, race, and family history of heart disease). Having any one risk factor increases your likelihood of developing cardiovascular problems; this likelihood increases as the number of risk factors increases.

Several risk factors are closely tied to diet, weight, and exercise. Most nutrition experts advise that reducing cholesterol and saturated fat is the most effective dietary step you can take for improving your health.

Cholesterol. Cholesterol, a fat-like substance produced by the liver, is necessary for normal biological function. It is an essential part of all cell membranes and a major component of brain and nerve cells. Cholesterol is the precursor of the steroid hormones and bile acids that aid digestion.

Because fats do not mix with liquids, the liver produces a protein that wraps the cholesterol molecule in a protective shell. This new molecule—a lipoprotein—can mix with the blood to carry cholesterol to all parts of the body, where it completes tasks necessary for normal biological function.

Lipoproteins have several forms: very low-density lipoprotein (VLDL), low-density lipoprotein (LDL), and high-density lipoprotein (HDL). VLDLs and LDLs ("bad cholesterol") carry large amounts of cholesterol and deposit it in the cells and artery walls. HDLs ("good cholesterol") pick up cholesterol and carry it to the liver, which removes it from the body. Measuring the proportions of these lipoproteins in the blood helps a physician assess a person's risk of developing atherosclerosis. A high level of LDLs increases the risk of heart disease, while a high level of HDLs reduces the risk. A low level of HDLs also increases risk.

Because cholesterol is absolutely necessary for life, the liver manufactures all the body needs. Extra cholesterol comes from eating foods of animal origin. The body cannot stop synthesizing cholesterol. If we eat large amounts of cholesterol-rich foods or high-fat foods (especially saturated fat) that increase the body's natural production of cholesterol, the amount of cholesterol in the bloodstream will increase.

In general, the higher the level of cholesterol in the blood, the higher the incidence of coronary artery disease. More than half the adults in the United States have total blood cholesterol levels that exceed the recommended levels. Making changes in the diet to control blood cholesterol is an effective means of reducing the risk or severity of heart disease. Every 1% reduction in total blood cholesterol cuts the risk of heart attack and sudden death by 2%. A low-fat (es-

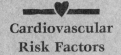

Cardiovascular Risk Factors

Factors You Cannot Control
Family history
Age and sex
Race

Factors You Can Control
Smoking
High blood cholesterol
High blood pressure
Diabetes
Obesity
Lack of exercise
Stress
Alcohol

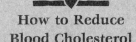

**How to Reduce
Blood Cholesterol**

- Eat fewer high-fat foods, especially those high in saturated fats.
- Replace part of the saturated fats in your diet with unsaturated fats.
- Eat fewer high-cholesterol foods.
- Choose foods high in complex carbohydrates.
- Lose weight if you are overweight.

**Guidelines of the
National Cholesterol
Education Program**

pecially low saturated fat), low-cholesterol diet helps reduce LDL levels. HDL levels can be increased by regular aerobic exercise and by maintaining desirable body weight.

Triglycerides. Body fat provides energy reserves, insulates the body, and cushions delicate organs. Fat is stored in the body in the form of triglycerides. They are also the primary form of dietary fat, containing monounsaturated, polyunsaturated, and saturated fatty acids. Like cholesterol, triglycerides are transported in the blood by lipoproteins (primarily by VLDLs).

In general, when HDL levels are high, triglyceride levels are low, and vice versa. High triglycerides may increase the risk of developing heart disease, pancreatitis, and other health problems. You should maintain triglyceride levels below 200 mg/dL.

Triglyceride levels can be affected by body weight, level of exercise, and the presence or absence of diabetes. Alcohol and simple sugars (sugar, honey, jellies, candy) also increase triglyceride levels.

Recommended Lipid Levels

	Desirable	Borderline	Undesirable
TC	< 200	200–239	≥ 240
LDL	< 130	130–159	≥ 160
HDL	> 60		< 35*
TC/HDL ratio	< 3.5		
TG	< 200	200–400	≥ 400–1000

*An HDL level below 35 mg/dL is considered a cardiovascular risk factor.
In milligrams per deciliter (mg/dL). *TC,* total cholesterol; *LDL,* low-density lipoprotein; *HDL,* high-density lipoprotein; *TG,* triglycerides; >, greater than; <, less than; ≥, greater than or equal to.
Adapted from National Cholesterol Education Program, June 1993

Recommended Lipid Levels for Children and Adolescents

	Desirable	Borderline High	High
TC	< 170	170–199	≥ 200
LDL	< 110	110–129	≥ 130

Cholesterol screening in children and adolescents (ages 2 to 18 years) is recommended when there is a family history of heart disease, or when a parent has high cholesterol.
National Cholesterol Education Program, 1991

The Food Guide Pyramid

The Arizona Heart Institute & Foundation endorses the concept of the Food Guide Pyramid developed by the United States Department of Agriculture and the Department of Health and Human Services. The Pyramid replaces the old familiar four food groups, which were usually depicted in boxes of equal size. The new Pyramid includes five major food groups, which together contain all the nutrients needed for good health.

The sizes of the groups as depicted in the Pyramid emphasize the relative amounts of each food group that should be eaten. Choose the majority of your foods from the base of the Pyramid and eat smaller amounts of the foods at the top of the Pyramid. You should eat more whole grains, vegetables, and fruits, less meat and dairy products, and only very small amounts of fats and sweets.

Carbohydrates

Carbohydrates provide the body with its main source of energy. Whole grains, vegetables, legumes (peas, dried beans, lentils), potatoes, and fruits are excellent sources of carbohydrates. The Arizona Heart Institute & Foundation recommends that more than half (60 to 70%) of daily calories should come from carbohydrates.

The simple carbohydrates are made up of one and two sugar molecules. These sugars are converted into glucose or blood sugar and then used as fuel by the body. Most sweeteners and candy are composed of sim-

Servings per Day at Three Calorie Levels

	1600	2200	2800
Starch	8	11	14
Vegetables	5	6	8
Fruits	3	4	6
Dairy	2–3	2–3	3
Protein	4	5	6
Fat	5	7	9

- *1600 calories:* Sedentary women, older adults
- *2200 calories:* Most children, teenage girls, active women, sedentary men
- *2800 calories:* Teenage boys, active men, some very active women

What is a Serving?

Starch

1 portion
80 calories
15 g carbohydrate
3 g protein
1 to 3 g dietary fiber
Size
1/2 C cereal, grain, or pasta
1 oz bread

Vegetables

1 portion
25 calories
5 g carbohydrate
2 g protein
2 to 3 g dietary fiber
Size
1/2 C cooked
1 C raw

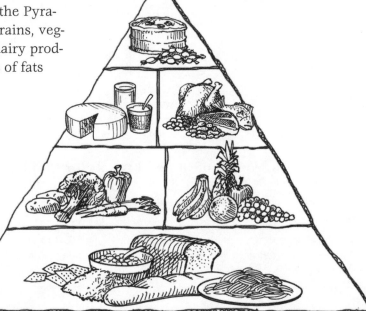

Number of Servings

Fats, sweets: Use Sparingly
Dairy: 2-3
Meats: 2-3 (AHI&F: 1-2)
Vegetables: 3-5 (AHI&F: 5-7)
Fuits: 2-4
Grains: 6-11

Fruit
1 portion
60 calories
15 g carbohydrate
2 to 3 g dietary fiber
Size
1/2 C fruit or juice
2 T dried

Dairy
1 portion
80 to 150 calories
12 g carbohydrate
8 g protein
Trace to 8 g fat
Size
1 C

Protein
1 portion
55 to 100 calories
7 g protein
Trace to 8 g fat
Size
1 oz, 1 egg, 2–3 egg whites
1/2 C dried beans
4 oz tofu

Fat
1 portion
45 calories
5 g fat
Size
1 tsp margarine, butter
1 tsp oil, mayonnaise
1 T salad dressing
1 T low-calorie mayonnaise

ple sugars and little else, which is why they're often called *empty calories.* Sugars (including honey, molasses, and other sweets), soft drinks, candy, jams and jellies, syrups, and sweet desserts should be eaten only occasionally.

Complex carbohydrates, such as starch, are composed of hundreds of sugar molecules hooked together to form long chains (like a beaded necklace). These sugars are also converted into glucose and then used as fuel by the body. Because the sugars are in long, complex chains, they are absorbed more slowly and are better for helping regulate blood sugar levels. In addition to energy, complex carbohydrates provide vitamins, minerals, and dietary fiber.

Breads, Cereals, Rice, & Pasta. Breads, cereals, rice, and pasta are excellent sources of complex carbohydrates, thiamin, niacin, and iron. The Arizona Heart Institute & Foundation recommends eating six to eleven servings daily from this group.

Whole grains make delicious main or side dishes. Eating more brown rice, amaranth, barley, bulgar, grits, and wheatberries is an excellent means of adding variety to your diet while meeting the daily requirement for this food group. Pasta is also a good choice; whole-wheat, quinoa, spinach, and other nutritious varieties of pasta are available.

Vegetables. Eating a variety of vegetables is important because different types provide different nutrients. The nutrients in vegetables may be protective against heart disease, cancer, and other diseases. Many vegetables are excellent sources of vitamin A (especially in the form of beta-carotene), vitamin C, potassium, and fiber. Vegetables are low in calories, are very low in fat and sodium, and have no cholesterol.

The cruciferous vegetables, including broccoli, cauliflower, Brussels sprouts, cabbage, rutabagas, and turnips, may reduce the risk of certain cancers. The cancer-preventive effects of these vegetables are not completely understood but are at least partly related to their dietary fiber, vitamin C and beta-carotene, and other anti-cancer compounds. For this reason, the Arizona Heart Institute & Foundation recommends five to seven servings of vegetables each day, more than the Pyramid suggests.

Fruits. Two to four servings of fruit each day supply valuable nutrients, especially vitamins A and C, potassium, and fiber. Whole fresh fruits have more fiber than pure fruit juices. Fruits are naturally sweet and make a perfect ending to a meal or a refreshing between-meal snack.

Dried fruits are a concentrated source of calories, nutrients, and fiber. They are an excellent addition to breakfast cereals, salads, and grain dishes.

Fiber. Fiber is the indigestible part of plants. It is necessary for optimum health and the prevention of certain diseases and conditions. A daily intake of 25 to 35 grams of fiber is desirable. The two types of dietary fiber—*insoluble* (which does not dissolve in water) and *soluble* (which does dissolve in water)—have different functions in the body. Both types are usually found together in foods, but one is usually predominant.

Insoluble fiber (better known as *bulk* or *roughage*) improves regularity by acting like a sponge in the intestines, soaking up water and making stools softer and larger, thereby making elimination easier. Insoluble fiber is effective in treating maladies such as constipation, hemorrhoids, and diverticulosis. By speeding transit time, it may also reduce your risk of colon and rectal cancer. The best sources of insoluble fiber are wheat bran, whole-wheat breads and cereals, legumes (kidney, pinto, lima, and black beans, peas, lentils), vegetables, and nuts.

Soluble fiber forms a gel in the intestines and is effective in helping to lower blood cholesterol levels and control blood glucose levels in diabetics by slowing down the absorption of blood sugar. Good sources of soluble fiber are oat bran, whole-grain oats, dried beans, peas, lentils, barley, corn, and some fruit (prunes, pears, apples) and vegetables (broccoli, cabbage, carrots).

Dairy

Milk, yogurt, and cheese provide protein, calcium, and riboflavin. Low-fat or nonfat dairy products have all the calcium but little or none of the fat found in whole-fat dairy products. Inadequate calcium intake is linked to osteoporosis (severe bone loss). The Arizona Heart Institute & Foundation recommends having two to three servings of nonfat or low-fat dairy products each day, unless you obtain your calcium from other sources.

Protein

Proteins are essential to all aspects of the body's development, growth, and maintenance, but they are needed in only small amounts. Meat, poultry, fish, dried beans, lentils, eggs, and nuts are rich in protein, B vitamins, iron, and zinc. Protein is also found in breads, cereals, and vegetables, although in smaller quantities. Only 10 to 15% of daily calories should come from protein. The Arizona Heart Institute & Foundation recommends limiting animal protein to less than six ounces per day, less than the Pyramid suggests. Limiting red meat consumption to less than 12 ounces per week is also recommended.

Vegetarians who do not eat animal foods obtain adequate protein if their diet is varied. Legumes are low in fat and high in com-

Goal

Nutrient	% of Total Calories
Carbohydrate	60–70
Fat	20–25
Saturated fat	7
Protein	10–15

To Achieve This Goal

Limit	To
Cholesterol	200–300 mg/day
Sodium	2400 mg/day
Animal protein	< 6 oz/day
Lean red meat	3/4 lb/week
Egg yolks	2–3/week
Low-fat cheese	3 oz/week

Try to obtain 25 to 35 grams of fiber per day by eating plenty of whole-grain breads and cereals, fruits, vegetables, dried beans, peas, and lentils.

Remember to drink at least eight cups of fluid per day, not including caffeinated beverages or alcohol.

Daily Fat Limit

The following guidelines show how many grams of fat and saturated fat you may eat each day, based on the number of calories in your daily diet. Fat should not exceed 20 to 25% of total calories, and saturated fat should not exceed 7% of total calories.

Total calories	Fat (g)*	Saturated fat (g)†
1000	22 to 28	8
1200	27 to 33	9
1400	31 to 39	11
1600	36 to 44	12
1800	40 to 50	14
2000	44 to 56	16
2200	49 to 61	17
2400	53 to 67	19
2600	58 to 72	20
2800	62 to 78	22
3000	67 to 83	23

* These amounts are 20 to 25% of total daily calories.
† Saturated fat is calculated as 7% of the total calories. The grams of fat in Column 3 are part of the amount in Column 2, not in addition to it.

plex carbohydrates and protein. Nuts and seeds, although high in monounsaturated fat (the "good" fat) are excellent sources of trace minerals, chromium and copper. As a delicious addition to salads and grains, dried beans, peas, lentils, nuts, and seeds provide an alternative source of protein in the diet.

Fats

Fat is not only implicated in heart disease, but also in certain types of cancer, hypertension, diabetes, and obesity. The Arizona Heart Institute & Foundation recommends that no more than 20 to 25% of daily calories come from fat, somewhat lower than the 30% most guidelines allow. Saturated fat—which is more dangerous than cholesterol in causing heart disease—should be limited to 7% of calories or less. Dietary cholesterol should not exceed 200 to 300 mg per day.

The obvious sources of fat, such as oils, butter, margarine, salad dressings, mayonnaise, and gravy, should be used sparingly. Consumption of hidden fats in meat, cream, whole-milk dairy products, doughnuts, cookies, cake, and other baked goods should also be limited.

Dietary fat has three forms: monounsaturated, polyunsaturated, and saturated. Their differences are due to their chemical structures, which make them either liquid or solid at room temperature. Unsaturated fats (the mono and poly forms) are liquid at room temperature. Saturated fats are solid at room temperature. The different types of fat have different effects on blood cholesterol.

Monounsaturated fats come from vegetable sources, such as olives, rapeseeds (canola), and peanuts; they lower LDL cholesterol without lowering HDL cholesterol. Most of the fat you eat should be monounsaturated. Polyunsaturated fat also comes from vegetable sources, such as sunflower seeds, safflower seeds, and corn; it may help lower LDL cholesterol, but it also lowers HDL cholesterol. Saturated fats are found in animal fats (meat, poultry, dairy products) and in certain vegetable sources (coconut, palm, palm kernel oils). Saturated fat raises blood cholesterol and should be avoided.

Shortening and other hardened (hydrogenated) vegetable oils should be limited as well. Partially hydrogenated vegetable oils—used in margarines and other processed foods—raise blood cholesterol levels like saturated fat, but probably not as much. Thus, substituting margarine for butter is not risk-free. Cutting back on total fat intake is the best solution.

Omega-3 fatty acids, a type of polyunsaturated fat found in deep cold-water fish, may protect against heart disease by making blood cells less "sticky" and therefore prevent clotting. They may help lower triglycerides and high blood pressure and may reduce the risk of cancer. Eating fish at least two or three times a week is recommended, especially those that are highest in omega-3 fatty acids: salmon, mackerel, whitefish, shad, and bluefish. Fish oil capsules are not recommended unless your doctor prescribes them—the amount needed could cost $1,000 a year, as well as increase the risk of hemorrhagic stroke and bleeding disorders in some people.

Vitamins & Minerals

Vitamins and minerals are essential for good health. Although they do not provide energy, they are necessary for many of the body's functions. Vitamins and minerals cannot be manufactured by the body and so must be obtained from a variety of foods. Healthy people who eat a varied diet of at least 1200 to 1400 calories each day generally meet their requirements without the use of supplements. Self-prescribing megadoses of vitamins can be dangerous.

Some groups of people are at high risk for particular nutrient deficiencies and, on the advice of their physicians, may need a supplement. The most common mineral deficiencies are calcium and iron.

Calcium. Inadequate calcium intake is linked to osteoporosis. Postmenopausal women are more likely to develop osteoporosis if they are thin, smoke, drink large amounts of alcohol, get little weight-bearing exercise, or have a family history of osteoporosis. The major food source of calcium is dairy products. Two to three servings of dairy products each day will contribute toward meeting your calcium needs, which range from 800 to 1200 mg per day for most people.

Nondairy foods that can contribute significant amounts of calcium to the diet include tofu (with calcium sulfate), sardines and salmon (with bones), spinach, turnip greens, kale, broccoli, figs, Swiss chard, chickpeas, sunflower seeds, and kidney beans.

Iron. Iron is an important component of hemoglobin, the compound in blood that carries oxygen to all the organs and muscles. Iron deficiency can result in anemia, which causes weakness, shortness of breath, lack of appetite, and lack of energy and concentration. Children, adolescents, and menstruating women are at greatest risk for iron deficiency. Although one of the best sources of iron is lean meat, dietary iron is also found in fish, poultry, whole grains, dried beans, peas, lentils, and green leafy vegetables. Serving these foods with vitamin C will increase the body's absorption of iron.

Antioxidant Vitamins. Certain vitamins may have previously unsuspected health

Children & Fat Intake

Cardiovascular disease begins early in life. Children over two years of age should limit fat to less than 30% of calories, with no more than 10% of calories from saturated fat.

Children under age two need fat for proper growth and development of the brain, bones, and muscles. They should not be on a fat-restricted diet.

benefits. Vitamins C and E and beta-carotene (which the body uses to produce vitamin A) may protect against heart disease, certain types of cancer, cataracts, and other disorders. These vitamins are called *antioxidants* because they counter the effects of free radicals—unstable oxygen molecules produced in the body during normal metabolic functions, as well as from cigarette smoke, alcohol, radiation, and pollutants. Over time, free radicals damage cells, and they may be one factor in the development of some chronic diseases and aging.

Beta-carotene and vitamin C are found in fruits and vegetables. Good sources include citrus fruits, strawberries, spinach, broccoli, kale, and sweet potatoes. Vitamin E is found in wheat germ, nuts, seeds, legumes, fatty fish, and polyunsaturated oils. Foods that are rich in antioxidant vitamins should be emphasized in the diet.

Water

Water is the most essential nutrient for life; it is used for digestion, absorption, circulation, elimination, and maintaining body temperature. Most people do not drink enough water because they only drink it when they feel thirsty. The body may already be suffering from dehydration by the time a thirst signal is delivered. Symptoms of dehydration include headache, cramps, increased body temperature, and loss of co-ordination.

The Arizona Heart Institute & Foundation recommends drinking at least eight cups of water every day in addition to all other beverages. Unsweetened, flavored mineral water or fruit juice diluted with seltzer or sparkling water is a good substitute for soft drinks. Beverages that contain caffeine or alcohol are dehydrating and do not contribute toward the daily fluid requirements.

Salt

Sodium, a mineral found in a wide variety of foods, helps regulate the amount of water in the body and maintains normal heart rhythm. Ingesting too much sodium can cause fluid retention and/or may aggravate high blood pressure in some people. Salt (sodium chloride) is unlikely to cause high blood pressure in people who are not already at risk for it, and restricting salt will not prevent high blood pressure. Americans consume a great deal of sodium from many sources. One teaspoon of salt (which is about half sodium) contains 2300 mg of sodium—almost the daily recommended limit of 2400 mg.

Eliminating salt from the diet does not mean that foods must be tasteless and unpalatable. Herbs, spices, chili peppers, and other seasonings enhance the natural flavors of other foods. Commercial salt substitutes and salt-free spice mixtures are also available.

Adding salt during cooking or at the table is not the only source of sodium in the diet. The majority comes from processed foods, including cheese, luncheon meats, bacon, sausage, canned soups and vegetables, packaged rice or potato mixes, and condiments (such as mustard, soy sauce, ketchup, pickles, and relish).

Coffee

Most studies show that it is safe to consume moderate amounts of filtered (not boiled) coffee—there is no increased risk of developing heart disease. The Arizona Heart Institute & Foundation recommends limiting coffee to one to two cups per day. People who have irregular heartbeats, stomach ulcers, trouble sleeping at night, or who experience coffee "jitters" would be better off avoiding caffeinated beverages altogether. Caffeine is also found in soft drinks, chocolate, and some over-the-counter medications.

Alcohol

Many magazines and television programs have reported that moderate alcohol consumption (especially red wine) helps pre-vent heart disease, perhaps by increasing HDL levels. Nevertheless, the harmful, addictive, even deadly, effects of alcohol far outweigh any potential benefit. Many people have unwisely increased their alcohol consumption in hopes of preventing heart disease; this practice is not recommended. Other methods for raising HDL levels, such as exercise, are far more effective and safe.

Alcoholic beverages should be consumed in moderation: no more than one drink per day for women and no more than two per day for men. One drink equals 12 ounces of beer, 5 ounces of wine, or 1-1/2 ounces of distilled spirits.

Food Labels

Most Americans like the convenience of packaged foods but, for a variety of reasons, are increasingly concerned about the ingredients. Learning how to read package labels will help you determine whether a food contains ingredients that you are avoiding or adding to your diet. Manufacturers must list the ingredients on the product label or wrapper in order of the amount (by weight) used in the food, with the largest amount first and the smallest last. An ingredient you are avoiding—such as salt—should be one of the last items named on the label or not be listed at all. An ingredient you are purposefully including in your diet—such as bran—should

Exercise and temperance can preserve something of our early strength even in old age.

Cicero

New food labels, mandatory as of May 1994, provide health and nutrition information that is both meaningful and reliable. Reflecting modern health concerns, they list the amount of fat, cholesterol, sodium, and fiber in the product.

Standard serving sizes and uniform definitions eliminate confusion for shoppers who want to compare the nutritional benefits of different brands. For example, the law gives "light" a specific dietary meaning—in the past, manufacturers could use the term to mean light in color, weight, calories, packaging, or anything else they wanted, sometimes misleading shoppers into buying products that were not what they appeared to be.

be near the beginning of the list. Obviously, a bran muffin that contains more sugar than bran is less nutritious than the advertising may imply.

The ingredient list and the food label provide the only reliable nutrition information. Neither the advertising claims nor the name and color are the best indicators of a bread's ingredients, for example. The first ingredient on the label should be a whole grain, such as 100% whole-wheat flour, stone-ground whole-wheat flour, cracked wheat, or whole oat flour. The bread should provide at least two grams of dietary fiber and no more than two grams of fat per serving.

When you are evaluating products for their calorie and fat content, you should check the serving size. A package of microwave popcorn might have 150 calories and 3 grams of fat per serving but include three servings per bag. If you eat the whole bag of popcorn by yourself, you'll have added 450 calories and 9 grams of fat to your daily intake. A six-ounce carton of yogurt might have fewer calories than an eight-ounce competing brand but actually have more calories per ounce than the larger carton.

Note the grams of fat in the product. To be certain you are eating less than 25% of calories from fat, choose items that have only 2 to 3 grams of fat or less per 100 calories. Thus, a 300-calorie frozen dinner

should have no more than 9 grams of fat. Be wary of products that claim to be 96% fat-free (or some other magic percentage). They may be 96% fat-free by weight but not by calories. Whole milk is 4% milkfat by weight and could be labeled 96% fat-free, even though 50% of its calories come from fat.

Weight Control & Exercise

The prevalence of obesity has doubled in America since 1900. One in eight Americans is obese (20% or more above desirable weight). Obesity is associated with high cholesterol levels, heart disease, stroke, high blood pressure, type II diabetes, certain cancers, gall bladder disease, osteoarthritis, and many other diseases.

However, some authorities believe that only certain subgroups of obese people are at risk for the specific conditions and diseases associated with obesity. Identifying body fat distribution patterns may help determine the risk for health problems and diseases associated with excess weight. It appears that people whose fat is distributed around the waist are at greater risk for these conditions than people whose fat is concentrated on the hips and thighs.

If you carry excess weight in your hips and thighs—just like your mother, sisters, and aunts—chances are that neither dieting nor exercise will significantly change your body shape. Constant dieting may be more detrimental to your health than just accepting your genetics. People who are not obese, especially if they do not have hypertension, diabetes, or cardiovascular disease, might actually be better off, from a health standpoint, if they do not diet. The physical and psychological consequences of repeated weight changes (yo-yo dieting) are possibly more damaging than maintaining some constant degree of overweight.

Body weight is the net balance of energy intake and energy expenditure. This balance is precise—most people tend to maintain their weight around a certain "set-point." Thus, it seems clear that body weight is under regulatory controls and that obesity is not just the direct result of gluttony or lethargy.

Eating disorders were discussed in medical textbooks centuries ago. In the past few decades, however, the incidence of anorexia and bulimia has reached a disturbingly high level. Extreme thinness should be discouraged for many reasons, but especially to help high-risk individuals from developing eating disorders.

Health has less to do with thinness than with lifestyle. Everyone is capable of developing healthy habits, which include good food choices and moderate exercise. Very few people are meant to be skinny. Regardless of how much you weigh, you still have a responsibility to take care of your health.

How to Reduce Body Fat. To reduce body fat, you must decrease energy intake, increase energy expenditure, or both. Successful long-term weight-loss programs combine a decrease in energy intake (the amount of food you eat) with an increase in energy expenditure (aerobic exercise) and include behavior modification. Once you lose the weight, you can't go back to your old eating habits, or you will regain the weight you lost.

To lose one pound of fat, a deficit of 3500 calories is necessary. By decreasing the food you eat each day by 250 calories and burning off 250 calories through exercise, you create a daily 500-calorie deficit; over the course of a week, this adds up to 3500 calories—or a loss of one pound of fat. In general, for a safe rate of weight loss, sedentary women should consume 1200 to 1500 calories per day and sedentary men, 1500 to 1800 calories per day (check with your registered dietitian for an appropriate calorie level to meet your individual needs). Losing one-half to one pound per week is a safe and effective goal. If you want to lose 20 pounds, expect it to take at least 20 weeks.

The principal means of increasing energy expenditure is by increasing your level of

Better to hunt in fields for health unbought,
Than fee the doctor for a nauseous draught.
The wise, for cure, on exercise depend;
God never made his work for man to mend.

Dryden

Benefits of Exercise

The following effects of regular exercise will give you increased energy, improved stamina, and greater self-confidence:

- *Increased heart and lung efficiency.* Exercise causes the heart and the lungs to work together more efficiently to circulate oxygen to the rest of the body. Your resting heart rate will be slower and your resting blood pressure lower.
- *Increased extremity circulation.* Conditioning im-

proves the heart's ability to circulate oxygen throughout the body.

- *Control of weight by increasing the number of calories burned.* Losing excess body weight will decrease the workload on the heart and may lower blood pressure in persons with high blood pressure.
- *Control of blood sugar levels in diabetics.* Exercise increases the body's ability to use glucose (blood sugar) and helps lower high levels of glucose.
- *Reduced cholesterol levels in the blood.* Regular aerobic exercise (such as walking, jogging, biking, swimming) can lower total cholesterol levels and increase HDL levels.
- *Control of stress.* Exercise provides a release for pent-up anxiety and frustration. It also helps fight depression.

physical activity. A general increase in daily physical activities, regular structured aerobic exercises, and muscle-toning exercises are recommended.

- *Daily activities.* Walk more, use the stairs, park in the space farthest from your destination, and do more manual chores around the house. Decreasing your dependence on automatic devices will help increase your energy expenditure. By following these suggestions and participating in other recreational activities, you can easily increase your general physical activity expenditure.
- *Structured exercise.* The number of calories you expend during exercise varies with the type, frequency, intensity, and duration of the activity. Individual differences in age, sex, body composition, and health status also affect your total energy expenditure. In general, walking or running one mile burns about 100 calories. In addition, for about two hours after you exercise, your metabolic rate will remain slightly (5 to 10%) elevated.
- *Muscle toning.* Muscular strength and conditioning programs are a beneficial part of any fitness plan. Even though this type of exercise burns few calories, it helps prevent the undesirable losses of lean body mass that are common to many weight-reduction programs.

Many people find it difficult to burn a significant number of calories through exercise. Those who expect immediate results may become discouraged. However, long-term weight maintenance is much more common in people who habitually exercise.

Weight reduction and/or maintenance is only one of the many benefits of a regular exercise program. Regular aerobic exercise (such as walking, jogging, and swimming) increases HDLs and lowers triglyceride levels. A carefully designed program of regular exercise lowers blood pressure, blood fat levels, and blood sugar levels; increases heart and lung efficiency; improves circulation; aids in weight management; helps control stress; and increases energy. Exercising 30 to 40 minutes (not counting warm-up and cool-down periods) three to five times per week is recommended. Consult your doctor before beginning any exercise program.

Changing habits that you have formed over many years can be challenging. Weight-management programs that integrate diet, exercise, and behavior modification require commitment. Slowly but progressively changing your habits will make these modifications a permanent part of your lifestyle. Some suggestions for making weight loss an easier, safer, and more effective process include:

- Eat a variety of nutritious foods in moderate amounts from the five basic food groups. Make sure these foods are low in fat because fat is a rich source of calories.

- Avoid fad diets. Most of them are not nutritionally sound and can cause numerous side effects, particularly those with fewer than 1200 calories per day.
- Exercise regularly if your doctor approves. Although physical activity alone rarely results in major weight loss, exercise helps control your appetite and burns off calories.
- Avoid diet pills. Studies show that most prescription diet medications have troublesome side effects and are notoriously ineffective in long-term weight loss.
- Don't cut out all dairy products in an attempt to reduce calories and fat. Dairy products are major sources of calcium and many other nutrients. Use nonfat and low-fat dairy products.
- Don't try to do it alone. Tell your family and friends about your weight loss plans and let them know how they can be most helpful to you. You might also join a self-help group devoted to weight loss. These groups provide companionship, support, and suggestions on dieting and long-term weight loss.
- To keep the pounds off, try to change your basic eating habits rather than simply "go on a diet." Keep a food diary of what, when, and why you eat to help you understand your eating patterns and the factors that influence them. Learn to recognize social and emotional "cues" to overeating and devise practical ways to counteract them.

Questions to Ask About a Weight Reduction Program

- Does the program combine diet, exercise, and behavior modification?
- Does the diet provide a minimum of 1200 calories per day?
- Is the diet well-balanced (that is, are all food groups represented)?
- Is 1 to 2 pounds per week the maximum rate of weight loss?
- Are the nutrition guidelines for heart disease and cancer risk reduction followed?
- Does the diet include foods that are acceptable, affordable, and available?
- Are aerobic and muscular toning exercises part of the program?
- What is the expertise of the person(s) promoting the program?
- Does the program promote magic foods, pills, potions, wraps, or other gimmicks?
- Will the program help you make permanent, healthful lifestyle modifications?

About this book

The Arizona Heart Institute Foundation Cookbook is designed as a browsing book. Open it to any page and you will find information about how to choose, store, cook, and season specific foods; kitchen tips; or health advice. Refer to the Index to find topics quickly, such as what fish to substitute when the type listed in a recipe is not available, which apples are best for cooking, or what variety of potato looks and tastes like it's already been buttered.

Nutrition Analysis

Each recipe in this cookbook has been analyzed for total calories, percentage of calories from fat, total fat, saturated fat, cholesterol, sodium, carbohydrate, protein, and fiber. Some of the recipes may be high in a nutrient that we recommend be limited. Keep in mind that a healthy balanced diet does not consist of just one food or dish but is the average of all the foods you eat over the course of one to three days. Even though one meal may be a little higher in fat or sodium, if it is part of an overall low-fat, low-sodium diet, it is perfectly acceptable.

Calories	%Fat	Fat (g)	Saturated Fat (g)	Cholesterol (mg)	Sodium (mg)	Carbohydrate (g)	Protein (g)	Fiber (g)
336	8	3	0.6	60	140	46	28	5

Exchanges: Starch 1-1/2, Fruit 1/2, Vegetable 3, Low-fat protein 3

Food Exchanges

Following each nutrition analysis is a line that lists the food exchange values of each serving. The exchange system enables you to make food choices easily and with maximum flexibility, while keeping your diet in proper balance throughout the day. The system was originally designed for diabetics, but it is widely used by many diet plans, with or without some modification.

In this system, foods that have comparable amounts of carbohydrate, protein, fat, and calories are grouped together. Any food in a group can be exchanged or traded for any other food in the same group. This permits you to control your diet but still be spontaneous in your food choices. If peaches are out of season, for example, you can exchange that choice for another fruit without compromising your nutrition objectives for the day. Remember that foods are grouped according to their nutritional similarities, not their volume; thus, 15 grapes have about the same nutrients as two tablespoons of raisins.

Recipes include a combination of ingredients and so most will count toward more than one exchange group. Some recipes may contain a food that is not reflected in the exchange list because the amount used is insignificant.

Hard-to-Find Ingredients

When you are cooking recipes in this book, feel free to change the ingredients to suit your personal preferences or to take advantage of the best-quality foods available. Many recipes include a suggestion list noting acceptable substitutes for vegetables, fruits, seasonings, or other ingredients. As a rule, it is better to substitute another type of fresh produce than to settle for poor-quality or canned fruits or vegetables. Some recipes specify a particular form or flavor of an ingredient that comes in many varieties, such as oil, honey, or mustard. Substituting another variety (using clover honey instead of tupelo, for example) usually will not affect the nutrition analysis or the final product. Be sure your substitutions are reasonable from a culinary standpoint: don't replace the apples in a Waldorf salad with bananas if you want to retain the character of the original recipe.

Some recipes in this cookbook call for ingredients that may be difficult to find in some parts of the country. Acceptable substitute ingredients may be noted in a suggestion list at the end of a recipe. The Culinary Glossary at the end of this book gives descriptions of unusual ingredients as well as cooking techniques. Margin text on the recipe pages includes many entries about specific grains, vegetables, fruits, and other food products—check the Index to find where a particular item is discussed.

Hundreds of food products and ingredients from around the world can be purchased by a simple telephone call. The following mail order companies specialize in exotic and hard-to-find foods, spices, and other ingredients. Most offer a free catalog

When I had to sit there and actually consider the nutritional makeup of every lousy item I planned to cook, I got really irritated, and I began to snap at my colleagues. It was like having to find out who built the bus I was planning to ride to work, or establishing the fiber content of my chair cushion before I sat down.

Al Sicherman
Caramel Knowledge

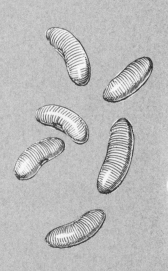

and a toll-free order number. We suggest that you order all of these catalogs promptly—you'll enjoy browsing and choosing recipes more when you know how easy it is to obtain the ingredients.

- **American Spoon Foods, Inc.**
  1668 Clarion Avenue
  P.O. Box 566
  Petoskey, MI 49770
  800–222–5886
  Free catalog; wide variety of preserves, jellies, fruit butters, and dried fruits.

- **Bean Bag Mail Order Co.**
  818 Jefferson Street
  Oakland, CA 94607
  800–845–2326
  Free catalog; about 80 varieties of commercial dried beans and 45 certified organic beans, with recipe suggestions.

- **Dean & Deluca**
  560 Broadway
  New York, NY 10012
  800–221–7714
  $3 catalog; hard-to-find gourmet foods and ingredients.

- **Ducktrap River Fish Farm, Inc.**
  57 Little River Drive
  Belfast, ME 04915
  800–828–3825
  Free catalog; salmon, trout, mackerel, shrimp, scallops, and other seafoods.

- **Falls Mill and Country Store**
  134 Falls Mill Road
  Belvidere, TN 37306
  615–469–7161
  Free price list; stone-ground grains, including cornmeal, grits, cracked wheat, whole-wheat flour, rye flour, and buckwheat flour.

- **Frieda's By Mail**
  P.O. Box 58488
  Los Angeles, CA 90058
  800–241–1771
  Free catalog; exotic fruits and vegetables from around the world.

- **G.B. Ratto & Co. International Grocers**
  821 Washington Street
  Oakland, CA 94607
  800–325–3483
  Free catalog; food products from around the world.

- **Ideal Cheese Shop**
  1205 Second Avenue
  New York, NY 10021
  800–382–0109
  $2 catalog (refundable); over 100 cheeses, including many low-fat varieties.

- **Malibu Greens**
  P.O. Box 6286
  Malibu, CA 90264
  800–383–1414
  Free catalog; gift baskets of fresh baby vegetables (does not ship in July or August).

- **Penzeys' Spice House Ltd.**
  P.O. Box 1488
  Waukesha, WI 53187
  414–574–0277
  Free catalog to users of this cookbook; over 200 spices and seasoning blends.
- **Rossi Pasta**
  P.O Box 759
  114 Greene Street
  Marietta, OH 45750
  800–227–6774
  Free catalog; 35 varieties of pasta.
- **Sehe-Ya Natural Pistachios**
  Steinway Groves
  Route 1, Box 17
  Cochise, AZ 85606
  602–826–3718 (accepts collect calls)
  Free brochure; lightly salted or unsalted pistachios, chili-flavored pistachios, pistachio brittle, gift packages, with recipes.
- **Simply Shrimp**
  7794 NW 44 Street
  Fort Lauderdale, FL 33351
  800–833–0888
  Free catalog; shrimp, grouper, snapper, swordfish, scallops, stone crab claws in season, and other seafoods.
- **Sultan's Delight**
  A Division of Nuts About Nuts, Inc.
  P.O. Box 090302
  Brooklyn, NY 11209
  800–852–5046 or 718–745–6844
  Free catalog; over 300 exotic Middle Eastern foods, spices, and other ingredients.

- **Sunrise Desert Foods**
  490 E. Pima Street
  Phoenix, AZ 85004
  800–266–4815
  Free catalog; products made from prickly pears, dates, pomegranates, wild oranges, jalapeño chili.
- **Texas Wild Game Cooperative**
  P.O. Box 530
  Ingram, TX 78025
  800–962–4263
  Free catalog; exotic game meats, including venison and cabrito (young goat), with recipes.
- **Uwajimaya**
  519 Sixth Avenue S.
  Seattle, WA 98104
  206–624–6248
  Free catalog; nearly 600 food products used in Japan, China, Thailand, Korea, and the Philippines.
- **Walnut Acres**
  Penns Creek, PA 17862
  1–800–433–3998
  Free catalog; organic whole foods, including cereals, grains, pancake and muffin mixes, fresh whole-grain breads and other baked goods, pastas, dried beans, prepared foods, and canned vegetables.
- **Wax Orchards**
  22744 Wax Orchards Road, SW
  Vashon, WA 98070
  800–634–6132
  Free catalog; low-calorie, low-fat fruit butters, preserves, ice cream toppings (five fat-free fudge toppings), and syrups; no-sugar fruit sweetener for use in baking and cooking, acceptable for diabetics; includes nutrition analysis of all products.

How to Modify a Recipe

Many of your favorite recipes can be converted to heart-healthy versions by changing the cooking technique or by changing one or more ingredients. Heart-healthy ingredients can be substituted when they do not compromise the basic structure or chemical balance of a recipe. Some ingredients cannot be replaced successfully, but they might be reduced or even eliminated.

- Use a nonfat, lower-fat, lower-calorie, or lower-sodium version of the ingredient (such as reduced-fat mayonnaise, low-sodium soy sauce, reduced-calorie syrup).
- Eliminate unessential high-fat ingredients (such as chocolate chips or coconut).
- Use a low-fat method of cooking, such as baking, broiling, grilling, poaching, steaming, or stir-frying.
- Use nonstick cookware and sauté foods in cooking spray and/or low-sodium broth or water instead of oil, butter, or margarine.
- Cook pasta, rice, grains, and vegetables without oil, butter, margarine, or salt.
- Buy only the leanest meats—select is most lean, choice is medium, and prime is the fattiest (with the greatest marbling).
- Buy the leanest chicken—fryers and broilers are more lean than roasters; hens and capons have the most fat. Turkey breast meat is more lean than chicken. White meat poultry is more lean than dark.
- Substitute poultry, fish, or shellfish for red meat.
- Remove the skin and visible fat from chicken and meat before cooking.
- Reduce or omit salt; use freshly ground black pepper, herbs, spices, lemon, and other complementary seasonings.
- To thicken sauces or cream soups, use buttermilk or evaporated skim milk instead of cream.
- To thicken vegetable soups, purée some of the vegetables and stir them back into the soup.
- Reduce the amount of fat in baked goods by one-fourth to one-third; a little water, skim milk, or fruit juice may be needed to maintain the moisture content.
- Replace the fat in baked goods with an equal amount of unsweetened applesauce, yogurt, or prune purée.
- Reduce the amount of sugar by one-third to one-half and add spices, extracts, or dried fruit as you like.

Be prepared to experiment. You may need to try several versions before hitting on the perfect recipe. Cooking times and assembly instructions may need to be modified along with the ingredients. Make written notes with each test so you can duplicate the successful result. With experience, you'll know how to modify recipes and create new ones with little trouble.

Heart-Healthy Substitutions

1 whole egg	2 egg whites
	1 egg white + 1 tsp oil
	1/4 C egg substitute
2 whole eggs	1 egg + 1 egg white
1 C whole milk	1 C skim or 1% milk
1 C light cream	1 C evaporated skim milk
	3 T oil + enough skim milk to make 1 C
1 C heavy cream	1 C evaporated skim milk
	2/3 C skim milk + 1/3 C oil
1 C whipped cream	1 C whipped evaporated skim milk
1 C evaporated milk	1 C skim evaporated milk
1 C whole milk yogurt	1 C low-fat or nonfat yogurt
1 C sour cream	1 C plain low-fat or nonfat yogurt
	1 C low-fat cottage cheese + 2 T lemon juice
	1 C buttermilk
1 C butter	1 C margarine
	3/4 C vegetable oil
	Baked goods: 1 C unsweetened applesauce
	Baked goods: 1 C prune purée
1 C shortening, lard	2/3 C vegetable oil
1 oz baking chocolate	3 T cocoa powder + 1 T oil
1 T salad dressing	1 T low-fat salad dressing
	1 T balsamic vinegar
White (all-purpose) flour	Replace 1/2 with whole-wheat flour or 1/3 with oat bran
Egg noodles	Noodles made without eggs
White rice	Brown rice (cooking time may require adjustment)
Cheese	Low-fat cheese made with part-skim milk
Peanut butter	Natural (non-hydrogenated) peanut butter
Mayonnaise	Low-fat or nonfat mayonnaise (and use nonfat yogurt for half)
Chicken broth	Defatted, low-sodium chicken broth
Bouillon cube	Low-sodium bouillon cube
Sugar	Reduce by one-third or one-half
Garlic salt	Garlic powder

I encourage my readers to "indulge" in treating themselves well. Of this I am 100 percent guilty as charged. I encourage them to reclaim a natural way of eating that respects their body's hunger signals, to accept and, yes, even love their natural size and shape, to celebrate the joy of movement in dance, exercise, or sport, to value who they are (not just what they look like), and to feel as good as they can feel and enjoy life as completely as they can.

I find that when people truly reach for these goals, they gradually learn to live well, which includes nourishing themselves well. They take good care of themselves, not out of duty or feelings of guilt, but out of a natural desire to be healthy and happy.

Susan Kano
Making Peace with Food

Abbreviations

Teaspoon	tsp
Tablespoon	T
Cup	C
Ounce	oz
Pound	lb
Pint	pt
Quart	qt
Gallon	gal

Dry Measurements

Dash	1/16 tsp
1/2 T	1-1/2 tsp
1 T	3 tsp
2 T	1 oz
4 T	1/4 C
5 T + 1 tsp	1/3 C
8 T	1/2 C
1 oz	2 T
2 oz	1/4 C
4 oz	1/2 C
6 oz	3/4 C
8 oz	1 C
16 oz	1 lb

Liquid Measurements

2 T	1 oz
16 oz	1 pint
2 C	1 pint
4 C	1 qt
2 pt	1 qt
4 qt	1 gal

Onion salt	Freeze-dried onion; onion powder
Ground beef	Ground turkey breast (half or more)
Tuna canned in oil	Tuna canned in water
Poultry	Skinless white meat poultry
Bacon	Canadian bacon, lean ham
Pork	Chicken, white meat
Chicken liver	Chicken, white meat
Veal cutlet	Turkey cutlets

Substitutes for Sugar in Baking

To replace 1 C of granulated sugar with a liquid sweetener (like honey), use the amount of sweetener shown in the second column and subtract the amount in the third column from the other liquids (milk, juice, etc.) used in the recipe:

Sweetener	Use	Reduce liquid by
Brown sugar	1 C firmly packed	—
Date sugar	2/3 C	—
Honey	1/2 C	1/4 C
Malt syrup	1 to 1-1/4 C	1/4 C
Maple syrup	1/2 to 1/3 C	1/4 C
Molasses	1/2 C	1/4 C

Note: Confectioners' sugar cannot be used as a substitute for table sugar in baking.

Emergency Substitutions

Breadcrumbs, dry, 1 C	3/4 C cracker crumbs
Buttermilk or sour milk, 1 C	1 C plain nonfat yogurt
	1 T vinegar or lemon juice + skim milk to equal 1 C
	1-3/4 tsp cream of tartar plus 1 C milk
Cake flour, 1 C	1 C minus 2 T sifted all-purpose flour
Cornstarch, 1 T	2 T all-purpose flour
	2 tsp arrowroot
Garlic, 1 small clove	1/8 tsp garlic powder
Ginger, fresh, 1 T minced	1/8 tsp ground ginger
Lemon juice, 1 tsp	1/2 tsp vinegar
Mustard, prepared, 1 T	1 tsp powdered mustard
Tomato juice, 1 C	1/2 C tomato sauce + 1/2 C water
Tomato sauce, 1 C	3/8 C tomato paste + 1/2 C water
Vinegar, 1 tsp	2 tsp lemon juice

An imaginary shelf labeled INDULGENCES *is a good idea. It contains the best butter, jumbo-sized eggs, heavy cream, marbled steaks, sausages and pâtés, hollandaise and butter sauces, French butter-cream fillings, gooey chocolate cakes, and all those lovely items that demand disciplined rationing. Thus, with these items high up and almost out of reach, we are ever conscious that they are not everyday foods. They are for special occasions, and when that occasion comes, we can enjoy every mouthful.*

Julia Child

A Low-Fat Cuisine

Coming to Arizona gave me an exciting opportunity to combine my background as a classically trained French chef with the abundance of ingredients found in the southwestern United States, which were new and unknown to me. The cuisine we developed at Vincent's is southwestern in nature but done with classical French techniques.

We offer a low-fat, low-cholesterol menu. Working with the Arizona Heart Institute & Foundation on this menu was a challenge because we were creating dishes that met their dietary guidelines but that I could still feel good about serving to my customers.

Southwestern ingredients are a natural for this type of cooking because chiles and peppers add an abundance of flavor without added fat. About 20% of our customers order from the Heart Smart Menu (but they still have a crème brulée for dessert!).

Vincent Guerithault

# n the Cover

Papaya Grapefruit Salad with Honey-Lime Vinaigrette
Black Bean Relish
Grilled Salmon with Jalapeño Honey Glaze
Pears Poached in Red Wine Sauce

The heart-healthy dinner shown on the cover was created by Vincent Guerithault especially for *The Arizona Heart Institute Foundation Cookbook*. Guerithault, chef-owner of Vincent Guerithault on Camelback in Phoenix, Arizona, serves on the Board of Directors of the Arizona Heart Institute Foundation.

Heart-healthy eating is easy when when you think about all your meals in the same way, emphasizing complex carbohydrates, fruits, and vegetables while limiting fat and protein, especially animal protein.

This complete dinner has 760 calories. About 60% of calories come from carbohydrate—an ideal amount. With 19 grams of dietary fiber, this meal provides 75% of the recommended 25 to 35 grams of fiber per day. It is also very low in fat, with just 17 grams. Only 20% of total calories come from fat, and only 3% of total calories come from saturated fat. The Arizona Heart Institute & Foundation recommends no more than 20 to 25% of total calories from fat, with just 7% of total calories from saturated fat. This meal is also low in cholesterol, containing only 60 mg of the 200 mg permitted each day. About 25% of the total calories come from protein. Very low in sodium, this meal has less than 100 mg, out of a daily limit of 2400 mg. It also provides a generous portion of fruit.

The Arizona Heart Institute & Foundation recommends that two out of three meals be vegetarian. Other foods served on the day of this meal should emphasize grains and vegetables.

Papaya Grapefruit Salad with Honey-Lime Vinaigrette

Vincent Guerithault

2 T honey
4 T lime juice
1 T walnut oil
1 T sherry wine vinegar
2 C chicory (or any favorite greens)
1 papaya, peeled, seeded, quartered
2 small grapefruit, peeled, segmented
1 tomato, peeled, seeded, diced

To make the vinaigrette, combine honey, lime juice, oil, and vinegar, mixing well with a whisk.

Place 1/2 C chicory on each serving plate. Very thinly slice the papaya on a bias and fan on top of lettuce. Place 5 grapefruit segments around the papaya. Top with diced tomato. Drizzle with Honey-Lime Vinaigrette.

Serves 4.

Calories	%Fat	Fat (g)	Saturated Fat (g)	Cholesterol (mg)	Sodium (mg)	Carbohydrate (g)	Protein (g)	Fiber (g)
135	25	4	0.4	0	11	27	2	4

Exchanges: Fruit 2, Fat 1

Legumes

Plants that produce pods with edible seeds are called *legumes*. This family includes kidney beans, pinto beans, soybeans, garbanzo beans, black beans, lentils, and peas. These complex carbohydrates provide soluble fiber, which helps reduce the levels of cholesterol in the blood.

Legumes are also a good source of protein, B vitamins, zinc, potassium, magnesium, calcium, and iron, which makes them a good substitute for meat and other animal proteins.

Black Bean Relish

Vincent Guerithault

3 C black beans, cleaned and soaked overnight in water to cover
1 C cooked white rice
1 C cooked corn, fresh or frozen
1 red bell pepper, seeded, diced
1 yellow bell pepper, seeded, diced
1 green bell pepper, seeded, diced
1 T diced red onion
3 T chopped cilantro
1 tomato, chopped
2 T olive oil
2 T sherry wine vinegar
Pepper to taste

Drain the black beans and rinse well. Put them in a stockpot and add water to cover. Bring to a boil; reduce heat and simmer for about 1 hour. When tender, drain and rinse well under cold water. Mix black beans with remaining ingredients and season to taste with pepper. Serve chilled.

Serves 12.

Calories	%Fat	Fat (g)	Saturated Fat (g)	Cholesterol (mg)	Sodium (mg)	Carbohydrate (g)	Protein (g)	Fiber (g)
228	12	3	0.5	0	4	41	11	9

Exchanges: Starch 2-1/2, Fat 1/2

Grilled Salmon with Jalapeño Honey Glaze

Vincent Guerithault

2 tsp chopped jalapeño pepper
3 oz honey
2 lb fresh salmon
Pepper to taste

Combine the chopped jalapeño and honey; set aside. Cut salmon into 6 portions (5 oz each). Season with pepper. Spray a medium-hot grill with nonfat cooking spray. Grill salmon for about 4 minutes on each side, or until firm in center. Brush one side with jalapeño honey glaze during the last 2 minutes of cooking.

Serves 6.

Calories	%Fat	Fat (g)	Saturated Fat (g)	Cholesterol (mg)	Sodium (mg)	Carbohydrate (g)	Protein (g)	Fiber (g)
270	31	9	1.7	60	84	12	34	0

Exchanges: Low-fat protein 5

Eskimos, Fat, & Heart Disease

The Eskimos who live in Greenland rarely develop heart disease, even though they eat large amounts of high-fat fish and whale blubber. Some fish oils contain a type of polyunsaturated fat called *omega-3 fatty acids*, which scientists think may help protect against atherosclerosis. These fats inhibit the body's ability to form life-threatening blood clots, which can cause a heart attack or stroke. Omega-3 fatty acids may also be associated with lower triglyceride and cholesterol levels.

Eating at least two to three servings of fish each week is strongly recommended. Fish is low in saturated fat and is a good source of protein.

Cold-water fish that use fat for warmth are good sources of omega-3 fatty acids. Salmon, mackerel, whitefish, shad, bluefish, and tuna contain this "good" fat.

Pears Poached in Red Wine Sauce

Vincent Guerithault

6 medium Anjou or Bosc pears
1 small orange
6 whole cloves
1 qt red cooking wine
1 C granulated sugar
1/2 stick whole cinnamon

With a potato peeler, remove some of the peel from the pears, leaving some skin intact. Pierce the cloves into the skin of the orange. Bring wine, sugar, cinnamon stick, and orange to a boil; gently add pears. Reduce heat to simmer and cook for about 30 minutes, or until pears are tender. Chill pears in their cooking liquid. Place 1 pear on each serving plate and spoon 1 to 2 T of liquid around each pear.

Serves 6.

Calories	%Fat	Fat (g)	Saturated Fat (g)	Cholesterol (mg)	Sodium (mg)	Carbohydrate (g)	Protein (g)	Fiber (g)
127	5	1	0	0	2	32	1	6

Exchanges: Fruit 2

Breads

Apple-Date Muffins

1-1/2 C oat bran
1/2 C whole-wheat flour
3 T brown sugar
2 tsp baking powder
1 tsp cinnamon
1/2 tsp nutmeg
1/2 C unsweetened apple juice
1/4 C skim milk
2 egg whites
2 T sunflower oil
2 T honey
1 C diced unpeeled Granny Smith apples
2 T chopped dates
2 T chopped pecans

Combine oat bran, flour, brown sugar, baking powder, cinnamon, and nutmeg; set aside. Mix apple juice, skim milk, egg whites, oil, and honey. Stir in flour mixture, apples, dates, and pecans. Spoon batter into a non-stick muffin pan, filling each cup about two-thirds full. Bake at 400° for 20 minutes.

Serves 12.

Calories	%Fat	Fat (g)	Saturated Fat (g)	Cholesterol (mg)	Sodium (mg)	Carbohydrate (g)	Protein (g)	Fiber (g)
120	31	4	0.5	0	78	23	4	3

Exchanges: Starch 1, Fruit 1/2, Fat 1/2

Preparing to Bake

All ingredients should be at room temperature. Take margarine, eggs, and milk out of the refrigerator about an hour before mixing. Separate eggs while cold; let the whites come to room temperature before using.

Dry ingredients are measured first to save work; if the wet ingredients are measured first, the utensils will have to be washed and dried before the dry ingredients can be measured. Salt, spices, baking soda, or baking powder are mixed with other dry ingredients before liquids are added so they will be evenly distributed throughout the final product.

The oven should be preheated to the specified temperature before the batter-filled pans are placed in it.

Arrange baking pans near the center of the oven to permit air to circulate freely so the food cooks evenly on the top and bottom. The rack should be placed in the middle position. Pans should not touch each other or the oven walls, nor should they be placed directly under another pan on a higher rack.

# Peach Muffins

2 C oat bran
1/2 C whole-wheat flour
2-1/2 tsp baking powder
1 tsp cinnamon
1 C finely chopped dried peaches
4 egg whites
3/4 C skim milk
1 T canola oil
1/2 C clover honey

Combine oat bran, flour, baking powder, cinnamon, and peaches. Beat egg whites, milk, oil, and honey; pour over dry ingredients and mix until just moistened. Pour equal amounts of batter into 12 muffin cups prepared with paper liners. Bake at 425° for 15 to 18 minutes.

Serves 12.

Suggestions

- Plump peaches in hot water, cinnamon-flavored brandy, or fruit juice for 15 to 30 minutes. Drain, pat dry, and chop.
- Other dried fruit (such as cherries, cranberries, apricots, pears, pineapple, or dates) can be substituted for the dried peaches.

Calories	%Fat	Fat (g)	Saturated Fat (g)	Cholesterol (mg)	Sodium (mg)	Carbohydrate (g)	Protein (g)	Fiber (g)
152	15	2	0.3	0	108	35	6	4

Exchanges: Starch 1, Fruit 1, Fat 1/2

Banana Muffins

2-1/4 C oat bran
2 tsp baking powder
1/4 tsp cinnamon
1 ripe banana, mashed
3/4 C skim milk
4 egg whites
2 T canola oil
1/3 C orange blossom honey
1/4 C raisins

Combine oat bran, baking powder, and cinnamon. Mix banana, milk, egg whites, oil, honey, and raisins. Add to dry ingredients, stirring just until moistened. Pour equal amounts of batter into 12 muffin cups prepared with paper liners. Bake at 425° for 15 to 18 minutes or until a toothpick inserted in the center of a muffin comes out dry.
Serves 12.

Suggestion
• Chopped dried apples can be added with the raisins.

The doctor is sure that my health is poor, he says that I waste away; so bring me a can of the shredded bran, and a bale of the toasted hay.

Walt Mason

Fiber
Dietary fiber is found in whole grains, fruit, and vegetables. Both types of fiber—water-insoluble and water-soluble—are important components of a healthy diet. Most fruits, vegetables, and whole grains contain some of both types of fiber. A diet high in insoluble fiber (wheat bran, nuts, whole grains, vegetables) may help reduce the risk of certain types of cancer. Soluble fiber (oat bran, fruit, legumes) may help lower blood cholesterol levels. Although advertising agencies have widely promoted oat bran and oat-

Calories	% Fat	Fat (g)	Saturated Fat (g)	Cholesterol (mg)	Sodium (mg)	Carbohydrate (g)	Protein (g)	Fiber (g)
122	27	4	0.4	0	92	25	5	3

Exchanges: Starch 1, Fruit 1/2, Fat 1/2

meal as "magic bullets" against cholesterol, fiber should be obtained from a wide variety of food sources spread over several meals throughout the day.

High-fiber foods are low in fat and calories, and they are often rich in antioxidants (beta-carotene and vitamins C and E). They are excellent choices for weight control.

The amount of fiber in the diet should be gradually increased to 20 to 35 grams per day. Liberal amounts of water and other beverages should be consumed throughout the day.

umpkin-Oat Muffins

1-1/3 C oat bran
1 C rolled oats
1-1/4 C skim milk
3/4 C whole-wheat flour
1/2 C brown sugar
1 T baking powder
2 tsp cinnamon
1/2 tsp nutmeg
1/2 tsp ginger
3/4 C puréed pumpkin
2 egg whites
2 T canola oil
1/2 C raisins

Combine oat bran, oats, and milk; set aside. Mix flour, sugar, baking powder, and spices; set aside. Blend pumpkin, egg whites, oil, and raisins; stir into oat mixture. Add flour mixture, stirring just until all ingredients are moistened. Spoon batter into 12 nonstick muffin cups; fill cups completely. Bake at 400° for 20 to 25 minutes.

Serves 12.

Calories	%Fat	Fat (g)	Saturated Fat (g)	Cholesterol (mg)	Sodium (mg)	Carbohydrate (g)	Protein (g)	Fiber (g)
170	20	4	0.5	0	124	34	6	3

Exchanges: Starch 1, Fruit 1, Fat 1/2

Raisin Bran Muffins

1/4 C raisins
2-1/4 C oat bran
2 tsp baking powder
2 tsp nonfat dry milk
1 C plain nonfat yogurt
1 C unsweetened applesauce
1/4 C molasses
1/4 C brown sugar
2 egg whites

Pour hot water to cover over raisins and set aside. Mix dry ingredients together; set aside. Drain raisins and mix with remaining ingredients. Add to dry ingredients and stir until just mixed. Spoon batter into 12 nonstick muffin cups. Bake at 400° for 20 to 25 minutes.

Serves 12.

Weight & Heart Disease

Obesity alone can lead to cardiovascular disease. Obesity is defined as being 20% above the normal weight for your age and height. Lack of exercise, overeating, or hypothyroidism can cause obesity. Excess weight makes the heart work harder to pump blood throughout the body, and it is commonly associated with high blood pressure and high fat (triglyceride and cholesterol) levels. Exercising and changing your eating habits can help you achieve your ideal weight. With your doctor's approval, losing one to two pounds per week is a realistic goal.

**Arizona Heart
Institute Foundation**
1–800–345–4278

Calories	%Fat	Fat (g)	Saturated Fat (g)	Cholesterol (mg)	Sodium (mg)	Carbohydrate (g)	Protein (g)	Fiber (g)
110	11	1	0.3	0	95	27	5	3

Exchanges: Starch 1, Fruit 1

Bananas

Eight or more bananas attached at the stem are called a *hand* of bananas; each one is called a *finger*. Bananas are high in potassium and carbohydrates, and they are low in fat.

The starch content in a banana turns to sugar during ripening, so a fully ripe banana is much sweeter than a partially ripe one. Unlike most fruit, bananas develop a better flavor when they ripen off the tree. Store bananas at room temperature until ripe. They will ripen faster in a brown paper bag, although the peel may stay a little green. Ripe bananas can be refrigerated for several days. They can be frozen and used in cooking after thawing.

Quick breads, muffins, and cakes are best made with very ripe bananas. Two to three mashed bananas equals one cup. Firm, slightly underripe bananas should be used if they will be baked or sautéed whole.

Bananas turn brown after they are cut, so they should be used immediately or brushed with lemon juice.

Banana Bread

1 C whole-wheat flour
1/4 C all-purpose flour
1/2 C oat bran
1-1/4 tsp baking powder
1-1/4 tsp baking soda
1/3 C sugar
1/3 C brown sugar
1/3 C margarine
2 egg whites
2 T skim milk
1 C mashed ripe banana

Stir together flours, oat bran, baking powder, and baking soda. Cream both sugars with margarine; add eggs and milk, beating until smooth. Add flour mixture and banana and beat until smooth. Spread batter in a nonstick 8 × 4 loaf pan. Bake at 350° for 60 to 65 minutes, or until a toothpick inserted in the center of the loaf comes out clean. Cool in the pan for 10 minutes. Remove from the pan and cool on a wire rack. Makes 1 loaf.

Serves 16.

Calories	%Fat	Fat (g)	Saturated Fat (g)	Cholesterol (mg)	Sodium (mg)	Carbohydrate (g)	Protein (g)	Fiber (g)
122	31	4	0.8	0	148	21	2	2

Exchanges: Starch 1/2, Fruit 1, Fat 1

# Cornbread

1-1/4 C yellow stone-ground cornmeal
3/4 C all-purpose flour
1 T sugar
1 T baking powder
1 C skim milk
2 egg whites, lightly beaten
1 T canola oil

Mix cornmeal, flour, sugar, and baking powder. Stir in remaining ingredients with a few rapid strokes. Spread batter in a 9 × 9-inch nonstick pan. Bake at 425° for 20 to 25 minutes.
Serves 12.

Suggestions
- For muffins, fill 12 muffin cups prepared with paper liners.
- Whole corn kernels and chopped red and green bell peppers can be stirred into the batter.

Calories	%Fat	Fat (g)	Saturated Fat (g)	Cholesterol (mg)	Sodium (mg)	Carbohydrate (g)	Protein (g)	Fiber (g)
106	13	1	0.2	0	115	19	3	1

Exchanges: Starch 1, Fruit 1/2

A stomach that is seldom empty despises common food.

Horace

Food Labels
Reading package labels will help you determine whether a food contains ingredients that you are avoiding or adding to your diet. The makers of most packaged foods list the ingredients on the product label or wrapper in order of the amount (by weight) used in the food, with the largest amount first and the smallest last. An ingredient you are avoiding—such as salt—should be one of the last items named on the label, or not be listed at all. An ingredient you are purposefully including in your diet—such as fiber-rich foods like bran—should be near the beginning of the list. Obviously, a bran muffin that contains more sugar than bran is less nutritious than the label claims.

Arizona Heart Institute Foundation
1–800–345–4278

Prunes

Prunes are dried freestone plums. They are high in fiber and sugar. They are an excellent source of vitamin A and also provide some B vitamins, iron, and potassium. Size does not indicate the flavor or quality of a prune. Stewed prunes have fewer nutrients than uncooked prunes.

Puréed prunes can replace the fat in baked goods. To make 1 cup of prune purée, blend 8 ounces of pitted prunes and 6 tablespoons of water in a food processor until smooth. Replace butter, margarine, or oil with an equal amount of prune purée. This substitution makes muffins, cakes, cookies, and other baked products 75 to 90% lower in fat, while keeping them moist and flavorful.

Prune Bread

1-1/2 C whole-wheat flour
1/2 C brown sugar
1-1/2 tsp cinnamon
1 C chopped pitted prunes
2 T chopped pecans
1 tsp baking soda
1 C skim milk
1 egg white

Mix flour, sugar, cinnamon, prunes, and pecans. Stir soda into milk. Stir milk and egg white into dry ingredients. Pour into a nonstick breadpan and let stand for 20 minutes. Bake at 350° for 50 minutes. Cool bread in the pan on a cooling rack; remove when completely cool.

Serves 16.

Suggestion

• Add 1 to 2 tsp grated orange or lemon rind to dry ingredients.

Calories	%Fat	Fat (g)	Saturated Fat (g)	Cholesterol (mg)	Sodium (mg)	Carbohydrate (g)	Protein (g)	Fiber (g)
101	8	1	0.1	0	66	22	3	2

Exchanges: Starch 1/2, Fruit 1

# Pumpkin-Raisin Bread

5 C flour
1 tsp baking soda
2 tsp cinnamon
3/4 tsp ground cloves
3/4 tsp ground ginger
1 C raisins
3-1/2 C cooked, mashed fresh pumpkin
1/2 C canola oil
1/2 C unsweetened applesauce
1-1/2 C sugar

Mix dry ingredients and raisins; set aside. Cream pumpkin with oil, applesauce, and sugar. Blend pumpkin mixture with dry ingredients. Pour into 3 medium nonstick bread pans. Bake at 350° for 1 hour and 15 minutes. Remove from pans and cool on a wire rack.

Serves 30 (10 slices per loaf).

Suggestions
• 1 can (29-oz) pumpkin can be substituted for the fresh pumpkin.
• Other winter squash can be substituted for the pumpkin.

*My only trial here was one which I have to encounter in whatever direction I travel in America, and which, though apparently a trivial matter in itself, has caused me infinite trouble, and no little compassion for the rising generation of the United States—I allude to the ignorant and fatal practice of the women of stuffing their children from morning till night with every species of trash which comes to hand…I once took the liberty of asking a young woman who was traveling in the same carriage with me, and stuffing her child incessantly with heavy cakes, which she also attempted to make mine eat, her reason for this system,—she replied, it was to "keep her baby good."
I looked at her own sallow*

Calories	%Fat	Fat (g)	Saturated Fat (g)	Cholesterol (mg)	Sodium (mg)	Carbohydrate (g)	Protein (g)	Fiber (g)
172	21	4	0.4	0	31	32	3	1

Exchanges: Starch 1, Fruit 1, Fat 1
Note: Occasional use

 # ucchini Bread

3 C whole-wheat flour
1 C sugar
1/2 C chopped walnuts
2 tsp cinnamon
1 tsp baking soda
1/4 tsp baking powder
1/4 tsp nutmeg
6 egg whites
1/2 C plus 1 T unsweetened applesauce
1/2 C buttermilk
2-1/2 C grated zucchini

Mix all dry ingredients; set aside. Blend egg whites, applesauce, and buttermilk; stir in zucchini. Combine with dry ingredients. Pour into a Bundt or tube pan lightly coated with cooking spray. Bake at 350° for 45 to 60 minutes.
Serves 20.

Calories	%Fat	Fat (g)	Saturated Fat (g)	Cholesterol (mg)	Sodium (mg)	Carbohydrate (g)	Protein (g)	Fiber (g)
131	16	2	0.3	0	71	25	4	3

Exchanges: Starch 1, Fruit 1/2, Fat 1/2

# Currant Toasting Bread

4 C all-purpose flour
2 T sugar
2 tsp baking soda
1/4 C margarine
2/3 C dried currants, plumped
1/2 C lemon juice
1 C skim milk

Mix flour, sugar, and soda. Cut in margarine until particles are the size of rice grains. Toss in currants. Mix lemon juice and milk. Add half to dry ingredients and mix quickly. Add remaining liquid and mix only until blended. Lightly knead dough about 10 times on a floured surface and shape into a round loaf. Transfer to a nonstick baking sheet. Bake for 35 to 40 minutes at 375°. Cool on a wire rack. Lightly toast slices of bread in an oven or toaster oven. Cut only as many slices as will be eaten at one time; store cut loaf tightly wrapped in freezer.

Serves 12.

Suggestions
- The lemon juice does not add flavor to this bread. For a lemony fragrance and taste, add the grated rind of one to two lemons. Serve with low-sugar blackberry jam.
- Make 12 biscuits by pulling off clumps of dough and placing them on a baking sheet. Flatten the tops slightly. Bake for 30 to 35 minutes, or until lightly browned.

Calories	%Fat	Fat (g)	Saturated Fat (g)	Cholesterol (mg)	Sodium (mg)	Carbohydrate (g)	Protein (g)	Fiber (g)
226	17	4	0.8	0	203	42	5	2

Exchanges: Starch 2, Fruit 1, Fat 1

Leaveners

Ingredients that lighten the texture and increase the volume of baked goods are called *leaveners.* When baking powder or baking soda is mixed with liquid, it produces carbon dioxide gas bubbles that cause the batter to rise during baking.

- *Baking soda:* This alkali must be used with an acid, such as sour milk, vinegar, or lemon juice, for it to have a leavening effect. Mix baking soda with the dry ingredients first, before adding any liquid. It has an immediate reaction when mixed with liquid, so the dough or batter must be baked immediately.

- *Baking powder:* When mixed with a liquid, baking powder begins to foam immediately, forming the gas bubbles that raise dough. Double-acting baking powder has one acid that acts at room temperature and another that works at high heat in the oven; use double-acting baking powder in all recipes unless specifically instructed otherwise.

Basic Biscuits

2-1/4 C all-purpose unbleached flour, divided
1 C plain nonfat yogurt
1 tsp sugar
2 tsp baking powder
1/2 tsp baking soda

Mix 1 C of flour with the yogurt; sprinkle sugar on top. Cover and let stand in warm place overnight.

Mix remaining 1-1/4 C flour, baking powder, and baking soda. Stir into yogurt mixture. On a lightly floured surface, pat the dough into an 8 × 4-inch rectangle. Cut into 8 squares. Transfer to a nonstick baking sheet. For crusty biscuits, leave at least 2 inches between biscuits. Bake at 425° until golden, about 12 minutes.

Serves 8.

Suggestions

- Add herbs, grated cheese, or ground nuts to the dry ingredients.
- Stir raisins, currants, finely chopped dried fruit, blueberries, or lightly sugared chopped raw cranberries into the dry ingredients.
- For drop biscuits, add a little extra liquid to the batter; drop by spoonfuls onto the baking sheet and bake as directed.
- Substitute whole-wheat flour for up to half of the all-purpose flour.

Calories	%Fat	Fat (g)	Saturated Fat (g)	Cholesterol (mg)	Sodium (mg)	Carbohydrate (g)	Protein (g)	Fiber (g)
148	2	0	0.1	1	170	30	5	1

Exchanges: Starch 2

# Scottish Scones

1-1/2 C all-purpose flour
1-1/4 C rolled oats
1/4 C sugar
1 T baking powder
1 tsp cream of tartar
1/4 C canola oil
1/3 C skim milk
1/4 C egg substitute
1/2 C dried currants, plumped

Vigorous Old Age
If you eat healthfully, exercise moderately, use medication prudently, don't smoke, and keep your stress in check, you stand the best chance of living your last years vigorously and independently.

Diethrich and Cohan
Women and Heart Disease

Mix dry ingredients together. Add oil, milk, and egg substitute; mix just until moist. Stir in currants. On a lightly floured surface, pat the dough to form an 8-inch circle. Transfer to a nonstick cookie sheet and cut into 12 wedges; do not separate. Bake at 425° for 12 to 15 minutes, or until light brown. Serve warm.

Serves 12.

Calories	%Fat	Fat (g)	Saturated Fat (g)	Cholesterol (mg)	Sodium (mg)	Carbohydrate (g)	Protein (g)	Fiber (g)
168	28	5	0.5	0	128	27	4	2

Exchanges: Starch 1, Fruit 1, Fat 1

Popovers

1/4 C egg substitute
1/2 C 2% milk
1/2 C sifted flour
1/4 tsp salt

Blend egg and milk. Combine flour with salt; sift over the egg and milk mixture. Beat well until the batter is free of lumps. Pour into 4 large muffin or popover tins lightly coated with cooking spray. Bake at 425° for 30 minutes. Remove from oven and immediately puncture each popover with a sharp paring knife to allow steam to escape. Serve hot.
    Serves 4.

Calories	%Fat	Fat (g)	Saturated Fat (g)	Cholesterol (mg)	Sodium (mg)	Carbohydrate (g)	Protein (g)	Fiber (g)
79	8	1	0.4	2	178	14	4	1

Exchanges: Starch 1

# Steamed Apple-Spice Bread

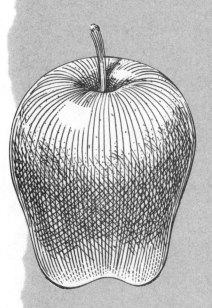

1 C sifted all-purpose flour
1-1/2 C unsifted whole-wheat flour
1/2 C cornmeal
1 tsp baking powder
1 tsp baking soda
1 tsp cinnamon
1/2 tsp nutmeg
1/2 tsp ground ginger
1/4 tsp ground cloves
1/4 C honey
3/4 C molasses
1-2/3 C skim milk
3/4 C unsweetened applesauce
1 C raisins

   Mix flours, cornmeal, salt, baking powder, baking soda, and spices in a large bowl. Combine honey, molasses, milk, and applesauce. Add to dry ingredients and stir until well mixed. Stir in raisins. Pour batter into four 1-lb coffee cans (lightly coated inside with cooking spray), filling each about two-thirds. Cover each can tightly with several layers of aluminum foil tied around the top with string.

   Use a deep kettle or roasting pan with a tight-fitting lid that is large enough

Fiber & Cholesterol

A healthy diet should include a wide variety of fibers. The most effective fibers for decreasing blood cholesterol are:

- Pectins, found in squash, apples, potatoes, bananas, oranges, cabbage, carrots
- Lignans, found in pears, eggplant, strawberries, radishes, whole-grain bread
- Gums, found in oatmeal, dried beans, and other legumes

Arizona Heart Institute Foundation
1–800–345–4278

to hold the four cans without touching. Place a rack in the bottom of the kettle; pour in boiling water to just below the level of the rack. Arrange the cans on the rack; they should not touch the sides of the kettle or each other. Cover the kettle and steam over low heat for 3 hours, pouring in more boiling water as needed (do not let the kettle boil dry). Remove the cans from the kettle and cool upright for 20 minutes. Remove bread from cans and allow to cool before slicing. The loaves can be frozen for up to 6 months when tightly wrapped in foil. Makes 4 loaves, 6 slices each.

Serves 24.

Suggestion

- Substitute any combination of chopped dried fruits for part or all of the raisins.

Calories	%Fat	Fat (g)	Saturated Fat (g)	Cholesterol (mg)	Sodium (mg)	Carbohydrate (g)	Protein (g)	Fiber (g)
118	3	0	0.1	0	65	27	3	1

Exchanges: Starch 1, Fruit 1

# Steamed Brown Bread

1 C whole-wheat flour
1 C all-purpose flour
1 C yellow cornmeal
2 tsp baking soda
1/2 tsp salt
2 C buttermilk
2/3 C molasses
1 C raisins

Lightly coat the inside of two 1-lb coffee cans with cooking spray. Line the bottom of each can with a piece of waxed paper cut to fit. Pour several inches of water into a large pot that has a rack in the bottom and is deep enough to hold both cans when covered with a lid. Bring the water to a boil.

Combine the flours with the cornmeal, baking soda, and salt. Stir in the buttermilk, molasses, and raisins, mixing well. Divide the batter between the two cans. Cover the open top of each can with a piece of foil coated with cooking spray, coated side down. Tie the foil in place with string. Place the cans, foil end up, on the rack in the pot and cover tightly with the lid. Steam the bread for 90 minutes to 2 hours. Add more water as necessary to keep the pot from

Boston Brown Bread
One cup of sweet milk,
One cup of sour,
One cup of corn meal,
One cup of flour,
Teaspoon of soda,
Molasses one cup;
Steam for three hours,
Then eat it all up.

Old Yankee Cookbook

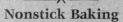

Nonstick Baking

- Lightly coat baking pans with cooking spray; non-stick pans such as Teflon and Silverstone may also require pretreatment.
- Line the bottom of each pan with waxed paper cut to fit.
- Use frilled paper liners for muffins and cupcakes.

boiling dry. Transfer the cans to a 350° oven and bake for 10 minutes.

Cool the bread in the can for 30 minutes. Remove the string and foil. Use a can opener to detach the lid from the bottom of the can; push the lid through the can, so it forces the bread out of the can. To serve, cut each loaf into 6 slices and then cut each slice in half.

Serves 24.

Calories	%Fat	Fat (g)	Saturated Fat (g)	Cholesterol (mg)	Sodium (mg)	Carbohydrate (g)	Protein (g)	Fiber (g)
105	4	0	0.2	1	140	23	3	1

Exchanges: Starch 1, Fruit 1/2

Pumpkin Streusel Coffee Cake

Cake

1/4 C margarine
1/4 C sugar
1 tsp vanilla
3/4 C egg substitute
1-1/4 C flour
3/4 C whole-wheat flour
1 tsp baking powder
1 tsp baking soda
1 C plain nonfat yogurt

Filling

1-3/4 C puréed pumpkin
1/4 C egg substitute
1/4 C sugar
1 tsp pumpkin pie spice

Streusel

1/4 C brown sugar
2 T margarine
1 tsp cinnamon
2 T rolled oats

Family History

If one or more members of your family (parent, sister, or brother) have a history of cardiovascular disease, your chances of developing heart disease are increased. Just because there is a family history, however, does not mean that you are doomed to develop the disease yourself. It's important to separate the hereditary from environmental influences. If those who had the disease were smokers, did not exercise, or had poor diets, these are all things that you personally can change so that your own risk may be far less than that of other family members.

**Arizona Heart
Institute Foundation**
1-800-345-4278

Cake: Cream margarine with 1/4 C sugar and vanilla. Beat in 3/4 C egg substitute. Combine flours, baking powder, and soda. Beat into creamed mixture in thirds, alternating dry ingredients with the yogurt.

Filling: Mix filling ingredients together well.

Streusel: Mix streusel ingredients together well.

Spoon half the cake batter into a 13 × 9 nonstick baking dish. Sprinkle half the streusel over the batter. Spread pumpkin filling over the streusel. Carefully spread the rest of the cake batter over the pumpkin. Sprinkle the remaining streusel on top. Bake at 325° for 50 to 60 minutes, or until a toothpick inserted in the center comes out clean.

Serves 12.

Calories	%Fat	Fat (g)	Saturated Fat (g)	Cholesterol (mg)	Sodium (mg)	Carbohydrate (g)	Protein (g)	Fiber (g)
209	26	6	1.3	0	226	34	6	2

Exchanges: Starch 2, Fat 1
Note: Occasional use

 **Workaday Pancakes**

1 C whole-wheat flour
1 tsp baking powder
1/2 tsp baking soda
1 C skim milk

Mix flour, baking powder, and baking soda. Stir in milk, mixing well. (Add a little more flour or milk if the batter is too thin or too thick.) Pour 1/4 C of batter onto a hot nonstick griddle or skillet; repeat with remaining batter to make 6 pancakes. When bubbles appear and begin to break, and when edges are dry, turn pancake and brown on the other side.
Serves 2.

Suggestion
• Fresh or dried fruit and spices to taste—such as blueberries, mashed bananas, puréed pumpkin, chopped dates or apricots, or cinnamon and raisins—can be stirred into the batter.

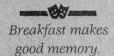

Breakfast

A high-fiber, low-fat breakfast is nourishing. Good nutrition helps the body perform more efficiently and resist infection. Eating breakfast improves mental ability throughout the day, including concentration and problem-solving skills. People who do not eat breakfast are more easily fatigued, and students may do poorly on tests.

Breakfast is an important meal, especially for people who are watching their weight. People who skip breakfast tend to eat more during the day or late at night and therefore gain weight more easily.

Calories	%Fat	Fat (g)	Saturated Fat (g)	Cholesterol (mg)	Sodium (mg)	Carbohydrate (g)	Protein (g)	Fiber (g)
248	5	1	0.3	2	461	50	12	7

Exchanges: Starch 3-1/2

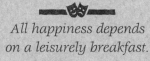

All happiness depends on a leisurely breakfast.

John Gunther

 **eekend Pancakes**

1/3 C all-purpose flour
2/3 C whole-wheat flour
1/4 C rolled oats
2 T wheat germ
2 tsp sugar
1 tsp baking powder
1/2 tsp baking soda
1 C buttermilk
1/4 C skim milk
2 tsp canola oil
1/2 tsp vanilla extract
1 tsp grated orange or lemon rind
3 egg whites, lightly beaten

Mix dry ingredients together. Add buttermilk, skim milk, oil, vanilla, and orange rind, stirring just to combine. Beat egg whites until fluffy; fold into batter. Let batter stand about 10 minutes. Cook pancakes on a hot nonstick griddle or skillet; turn when the tops are bubbly and a few bubbles have broken.
Makes 12.

Suggestion
• Fresh or dried fruit and spices can be stirred into the batter before cooking.

Calories	%Fat	Fat (g)	Saturated Fat (g)	Cholesterol (mg)	Sodium (mg)	Carbohydrate (g)	Protein (g)	Fiber (g)
70	17	1	0.2	1	104	11	4	1

Exchanges: Starch 1

Blueberry-Banana Pancakes

A good, honest,
wholesome, hungry
breakfast.

Walton
The Compleat Angler

1-1/2 C rolled oats
2-1/2 C skim milk
2 egg whites
1 C whole-wheat flour
2 tsp baking powder
1 tsp baking soda
1 tsp cinnamon
1 very ripe banana, well mashed
1/2 C blueberries

Mix oatmeal, milk, and egg whites; let stand for 30 to 60 minutes. Stir the flour, baking powder, baking soda, and cinnamon together. Mix dry ingredients and banana with oatmeal-milk mixture, stirring just until the dry ingredients are moistened. Pour 5-inch circles of batter onto a hot nonstick griddle or skillet. Immediately sprinkle a spoonful of blueberries on top of each pancake. Turn each pancake when the top is bubbly and a few bubbles have broken.
Serves 12.

Suggestion
• Serve with Blueberry Topping (page 416).

Calories	%Fat	Fat (g)	Saturated Fat (g)	Cholesterol (mg)	Sodium (mg)	Carbohydrate (g)	Protein (g)	Fiber (g)
107	8	1	0.2	1	100	20	5	2

Exchanges: Starch 1-1/2

And then I'm frightened of eggs, worse than frightened; they revolt me. That white round thing without any holes...Brr! Have you ever seen anything more revolting than an egg yolk breaking and spilling its yellow liquid? Blood is jolly, red. But egg yolk is yellow, revolting. I've never tasted it.

Alfred Hitchcock

How to Freeze Egg Whites

Stir the separated whites lightly to blend and then strain them through a medium strainer. Freeze, covered tightly, in measured quantities. Thaw egg whites in a closed container in the refrigerator. They must be cooked within 24 hours; do not use thawed egg whites to prepare foods that will not be cooked before serving.

French Toast

1 egg
4 egg whites
1/4 C skim milk
1/2 tsp almond extract
2 T brown sugar
1/4 tsp cinnamon
6 slices whole-wheat bread

Beat egg and egg whites well. Mix in milk, extract, sugar, and cinnamon. Dip each slice of bread in egg batter. Cook in a preheated nonstick skillet over medium-high heat for 2 to 3 minutes on each side, or until golden brown. Serve hot.

Serves 6.

Suggestions

- Serve with Honey-Ginger Applesauce (page 356), Cherries Sauce (page 417), Melba Sauce (page 419), Ginger Pears (page 418), Orange Dressing (page 480), or fresh fruit with a light dusting of powdered sugar.
- Use Cinnamon Swirl Bread (page 66) or Brandied Raisin Bread (page 65) instead of whole-wheat bread.
- Vanilla or other extracts can be substituted for the almond extract.

Calories	%Fat	Fat (g)	Saturated Fat (g)	Cholesterol (mg)	Sodium (mg)	Carbohydrate (g)	Protein (g)	Fiber (g)
114	13	2	0.5	36	204	19	7	2

Exchanges: Starch 1-1/2

# **W**hole-Wheat Crêpes

5 egg whites
1 T canola oil
1 T nonfat dry milk powder
1-1/2 C whole-wheat flour
1/4 tsp salt

Beat egg whites with oil and nonfat dry milk. Add flour and blend until smooth. Let batter stand for 1 hour at room temperature. Pour 1 T of batter into a hot, nonstick crêpe pan, quickly tilting pan to spread batter evenly across the entire pan; crêpe with be very thin. Cook until lightly brown. Turn the crêpe and lightly cook the other side. Repeat with remaining batter, making 6 crêpes. Cool crêpes on a wire rack.

Fill with vegetables, fruit, or frozen yogurt, as desired.

Makes 6.

Suggestions
• Add grated Parmesan cheese or herbs to the batter.
• Substitute cornmeal for up to 1/2 C whole-wheat flour.

Crêpes

Crêpes—thin, tender pancakes—are elegant at any meal. They can be served hot or cold, with sweet or savory fillings. Crêpes are appropriate for an appetizer, a main course, a dessert, or a snack.

Make large batches of crêpes and freeze extras. Crêpes can be kept in the refrigerator for two or three days, or frozen for up to four months. They can be stacked directly on top of one another for storage—they'll separate easily when thawed to room temperature. Waxed paper can be used to separate crêpes into groups of two or more, making it easy to remove and thaw only the number needed for one occasion.

Most filled crêpes can be frozen (exceptions include fillings that contain potatoes, mayonnaise, cooked egg white, raw vegetables, or cream-type bases). They should be thawed at room temperature for one hour and baked a few minutes longer than fresh crêpes.

Calories	%Fat	Fat (g)	Saturated Fat (g)	Cholesterol (mg)	Sodium (mg)	Carbohydrate (g)	Protein (g)	Fiber (g)
138	18	3	0.3	0	140	22	7	3

Exchanges: Starch 1-1/2, Fat 1/2

How to Fold Crêpes

- *Rolls:* Place a line of filling down the center of the crêpe and then roll it up into a cigar shape.
- *Triangles:* Spread a spoonful of filling in one quadrant or half of the crêpe and then fold it in quarters, for a triangular shape.
- *Pockets:* Place a spoonful of filling in the center of the crêpe and fold up four sides to form a rectangular pocket; serve seam-side down.
- *Stacks:* Stack three or four crêpes with a layer of filling in between each crêpe; serve the entire stack as a main course or dessert, or cut it into wedges to serve as appetizers or snacks.

Dessert Crêpes

3 egg whites
1-1/2 C all-purpose flour
1 C skim milk
1/2 tsp grated lemon or orange rind
1/2 tsp sugar
1 T canola oil

Process all ingredients except oil in a blender for 15 seconds. Scrape sides of blender jar with a rubber spatula. Restart blender; immediately add oil and process for 10 seconds. Allow batter to rest for 1 hour.

Working very quickly, pour 1/4 C of batter into a hot, nonstick crêpe pan, tilt and swirl pan to spread batter evenly across the entire pan, and pour excess batter back into the blender jar, drawing the edge across the lip of the jar to remove drips. Cook until lightly brown, about 30 seconds. Turn the crêpe and lightly cook the other side. Repeat with remaining batter. Cool crêpes on a wire rack.

Serves 6.

Suggestion

- Omit citrus rind; add flavoring to taste, such as orange liqueur, creme de cacao, kirsch, unsweetened cocoa powder, vanilla or almond extract, finely grated semisweet chocolate, or nuts.

Calories	%Fat	Fat (g)	Saturated Fat (g)	Cholesterol (mg)	Sodium (mg)	Carbohydrate (g)	Protein (g)	Fiber (g)
158	15	3	0.3	1	49	26	6	1

Exchanges: Starch 1-1/2, Fat 1/2

Whole-Wheat Bread

3 C warm water
3 pkg (1/4 oz each) yeast
1 T molasses
6-1/2 C whole-wheat flour
2 T canola oil
1 tsp salt

Combine water, yeast, and molasses in a large mixing bowl. Allow to rest for 5 minutes. When the yeast begins to foam, stir in 3 C of flour. Cover the bowl with a towel and allow the dough to rest in a warm place until doubled in size, about 1 hour.

Stir oil and salt into the dough. Mix in 3 C of flour. Transfer the dough to a lightly floured board or work surface and knead the dough until it is smooth and elastic, about 10 minutes. Add more flour as needed to keep the dough from sticking to the work surface.

Divide the dough in half and shape into 2 loaves. Place each loaf in a non-stick 9 × 5 inch bread pan. Cover and allow to rise for 1 hour.

Bake at 375° for 50 minutes, or until the bread is nicely browned. If the crust browns too fast, cover it with aluminum foil during the last 5 to 10 minutes. Remove bread from pans and tap the bottom of the loaf. The bread is done if it sounds hollow. Makes 2 loaves.

Serves 24.

Calories	%Fat	Fat (g)	Saturated Fat (g)	Cholesterol (mg)	Sodium (mg)	Carbohydrate (g)	Protein (g)	Fiber (g)
125	13	2	0.2	0	91	24	5	4

Exchanges: Starch 1-1/2

"...bread...has been the symbol of goodness... warmth and security since long before Biblical times. It is the most exciting food a woman can prepare for those she loves."

Fleischmann's Yeast

Yeast Breads

Yeast is made up of tiny one-celled fungi. They multiply rapidly when given moisture, warmth, and food. The yeast cells feed on sugar, which is chemically converted to alcohol and carbon dioxide, a gas that makes the bread rise. Yeast also adds a sweet, nutty flavor and a rich aroma to the bread.

The recipes in this book use traditional yeast, which is usually softened in warm liquid before it is added to the bread dough. If the liquid is too hot, it will kill the yeast; if it is too cool, the yeast will not grow properly. Unless a recipe or type of yeast gives different instructions, use liquids at 105° to 115°; allow the yeast to soak for about 10 minutes, or until it is foamy.

Dry yeast is granulated; it is usually sold in small foil envelopes and can be stored at room temperature for many months (the packages are printed with an expiration date). Compressed or fresh yeast is sold as small moist cakes; it can be stored in the refrigerator for two weeks or in the freezer for up to six months. To test the potency of stored yeast, mix a small amount with an equal amount of sugar and stir it with warm water; it should become foamy within five minutes.

Sugar, molasses, brown sugar, or honey can be used as food for the yeast. Salt is often added to bread dough to control the yeast's growth, slowing the rising time.

Water, skim milk, reconstituted dry milk, evaporated milk, or potato water can be used to make bread. Water makes a crusty loaf; milk provides a soft crust.

 randied Raisin Bread

1-1/2 C raisins
3/4 C ginger-flavored brandy
2 C skim milk, scalded
2 pkg (1/4 oz each) yeast
1 T honey
3 C whole-wheat flour
3-1/2 C all-purpose flour
2 T canola oil
1 tsp salt

Plump raisins in brandy for 48 to 72 hours, stirring occasionally (most of the brandy will be absorbed). Combine milk, yeast, and honey in a large mixing bowl. Allow to rest for 5 minutes. Stir the two flours together. When the yeast begins to foam, stir in 3 C of flour mixture. Cover with a towel and allow the dough to rest in a warm place until doubled in size, about 1 hour. Stir oil, salt, raisins, and any unabsorbed brandy into the dough. Mix in 3 C of flour. Transfer the dough to a lightly floured work surface and knead the dough until it is smooth and elastic, about 10 minutes. Add more flour as needed to keep the dough from sticking. Divide the dough in half and form into 2 loaves. Place each loaf in a nonstick 9 × 5 inch bread pan. Cover and allow to rise for 1 hour. Bake at 375° for 50 minutes, or until the bread is browned.

Serves 24.

Calories	%Fat	Fat (g)	Saturated Fat (g)	Cholesterol (mg)	Sodium (mg)	Carbohydrate (g)	Protein (g)	Fiber (g)
187	8	2	0.2	0	104	37	5	3

Exchanges: Starch 1-1/2, Fruit 1

# Cinnamon Swirl Bread

1 pkg (1/4 oz) yeast
1/4 C hot water
2 C skim milk, scalded
2 T margarine
1 T sugar
2 tsp vanilla extract
Grated rind of 1 orange
6-1/2 C all-purpose flour
1 tsp salt
1/2 C raisins
1-1/2 T cinnamon
1/2 C sugar
4 tsp orange juice

Dissolve yeast in hot water; allow to rest for 5 minutes, or until foamy. Combine milk, margarine, 1 T sugar, vanilla, and orange rind in a large mixing bowl, stirring until margarine is melted. Stir in yeast. Mix in 3 C of flour. Cover with a towel and allow the dough to rest in a warm place until doubled in size, about 1 hour.

Stir salt and raisins into the dough. Mix in 3 C of flour. Transfer the dough to a lightly floured board or work surface and knead the dough until it is smooth

Wheat Flour
Gluten is a protein that gives dough enough strength and elasticity to trap the carbon dioxide gases produced by yeast. It helps bread and other baked goods rise and gives them a light structure. Different flours have different amounts of gluten; those that have the most gluten produce the highest-rising breads. All-purpose white flour has more gluten than whole-wheat flour. Thus, a loaf of bread made with all whole-wheat flour will not rise as high as one made with half or all white flour.

The three basic types of wheat flour are *hard* (higher gluten content, higher protein content; best for bread baking), *soft* (lighter color; used in pastry making, called *pastry flour*), and *durum* (the hard, dense, starch kernel; used in pasta-making because it holds its shape while cooking in boiling water).

Whole-wheat flour contains the entire wheat kernel, including the bran and the germ. It is a much better source of fiber and vitamins B and E than refined flour. Whole grain flours should never be sifted. Labels that list wheat flour as an ingredient mean refined white flour; look for labels that list whole-wheat flour to get the nutritional benefit of the whole grain.

Whole-grain flours stay fresh for only a month at room temperature. Taste a pinch of flour to test it for freshness; it should not be bitter. Store whole-grain flours in airtight containers in the refrigerator or freezer (whole wheat will keep for up to a year; other whole-grain flours should be used within two to three months). Bring the flour to room temperature before using.

The bran, germ, and 83% of the nutrients are removed in refining white flour. Store white and other refined flours in airtight containers at room temperature in a cool, dry, dark place for six to twelve months. To help prevent insect infestations, put a bay leaf in the container of flour.

and elastic, about 10 minutes. Add more flour as needed to keep the dough from sticking to the work surface.

Divide the dough in half. Roll each half into a 15 × 7-inch rectangle, about 1/2-inch thick. Mix cinnamon with 1/2 C sugar; sprinkle half of the mixture evenly over each rectangle of dough. Sprinkle 2 tsp of orange juice on each rectangle, and smooth the damp cinnamon mixture with a spatula. Starting at the narrow side, tightly roll up each rectangle of dough like a jelly roll. Seal the seam. Make a light indentation at each side of the roll (about 1 inch from each end, or enough to include all the rough edges) and fold under the edges. Place each roll, sealed edge down, in a nonstick 9 × 5-inch bread pan. Cover and allow to rise for 1 hour.

Bake at 375° for 50 minutes, or until the bread is nicely browned. If the crust browns too fast, cover it with aluminum foil during the last 5 to 10 minutes. Remove bread from pans and tap the bottom of the loaf. The bread is done if it sounds hollow. Makes 2 loaves.

Serves 24.

Suggestion
• Omit orange rind; substitute water or apple juice for orange juice.

Calories	%Fat	Fat (g)	Saturated Fat (g)	Cholesterol (mg)	Sodium (mg)	Carbohydrate (g)	Protein (g)	Fiber (g)
160	8	1	0.2	0	113	32	4	2

Exchanges: Starch 2

# **W**hole-Wheat Pita Bread

1 cake or pkg yeast
Pinch of sugar
1-1/4 C warm water, divided
1-3/4 C all-purpose flour
1-1/4 C whole-wheat flour
2 T olive oil
1/2 tsp salt

Dissolve yeast and sugar in 1/4 C warm water. Set aside for 10 minutes. Combine both flours, salt, and oil in a small bowl. Add remaining water and yeast mixture, stirring until the dough forms a ball. Transfer the dough to a floured surface. Knead until the dough is smooth and satiny, about 10 minutes. Use more flour as necessary while kneading. Divide the dough into 6 balls, rolling or pressing each into 1/4-inch thick rounds. Cover with a towel and let rise in a warm place for 45 minutes.

Transfer the pitas to a baking sheet sprinkled with cornmeal. Bake at 500° for 12 to 15 minutes, or until puffed and golden. Remove from oven and immediately puncture each pita with a sharp paring knife to allow steam to escape; place hot pitas in a covered pan to cool.

Serves 6.

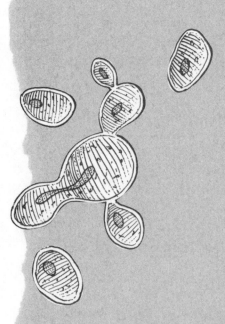

Calories	%Fat	Fat (g)	Saturated Fat (g)	Cholesterol (mg)	Sodium (mg)	Carbohydrate (g)	Protein (g)	Fiber (g)
261	18	5	0.8	0	181	47	8	4

Exchanges: Starch 3, Fat 1

Oats

A hulled, crushed oat grain that still has its bran and germ is called a *groat*. Rolled oats are groats that have been sliced, steamed, crushed between rollers, and dried. Flatter, more finely rolled oats cook more quickly than thicker, old-fashioned rolled oats but have the same nutritional value.

Oat flour (finely ground oatmeal) is chewy and sweet. It has little gluten, so it must be used with wheat flour to make yeast breads.

Oat bran contains soluble fibers that may help lower blood cholesterol when eaten in huge quantities. Oats are a high-carbohydrate food that contains B vitamins and dietary fiber.

Oatmeal Pita Bread

1 cake or pkg yeast
Pinch of sugar
1 C warm water
1 C all-purpose flour
1-1/4 C whole-wheat flour
3/4 C rolled oats
1/2 tsp salt
2 T safflower oil

Dissolve yeast and sugar in 1/4 C warm water. Set aside. Combine both flours, oatmeal, and salt in a small bowl. Add oil to yeast mixture. Add to dry ingredients and stir until coarse mixture forms. Add remaining 3/4 C water and stir until the dough forms a ball. Transfer the dough to a floured surface. Knead until the dough is smooth and satiny, about 10 minutes. Use more flour as necessary while kneading. Divide the dough into 6 balls, rolling or pressing each into 1/4-inch thick rounds. Cover with a towel and let rise in a warm place for 45 minutes.

Transfer the rounds to a baking sheet sprinkled with cornmeal. Bake at 500° for 12 to 15 minutes, or until puffed and golden. Remove from oven and immediately puncture each pita with a sharp paring knife to allow steam to escape; place the hot pitas in a covered pan to cool.

Serves 6.

Calories	%Fat	Fat (g)	Saturated Fat (g)	Cholesterol (mg)	Sodium (mg)	Carbohydrate (g)	Protein (g)	Fiber (g)
244	22	6	0.6	0	181	41	8	5

Exchanges: Starch 3, Fat 1

Whole-Wheat Tortillas

2 C whole-wheat flour
1 C all-purpose flour
1 tsp baking powder
1/4 C canola oil
1 C very hot water (tap water is not hot enough)

Mix dry ingredients; stir in oil. Add hot water and stir with a fork until dough can be kneaded. Knead for 5 minutes. Form dough into 10 balls. Roll balls into flat, round tortillas, using a floured rolling pin and working on a lightly floured surface. Cook tortillas over medium-high heat on a griddle or in an electric skillet for about 1 minute on each side, turning them over when bubbles appear.

Serves 10.

Calories	%Fat	Fat (g)	Saturated Fat (g)	Cholesterol (mg)	Sodium (mg)	Carbohydrate (g)	Protein (g)	Fiber (g)
175	31	6	0.5	0	40	27	5	3

Exchanges: Starch 2, Fat 1

- *Graham flour:* Coarse whole-wheat bread flour.
- *Self-rising flour:* Contains baking powder and soda; very high in sodium.
- *Unbleached flour:* White flour is bleached with chlorine dioxide to age it artificially and to make it snowy white; unbleached white flour has a natural creamy color and a more natural flavor. Flour must be aged to strengthen the gluten content; by shortening the aging period with chemicals, the manufacturer reduces the expense of storage. Bleaching destroys vitamin E.
- *Wheat germ:* The germ or embryo of the wheat grain; adds a pleasant nutty flavor to baked goods. Highly nutritious; contains B vitamins, dietary fiber, and oils (which are rich in vitamin E and essential fatty acids). The high oil content makes it very perishable; store wheat germ in the refrigerator in an airtight container for up to two weeks.
- *Whole white wheat:* A new flour that is lighter, sweeter, and milder than regular whole wheat. It produces a lighter product, more like refined all-purpose flour.

Whole-Wheat Bagels

1 pkg active dry yeast
2/3 C warm water
2 C whole-wheat flour
1 C water
1-1/2 tsp salt
3 T sugar
2 C enriched all-purpose flour
1 tsp sugar
1 egg white, lightly beaten

Dissolve yeast in 2/3 C warm water. Add whole-wheat flour, 1 C water, salt, and 3 T sugar. Stir until smooth. Blend in all-purpose flour and knead, adding more flour if necessary, until dough is smooth but not sticky. Cover and let rest for 15 minutes. Divide dough into 12 pieces and shape into balls. Using the handle of a wooden spoon or your thumb, punch a hole in the center of each ball and pull, forming a uniform doughnut shape. Place on a floured surface, cover, and let rise for 30 minutes. Bring a large skillet of water to a boil. Drop bagels a few at a time into the simmering water; after they rise to the top, turn and simmer for about 3 minutes. Remove from water, pat dry, and place on a nonstick baking sheet. Brush with egg white. Bake at 375° for 30 minutes or until golden.
Serves 12.

Calories	%Fat	Fat (g)	Saturated Fat (g)	Cholesterol (mg)	Sodium (mg)	Carbohydrate (g)	Protein (g)	Fiber (g)
160	3	1	0.1	0	273	34	6	3

Exchanges: Starch 2

Pizza Crust

"Give us this day our daily bread" is probably the most perfectly constructed and useful sentence ever set down in the English language.

P.J. Wingate

1 T sugar
1 T canola oil
1 C boiling water
1 pkg (1/4 oz) dry yeast softened in 1/4 C lukewarm water
1-1/2 C all-purpose flour
1-1/2 C whole-wheat flour

Combine sugar, salt, oil, and boiling water in large mixing bowl. Stir until sugar dissolves. Cool to lukewarm and add yeast. Stir flours together. Add 1-1/2 C flour mixture and beat until smooth. Add enough of remaining flour to make a dough that is easy to handle. Transfer to a floured work surface and knead until smooth and elastic. Stretch dough into a 12-inch pizza pan. Cover and let rise about 15 minutes. Use sauces, toppings, and cheeses as desired. Bake at 425° for 25 minutes, or until lightly browned.

Serves 8.

Suggestions
• Add 1 clove minced garlic and 2 tsp oregano or basil to the dry ingredients.
• Add 1/2 C freshly grated Parmesan cheese to the dry ingredients.

Calories	%Fat	Fat (g)	Saturated Fat (g)	Cholesterol (mg)	Sodium (mg)	Carbohydrate (g)	Protein (g)	Fiber (g)
185	12	2	0.2	0	2	36	6	4

Exchanges: Starch 2-1/2, Fat 1/2

Grains
Oats
Barley
Cornmeal
Quinoa
Wheat
Rice
Wild Rice

Legumes
Dried Beans
Tofu

rains & Legumes

 # uesli

1/2 C oat bran
1 C rolled oats
1 C plain low-fat yogurt
1 T unsalted sunflower seeds
2 kiwis, sliced

Mix oat bran, oats, and yogurt. (Thin with skim milk if desired.) Refrigerate overnight in a tightly covered container. Spoon into 2 cereal bowls and top with sunflower seeds and kiwis.
Serves 2.

Suggestions
• Other fresh or dried fruit may be substituted for the kiwi.
• Cinnamon or other spices to taste may be stirred into the muesli.

Calories	%Fat	Fat (g)	Saturated Fat (g)	Cholesterol (mg)	Sodium (mg)	Carbohydrate (g)	Protein (g)	Fiber (g)
360	21	8	2.2	7	92	63	19	9

Exchanges: Starch 3, Fruit 1, Dairy 1

Breakfast cereals that come in the same colors as polyester leisure suits make oversleeping a virtue.

Fran Lebowitz

Percentage of Calories from Sugar in Cereals

Puffed Rice	0
Puffed Wheat	0
Shredded Wheat	0
Cheerios	4
Rice Chex	7
Corn Flakes	8
Corn Chex	11
Special K	11
Grape-Nuts	11
Wheat Chex	12
40% Bran Flakes	22
Bran Buds	40
Cap'n Crunch	40
Cocoa Krispies	40
Honeycomb	40
Raisin Bran	40
Frosted Flakes	44
Fruity Pebbles	44
Lucky Charms	44
Trix	44
Fruit Loops	47
Alphabits	51
Apple Jacks	51
Sugar Smacks	55

Dietary Fiber in Cereals

Fiber One	13
Unprocessed bran	12
All-Bran	9
40% Bran Flakes	5
Wheatena	4
Wheat germ	4
Grape-Nuts	3
Oatmeal	3
Shredded Wheat	3
Wheat Chex	3
Wheaties	3
Cheerios	2
Corn grits	2
Corn Flakes	1
Special K	1
Cream of Wheat	1
Oat bran	0.5
Rice Krispies	0

Grams per ounce

Fruited Oatmeal

1-1/2 C water
1-1/3 C rolled oats
1/4 C dried apricots, chopped
1/2 C dates, chopped
1 small apple, peeled, cored, and chopped
1/4 C pecans, chopped

Bring water to a boil in a saucepan. Add oats and cook over medium heat for 1 minute, stirring constantly. Stir in dried fruit and apple. Cover and cook over low heat for 5 minutes, stirring occasionally, until desired consistency is reached. Stir in nuts.
Serves 4.

Suggestions
- Serve with skim milk and honey.
- Other dried fruits, such as figs, raisins, currants, pears, or prunes, may replace part or all of the apricots and dates.

Calories	%Fat	Fat (g)	Saturated Fat (g)	Cholesterol (mg)	Sodium (mg)	Carbohydrate (g)	Protein (g)	Fiber (g)
252	25	7	0.7	0	3	45	6	5

Exchanges: Starch 1-1/2, Fruit 1-1/2, Fat 1

Barley Pilaf with Sun-Dried Cranberries

Rozanne Gold

1/2 C sun-dried cranberries
3 C chicken broth
1 C finely chopped onion
1 C finely chopped carrot
3 cloves garlic, minced
1 tsp dried thyme leaves
1/2 lb barley
1/2 lb mushrooms, coarsely chopped
1/2 C finely chopped parsley
Pepper to taste

Soak cranberries in 1 C hot water for 30 minutes. Heat chicken broth in a large enamel pot. Add onions, carrots, garlic, and thyme. Cover and cook 15 minutes, or until soft. Add barley and mushrooms. Cover and simmer for 40 minutes, stirring often. Add cranberries with water, stir, cover, and continue to cook for 15 minutes, or until barley is soft and liquid is absorbed.

Serves 6.

Calories	%Fat	Fat (g)	Saturated Fat (g)	Cholesterol (mg)	Sodium (mg)	Carbohydrate (g)	Protein (g)	Fiber (g)
210	5	1	0.3	0	52	45	6	7

Exchanges: Starch 2, Vegetable 3

Barley

Once a staple grain in Europe, whole hulled barley is a good source of B vitamins, potassium, and protein.

The tough, sharp hulls adhere tightly to the barley grain. It must be milled or "pearled" many times to remove the hull. This process also removes the nutritious germ and bran layers. A naturally hull-less variety of barley is now available.

This mild-flavored grain has a chewy texture when cooked. It is good in soups or mixed with other grains (try using barley to replace half the rice in recipes). Steamed barley is good with lamb.

Whole grains contain small amounts of fat and will become rancid if improperly stored. Like other whole-grain cereals (buckwheat, hominy, millet, oats, rice, rye, wheatberries), barley can be stored tightly covered in the refrigerator for four to five months, or at room temperature for one month. Pearl barley and hominy can be stored at room temperature, in a cool, dry place, for up to one year.

# **Barley Patties**

1 C cooked barley, divided
1/3 C minced onion
1/3 C finely chopped green pepper
1/2 tsp dried thyme
1-1/2 C finely chopped mushrooms
2 T minced fresh parsley
1 T ground pecans
1/3 C whole-wheat cracker crumbs
Whole-wheat flour

Process 3/4 C of barley in a blender until smooth. Stir in remaining barley. Sauté onions, pepper, and thyme in cooking spray over medium heat. Add mushrooms. Cook until tender and lightly browned. Drain. Mix with barley, parsley, nuts, and cracker crumbs. Add more cracker crumbs if needed to form a stiff mixture. Form into 4 patties. Coat lightly with flour, dusting off excess. Using the same skillet, with more cooking spray if needed, brown patties on both sides; serve hot.

Serves 4.

Suggestions
- Serve on buns with lettuce, watercress, finely grated carrot, tomato, Almost Guacamole (page 440), or Pineapple Salsa (page 466).
- Recipe can be doubled or tripled and patties frozen for cooking later.

Calories	%Fat	Fat (g)	Saturated Fat (g)	Cholesterol (mg)	Sodium (mg)	Carbohydrate (g)	Protein (g)	Fiber (g)
98	23	3	0.4	0	53	17	3	3

Exchanges: Starch 1, Fat 1/2

# Rosemary Polenta

Sean Kavanaugh

1 clove garlic, chopped
2 cloves shallots, chopped
1 C polenta cornmeal
Chopped rosemary to taste
3 C chicken stock or low-sodium broth
Freshly ground black pepper to taste

Sauté garlic and shallot. Add polenta, rosemary, chicken stock, and pepper. Cook until thickened and then pour onto a sheet pan. Serve with Mesquite-Smoked Tomato Sauce (page 445).

Serves 4.

Calories	%Fat	Fat (g)	Saturated Fat (g)	Cholesterol (mg)	Sodium (mg)	Carbohydrate (g)	Protein (g)	Fiber (g)
152	8	1	0.3	0	44	29	5	3

Exchanges: Starch 2

Polenta & Cornmeal

Polenta is a hearty dish made of coarsely ground cornmeal. Refined cornmeal does not have the hull or germ; look for whole yellow or whole white cornmeal. Yellow cornmeal has more vitamin A than white. Blue cornmeal is high in protein; it is often used in chips, tortillas, and pancakes.

To cook polenta, bring two quarts of cold water to a boil. Slowly pour in one pound of polenta cornmeal, stirring constantly; continue stirring until the polenta is cooked. If lumps form, use a spoon to press them against the side of the pot and stir gently. Leave the cooked polenta over the heat without stirring; scrape it from the sides of the pot so that steam can form under the polenta; this will help loosen it from the bottom of the pot. Pour the polenta onto a large serving dish and serve immediately.

Cold polenta can be stored in the refrigerator for four to five days; it can be cut into strips, baked, and served with a hearty sauce, fresh fruit or preserves, or made into canapes.

Exercise & Energy

People who exercise regularly feel better and have more energy. Lack of exercise causes poor circulation, loss of muscle tone and strength, and weight gain. Brisk walking, jogging, swimming, and bicycling are the best exercises for burning off calories, controlling weight, and improving the function of the heart and lungs. Inactive people should start with mild activity. Always check with a doctor before starting an exercise program.

**Arizona Heart
Institute Foundation**
1-800-345-4278

Sweet Red Pepper & Black Olive Polenta

Maureen Pothier

2 C water
1 C chicken stock
Large pinch salt
1/2 C polenta (or yellow cornmeal)
1/2 tsp white pepper
1/4 C grated Gruyère cheese
1/3 C finely diced sweet red pepper
1/4 C finely diced Calamata olives

Bring water and chicken stock to a rapid boil in a heavy saucepan. Add salt; slowly sprinkle in polenta, stirring constantly and briskly with a wooden spoon to prevent lumping. Cook over medium heat, stirring constantly, until the polenta is very thick, about 20 minutes. Add white pepper and Gruyère; mix well. Gently fold in sweet red pepper and olives. Serve immediately.

Serves 2.

Calories	%Fat	Fat (g)	Saturated Fat (g)	Cholesterol (mg)	Sodium (mg)	Carbohydrate (g)	Protein (g)	Fiber (g)
107	28	3	1.4	6	107	15	4	1

Exchanges: Starch 1, Fat 1/2

Polenta & Mushrooms

Michael Lomonaco

1 C cornmeal
2 C water
1/2 tsp dried thyme leaves
2 T chopped fresh parsley
1/2 tsp dried oregano leaves
Pepper to taste
1 C dry sautéed shiitake mushrooms
1/2 C plain nonfat yogurt

In a non-stick pot, bring the water to a boil. Using a wire whisk, stir in the cornmeal slowly to avoid lumps. Return to a boil and reduce heat; simmer for 15 minutes. After the polenta has cooked, stir in the herbs, mushrooms, and yogurt. Cook for 5 minutes.

Line a baking pan with nonstick or waxed paper. Pour the polenta into the pan; set aside to cool. Cut the firm, cool polenta into pieces, which can be easily broiled, toasted, or grilled. Serve with tomato sauce or as a side dish with vegetable stew or chili.

Serves 6.

*Happiness lies,
first of all, in health.*

G.W. Curtis
Lotus-Eating: Trenton

High-Carbohydrate Diet
As you reduce the amount of fat and protein you eat, you will need to increase your complex carbohydrates (beans, grains, and other starchy vegetables), other vegetables, and fruits.

Diethrich and Cohan
Women and Heart Disease

Calories	%Fat	Fat (g)	Saturated Fat (g)	Cholesterol (mg)	Sodium (mg)	Carbohydrate (g)	Protein (g)	Fiber (g)
104	5	1	0.1	0	18	21	4	2

Exchanges: Starch 1, Vegetable 1

Quinoa

Quinoa (pronounced *keen-wa*) was the staple food of the ancient Incas. It is grown in the mountain regions of Peru and Bolivia. It is rich in essential nutrients and is an excellent vegetable source of protein: quinoa has more protein than other grains and contains eight essential amino acids.

This quick-cooking grain has a light nut-like flavor that takes on the taste of the seasonings used with it. Quinoa can be used in place of any other grain. It can be boiled like rice, added to soup or stew, or ground into a flour.

Quinoa grains are naturally coated with an inedible substance called *saponin,* which has a very bitter flavor. The grain must be washed thoroughly before cooking.

To cook quinoa, bring 2 cups of water and 1 cup of quinoa to a boil in a 1-1/2 qt saucepan. Reduce heat and simmer about 10 to 15 minutes, or until the water is absorbed.

uinoa-Stuffed Acorn Squash

2 medium acorn squash, halved and seeded
2 tsp margarine
2/3 C quinoa, well rinsed (see margin)
1 T canola oil
1/4 C minced onion
1/4 C minced carrot
1/4 C minced celery
1/4 C minced fresh ginger
2 tsp minced garlic

Place squash, cut side up, in a shallow baking pan. Dot with margarine. Cover and bake at 400° until squash is tender, about 45 minutes.

Place quinoa in a saucepan, add water to cover, and bring to a boil. Reduce heat and simmer, covered, until quinoa has popped open and is tender. Drain. Sauté vegetables in oil until soft. Add ginger and garlic; continue sautéing until very soft and fragrant. Stir in quinoa. Spoon quinoa filling into squash halves. Bake at 375° until hot, about 20 minutes.

Serves 4.

Calories	%Fat	Fat (g)	Saturated Fat (g)	Cholesterol (mg)	Sodium (mg)	Carbohydrate (g)	Protein (g)	Fiber (g)
180	14	3	0.7	0	18	36	6	9

Exchanges: Starch 2-1/2

Aromatic Couscous

Rozanne Gold

1/2 C couscous
1 C no-salt chicken stock
1/2 C water
1/4 C low-sodium tomato sauce
2 oz (about 1/3 C) minced zucchini
1-1/2 oz (about 1/3 C) minced carrot
1 clove garlic, minced
1/2 tsp ground cumin
1/4 tsp ground coriander
1/8 tsp allspice
Freshly ground black pepper
1/16 tsp cayenne pepper
3 T chopped parsley

Bring chicken stock, water, tomato sauce, zucchini, carrot, garlic, and spices to a boil. Boil for 2 minutes. Add couscous. Reduce heat to medium and cook for 3 minutes, or until most of the water is absorbed and the couscous is fluffy. Cover, remove from heat, and let steam for 2 minutes. Stir in parsley, mixing gently. Makes 2 C.
Serves 2.

Couscous

Couscous is made of finely cracked wheat or millet that is steamed, dried, and some-what refined into tiny pellets. It does not include the germ or the bran of the wheat kernel.

This grain is widely used in the Middle East. The seasonings vary from one country to another: saffron is popular in Morocco, tomatoes in Algeria, and harissa sauce in Tunisia.

To cook couscous, bring 1-1/2 cups of water to a boil. Stir in 1 cup of couscous. Reduce heat and cook, covered, for 5 minutes. Fluff with a fork before serving.

Calories	%Fat	Fat (g)	Saturated Fat (g)	Cholesterol (mg)	Sodium (mg)	Carbohydrate (g)	Protein (g)	Fiber (g)
106	4	1	0.1	0	29	21	4	2

Exchanges: Starch 1, Vegetable 1

emon Couscous with Fish

1/2 C sliced onion, separated into rings
1/2 C white wine
1/4 C lemon juice
1/2 tsp grated lemon rind
1/8 tsp salt
Freshly ground black pepper to taste
1 lb mahi-mahi or other mild fish
1 C water
1 C uncooked couscous
1 small can tomatoes, drained, chopped
4 lemon slices, for garnish
2 T chopped fresh parsley

Sauté onion in margarine over medium-high heat for 1 to 2 minutes. Stir in wine, lemon juice, lemon rind, salt, and pepper. Bring to a boil; add fish. Cook, covered, over medium-high heat for 8 to 9 minutes, or until fish flakes easily with a fork. Remove fish and onion rings from skillet; keep warm. Add water to cooking liquid to make 1-1/2 C; bring to a boil. Stir in couscous and remove from heat. Cover; let stand 5 minutes. Stir in tomatoes and juice of 1 lemon. Serve couscous with fish and onions, garnished with lemon slices and parsley.
Serves 4.

Calories	%Fat	Fat (g)	Saturated Fat (g)	Cholesterol (mg)	Sodium (mg)	Carbohydrate (g)	Protein (g)	Fiber (g)
334	16	6	1.1	37	56	40	27	2

Exchanges: Starch 2-1/2, Low-fat protein 3

# **T**abbouleh

3/4 C cracked wheat, soaked in 1-1/2 C water and drained
2 to 3 bunches fresh parsley, stems removed, chopped
3/4 C chopped fresh mint, stems removed, chopped
1 large onion, finely diced
2 medium tomatoes, diced
1-1/2 T olive oil
Juice of 1 lemon
1/2 tsp ground cinnamon
1/2 tsp pepper
2 heads romaine lettuce, cleaned and separated

Mix cracked wheat, parsley, mint, onions, and tomatoes. Add oil, lemon juice, and seasonings, tossing lightly. Serve over lettuce leaves.
Serves 8.

Bulgar Wheat

Bulgar wheat is widely used in Syrian and Lebanese cooking. It is a whole-wheat kernel that is steamed, dried, and crushed; the texture can range from fine to coarse. It has a nutty, sweet taste. Nutrients are preserved, but the cooking time is decreased to about 15 minutes. Cracked wheat is similar to bulgar wheat; it is made from whole wheatberries, cracked into fragments that range from fine to coarse.

Calories	%Fat	Fat (g)	Saturated Fat (g)	Cholesterol (mg)	Sodium (mg)	Carbohydrate (g)	Protein (g)	Fiber (g)
114	27	3	0.5	0	40	19	5	7

Exchanges: Starch 1-1/2, Fat 1/2

 # Tabbouleh with Chickpeas

1 C medium-cracked bulgar
1-1/4 C cold water
Juice of 2 lemons
1 C dried chickpeas, soaked overnight and cooked until tender
1/2 C freshly chopped mint
2 medium tomatoes, peeled, seeded, and cut into strips
6 scallions, trimmed and thinly sliced
1 T olive oil
Freshly ground black pepper to taste

Place the bulgar, cold water, and lemon juice in a large bowl. Allow bulgar to absorb liquid for 30 minutes, stirring once or twice. Drain. Toss bulgar with the remaining ingredients. Set aside for 15 to 30 minutes to allow flavors to blend. Garnish with fresh mint before serving.

Serves 4.

Suggestion

• A half-pint of cherry tomatoes, halved, may be substituted for the medium tomatoes.

Calories	%Fat	Fat (g)	Saturated Fat (g)	Cholesterol (mg)	Sodium (mg)	Carbohydrate (g)	Protein (g)	Fiber (g)
264	22	7	0.8	0	28	43	12	9

Exchanges: Starch 2-1/2, Vegetable 1, Fat 1

Rice Tabbouleh

Sanford D'Amato

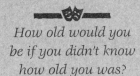
2 T finely diced onions
1/4 C rice
1/3 C chicken stock, hot
1/4 bay leaf
2 plum tomatoes, cored, scored at opposite end
1 scallion, small dice
1/4 tsp ground coriander
1 C parsley tops (no stems), chopped coarsely and loosely packed
1 T lemon juice
Freshly ground black pepper to taste

Sauté onions in a medium-hot pan until transparent. Add rice and sauté for 30 seconds. Add hot chicken stock and bay leaf and bring to a boil. Cover with waxed paper cut to fit the pan. Bake at 350° for 5 to 7 minutes, until liquid is absorbed. Place in bowl and refrigerate. Plunge tomatoes into boiling water for 17 seconds. Put into ice water; peel, seed, and cut into small dice. Add with remaining ingredients to rice. Let set for at least 2 hours.

Serves 3.

Calories	%Fat	Fat (g)	Saturated Fat (g)	Cholesterol (mg)	Sodium (mg)	Carbohydrate (g)	Protein (g)	Fiber (g)
92	6	1	0.1	0	207	19	3	3

Exchanges: Starch 1

Orange-Raisin Rice

1/3 C minced onion
1 C rice
2 T yellow raisins
1/4 C sliced almonds
1 C low-sodium chicken broth
1 T finely grated carrot
1 tsp grated orange rind
1/2 C orange juice
Freshly ground black pepper

In a medium saucepan, sauté the onion in cooking spray until soft. Add rice, raisins, almonds, broth, carrot, orange rind, and orange juice. Bring to a boil; reduce heat and simmer, covered, until all liquid is absorbed, about 20 minutes. Season to taste with pepper. Lightly fluff rice with a fork and serve hot.
    Serves 4.

Calories	%Fat	Fat (g)	Saturated Fat (g)	Cholesterol (mg)	Sodium (mg)	Carbohydrate (g)	Protein (g)	Fiber (g)
278	18	5	0.6	0	21	51	7	2

Exchanges: Starch 3, Fruit 1/2, Fat 1

Basmati Rice

2 C water
1 C Basmati rice, very well rinsed and drained (see margin)
1/3 C minced scallions
3 T minced fresh parsley

   Bring water to a boil and stir in rice. Reduce heart and simmer, covered, for 15 minutes. Remove pan from heat and let stand covered for 5 minutes. Stir in scallions and parsley. Serve promptly.
   Serves 4.

Rice

White rice is also called *polished rice*. Removal of the outer brown layers to make white rice removes the bran and germ, including the vitamins, minerals, and protein. Converted rice is parboiled under pressure before milling; it has more vitamins and minerals than regular white rice. Converted rice is cream colored, not bright white. Quick-cooking rice has been cooked and dehydrated; it absorbs water almost instantly during cooking.

   White rice can be stored at room temperature in the original container for several weeks, or in an airtight container indefinitely. Cooked rice can be stored in an airtight container in the refrigerator for a week.

   Brown rice is a good source of B vitamins. It also has protein, and dietary fiber. It has a nutty flavor. Instant brown rice has been cooked and dried and still has most of its nutrients; it is faster cooking than regular brown rice. Long-grained brown rice is most like the texture of white rice. Raw

Calories	%Fat	Fat (g)	Saturated Fat (g)	Cholesterol (mg)	Sodium (mg)	Carbohydrate (g)	Protein (g)	Fiber (g)
187	2	0	0.1	0	6	41	4	1

Exchanges: Starch 3

brown rice can be stored at room temperature for a month or in an airtight container in the refrigerator for six months.

Short-grained rice is chewier and stickier than other varieties. Do not wash it before cooking, or it will be dry and not sticky. Cooked medium-grained rice is fluffier than short-grain varieties. Cooked long-grain rice has dry, separate grains.

- *Arborio rice:* Short-grained rice grown in Italy; plump grains and a creamy, al dente texture. Used to make risotto; very nice in rice pudding.
- *Basmati rice:* Long-grained rice grown in India; prized for its nutty flavor and aroma (*basmati* means "queen of fragrance"). Available in large supermarkets or Indian and Middle Eastern markets.

Brown Rice Curry

1 medium onion, sliced vertically (not in rings)
2 garlic cloves, minced
1 can (13-3/4 oz) low-sodium chicken broth
1 C brown rice, raw
1 T curry powder
1 tsp dry mustard
1 tsp ground thyme
1 C finely diced carrots
1/2 C thinly sliced celery
1/3 C raisins
1 lb fresh spinach, stems removed

In a 3-qt saucepan, sauté onion and garlic in 1/4 C broth. To the remaining broth, add water to make 2-2/3 C liquid. Pour over onion and bring to a boil. Add rice, curry powder, mustard, and thyme. Reduce heat and simmer, covered tightly, for 40 minutes. Add carrots, celery, raisins, and spinach. Simmer, covered, until carrots are cooked and all liquid is absorbed, about 10 to 15 minutes.

Serves 4.

Calories	%Fat	Fat (g)	Saturated Fat (g)	Cholesterol (mg)	Sodium (mg)	Carbohydrate (g)	Protein (g)	Fiber (g)
269	8	2	0.5	0	110	56	8	6

Exchanges: Starch 2-1/2, Fruit 1, Vegetable 1

 **egetable Rice**

1 C water
1/2 C quick-cooking brown rice
1/4 C low-fat, low-salt Italian dressing
3/4 C finely chopped red bell pepper
1/2 C finely chopped broccoli
1/3 C grated carrot
1/2 C chopped fresh parsley
2 tsp lemon juice

Bring water, rice, and Italian dressing to a boil over medium-high heat. Reduce heat and simmer, covered, for 25 minutes or until the rice is tender and liquid is absorbed. Stir in remaining ingredients. Cover and let stand 10 minutes before serving.

Serves 6.

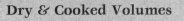

Dry & Cooked Volumes

Dry	Cooked
1 C bulgar	3 C
1 C long-grain rice	3 C
1 C quick-cooking rice	2 C
8 oz spaghetti	4 C
1 C macaroni	2-1/2 C
1 C noodles	3 C
1/4 C popcorn	5 C

Calories	%Fat	Fat (g)	Saturated Fat (g)	Cholesterol (mg)	Sodium (mg)	Carbohydrate (g)	Protein (g)	Fiber (g)
78	18	2	0.2	1	89	15	2	2

Exchanges: Starch 1

Spanish Rice

1 C quick-cooking brown rice
1 clove garlic, minced
1 medium onion, sliced
1 medium green pepper, chopped
1 can (16 oz) unsalted tomatoes, drained (reserve liquid)
3/4 tsp chili powder
1/4 tsp marjoram leaves

Add enough water to the liquid drained from the tomatoes to make 2 cups; set aside. Brown the rice in a 10-inch skillet, adding garlic when rice is nearly browned. Stir in remaining ingredients, including liquid, and bring to a boil. Reduce heat and simmer, covered, for about 15 minutes, or until rice has absorbed all the liquid. Remove from heat and let stand, covered, for 10 minutes before serving.

Serves 6.

Calories	%Fat	Fat (g)	Saturated Fat (g)	Cholesterol (mg)	Sodium (mg)	Carbohydrate (g)	Protein (g)	Fiber (g)
142	8	1	0.2	0	20	30	4	3

Exchanges: Starch 1-1/2, Vegetable 1

Brown Rice Pizza

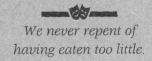
1-1/2 C cooked brown rice, prepared without salt or fat
1 C shredded part-skim mozzarella cheese, divided
1/4 C egg substitute
1 tsp dried oregano, divided
1 C fresh broccoli florets
1 medium red bell pepper, sliced in rings
1 C sliced fresh mushrooms
1 small onion, sliced
1 can (8 oz) no-salt-added tomato sauce

Mix rice, 1/2 C cheese, egg substitute, and 1/2 tsp oregano. Press into a 10- or 12-inch pizza pan lightly coated with cooking spray. Bake at 400° for 25 minutes.

Sauté broccoli, bell pepper, mushrooms, and onions over medium-high heat until crisp-tender.

Combine tomato sauce and remaining 1/2 tsp oregano; spread evenly over baked crust. Top with sautéed vegetables. Sprinkle remaining cheese on top of the pizza. Bake at 400° for 10 minutes, or until the pizza is hot and the cheese is melted.

Serves 4.

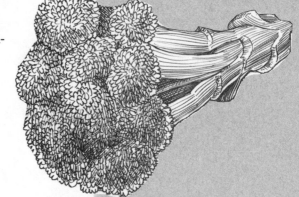

Calories	%Fat	Fat (g)	Saturated Fat (g)	Cholesterol (mg)	Sodium (mg)	Carbohydrate (g)	Protein (g)	Fiber (g)
203	26	6	3.3	15	203	26	13	3

Exchanges: Starch 1, Vegetable 2, Medium-fat protein 1

Wild Rice & Carrots

Wild Rice

Wild rice is really the fruit seed of an aquatic grass; it is not a member of the rice family. This grass grows wild alongside lakes in Minnesota, Wisconsin, and Canada. Most wild rice is grown on Indian reservations; it is harvested by hand by Indians who beat the grasses so the seeds fall into their boats.

Wild rice is a good source of protein and B vitamins. It has a nutlike flavor, a nice texture, and dark brown color. It is often mixed with other varieties of rice, primarily because it is very expensive. It must be washed well in cold water before using.

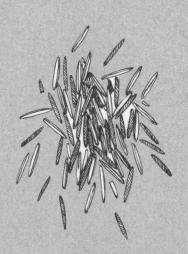

1/2 C chopped unpeeled apple
1/2 C sliced green onions
1 C shredded carrot
1/2 C plus 3 T quick-cooking wild rice, uncooked
1/2 C plus 3 T water
2 T lemon juice
1/2 tsp ground cardamom
1/2 tsp freshly ground black pepper

Mix all ingredients in a microwave-safe 2-qt casserole; cover tightly. Microwave on HIGH for 2 minutes; stir. Continue cooking on HIGH until mixture boils, about 3 minutes. Continue cooking on LOW (10% power) for about 5 minutes. Cool for 10 minutes, covered. Stir well before serving.

Serves 4.

Calories	%Fat	Fat (g)	Saturated Fat (g)	Cholesterol (mg)	Sodium (mg)	Carbohydrate (g)	Protein (g)	Fiber (g)
138	3	1	0.1	0	25	30	5	2

Exchanges: Starch 1-1/2, Vegetable 1

Black Beans

Karla A. Graves

1 lb dried black beans, rinsed, stones removed
1 onion, diced
1 bunch cilantro, cleaned and chopped
1 C chopped tomatoes
2 cloves garlic, diced
1/4 tsp salt
1 jalapeño pepper, diced (optional)

Cook beans, in water to cover, until soft. Add remaining ingredients and cook an additional 30 minutes. Serve with Snapper Soft Tacos with Two Salsas (page 276).

Serves 16 (1/2 C each).

Suggestion
• Do not add salt to beans during cooking or they may become tough.

(page 276).

Cooked Volumes of Dried Beans

1 cup dried	Cups cooked
Baby lima beans	3-1/2
Black beans	4
Black-eyed peas	4
Garbanzo beans	4
Great Northern beans	4
Kidney beans	4
Lentils	4-1/2
Lima beans	2-1/2
Pink beans	4
Pinto beans	4
Red beans	4
Navy beans	4
Split peas	4-1/2

Calories	%Fat	Fat (g)	Saturated Fat (g)	Cholesterol (mg)	Sodium (mg)	Carbohydrate (g)	Protein (g)	Fiber (g)
107	5	1	0.1	0	44	20	7	6

Exchanges: Starch 1, Vegetable 1

*Beans, beans, the musical
fruit,
The more you eat, the more
you toot.
The more you toot, the
better you feel,
Beans, beans at every meal.*

American Doggerel

How to "De-gas" Beans

Beans contain complex sugars that are indigestible for most people. Bacteria in the intestine digest these sugars for us, and the by-product of their metabolism is intestinal gas.

People who frequently eat beans adapt and do not have problems with gas, usually within two to four days of eating 1-1/2 C beans per day.

About 90% of the gas-producing sugars can be eliminated by presoaking the beans. First rinse the beans and drain well. Pour boiling water over the beans and soak for four hours. Drain the beans and cook with fresh water. Some of the vitamins and minerals are lost with this method.

Black Beans & Rice

1 C chopped onion
1/2 C chopped green pepper
2 C cooked brown rice, prepared without salt or fat
1/2 tsp ground cumin
1/8 tsp dried coriander
2 C hot cooked black beans
3/4 C chopped tomato
1/4 C chopped green scallions, green tops only

Sauté onion and green pepper in cooking spray over medium-high heat until tender. Stir in remaining ingredients. Cook until thoroughly heated, about 3 minutes. Serve hot black beans over rice. Garnish with tomato and scallions.
Serves 8.

Suggestions
• Stir tomatoes into black beans and cook briefly, until tomatoes are hot but not soft.
• Add chili powder or other seasonings to taste.

Calories	%Fat	Fat (g)	Saturated Fat (g)	Cholesterol (mg)	Sodium (mg)	Carbohydrate (g)	Protein (g)	Fiber (g)
134	6	1	0.2	0	6	27	6	5

Exchanges: Starch 1-1/2, Vegetable 1

Tortas de Lentejas

Rick Bayless

10 oz (1-3/4 C) red lentils, cleaned of debris
1 medium white onion, sliced in rings
6 cloves garlic, unpeeled
1/4 C grated queso añejo or Parmesan cheese
1/2 C finely chopped cilantro
1/2 tsp freshly ground black pepper
Salt, if necessary
4 egg whites
3 T buttermilk
2 C dry bread crumbs
18 oz Roasted Tomato-Chipotle Sauce (page 444)
Cilantro sprigs

Bring 2 qt water to a boil in a large saucepan. Add the lentils and simmer over medium heat until quite tender, about 15 minutes. Strain; spread lentils in a thin layer on a baking sheet to cool completely. Spray onions with cooking spray and grill them on a charcoal or gas grill until well-browned and tender (or cook them in a large skillet in a single layer over medium heat). Cool and finely chop. Meanwhile, roast the unpeeled garlic in a dry pan, turning regularly until soft, about 15 minutes. Cool, peel, and mince.

Combine lentils, onion, garlic, cheese, cilantro, and pepper. Form into 12 discs, about 2 inches in diameter and 1/2-inch thick. Freeze until firm if time permits (will make breading easier).

Beat the eggs and buttermilk in a flat dish. Spread the bread crumbs in another flat dish. Carefully dip each cake in the egg mixture, then dredge in the crumbs, patting them firmly in place. Refrigerate if not cooking immediately.

Heat a large (preferably nonstick) skillet over medium heat; add cooking spray. In batches, fry the cakes in an uncrowded single layer until brown and crusty, about 3 minutes per side. Remove and drain on paper towels.

Bring the Roasted Tomato-Chipotle Sauce to a boil. Spoon equal amounts onto 6 warm dinner plates. Top with 2 lentil cakes, slightly overlapping. Garnish with cilantro sprig.

Serves 6.

Calories	%Fat	Fat (g)	Saturated Fat (g)	Cholesterol (mg)	Sodium (mg)	Carbohydrate (g)	Protein (g)	Fiber (g)
330	9	3	1.2	5	304	55	22	10

Exchanges: Starch 2

# **S**weet & Sour Tofu

1 clove garlic, crushed
1/2 tsp ground ginger
1 T orange blossom honey
1 scallion, chopped
1 T no-salt-added tomato paste
1 T vinegar
1 T lemon juice
1 tsp sesame oil
1/3 C low-sodium soy sauce
1 medium onion, sliced
1 lb firm tofu, cut into bite-sized cubes
1 medium red bell pepper, sliced
1 medium green bell pepper, sliced
10 oz mushrooms, quartered
2 tsp canola oil
2 T cornstarch
1/2 C unsweetened orange juice
4 C hot cooked brown rice

Combine garlic, ginger, honey, scallion, tomato paste, vinegar, lemon juice, sesame oil, and soy sauce. Pour over tofu and marinate for at least 1 hour or overnight in the refrigerator; drain, reserving marinade. Sauté onion and bell

Soybeans & Tofu

Soybeans offer the highest quality vegetable protein. Soy foods include sprouts, tofu (or soybean curd), bean cakes, soymilk, miso, and tempeh.

Tofu is an excellent source of calcium if it is processed with calcium sulfate; it is a low-saturated-fat, no-cholesterol, high-protein, low-sodium food. It has the consistency of custard pressed into creamy cakes, and it is sold in four degrees of firmness.

Tofu is packed in plastic containers filled with water. It is very perishable. Store it in the refrigerator, and change the water every day (use spoons, not fingers, to lift the curd). Use the tofu within a week. Discard the whole block if any moldy spots appear; do not trim off bad spots to use the rest.

Tofu requires seasonings, sauces, and marinades to give it flavor. It is a good substitute for ricotta and cottage cheese.

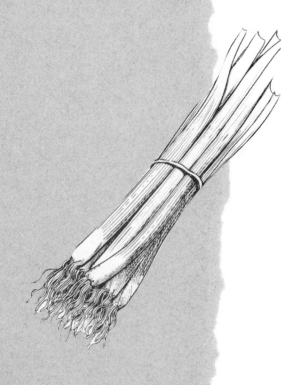

peppers in oil until crisp-tender; remove from skillet and set aside. Pour marinade into skillet and heat until almost boiling. Mix orange juice and cornstarch; stir into marinade. Cook until mixture boils and is thickened and translucent. Add tofu, onion, and pepper. Reduce heat to low and cook for a few minutes, until tofu is warm. Serve over hot brown rice.

Serves 6.

Suggestion
• Sprinkle sesame seeds over each serving.

Calories	%Fat	Fat (g)	Saturated Fat (g)	Cholesterol (mg)	Sodium (mg)	Carbohydrate (g)	Protein (g)	Fiber (g)
288	23	7	1.0	0	550	46	12	5

Exchanges: Starch 2-1/2, Vegetable 1, Low-fat protein 1, Fat 1

Tofu Burgers

1/2 lb tofu, drained, pressed, and mashed
2 T tahini
1/3 C finely chopped onion
2 tsp oregano
2 T finely chopped or ground sunflower seeds
1/4 C unsalted whole-wheat cracker crumbs
1 T low-sodium soy sauce
Freshly ground black pepper to taste
Whole-wheat flour

Mix tofu with tahini until smooth; set aside. Sauté onion and oregano in cooking spray until tender and lightly browned. Add to tofu along with sunflower seeds, cracker crumbs, soy sauce, and pepper, blending well. Add more cracker crumbs if needed to make a firm mixture. Shape into 6 patties. Dredge both sides in whole-wheat flour, dusting off excess flour. Brown patties on each side in cooking spray over medium heat.

Serves 6.

Suggestion
• Serve with Whole-Wheat Pita Bread (page 68) and Roasted Red Pepper Spread (page 448) or Tomato Salsa (page 455).

Calories	%Fat	Fat (g)	Saturated Fat (g)	Cholesterol (mg)	Sodium (mg)	Carbohydrate (g)	Protein (g)	Fiber (g)
67	53	4	0.5	0	150	5	5	1

Exchanges: Starch 1/2, Medium-fat protein 1/2

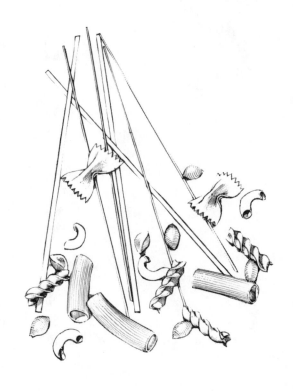

Pasta

Angel Hair Pasta with Basil

2 T finely chopped garlic
2 T finely chopped shallots
2 T chopped fresh basil
1/3 C plum tomatoes, peeled, seeded, and diced
1 lb angel hair pasta, cooked al dente and drained
Freshly ground black pepper to taste
4 sprigs fresh basil
1/3 C freshly grated Parmesan cheese

Sauté garlic, shallots, basil, and tomatoes for 2 to 3 minutes, or until the tomatoes are tender. Toss the tomatoes with the hot pasta and black pepper. Garnish with fresh basil sprigs. Serve with Parmesan cheese on the side.
Serves 6.

Shallots

Shallots are widely used in European cooking, primarily in sauces and slow-cooked meat dishes. These tiny bulbs can be gray, pink, or golden brown. They look like miniature onions but separate into two or three cloves, like garlic.

Shallots are less pungent and faster-cooking than onions. The elongated varieties generally have a stronger taste than the round ones, and the reddish ones are stronger flavored than the brown ones.

Shallots should be stored like onions. Chopped shallots freeze well but lose most of their flavor when dried.

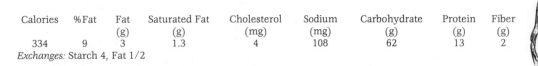

Calories	%Fat	Fat (g)	Saturated Fat (g)	Cholesterol (mg)	Sodium (mg)	Carbohydrate (g)	Protein (g)	Fiber (g)
334	9	3	1.3	4	108	62	13	2

Exchanges: Starch 4, Fat 1/2

How to Cook Pasta

Use at least 8 quarts of rapidly boiling water to cook 1 pound of pasta. Instead of salt, add herbs, a bay leaf or clove, strips of citrus peel, or lemon juice to the water.

Homemade pasta does not stick during cooking. To keep commercial pasta from sticking together, some cooks add oil to the water. This high-fat practice is unnecessary. When the water has reached a full rolling boil, drop in the pasta and immediately begin stirring. Keep the pasta constantly moving until the water returns to a full boil. Make sure the water continues to boil throughout the cooking period—it will keep the pasta in constant motion so that it cannot clump and stick.

To test pasta, remove a piece from the boiling water and taste it; it should be tender but firm, without a hard core. Overdone pasta is unpleasantly mushy. Test frequently until it is just done. Drain well before serving or mixing with sauce.

Potato-Herb Raviolini

Laura Brennan

1 head garlic
Scant tsp olive oil
2 medium Idaho or baking potatoes
1 heaping tsp chopped fresh tarragon
2 sheets fresh pasta (commercial or homemade), about 12 × 13 inches

Cut the head of garlic in half (widthwise), rub with the olive oil, and season with salt and pepper. Roast, wrapped in aluminum foil, at 350° for 30 to 40 minutes, or until soft.

Bake the potatoes until soft; peel and rice them when cool enough to handle. To the riced potatoes, add 3 to 5 mashed cloves of the roasted garlic, the chopped tarragon, and pepper to taste.

Using a raviolini or small ravioli mold, make 36 raviolini, filling the pasta with potato-herb mixture. Cook in boiling water for 3 to 4 minutes. Drain, refresh in cold water, and set aside until ready to use. Serve with Braised Haddock with Leeks (page 260).

Serves 6.

Calories	%Fat	Fat (g)	Saturated Fat (g)	Cholesterol (mg)	Sodium (mg)	Carbohydrate (g)	Protein (g)	Fiber (g)
62	13	1	0.1	0	2	12	2	1

Exchanges: Starch 1

Pasta Primavera

1/2 lb asparagus, diagonally sliced into 1-inch pieces
1/2 C broccoli florets
1/2 C snow peas, sliced diagonally into 1-inch pieces
1/2 C yellow squash
1/2 C sliced red bell pepper
1/2 lb mushrooms, sliced
1 clove garlic, minced
1 T water
1/2 C hot water
2 T dry white wine
1/2 tsp low-sodium chicken bouillon granules
3/4 C skim milk
1 T all-purpose flour
8 oz hot cooked linguini, prepared without fat or salt, drained
1/2 C plus 1 T grated Parmesan cheese, divided
1 T chopped fresh parsley
1 -1/2 tsp chopped fresh basil
1/8 tsp pepper

Steam asparagus, broccoli, snow peas, squash, and bell peppers for 15 to 20 minutes or until crisp-tender. Sauté mushrooms and garlic over medium-high heat for 5 minutes, or until mushrooms are tender. Add steamed vegetables

Pasta Shapes
Different pasta shapes are intended for use with different types of sauces. In general, thin, smooth sauces should be serve with strings and flat pasta shapes. Thick, chunky sauces should be served with twisting or other complicated pasta shapes, which will catch and hold the chunks.

- *Angel hair:* Long, extremely thin strings.
- *Cannelloni:* Rolled stuffed squares.
- *Conchiglie:* Seashell shape.
- *Fettucini:* Long, flat strands, about one-fourth inch wide.
- *Frafalle:* Bow shape.
- *Gramigna:* "Weeds," formless, twisting shapes made of short pieces of spaghetti.
- *Lasagna:* Long, wide strips, usually with ruffled edges.
- *Linguini:* Long, flat strings, about one-eighth inch thick and slightly wider.
- *Orzo:* Tiny rice-shaped pasta; can be substituted for rice.

- *Penne:* Ridged short tubes with ends cut diagonally.
- *Radiatore:* Small round wheels.
- *Rigatoni:* Ridged short tubes with ends cut straight.
- *Rotille:* Small corkscrew shape.
- *Spaghetti:* Long, thin strings, about one-eighth inch in diameter.
- *Vermicelli:* Very thin spaghetti.

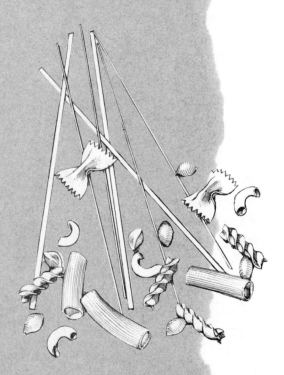

and 1 T water. Reduce heat and simmer, uncovered, for 5 minutes. Set aside.

Bring 1/2 C hot water, wine, and bouillon granules to a boil; cook until mixture is reduced to 2 T.

Mix milk with flour and slowly add to wine mixture, stirring constantly. Cook over medium heat, stirring constantly, for 5 minutes or until thick and bubbly. Pour over hot linguini and toss lightly. Add 1/2 C Parmesan cheese, parsley, basil, and pepper; toss. Spoon vegetables over the linguini and top with remaining Parmesan.

Serves 6.

Calories	%Fat	Fat (g)	Saturated Fat (g)	Cholesterol (mg)	Sodium (mg)	Carbohydrate (g)	Protein (g)	Fiber (g)
234	15	4	2.0	8	196	38	12	3

Exchanges: Starch 2, Vegetable 1, Medium-fat protein 1/2

# Arizona Pasta Primavera

1 medium yellow bell pepper, seeded and diced small
1 medium red bell pepper, seeded and diced small
1 poblano chili pepper, minced, or to taste
1 small can chopped green chili, or to taste
1 medium zucchini, thinly sliced
1 T fresh garlic, minced
6 plum tomatoes, peeled and coarsely chopped (save juices)
1/4 C fresh or frozen corn
2 T chopped fresh cilantro
1 tsp ground cumin
3 T dry white wine
Freshly ground black pepper to taste
1/2 lb tri-color rotilli pasta, cooked al dente and drained (4 C cooked)
4 T Parmesan cheese, freshly grated

Sauté bell peppers, poblano and green chili peppers, zucchini, and garlic for 2 to 3 minutes, or until the peppers are tender. Add the tomatoes (with juices), corn, cilantro, and cumin. Sauté for 2 minutes. Add the white wine and cook until the pan is deglazed. Season with pepper. Toss the sauce with the cooked pasta. Serve hot, garnished with Parmesan cheese.
Serves 4.

Calories	%Fat	Fat (g)	Saturated Fat (g)	Cholesterol (mg)	Sodium (mg)	Carbohydrate (g)	Protein (g)	Fiber (g)
549	8	5	1.6	5	342	105	20	7

Exchanges: Starch 5-1/2, Vegetable 3, Medium-fat protein 1/2

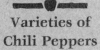
Varieties of Chili Peppers

• *Anaheim:* Mild to slightly hot large peppers (six to seven inches long); light green to dark bright green, and red when ripe; one of the most popular chili peppers, the mildest variety. Often used in salsa.

• *Ancho:* Mild to slightly hot dried poblano chili (three to five inches long, about three inches wide); dark brown that becomes red when reconstituted.

• *Cascabel:* Moderately hot short, round red pepper; often used in sauces.

• *Cayenne:* Fiery long, thin pepper (three to eight inches long); bright green to bright red; can replace jalapeños or serranos.

• *Chipotle:* Extremely hot smoke-dried jalapeño pepper (two to three inches long); brown or brick red; good in chili, barbecue sauce, beans, and corn.

• *Fresno:* Mild and sweet; small, slender, green or greenish-red.

- *Hungarian Yellow Wax:* Very hot, stinging banana pepper (four to six inches long); pale chartreuse to orange, ripening to red—flavor at its peak when orange.
- *Jalapeño:* Very hot; short and fat chili; dark green or purple, ripening to gold or red; very popular variety used in salsa, soup, meat or chicken dishes, and nachos. One of the hottest chilies. Easy to peel.
- *Pequin:* Extremely hot tiny pepper; used in Tabasco sauce and cayenne.
- *Poblano:* Mild to fairly hot heart-shaped chili (four to five inches long); dark green, and reddish brown when ripe; good stuffed and baked when green, or roasted and peeled for use in soups, stews, and sauces; dried poblanos are called *ancho peppers.*
- *Serrano:* Hot to extremely hot small pointed peppers; light green to dark green, and red when ripe; often used in place of jalapeños; good in guacamole, relishes, sauces, and pickles.

Fresh Tomato Sauce & Vermicelli

24 large, ripe Italian plum tomatoes, peeled, seeded, and diced (drain and save juices)
1 small yellow onion, diced small
2 cloves garlic, minced
1/4 C fresh basil, chopped
6 C hot cooked vermicelli (about 10 oz uncooked)

Sauté the onion and garlic for 6 to 8 minutes, or until the onion is tender. Add the drained tomato juices and simmer over low heat for 5 to 10 minutes. Stir in the tomatoes and simmer for 1 hour, stirring occasionally. Serve over vermicelli.

Serves 6.

Calories	%Fat	Fat (g)	Saturated Fat (g)	Cholesterol (mg)	Sodium (mg)	Carbohydrate (g)	Protein (g)	Fiber (g)
279	7	2	0.3	0	39	57	10	7

Exchanges: Starch 2-1/2, Vegetable 4

Seashells Alfredo

1/4 C chopped scallion
2 cloves garlic, minced
1 T flour
1 can (12 oz) evaporated skim milk
1/4 C freshly grated Parmesan cheese
1/4 C freshly grated Romano cheese
1/2 tsp dried parsley
1/2 tsp dried thyme
1/2 tsp dried basil
1/4 C finely chopped red bell pepper
6 C hot cooked macaroni shells

Sauté scallion and garlic for 2 minutes. Stir in flour and cook briefly. Gradually stir in milk and bring to a boil, stirring constantly. Cook over medium-low heat until thick, about 3 minutes. Remove from heat and stir in cheeses, herbs, and red pepper. Serve immediately over macaroni shells.

Serves 6.

"How long does getting thin take?" asked Pooh anxiously.

A.A. Milne
Winnie-the-Pooh

Weekly Weight Loss
Many people enter a weight reduction program with unrealistic expectations, especially about the rate of weight reduction. A one-half to one pound rate of weight loss per week has been established as both safe and effective. If you want to lose 20 pounds, expect it to take 20 weeks.

Arizona Heart Institute Foundation
1–800–345–4278

Calories	%Fat	Fat (g)	Saturated Fat (g)	Cholesterol (mg)	Sodium (mg)	Carbohydrate (g)	Protein (g)	Fiber (g)
292	11	4	1.8	9	194	49	15	2

Exchanges: Starch 3, Dairy 1

Broccoli Fettucini Alfredo

1/4 C low-calorie tub margarine
1/4 C all-purpose flour
2 C evaporated skim milk
1/2 C grated Parmesan cheese
1/4 C chopped fresh parsley
1/4 tsp nutmeg
Freshly ground black pepper to taste
4 C cooked fettucini (about 3-1/2 oz uncooked)
2 C fresh broccoli florets, steamed
1 C chopped fresh mushrooms, sautéed

Melt margarine; add flour and cook, stirring constantly, for about 2 minutes. Stir in milk and cook until thickened slightly. Add Parmesan cheese, parsley, nutmeg, and pepper, stirring constantly until cheese is melted and sauce is smooth and thick. Toss with fettucini, broccoli, and mushrooms. Serve immediately.

Serves 6.

Calories	%Fat	Fat (g)	Saturated Fat (g)	Cholesterol (mg)	Sodium (mg)	Carbohydrate (g)	Protein (g)	Fiber (g)
302	23	8	2.4	44	330	42	16	3

Exchanges: Starch 2, Dairy 1, Fat 1

# Garden Lasagna

12 spinach lasagna noodles (about 1 lb), cooked and drained
1-1/2 lb zucchini, coarsely grated
Freshly ground black pepper to taste
1/2 lb skim-milk ricotta cheese
1/2 lb low-fat cottage cheese
2 C grated Parmesan cheese
3/4 lb skim-milk mozzarella cheese, thinly sliced
1/2 C chopped fresh basil
Double Red Sauce (page 447)

Set aside 1 C of zucchini. Coat the bottom and sides of a 13 × 9 baking dish with cooking spray. Cover the bottom of the pan with a layer of lasagna noodles. Spread half the zucchini over the pasta and sprinkle with a little pepper. Top with 2 more pasta strips, then half the ricotta, half the cottage cheese, and half the Parmesan. Add 2 pasta strips, followed by half the mozzarella, half the Double Red Sauce, and half the basil. Repeat layers in the same order with the remaining ingredients, reserving some basil for final garnish.

Bake at 375° for 20 minutes. Lightly coat the reserved zucchini with cooking spray, tossing lightly; arrange it in decorative rows or in a border on top of the lasagna. Bake 5 minutes. Sprinkle reserved basil on top; cool for 10 minutes before cutting.

Serves 12.

Calories	%Fat	Fat (g)	Saturated Fat (g)	Cholesterol (mg)	Sodium (mg)	Carbohydrate (g)	Protein (g)	Fiber (g)
307	37	13	7.5	53	754	25	24	3

Exchanges: Starch 1, Vegetable 2, Medium-fat protein 2

Cheese

Cheese is one of the most popular foods in the world—more than 2,000 kinds are made. Milk is coagulated or separated into curds (semi-solids) and whey (liquid), and the cheese is made from the curds. Cheese can be fresh or matured (ripened). Ripened cheeses contain more salt, which removes moisture and acts as a preservative. Processed cheeses and cheese foods are very high in sodium. Lower-fat, reduced-sodium cheeses are available; read labels carefully.

Cheese is a concentrated source of calcium, protein, and riboflavin. Hard cheeses are a better source of calcium than softer cheeses.

Cheese is also high in fat and cholesterol. High-fat (more than 8 grams of fat per ounce) cheeses include American, blue, Cheddar, Colby, havarti, and Muenster. Moderately high-fat (6 to 8 grams of fat per ounce) cheeses include provolone, Romano, mozzarella, Neufchatel, Camembert, and feta. Cheeses that have less than 5 grams of fat per ounce are usually made with part-skim milk; they include low-fat cottage cheese, farmer cheese, part-skim mozzarella, and part-skim ricotta. Many traditionally high-fat cheeses are now made with part-skim milk, which lowers their fat content; this varies from one variety and maker to another, so read the labels carefully.

Store cheese tightly wrapped in the refrigerator; cut only the amount that will be eaten at one time. Although it grates more easily when it is cold, cheese tastes best at room temperature. When cooking with cheese, add it at the last minute and heat only long enough to melt the cheese.

Discard moldy cheese (unless mold is a characteristic of the cheese, such as Roquefort or Stilton).

Lasagna Florentine

1 large onion, finely chopped
4 cloves garlic, minced
1 can (16 oz) unsalted tomatoes with liquid, chopped
1 can (6 oz) unsalted tomato paste
1/2 tsp oregano
1/8 tsp basil
1/8 tsp marjoram
6 C cooked spinach lasagna, prepared without fat or salt (about 10 oz uncooked)
1 lb fresh spinach, lightly steamed, chopped, and drained
2 C low-fat (1%) cottage cheese
1 C part-skim ricotta cheese
3 T grated Romano cheese
1 T minced fresh parsley
4 oz part-skim mozzarella cheese, shredded

Sauté onion and garlic briefly. Add tomatoes, tomato paste, and herbs. Simmer for 30 minutes. Mix cheeses (except mozzarella) with parsley. Spread a thin layer of tomato sauce in the bottom of a 9 × 13-inch baking pan. Layer with one-third the lasagna noodles, half the cheese, half the spinach, and one-third the tomato sauce. Repeat layers. Top with the remaining lasagna noodles and tomato sauce. Sprinkle with mozzarella. Bake at 350° for about 40 minutes.
Serves 9.

Calories	%Fat	Fat (g)	Saturated Fat (g)	Cholesterol (mg)	Sodium (mg)	Carbohydrate (g)	Protein (g)	Fiber (g)
273	23	7	3.7	48	369	34	20	4

Exchanges: Starch 1-1/2, Vegetable 2, Low-fat protein 2

# **S**tuffed Shells

1-3/4 C finely chopped red bell pepper
1/2 C chopped onion
2 cloves garlic, minced
1 can (14-1/2 oz) no-salt-added whole tomatoes, undrained
1 can (8 oz) no-salt-added tomato sauce
1/2 tsp oregano
1/4 tsp salt
12 jumbo pasta shells, cooked without salt or fat, drained
3/4 C part-skim ricotta cheese
3/4 C low-fat cottage cheese
1/2 C grated Parmesan cheese
1/2 C chopped fresh basil
1/2 C chopped fresh parsley

Sauté bell pepper, onion, and garlic until tender. Purée sautéed vegetables with tomatoes in a blender or food processor. Combine with tomato sauce, Italian seasoning, and salt; bring to a boil. Reduce heat and simmer, uncovered, for 20 minutes. Spread 1/2 C of tomato sauce into an 11 × 7-inch baking dish; set aside. Process cheeses, basil, and parsley in a blender until smooth. Spoon equal amounts into pasta shells. Arrange filled shells in the baking dish. Pour remaining tomato sauce over shells. Bake, covered, at 400° for 40 minutes.
Serves 6.

Calories	%Fat	Fat (g)	Saturated Fat (g)	Cholesterol (mg)	Sodium (mg)	Carbohydrate (g)	Protein (g)	Fiber (g)
213	25	6	3.4	17	336	26	15	3

Exchanges: Starch 1, Vegetable 2, Medium-fat protein 1

- *Cottage cheese:* Lumpy; moist, mild flavor. Store it upside down in its own container in the refrigerator for two to three weeks.
- *Cream cheese:* Fresh unripened cheese made from cow's milk; soft and spreadable. Store tightly wrapped in the refrigerator for up to two weeks.
- *Farmer's cheese:* Bland, smooth cheese pressed into a block that can be sliced. Store tightly wrapped for two weeks in refrigerator.
- *Feta:* Greek. White, crumbly, soft cheese made from ewe's milk (sometimes goat). Sharp, salty taste. Good in savory stuffings and salads.
- *Mascarpone:* Delicately flavored, rich double-cream cheese. May be soft or firm. Very good with fruit.
- *Monterey Jack:* Cheddar-type cheese. Bland; smooth texture.

- *Mozzarella:* Italian. Unripened curd cheese. Originally made from buffalo's milk; now made from cow's milk. Soft; moist texture; mild and creamy. Good for cooking.
- *Parmesan:* Italian. A granular type of cheese used for grating and cooking. Refrigerate lightly wrapped for several months.
- *Ricotta:* Italian. Fresh unripened cheese made from whey of cow's milk. Smooth texture; mild, sweeter than cottage cheese. Made by draining cottage cheese for a longer period. Used in sweet and savory dishes. Store in refrigerator for up to one week.
- *Sapsago:* Swiss. A hard cheese made from soured skim milk and whole milk. Clover added to the curd gives it a pale green color. Good all-purpose cooking cheese; grate before using.

 # asta with Grilled Eggplant

1/2 C chopped parsley
1 T olive oil
1/4 C red wine vinegar
2 tsp capers, drained
2 cloves garlic, minced
1 tsp Worcestershire sauce
1-1/2 lb eggplant, peeled and cut into 1/2-inch thick slices
4 C cooked bowtie pasta, drained and rinsed
6 plum tomatoes, seeded and chopped

Process parsley, oil, vinegar, capers, garlic, and Worcestershire sauce in a blender until smooth to make a dressing; set aside. Grill or broil eggplant slices for 5 to 10 minutes on each side, or until tender. Cool and dice. Toss eggplant, pasta, and tomatoes with dressing. Serve at room temperature.

Serves 8.

Suggestion
- Zucchini, cut in half lengthwise, can be substituted for the eggplant.

Calories	%Fat	Fat (g)	Saturated Fat (g)	Cholesterol (mg)	Sodium (mg)	Carbohydrate (g)	Protein (g)	Fiber (g)
150	15	3	0.4	0	21	28	5	3

Exchanges: Starch 1-1/2, Vegetable 1

Chicken & Rigatoni

3 skinless, boneless chicken breast halves (4 oz each) cut into 1-inch cubes
2 medium red bell peppers, seeded and diced
2 medium yellow bell peppers, seeded and diced
10 oz fresh mushrooms, sliced
2 cloves garlic, minced
3 T dry white wine
1/2 C low-sodium chicken broth
6 oz rigatoni, cooked without salt and fat, drained
1/2 C sliced scallions
1/2 C freshly grated Parmesan cheese
1/8 tsp freshly ground black pepper
1/4 C chopped fresh parsley

   Sauté chicken, peppers, mushrooms, and garlic until chicken is lightly browned. Add wine and cook briefly, until wine evaporates. Add chicken broth. Reduce heat and simmer, uncovered, 2 minutes. Remove from heat and gently toss with rigatoni and remaining ingredients.
   Serves 4.

Calories	%Fat	Fat (g)	Saturated Fat (g)	Cholesterol (mg)	Sodium (mg)	Carbohydrate (g)	Protein (g)	Fiber (g)
369	18	7	3.3	56	291	43	32	3

Exchanges: Starch 2, Vegetable 2, Low-fat protein 3

Vegetable Soups

Beet
Broccoli
Cabbage
Carrot
Corn
Garlic
Kale
Pea
Pepper
Potato
Pumpkin
Tomato
Watercress
Zucchini
Mixed Vegetable

Grain & Legume Soups

Wild Rice
Dried Beans
Peanut

Shellfish Soups

Chicken Soups

Fruit Soups

Peach
Cantaloupe

Soups

Cold Lithuanian Beet Borscht

Joyce Goldstein

6 to 7 large beets
1/2 C red wine
2 tsp butter or olive oil
2 red onions, diced (about 3 C)
1 to 1-1/2 C defatted chicken stock, vegetable stock, or water
3 to 4 C buttermilk
Pepper
1 to 2 T fruit vinegar or lemon juice, optional
Pinch of sugar, optional
1-1/2 C diced, peeled, and seeded cucumbers
1/2 C minced green onions
6 small boiled potatoes, diced coarsely

Wash the beets. Peel one and grate it into a bowl. Cover with a little red wine. Cover the other beets with cold water and bring to a boil. Reduce heat and cook until beets are tender. Refresh in cold water and peel while still warm. Cut one cooked beet into fine julienne strips and set aside.

Melt the butter in a small saucepan. Add the onions and cook until tender and translucent. Add just enough chicken stock to cover. Bring to a boil. Slice the remaining cooked beets. Purée beet slices, cooked onions, stock, and grated beet and red wine in a blender. Transfer to a bowl. Add buttermilk. Season with pepper. Adjust seasoning—you may need a few tablespoons of fruit vine-

Beets

Beets are a round root vegetable. They are usually garnet red but can range from deep red to white. Larger beets are less tender than small ones. Beets are most often used to make soups or salads.

Remove the green tops, leaving two inches of stem, and store unwashed beets in a plastic bag in the refrigerator for seven to ten days (greens should be wrapped separately). Beet greens are an excellent source of beta-carotene, calcium, and iron; they can be cooked like spinach or other greens.

Boil beets in their skins and with the stem ends to preserve their bright color. Adding an acid—like lemon juice, vinegar, or a little cream of tartar—to the cooking water will also help keep beets red.

Baked beets are even better than boiled. Scrub the beets well but don't peel them. Bake at 325° for an hour, or until the peel is wrinkled. Remove the peel before serving.

Add beets to other ingredients just before serving—their color stains everything. Don't use plastic or wooden bowls for mixing or serving beets. The stains are difficult or impossible to remove.

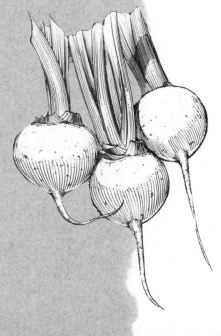

gar or lemon juice and a little sugar. The balance of sweet and sour is very personal. Add the julienne of beet and chill the soup.

To serve, ladle soup into 6 large bowls. Garnish with cucumbers, green onions, and potatoes.

Serves 6.

Suggestion

• Include a dollop of nonfat yogurt with the garnish.

Calories	%Fat	Fat (g)	Saturated Fat (g)	Cholesterol (mg)	Sodium (mg)	Carbohydrate (g)	Protein (g)	Fiber (g)
203	13	3	1.7	8	221	36	9	5

Exchanges: Starch 1, Vegetable 3, Dairy 1/2

# Broccoli Soup

1-1/2 C chopped onion
1 bay leaf
1/2 medium green pepper, chopped
4 C chopped fresh broccoli
2-1/2 C water
2 C evaporated skim milk
Pinch of nutmeg
1/2 tsp thyme
1/2 tsp basil
Freshly ground black pepper to taste
1-1/2 C fresh broccoli florets, cut bite-sized
1 T lemon juice
1/2 C plain nonfat yogurt
Watercress sprigs
8 very thin lemon slices

Sauté onion with bay leaf until onion is translucent. Add green pepper, 4 C chopped broccoli, and water. Cook, covered, about 10 minutes, or until broccoli is tender but not soft. Remove pot from heat and cool for 15 to 20 minutes. Discard bay leaf.

Cruciferous Vegetables

Cruciferous vegetables get their name from their flowers, which have four petals that look something like a cross or crucifix. They contain a variety of compounds, called *indoles*, that appear to protect against certain forms of cancer, particularly of the stomach and large intestine.

There is some evidence that the more cruciferous vegetables a person eats, the lower the risk of cancer. Although this theory has not yet been proved, eating more of these vegetables will certainly not harm you and it may do some good.

Arugula
Broccoli
Brussels sprouts
Cabbage
Cauliflower
Collards
Horseradish
Kale
Kohlrabi
Mustard greens
Radish
Rutabaga
Turnip
Watercress

Purée the cooked vegetables, milk, and herbs in a food processor or blender. Return mixture to pot. Stir in 1-1/2 C broccoli florets and lemon juice; heat over medium heat until florets are tender, about 4 minutes. Stir in yogurt and heat; do not boil. Adjust seasonings to taste. Garnish individual servings with watercress and a lemon slice.

Serves 8.

Suggestion

• For a richer flavor, substitute low-sodium chicken broth for the water.

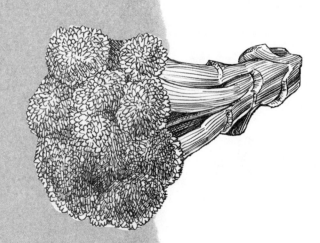

Calories	%Fat	Fat (g)	Saturated Fat (g)	Cholesterol (mg)	Sodium (mg)	Carbohydrate (g)	Protein (g)	Fiber (g)
88	3	0	0.1	3	100	15	8	2

Exchanges: Vegetable 1, Dairy 1

# Cabbage Patch Soup

4 C chopped green cabbage
3 C chopped carrot
1/4 C chopped onion
1 can (28 oz) no-salt-added tomatoes with juice
2 tsp chopped parsley
1 tsp tarragon
1 tsp basil
2 T lemon juice
Caraway seeds

Bring cabbage, carrot, onion, tomatoes with juice, parsley, tarragon, basil, and enough water to cover to a boil. Reduce heat and simmer, covered, until vegetables are tender but not mushy. Purée in a blender or food processor until almost smooth and return to pot. Stir in lemon juice. Adjust seasonings to taste. Heat to serving temperature. Garnish individual servings with a light sprinkling of caraway seeds.

Serves 6.

Risk Factors

Cardiovascular risk factors are conditions that increase the chance that a person will develop heart disease. The three greatest risk factors for cardiovascular disease that can be controlled are cigarette smoking, high blood pressure, and high blood cholesterol. Most other risk factors can also be managed (obesity, lack of exercise, diabetes, stress), but a few are beyond your control—age, sex, race, and family history of heart disease. While any one risk factor will increase your likelihood of developing cardiovascular problems, the more risk factors you have, the more concerned you should be about prevention.

**Arizona Heart
Institute Foundation**
1–800–345–4278

Calories	%Fat	Fat (g)	Saturated Fat (g)	Cholesterol (mg)	Sodium (mg)	Carbohydrate (g)	Protein (g)	Fiber (g)
80	7	1	0.1	0	60	19	2	4

Exchanges: Fruit 1/2, Vegetable 2

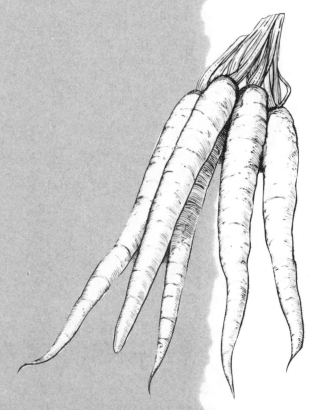

arrot Soup

1 medium onion, chopped
1 large clove garlic, minced
6 C sliced carrots
2 C diced potatoes
Pinch of nutmeg
Freshly ground black pepper to taste
3 C low-sodium chicken broth
Parsley sprigs

Sauté onion and garlic until soft. Stir in remaining ingredients; add water to cover if necessary. Bring to a boil; reduce heat and simmer, covered, for 30 minutes. Purée soup in a blender or food processor until smooth. Adjust seasonings to taste. Serve hot. Garnish individual servings with parsley.

Serves 11.

Suggestions

- Add honey, sherry, or other flavorings to taste.
- Turnips, parsnips, or fennel can be substituted for part or all of the potato.

Calories	%Fat	Fat (g)	Saturated Fat (g)	Cholesterol (mg)	Sodium (mg)	Carbohydrate (g)	Protein (g)	Fiber (g)
60	8	1	0.2	0	50	13	2	2

Exchanges: Vegetable 2-1/2

Two Soup Combination: Carrot & Ginger, Parsnip & Herb

Steven Allen

Carrot & Ginger Soup
4 medium carrots, peeled
2-1/2 C Pritikin chicken broth
1-1/2 T chopped onion
1 small celery stalk, sliced
1/2 root parsley, peeled and sliced
1/4 bay leaf
1 tsp thyme leaves
1/2 T grated ginger root
1/4 tsp white pepper
1/2 tsp ground cumin
1 C plain nonfat yogurt, divided

Cut grooves lengthwise in one of the carrots and slice 12 thin rounds to resemble flower petals. Cook them in the chicken broth until tender; remove carrots from broth and reserve for garnish. Slice the rest of the carrots. Simmer carrots, onion, celery, root parsley, bay leaf, and thyme in broth until all vegetables are tender. Transfer to a blender; add ginger root, pepper, and cumin. Purée until smooth. Return to cooking pot and add 3/4 C yogurt. Taste and adjust seasoning. Reheat when ready to serve.

weight if you are to embark on a lifestyle that will keep those pounds from returning.

- Standardized programs that do not tailor the diet to the individual's own health needs can be dangerous.
- A support system is crucial to facilitate and maintain weight loss. Solo programs can be defeating and demoralizing.

Edward B. Diethrich, MD
Heart Test

Parsnip & Herb Soup

3 medium parsnips, peeled and sliced
2-1/2 C Pritikin chicken broth
1 T lemon juice
White pepper to taste
1/4 C chopped herbs (parsley, chives, thyme, tarragon, celery leaves)
1/4 C spinach leaves, cleaned, stems removed

Slowly simmer parsnips in chicken broth until tender. Add lemon juice and white pepper; transfer to a blender. Add herbs and spinach; purée until smooth. Return to cooking pot. Taste and adjust seasonings. Keep warm.

To serve Two Soup Combination: Using 2 small ladles (one in each hand), pour 3 oz of each soup simultaneously in serving dishes. Garnish with dollops of yogurt, carrot flowers, and herbs.

Serves 6.

Suggestion

- Any fat-free, low-sodium chicken broth may be substituted for the Pritikin broth.

Calories	%Fat	Fat (g)	Saturated Fat (g)	Cholesterol (mg)	Sodium (mg)	Carbohydrate (g)	Protein (g)	Fiber (g)
112	9	1	0.3	1	125	21	6	4

Exchanges: Vegetable 4

Salmon Corn Chowder

*Corn, which is
the staff of life.*

Edward Winslow
1624

1 C fresh or frozen corn
1/4 C diced celery
1/4 C diced carrots
1/8 C diced yellow onions
1/2 C diced yellow bell peppers
1/2 C diced poblano chili peppers, or to taste
2 T fresh garlic, minced
1/2 C dry white wine
1/4 C red chili powder, or to taste
1 T ground cumin
1 T fresh basil, chopped
1 tsp fresh oregano, chopped
1 bay leaf
8 oz salmon, cleaned, deboned, and cubed
2 qt low-sodium vegetable broth
1 T freshly ground black pepper
1 T flour

Sauté corn, celery, carrots, onions, bell peppers, chili peppers, and garlic for 3 to 5 minutes, or until the onions are translucent. Add the wine, chili powder, cumin, basil, oregano, and bay leaf. Sauté for 3 minutes. Stir in salmon, vegeta-

Sweet Corn or Maize

Yellow corn has more vitamin A than white corn. Blue corn is higher in protein, potassium, and manganese than yellow corn. All corn is an excellent source of carbohydrate and fiber.

Fresh corn will squirt milky liquid when a kernel is pierced. The kernels should be tightly spaced in straight rows; older corn has gaps between kernels. Medium-size kernels have the best flavor. The husk should be bright green, and the silk should be dry and golden.

Purists say that corn should not be picked until the water in the cooking pot is boiling. When corn is picked, a chemical reaction changes its sugar to starch, making the corn taste less sweet. The longer it is off the stalk, the less sweet it will be. Refrigeration slows down the conversion of sugar to starch (it will lose half of its sugar within 24 hours at room temperature). Chilling slows down this process, so (unless you can get corn straight from the field) buy corn that is kept in a refrigerated display in the grocery. Store corn in the refrigerator if it can't be cooked and eaten immediately. Stand the cobs upright in a container of water (about an inch deep) to help preserve the flavor for a day or two.

Popcorn kernels contain moisture. When they are heated, the moisture changes to steam and the internal pressure causes the corn to pop. Popcorn that is not stored tightly sealed will lose its internal moisture and won't pop when cooked. Regular corn will never pop.

ble broth, and black pepper. Simmer for 1 hour. Mix the flour with a little broth to make a paste. Stir into the soup and simmer for 30 minutes. Discard bay leaf before serving.

Serves 6.

Suggestions
• Add red chili powder in small amounts, tasting after each addition, until the desired strength is reached; less or more than the amount specified may be used.
• Canned salmon, cleaned and flaked, can be substituted for the fresh salmon.
• A mixture of 1/4 C vinegar and 1/4 C water can be substituted for the white wine.

Calories	%Fat	Fat (g)	Saturated Fat (g)	Cholesterol (mg)	Sodium (mg)	Carbohydrate (g)	Protein (g)	Fiber (g)
156	27	5	1.0	14	158	16	14	4

Exchanges: Starch 1/2, Vegetable 2, Low-fat protein 1

Roasted Garlic Soup with Swiss Chard Timbale

John Novi

2 tsp olive oil
2 C peeled garlic cloves
3 C whole plum tomatoes, crushed
6 qt chicken stock
4 T mushroom soy
2 T white pepper
3 lb washed Swiss chard leaves, stems removed
1 C Spanish olives, pitted, chopped
1/2 C capers, nonpareils preferred
3 T nuoc-nam
15 anchovies, rolled and stuffed with red pimiento (optional)

Toss the garlic with about 1 tsp of olive oil and place it on a cookie sheet. Roast at 350° for about 20 minutes, or until all the garlic is golden brown. Transfer the roasted garlic to a food processor and add 1 tsp of olive oil. Turn the machine on and purée until the garlic is as smooth as peanut butter, about 6 to 8 minutes.

Mix 1 C garlic purée, tomatoes, and stock in a stainless steel soup pot, whisk it frequently, and bring the mixture to a boil. Reduce heat to simmer and add

Swiss Chard

Swiss chard is actually a type of beet, but it is used for its leaves and stems, not the root. It can be green or red; yellowing indicates bitterness. Swiss chard has a delicate flavor. It is rather like fresh spinach but not as sharp. It is sometimes slightly bitter or tart. It is an excellent source of vitamins A and C, calcium, and iron. Swiss chard can be stored in the refrigerator, wrapped in plastic, for up to three days.

The leaves can be used like spinach and the stalks like celery. Very fresh Swiss chard is good steamed and served plain. Nutmeg is a good seasoning for Swiss chard.

Raw young leaves are good in salads. Smaller leaves are best, but they are usually found only in home gardens; most groceries stock leaves that are 10 to 12 inches long. Large, mature leaves can be stuffed like cabbage.

As with spinach, cook Swiss chard with only the amount of water that clings to the leaves during washing. If salt is added during cooking, the leaves will turn dark. Swiss chard can be added to soups or stir-fries, or grilled like radicchio.

Dandelion

Dandelion is a wild meadow plant that has a bitter flavor. Its flavor is best in the early spring. Smaller leaves are less bitter and more tender than large ones. They should be stored like other greens and used in two or three days.

Dandelion greens can be used raw or cooked. They are good in salads when mixed with mild-flavored greens or collards, chard, kale, or mustard greens. They can be substituted for part or all of the spinach in recipes.

the soy and white pepper. Cook for about 25 minutes. Pour the soup through a fine sieve.

To make the timbale, cook Swiss chard in boiling water for about 5 minutes. Drain and then plunge into cold water. Drain again and chop it fine; place it in a mixing bowl. Toss in the capers, olives, and nuoc-nam and place the mixture into 15 individual timbales. Steam the Swiss chard timbales and, when hot, unmold them. Place each timbale in the center of a soup bowl and pour hot garlic soup around it. Garnish the top of each timbale with one anchovy or a slice of roasted red pepper.

Serves 15.

Suggestions

- This soup is great made with spinach, dandelion, or any other green. Great all year round.
- Any light soy sauce can be substituted for the mushroom soy.
- 15 slices of roasted red pepper can be substituted for the anchovies.

Calories	%Fat	Fat (g)	Saturated Fat (g)	Cholesterol (mg)	Sodium (mg)	Carbohydrate (g)	Protein (g)	Fiber (g)
97	25	3	0.7	0	279	12	7	1

Exchanges: Vegetable 2-1/2, Fat 1/2

Kale & Potato Soup

4 medium white potatoes, peeled and diced
8 C water
1/4 tsp salt
1/2 tsp freshly ground black pepper
2 lb fresh kale, cut in thin shreds
3 cloves garlic, minced

Simmer potatoes in water until tender, about 20 to 30 minutes. Remove potatoes from pot, reserving liquid. Mash the potatoes and return them to the pot with liquid. Add salt and pepper and simmer for 20 minutes. Add kale and garlic; simmer for about 25 minutes. Adjust seasonings to taste. Serve hot.
Serves 8.

Carotene

Carotene is converted by the body into vitamin A. This chemical gives carrots, pumpkins, and other vegetables a bright orange to yellow-orange color. Dark green leafy and deep orange vegetables and fruits are rich in carotenoids:

> Apricots
> Bell pepper, red
> Broccoli
> Brussels sprouts
> Cabbage, green
> Carrots
> Beet greens
> Mustard greens
> Kale
> Spinach
> Sweet potatoes
> Tomatoes
> Winter squash

Calories	%Fat	Fat (g)	Saturated Fat (g)	Cholesterol (mg)	Sodium (mg)	Carbohydrate (g)	Protein (g)	Fiber (g)
76	3	0	0.0	0	91	17	3	3

Exchanges: Starch 1, Vegetable 1

Fennel

Fennel is a celery-like shoot that has a white or light green bulb, firm darker green stalks, and fragrant leaves. Also called *anise*, fennel has a faint sweet, licorice flavor, which is more delicate when cooked. Store fennel wrapped in plastic in the refrigerator for one to two days.

Florence fennel has a broad, bulbous base and is used like a vegetable. Common fennel is often used as an herb to flavor fish or soup. Fennel reduces the oiliness of salmon, mackerel, and other high-fat fish. It is also good with tomatoes, lentils, rice, and potatoes. Sage, sweet basil, marjoram, and tarragon are good companion seasonings. Cooked fennel can be puréed and used as a soup base. It can also be served raw in salads or sandwiches, or grilled.

Fennel seeds are often used in cookies, breads, and other baked goods; they should be lightly crushed for maximum flavor. Fennel leaves can be brewed for tea.

Sweet Pea & Fennel Soup

Michael Hutchings

1 C Florence fennel bulb, sliced
1/2 C sliced onions
1 tsp butter or olive oil
1 qt white stock or water
2 C shelled peas (fresh or frozen)
Pinch salt
Pinch white pepper
1 tsp mint leaves
1 C croutons

Use a heavy-bottomed stock pot or steam-jacketed kettle. Sweat the fennel and onion in butter or olive oil until tender. Add stock and bring to a boil. Cook for 10 minutes, or until the vegetables are tender. Add the peas and cook for an additional 10 to 15 minutes, or until tender. Purée the soup in a high-speed blender. Pass through a medium-fine strainer into a bowl. Set on crushed ice to cool, stirring occasionally, if the soup will not be served immediately. To serve, reheat the soup. Season with salt and pepper. Garnish each serving with mint. Serve with croutons.

Serves 10.

Suggestions
- Stir in 1/2 C evaporated skim milk before serving.
- This soup is also good thinned and served chilled in the summer.

Calories	%Fat	Fat (g)	Saturated Fat (g)	Cholesterol (mg)	Sodium (mg)	Carbohydrate (g)	Protein (g)	Fiber (g)
60	20	1	0.7	0	84	9	3	2

Exchanges: Vegetable 2

Pepperpot Soup

*The greatest animal
in creation,
the animal who cooks.*

Douglas Jerrold

Bell Peppers

Sweet or bell peppers
come in many colors,
shapes, and sizes. All are
green before they ripen and
turn red, yellow, orange, purple, chocolate brown, or
creamy white. Some purple
varieties lose their color in
cooking; Purple Beauty retains its vivid color when

6 C low-sodium chicken broth
1/2 C rice
1 tsp paprika
Freshly ground black pepper to taste
3/4 tsp cinnamon
1/2 tsp onion powder
1/2 tsp garlic powder
1/4 tsp ground cloves
2 medium tomatoes, peeled, chopped
2 large peppers, chopped (choice of colors)
1 large onion, chopped
2 carrots, chopped
1/2 C dry white wine
Minced fresh parsley

Bring first 8 ingredients to a boil in large saucepan. Mix in tomatoes, peppers, onion, and carrots. Reduce heat and simmer until vegetables and rice
are tender, about 20 minutes. Add wine and bring to simmer. Garnish each
serving with minced parsley.

Serves 8.

Calories	%Fat	Fat (g)	Saturated Fat (g)	Cholesterol (mg)	Sodium (mg)	Carbohydrate (g)	Protein (g)	Fiber (g)
100	9	1	0.3	0	194	19	4	2

Exchanges: Starch 1, Vegetable 1

cooked. Green peppers will not ripen and change their color after picking.

Store peppers in the refrigerator, preferably in the butter compartment. Green peppers keep longer than other colors because their sugar content is lower. Peppers are high in vitamin C; red ones are also high in vitamin A. Remove the core, seeds, and membranes before using.

These mild peppers are served raw or cooked in stews, sauces, soups, salads, and rice. They are also good stuffed and baked—cut off the tops of parboiled peppers and stand them upright in muffin tins for filling and baking; the peppers will hold their shape better if they are cooked in muffin tins instead of in a baking pan.

 # otato Soup

4 medium white potatoes, peeled and thinly sliced
1 medium onion, thinly sliced
4 stalks celery with leaves, thinly sliced
1 bay leaf
1/4 tsp salt
3 C skim milk
Freshly ground black pepper to taste

In a large saucepan, sauté vegetables for 3 to 5 minutes. Add enough hot water to cover vegetables. Add bay leaf and salt; cook until vegetables are tender. Remove bay leaf. Using an electric mixer, mash vegetables in cooking liquid (or transfer to a food processor or blender and purée; return to cooking pot). Stir in milk and season with pepper. Heat to serving temperature.
Serves 6.

Suggestions
• Omit bay leaf; season with rosemary.
• Leave a slightly chunky texture instead of making a perfectly smooth soup.

Calories	%Fat	Fat (g)	Saturated Fat (g)	Cholesterol (mg)	Sodium (mg)	Carbohydrate (g)	Protein (g)	Fiber (g)
107	3	0	0.2	2	178	21	6	2

Exchanges: Starch 1, Dairy 1/2

# Pumpkin-White Bean Chowder

Stephan Wayne Pyles

2-1/2 qt chicken stock
1-1/2 C white beans, soaked overnight and drained
1 medium pumpkin (about 5 to 6 lb)
8 oz Canadian bacon or ham
1 medium onion, diced
2 stalks celery, diced
1 carrot, diced
1 red bell pepper, seeded and diced
1 yellow bell pepper, seeded and diced
2 cloves garlic, finely minced
2 T fresh thyme, chopped
1/4 C white wine
4 slices French or sourdough bread
1 T olive oil
1 T roasted garlic
1 pomegranate
1/2 C crème fraîche
1 T heavy cream
4 T chives, chopped

Bring 1/2 qt (2 C) of the chicken stock to a boil and add the soaked beans. Lower the heat and simmer for 30 to 45 minutes, until tender.

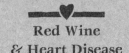
Red Wine
& Heart Disease

French cooking contains large amounts of butter, cream, and eggs—the antithesis of a heart-healthy diet. Even though they eat large amounts of saturated fat, exercise less than Americans, and drink large quantities of alcohol, the French have the second lowest rate of heart disease among industrialized nations (Japan has the lowest rate). Popular reports attribute this seeming paradox to the consumption of wine, especially red wine.

The truth lies in timing, not in drinking. French food consumption has changed significantly in recent years. In 1961, fat supplied only 28% of calories in the French diet. That amount has steadily increased, rising to 39% by 1988, largely because the

French are eating more meat and dairy products than in the past. They have been eating as much fat as Americans only since the mid-1980s. In contrast, fat supplied 39% of calories in American diets as long ago as 1923.

Because heart disease takes many years to develop, the consequences of the relatively new French diet have not yet started to appear. Red wine may or may not have a protective effect against heart disease; a low-fat diet definitely does.

Meanwhile, slice the pumpkin into 4 pieces and remove seeds. Place 3 pieces, skin-side down, on a cookie sheet and bake at 350° for 30 minutes. Have a bowl of very cold water ready. Peel the reserved piece and cut into 1/4-inch dice. Bring a pan of water to the boil and cook the diced pumpkin until tender, about 1 minute. Drain and then plunge boiled, diced pumpkin into the bowl of cold water. When cold, drain and set aside.

Cook the Canadian bacon in a large saucepan over medium heat for 1 minute. Add the onion, celery, carrot, bell peppers, garlic, and thyme. Cook for about 3 to 5 minutes, or until vegetables become translucent. Add white wine and remove pan from heat.

Remove skin and seeds from roasted pumpkin. Cut into pieces and add to vegetables. Return pan to heat, add remaining 2 qt chicken stock and simmer for 45 minutes. Ladle soup into a blender and purée. Pass through a strainer and return to a clean saucepan. Add reserved diced pumpkin and white beans. Heat thoroughly.

To make the croutons, cut the crust off the bread and cut the bread into 1/2-inch cubes. Combine the olive oil, salt, and roasted garlic in a mixing bowl; add the bread cubes. Mix thoroughly so the croutons are well seasoned. Place on a sheet pan and bake 350° until croutons are golden brown, about 5 to 7 minutes.

To make pomegranate crème fraîche, cut the pomegranate into quarters and reserve one of the quarters for garnish. Squeeze the other three quarters into a saucepan and reduce to a syrupy glaze over medium heat. Let cool, then whisk in a mixing bowl together with the crème fraîche and heavy cream. Remove seeds from the reserved pomegranate quarter to use for garnish.

To serve, ladle soup into warm bowls and garnish with croutons, pomegranate crème fraîche, chives, and a few of the reserved pomegranate seeds.

Serves 6 to 8.

Calories	%Fat	Fat (g)	Saturated Fat (g)	Cholesterol (mg)	Sodium (mg)	Carbohydrate (g)	Protein (g)	Fiber (g)
442	25	12	5.2	35	618	63	25	10

Exchanges: Starch 3-1/2, Vegetable 2, Low-fat protein 1, Fat 2

# hilled Tomato Bouillon with Tomato & Vodka Granite

Terrance Brennan

6 large vine-ripened tomatoes, roughly chopped
1/2 medium carrot, chopped
1/2 red onion, peeled, chopped
1 celery stalk, chopped
1 small garlic clove
2 T sherry vinegar
6 drops Tabasco sauce
Pepper to taste
1 oz Absolut Peppar Vodka
2 T chopped fresh basil
2 large tomatoes, peeled and julienned
6 basil tops (not stems)

Place the chopped tomatoes in a colander over a bowl or pan and let stand for 3 hours at room temperature. Reserve 1/2 C of the tomato water that collects in the bowl.

To make the bouillon, roughly cut up tomatoes, carrot, onion, and celery. Put vegetables and garlic through a vegetable juicer. Strain through a chinois. Add the reserved tomato water, sherry vinegar, Tabasco, and pepper to taste. Refrigerate for 3 hours.

Tomatoes

When tomatoes ripen on the vine, they produce ethylene gas, which turns them red; they also have better flavor, fragrance, and texture. Partially vine-ripened tomatoes can finish ripening at room temperature in a paper bag; a few holes should be punched in the bag so the tomatoes can breathe. Placing an apple (which naturally produces ethylene gas) in the bag will make the tomatoes ripen faster. Fresh tomatoes taste best if they have never been refrigerated. Tomatoes that have been refrigerated will never become ripe.

Commercial growers usually pick mature tomatoes while they are hard and green because they can be shipped more easily than soft, ripe tomatoes. Artificial treatment with ethylene gas turns the tomatoes red (hard-ripened). Most grocery-store tomatoes are hard-ripened; they are not as flavorful as a vine-ripened tomato.

Sun-dried tomatoes can be stored in the refrigerator for six to nine months; they should be plumped in boiling water before using.

To peel a tomato, drop it in boiling water briefly and then immediately plunge it into cold water. The skins will slip off easily. Use the small, pear-shaped Italian plum tomatoes for making sauce; they contain less water and more sugar than other tomatoes.

Tomatoes contain vitamins A and C and potassium. Most of the vitamin C is found in the "jelly" around each seed; for better nutrition, do not remove the seeds before cooking or serving.

To make the granite, mix 1 C of the tomato bouillon with vodka and 2 T chopped basil. Pour into a shallow 10 × 12-inch pan and freeze. Scrape with a fork about every 20 minutes. Repeat until frozen, about 1 hour.

To serve, divide the granite and julienned tomatoes among six chilled bowls. Ladle 6 ounces of chilled bouillon into each bowl. Garnish with basil tops. Serve immediately.

Serves 6.

Calories	%Fat	Fat (g)	Saturated Fat (g)	Cholesterol (mg)	Sodium (mg)	Carbohydrate (g)	Protein (g)	Fiber (g)
60	13	1	0.1	0	37	13	2	2

Exchanges: Vegetable 2-1/2

Fresh Tomato Soup

2 lb Italian plum tomatoes, peeled and quartered
1 medium onion, chopped
1 stalk celery, chopped
2 C low-sodium chicken broth
1 T no-salt-added tomato paste
1/2 tsp dried basil
1/2 tsp dried thyme
1/4 tsp freshly ground black pepper

Simmer all ingredients for 30 minutes, breaking up tomatoes with a spoon during cooking. Strain to remove seeds. Serve hot or cold.
Serves 6.

Suggestions
- Six medium tomatoes may be substituted for the plum tomatoes.
- Low-sodium beef broth may be substituted for the chicken broth.
- Leftover soup can be served as a sauce over pasta, meat, or vegetables, or as a topping for savory crêpes.

Calories	%Fat	Fat (g)	Saturated Fat (g)	Cholesterol (mg)	Sodium (mg)	Carbohydrate (g)	Protein (g)	Fiber (g)
48	15	1	0.2	0	38	9	2	3

Exchanges: Vegetable 2

I promise to keep on living as though I expected to live forever. Nobody grows old by merely living a number of years. People grow old only by deserting their ideals. Years may wrinkle the skin, but to give up interest wrinkles the soul.

Douglas MacArthur

A Positive Attitude

Most of all, persevere in thinking and acting as a confident, physically fit, positive-minded individual. It isn't easy to change a negative self-image into a new one. Don't expect transformations overnight. But start now. You won't learn how to think and act like a thin, fit person just by losing a few pounds. Losing weight will only make you look fit. Being and staying fit as a total person must register in your mind, not just on the bathroom scale.

Edward B. Diethrich, MD
Heart Test

Eat well of the cresses.

John Grange

Watercress

Watercress has a spicy, slightly peppery, pungent flavor. Its stems look like parsley, and the leaves are small and round. To store, stand the bunch of watercress upright in a glass of water and place the glass in a plastic bag. It will keep in the refrigerator for five to seven days.

Watercress is often served raw in salads or sandwiches, or as a garnish. It can also be used in soups and stir-fry recipes.

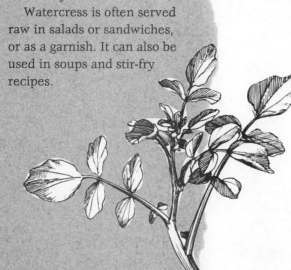

Watercress Soup

Michael Hutchings

12 oz baking potatoes, peeled and sliced into 1/4-inch rounds
7 C boiling water
1/2 lb watercress, trimmed and thoroughly washed
Salt
White pepper to taste
1 C croutons

Cook the potatoes in boiling water until tender. Sweat the watercress in a soup pot until limp. Add the potatoes and cooking water. Cook over high heat until the vegetables are tender. Purée in a food processor and pass through a fine sieve. Adjust seasoning. Cool over ice. Serve cold with croutons on the side.

Serves 8.

Suggestion
- Spinach can be substituted for the watercress. Season to taste with freshly grated nutmeg.

Calories	%Fat	Fat (g)	Saturated Fat (g)	Cholesterol (mg)	Sodium (mg)	Carbohydrate (g)	Protein (g)	Fiber (g)
54	17	1	0.8	0	69	10	2	1

Exchanges: Starch 1/2

# **Zucchini-Rice Soup**

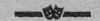
3 large or 4 medium zucchini, chopped
1/2 C chopped onion
2 cans (10 oz each) low-sodium chicken broth
2 C cooked brown rice
1/2 tsp rosemary
2 T lemon juice
1 C plain nonfat yogurt

Simmer zucchini and onion in chicken broth for 15 minutes or until zucchini is tender (add water just to cover zucchini if necessary). Purée soup in a blender or food processor; return to pot. Stir in rice, rosemary, lemon juice, and yogurt. Adjust seasonings to taste. Heat to serving temperature; do not boil.

Serves 8 (1 C each).

Calories	%Fat	Fat (g)	Saturated Fat (g)	Cholesterol (mg)	Sodium (mg)	Carbohydrate (g)	Protein (g)	Fiber (g)
96	8	1	0.2	1	46	18	4	2

Exchanges: Starch 1, Vegetable 1

Gazpacho

2 cloves garlic
2 cucumbers, peeled and chopped
5 medium tomatoes, peeled
6 scallions (reserve green tops)
1 medium green pepper, diced
1-1/4 C no-salt-added tomato juice
1/4 tsp pepper
1/4 C red wine vinegar

Finely chop the garlic, cucumber, tomatoes, and white part of scallions in a blender or food processor. Add green pepper, tomato juice, pepper, and vinegar. Chill for at least 4 hours; serve cold. Garnish each serving with chopped scallion tops.

Serves 6 (1 C each).

Suggestion
• For a spicier soup, add a little salsa, chili pepper, or Tabasco sauce.

Calories	%Fat	Fat (g)	Saturated Fat (g)	Cholesterol (mg)	Sodium (mg)	Carbohydrate (g)	Protein (g)	Fiber (g)
51	9	1	0.1	0	19	12	2	2

Exchanges: Vegetable 2

Alphabet Soup

Manners in eating
count for something.

Ovid

1 onion, chopped
1 clove garlic, chopped
2 celery stalks, chopped
9 C low-sodium beef broth
1/4 C lentils
1/4 C split peas
1/4 C barley
1 can (8 oz) low-sodium tomato sauce
3 C mixed vegetables (such as string beans, carrots, corn, potatoes, spinach)
2 tsp basil
1 tsp oregano
1/2 C alphabet macaroni
1/2 green cabbage, coarsely shredded

Sauté onion, garlic, and celery until tender but not brown; set aside. Bring broth to a boil. Add lentils, split peas, and barley. Cook for 15 minutes. Add onion mixture, tomato sauce, mixed vegetables, and herbs. Cook for 15 minutes, or until lentils and split peas are tender. Stir in macaroni and cabbage; cook until tender. Add more water during cooking if necessary. Serve hot.
Serves 12.

Calories	%Fat	Fat (g)	Saturated Fat (g)	Cholesterol (mg)	Sodium (mg)	Carbohydrate (g)	Protein (g)	Fiber (g)
114	9	1	0.3	0	75	21	7	4

Exchanges: Starch 1, Vegetable 1

inestrone Soup

1 small zucchini, diced
1 small yellow squash, diced
1 small carrot, diced
1 fennel bulb, diced
1 small red onion, diced
1/2 medium red bell pepper, diced
1/2 medium green bell pepper, diced
1 stalk celery, diced
1 T chopped fresh garlic
1/4 C chopped fresh basil
1/4 C chopped fresh parsley
2 qt low-sodium chicken broth
1 C bowtie macaroni
2 T lemon juice
Freshly ground black pepper to taste

Sauté zucchini, squash, carrots, fennel, onion, bell peppers, celery, and garlic for 6 to 8 minutes, or until tender. Stir in half of both the basil and parsley. Add the chicken broth and bowtie macaroni and bring to a boil. Reduce the heat to low and simmer for 30 minutes. Stir in the lemon juice, black pepper, and the remaining basil and parsley.

Serves 8.

Calories	%Fat	Fat (g)	Saturated Fat (g)	Cholesterol (mg)	Sodium (mg)	Carbohydrate (g)	Protein (g)	Fiber (g)
115	11	1	0.4	0	69	20	6	2

Exchanges: Starch 1, Vegetable 1

Vegetable Gumbo

Michael Lomonaco

2 onions, diced
4 ribs celery, diced
2 red bell peppers, diced
2 green bell peppers, diced
1 can (18 oz) plum tomatoes
1/2 lb okra, sliced
10-oz pkg spinach, chopped
1 small head cabbage, shredded
3 garlic cloves, crushed
3 cloves and 2 bay leaves, tied in a small cheesecloth sachet
6 basil leaves, chopped
2 oz file powder (filé)
1 tsp black pepper
1/2 tsp cayenne pepper
1 qt hot Vegetable Stock (page 484)
2 C cooked rice

In a large nonstick casserole, combine the onions, celery, bell peppers, tomatoes, okra, spinach, and cabbage. Cook over low heat until the vegetables are wilted and the onions become translucent, about 15 minutes. Add the garlic, herbs, and spices; continue to cook for 5 minutes. Add the hot Vegetable Stock

Okra

The bright green pods of okra have a velvety, furry skin; they are actually unripe seed capsules. Buy young, tender pods that are less than three or four inches long. They can be stored in the refrigerator for up to three days; the pods should be kept dry as moisture makes them slimy. Okra contains fair amounts of vitamin C, vitamin A, calcium, and B vitamins.

Okra is widely used in Southern cooking and in dishes from Greece, Turkey, India, the Middle East, Africa, and the Caribbean. It is an essential ingredient in gumbo. It is used to thicken soups and stews; add 1 cup or more of sliced okra for the last 10 minutes of cooking. Do not slice okra or remove the stems until just before using it.

Okra can be boiled, baked, or stuffed. When cooked briefly, it has a delicate flavor and a crisp texture (like fresh green beans). It is good with tomatoes, bell peppers, eggplant, zucchini, black-eyed peas, and corn.

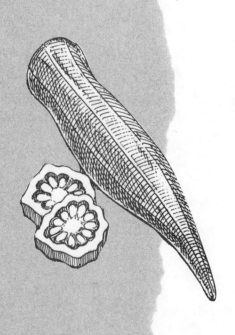

and bring to a boil. Reduce heat and simmer for 45 minutes. Stir in the rice and cook for 5 minutes. Serve hot.

Serves 4.

Suggestion

- The fresh or frozen homemade Vegetable Stock can be replaced with low-salt vegetable broth from a health food store.

Calories	%Fat	Fat (g)	Saturated Fat (g)	Cholesterol (mg)	Sodium (mg)	Carbohydrate (g)	Protein (g)	Fiber (g)
291	9	3	0.6	0	189	60	13	12

Exchanges: Starch 2, Vegetable 6

Wild Rice Soup

2 T chopped onion
3 T chopped fresh mushrooms
3 T finely grated carrot
1/4 C flour
4 C low-sodium chicken broth, defatted
Dash of salt
1/4 C sherry
1/2 C cooked wild rice
1 C skim milk
1/2 C puréed pumpkin, fresh or canned
Chopped parsley

Sauté onion, mushrooms, and carrot until onion is translucent. Stir in flour and cook for 15 minutes. Add chicken broth and cook for 8 to 10 minutes, stirring frequently. Add salt, sherry, rice, milk, and pumpkin. Cook, stirring, until heated to serving temperature. Serve immediately, garnished with freshly chopped parsley.
Serves 6.

A Very-Low-Fat Diet

The food plan in the Diethrich Program...contains approximately 10 percent fat....It includes virtually no meat, no fish, no egg yolks, no dairy products (except skim milk and nonfat yogurt), and no butter, margarine, oils, or mayonnaise.

Instead, participants indulge in virtually limitless quantities of pasta, rice and other grains, beans, vegetables, and fruits in a wide variety of combinations and preparations. Hundreds of people on similar programs throughout the country affirm that eating this way allows for tasty, varied, interesting meals and that they successfully made the adjustment without feeling deprived....

Whether you should adopt such a strict program or begin on a more modest one is a decision you and your doctor will have to make based on your cholesterol level, health, and personality.

Diethrich and Cohan
Women and Heart Disease

Calories	%Fat	Fat (g)	Saturated Fat (g)	Cholesterol (mg)	Sodium (mg)	Carbohydrate (g)	Protein (g)	Fiber (g)
80	10	1	0.3	1	63	13	5	1

Exchanges: Starch 1

Fiber Content of Beans

Adzuki beans	7.2
Black-eyed peas	5.5
Lentils	4.9
Navy beans	4.7
Broad beans	4.3
Black beans	3.6
Pinto beans	3.4
Kidney beans	3.2
Lima beans	3.1
Great Northern beans	3.0
Garbanzo beans	2.8
Peas, canned	2.7
Split peas	1.7

Grams per 1/2 C serving

Black Bean Soup

1 C dried black beans, soaked overnight and drained
3 C water
4 C reduced-sodium chicken broth
1 medium onion, finely chopped
1/2 to 1 clove garlic, minced
1/2 C finely grated carrot
1/3 C chopped green pepper
1/4 tsp oregano
1/4 tsp parsley
1/4 tsp cumin
Freshly ground black pepper to taste
1 bay leaf studded with 1 whole clove

Bring beans, water, and broth to a boil; reduce heat and simmer, covered, until beans are tender, about 2 to 3 hours. Sauté onions and garlic until onion is tender but not brown. Add garlic, carrot, and green pepper; cook until tender. Stir into beans. Add spices and simmer gently for 30 minutes. Add water, broth, or white wine during cooking if necessary. Discard bay leaf and clove.
Serves 4.

Suggestion
• Add chopped chili pepper to taste.

Calories	%Fat	Fat (g)	Saturated Fat (g)	Cholesterol (mg)	Sodium (mg)	Carbohydrate (g)	Protein (g)	Fiber (g)
220	7	2	0.5	0	79	38	14	9

Exchanges: Starch 2, Vegetable 1, Low-fat protein 1

Hoppin' John

*If pale beans bubble for you
in a red earthenware pot,
you can often decline the
dinners of sumptuous hosts.*

Martial

1 lb fresh black-eyed peas
1 medium onion, minced
1/2 clove garlic, minced
2 C canned stewed tomatoes
2 C white rice, cooked
1/4 C chopped parsley
1/4 C chopped scallions, green tops only

Bring peas, onion, garlic, and 1 qt of water to a boil. Reduce heat and simmer until beans are tender. Add remaining ingredients, stirring well. Simmer just until thoroughly heated.
Serves 8.

Suggestions
• Be sure to use fresh, not dried, black-eyed peas in this recipe.
• Serve with cornbread and greens.

How to
Cook Dried Beans
Dried beans should be simmered, not boiled, to prevent them from sticking to pot. Stir them gently with a wooden spoon during cooking so the skins are not broken. They will be tender sooner if they are cooked without salt.

One cup of small dried beans will make about 2-1/2 cups of cooked beans; one cup of large dried beans makes about 2 cups cooked.

Calories	%Fat	Fat (g)	Saturated Fat (g)	Cholesterol (mg)	Sodium (mg)	Carbohydrate (g)	Protein (g)	Fiber (g)
170	11	2	0.4	0	54	34	5	4

Exchanges: Starch 2, Vegetable 1

Chili with Beans

2 medium onions, chopped
4 stalks celery, thinly sliced
1/2 C no-salt-added catsup
2 tsp dry mustard
2 cans (20 oz each) no-salt-added tomatoes
2 cans (20 oz each) no-salt-added red kidney beans
1 can (20 oz) Great Northern beans
2 T chili powder, or to taste

Sauté onions until translucent. Stir in remaining ingredients except chili powder. Add chili powder by teaspoons, stirring and tasting after each addition until the desired zippiness is reached. Simmer for 30 minutes.

Serves 8.

Suggestion

• Pinto beans may be substituted for part or all of the kidney beans and/or the Great Northern beans.

Calories	%Fat	Fat (g)	Saturated Fat (g)	Cholesterol (mg)	Sodium (mg)	Carbohydrate (g)	Protein (g)	Fiber (g)
255	6	2	0.2	0	177	49	15	13

Exchanges: Starch 2-1/2, Vegetable 2

Chili Mac

3 C chopped onion
3 cloves garlic, minced
2 cans (15-1/2 oz each) pinto beans, undrained
2 cans (14-1/2 oz each) stewed tomatoes, undrained and chopped
1-1/2 T chili powder
2 T no-salt-added tomato paste
2 tsp ground cumin
1 C cooked elbow macaroni
1/2 C no-salt-added tomato juice
1/2 C shredded low-fat cheddar cheese

Sauté onion and garlic until tender. Add remaining ingredients, except cheese, and stir well. Reduce heat and simmer, uncovered, for 15 minutes, stirring frequently. Add a little water or tomato juice if mixture is too thick. Top individual servings with grated cheese.
Serves 8.

Calories	%Fat	Fat (g)	Saturated Fat (g)	Cholesterol (mg)	Sodium (mg)	Carbohydrate (g)	Protein (g)	Fiber (g)
257	17	5	1.4	4	316	44	12	9

Exchanges: Starch 2, Vegetable 3, Fat 1

Seaside Chili

1-1/2 C chopped onions
1/2 C chopped celery
2 C peeled, seeded, and chopped tomatoes, fresh or canned
1-1/4 lb minced raw clams
1/3 C clam juice, reserved from raw clams
1 C water
1/2 tsp ground cumin
3 cloves garlic, minced
3 T chili powder
1 can (1-lb) butter beans, undrained
1/2 C zucchini, grated
2 C cooked small seashell macaroni

Sauté onions and celery until tender. Add tomatoes and cook 1 minute. Stir in clams, juice, water, and spices. Simmer for 1 hour. Add beans and zucchini; simmer, covered, for 15 minutes. Top each serving with seashell macaroni.
Serves 4.

Suggestions
- Bottled clam juice or fish stock may be used to supplement or to replace the fresh clam juice.
- Pinto or kidney beans may be substituted for the butter beans.

Calories	%Fat	Fat (g)	Saturated Fat (g)	Cholesterol (mg)	Sodium (mg)	Carbohydrate (g)	Protein (g)	Fiber (g)
426	10	4	0.6	74	400	57	41	11

Exchanges: Starch 3, Vegetable 3, Low-fat protein 4

Chunky Peanut Soup

1 small onion, diced
2 stalks celery, diced
3 T all-purpose flour
2 qt low-sodium chicken broth
2 tsp curry powder
2 cloves garlic, minced
1 tsp ginger
1/4 tsp cayenne pepper
1 jar (8 oz) unsalted old-fashioned chunky peanut butter
1 T lemon juice

Sauté onion and celery until soft, about 5 minutes. Gradually stir in chicken broth and simmer 30 minutes. Mix flour with 1/2 C of the hot chicken broth; stir into the pot of soup. Stir in curry powder, garlic, ginger, cayenne pepper, peanut butter, and lemon juice. Simmer gently for 15 minutes. Serve hot.
Serves 12.

Suggestions
• Use as a topping for baked potatoes or over rice.
• Strain soup and use as a peanut sauce for chicken or vegetable recipes.

Nuts & Seeds
The most heart-healthy nuts are walnuts, pecans, almonds, and chestnuts. They are high in polyunsaturated fat and low in saturated fat.

Chestnuts, roasted	8
Coconut, shredded*	63
Cashews, dry roasted*	71
Peanuts, dry roasted†	71
Peanuts, oil roasted†	71
Pistachios*	71
Sesame seeds	72
Almonds, blanched	75
Pumpkin seeds	75
Sunflower seeds	76
Walnuts, black	83
Walnuts, English	84
Pine nuts	85
Hazelnuts and filberts†	86
Brazil nuts†	87
Macadamia nuts*	92
Pecans, roasted	92

Percent calories from fat
* High in saturated fat, low in poly-unsaturated fat
† Primarily monounsaturated fat

Calories	%Fat	Fat (g)	Saturated Fat (g)	Cholesterol (mg)	Sodium (mg)	Carbohydrate (g)	Protein (g)	Fiber (g)
135	67	10	2.0	0	41	6	7	1

Exchanges: Starch 1/2, High-fat protein 1

Oyster & Scallop Stew with Vegetables

George Haidon

1/2 tsp margarine
2 T finely diced mixed carrots, celery, leeks
2 oz raw scallops, sliced thin
3 oysters, shucked, with juice
2 tsp chopped parsley

Melt the margarine in a heavy skillet. Add diced vegetables and cook slowly; do not brown. Add the scallops and oysters, with their juice. Moisten with enough water to cover. Boil for 2 minutes. Check seasoning. Add chopped parsley. Serve hot.

Serves 1.

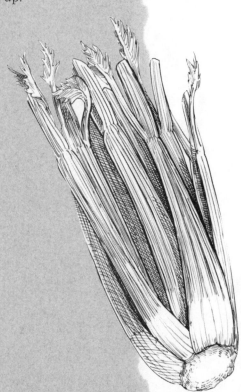

Calories	%Fat	Fat (g)	Saturated Fat (g)	Cholesterol (mg)	Sodium (mg)	Carbohydrate (g)	Protein (g)	Fiber (g)
120	29	4	0.7	42	241	5	16	1

Exchanges: Vegetable 1, Low-fat protein 2

Seafood Gumbo

2-1/3 C sliced okra
2 C chopped onion
2 C diced green bell pepper
2 C diced celery
1/4 C + 2 T all-purpose flour, browned
1/2 C water
2 large cloves garlic, crushed
1/4 C chopped fresh parsley
2 T lemon juice
1/2 tsp dried whole oregano
1/2 tsp poultry seasoning
1/2 tsp dried whole thyme
1/4 tsp ground red pepper
1/8 tsp ground cumin
1/8 tsp liquid smoke
2 C low-sodium chicken broth
1 can (14-1/2 oz) no-salt-added whole tomatoes, undrained and chopped
8 oz bottled low-sodium clam juice
1 bay leaf
1 lb small fresh shrimp, peeled and deveined
12 oz fresh Standard oysters, drained (reserve liquid)
3/4 lb fresh lump crabmeat, drained
5-1/2 C hot cooked brown rice, prepared without salt or fat

High Blood Pressure

Blood pressure is the amount of force necessary to pump blood through the body. High blood pressure (hypertension) may injure the arterial walls, making them prone to atherosclerosis. At the same time, it causes the heart to work harder. High blood pressure may damage body organs, causing stroke, heart attack, and heart and kidney failure.

In most cases, the cause of high blood pressure is unknown. Most people with high blood pressure do not have any symptoms. Early detection and effective treatment are essential. Your physician may

prescribe exercise, a low-salt diet, weight loss, and/or medication. Since this condition may be inherited, if you have high blood pressure, everyone else in your family should have their blood pressure checked regularly.

Blood pressure readings fluctuate and may vary according to age, sex, and other conditions, such as pregnancy. Your doctor can determine your normal level and show you how to maintain a lower blood pressure. High blood pressure is usually not "cured." It is controlled by treatment that may be required for the rest of your life. However, by controlling high blood pressure, you can live a normal and productive life. Keeping your blood pressure at a normal level is also an effective way to prevent heart disease and stroke. Sometimes reducing your weight by 10% and engaging in regular exercise is enough to control high blood pressure.

Arizona Heart
Institute Foundation
1-800-345-4278

Add water to reserved oyster liquid to equal 3/4 cup. Set aside.

Sauté okra, onion, bell pepper, and celery until tender, stirring frequently. Stir in browned flour. Add reserved oyster liquid and all remaining ingredients except seafood and rice. Bring to a boil, stirring constantly. Reduce heat and simmer, uncovered, for 1 hour.

Stir in shrimp, oysters, and crabmeat. Simmer, covered, until shrimp are done and edges of oysters begin to curl. Discard bay leaf. Serve over rice.

Serves 12.

Calories	%Fat	Fat (g)	Saturated Fat (g)	Cholesterol (mg)	Sodium (mg)	Carbohydrate (g)	Protein (g)	Fiber (g)
215	11	3	0.6	76	186	32	16	4

Exchanges: Starch 1-1/2, Vegetable 1, Low-fat protein 2

Pickle Soup

1/2 lb raw chicken breast, cubed
1/2 C chopped celery
1/3 C chopped carrot
2/3 C chopped onion
1 C diced potato
1 clove garlic, minced
1/4 tsp salt
1/4 tsp black pepper
1 tsp minced parsley
4 C water
1/3 C grated low-sodium dill pickle

Simmer all ingredients except pickle until tender. Just before serving, stir in grated pickle. Serve hot.

Serves 4.

I seem to have lost some weight and I don't wish to mar my image. I cannot reveal exactly how much weight. I can only say that had I lost ten more pounds, I would have had to file a missing persons report.

Alfred Hitchcock

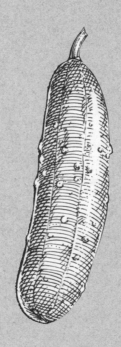

Calories	%Fat	Fat (g)	Saturated Fat (g)	Cholesterol (mg)	Sodium (mg)	Carbohydrate (g)	Protein (g)	Fiber (g)
118	13	2	0.5	31	186	12	14	2

Exchanges: Starch 1/2, Vegetable 1, Low-fat protein 2

 Chicken Potage

4 whole skinless chicken breasts

2 tsp low-sodium chicken bouillon granules

1 C grated raw potato

1 clove elephant garlic, thinly sliced

1 medium onion, chopped

1/2 C thinly sliced celery

1 C thinly sliced carrots

1 C thinly sliced fresh mushrooms

2 T chopped fresh parsley

1 tsp crushed rosemary

Freshly ground black pepper to taste

2 C skim milk

2 T cornstarch mixed with 3 T cold water

3/4 C green peas

Cook chicken in 2 qt water. Reserve 1-1/2 qt cooking liquid. Remove chicken from bones and dice. Add bouillon to cooking liquid. Simmer potato in 2 C of the broth until tender, about 15 minutes. Purée potato with liquid; stir into reserved broth. Add remaining vegetables and seasonings, except peas. Simmer, covered, until vegetables are tender. Add milk; stir in the cornstarch and water mixture. Add chicken and peas. Simmer until slightly thick, about 5 minutes.

Serves 10 (1 C each).

Calories	%Fat	Fat (g)	Saturated Fat (g)	Cholesterol (mg)	Sodium (mg)	Carbohydrate (g)	Protein (g)	Fiber (g)
192	17	4	1.1	54	130	13	26	2

Exchanges: Vegetable 2, Low-fat protein 3

# **P**each "Consommé" with Summer Berries & Fruit

Terrance Brennan

5 C water
1 C dry white wine
1-1/2 C sugar
3 C ripe peaches, peeled and minced
2 cloves
1 bay leaf
1 tsp crushed cardamom seeds
6 peppercorns
1/4 tsp lemon zest
1/4 tsp orange zest
1/2 vanilla bean, split and scraped
2 C favorite mixed berries (at least 3 types)
2 peaches, thinly sliced into 18 pieces
3 Black Mission figs, quartered
1 star fruit, thinly sliced in 18 pieces
6 oz fruit or lemon sorbet
6 fresh mint sprigs

In a medium nonreactive stockpot, bring water, wine, and sugar to a simmer and cook for 3 minutes. Add peaches, cloves, bay leaf, cardamom, pepper-

Berries

Berries contain vitamin C, potassium, and fiber. Strawberries have the most vitamin C per serving. Berries should be used within a day or two of picking for the best flavor and texture. They are ripe and soft when picked.

Store berries unwashed and uncovered in the refrigerator for one or two days. Because berries crush easily, they should not be stored in tall, narrow containers; spread them in a single layer if possible. Berries can be frozen whole for up to four months. Wash them and remove the stems just before using.

Chill berries before washing to keep them from getting mushy. Serve berries with a little dry or sweet white wine instead of cream for dessert.

Vanilla Beans

Vanilla beans, the cured pods of an orchid, are expensive; fortunately, they can be used repeatedly. They can be used whole or split in half. Cutting the bean lengthwise releases tiny, dark beans that intensify its flavoring power. Recipes may specify that the cut edge should be scraped with a sharp paring knife to detach the beans first (use them; don't discard them).

A vanilla bean may be added to milk, custard, pudding, or poaching liquids during cooking, replacing vanilla extract. The bean should be saved, washed in cold water, patted dry, and stored in an airtight container in the refrigerator.

A vanilla bean can also be buried in a container of sugar for storage; this keeps the bean from drying out and flavors the sugar as well. The bean can be reused and reburied for as long as it is fragrant and flavorful. Vanilla-flavored sugar can be used in preparing baked goods, desserts, or beverages.

corns, lemon and orange zest, and vanilla bean and simmer for 5 minutes. Cover and let stand overnight at room temperature. Strain through a cheesecloth and chill.

Combine the berries, peaches, figs, and star fruit. Divide among 6 chilled soup bowls. Ladle Peach Consommé into bowls. Place a scoop of sorbet in the center of each bowl and garnish with mint sprigs. Serve immediately.

Serves 6.

Suggestion

• Peach Consommé can be stored in the refrigerator for 3 days.

Calories	%Fat	Fat (g)	Saturated Fat (g)	Cholesterol (mg)	Sodium (mg)	Carbohydrate (g)	Protein (g)	Fiber (g)
335	2	1	0.1	0	12	84	2	4

Exchanges: Fruit 5-1/2
Note: Not appropriate for diabetics

hilled Cantaloupe Soup

6 ripe cantaloupes, halved and seeded
3/4 C dry sherry
1/2 C sugar
1-1/2 C orange juice
Mint sprigs

   Scoop pulp from each cantaloupe half, leaving 1/2-inch thick shells. Cut a thin slice from the bottom of each shell so that they can be used as serving bowls. Purée pulp, sherry, sugar, and orange juice in a blender or food processor. Adjust sweetness to taste. Chill thoroughly. Serve in cantaloupe bowls, garnished with fresh mint.
   Serves 12.

Melons

   About 20 varieties of melons are available. They are more than 90% water. All melons are good sources of potassium and vitamin C. Yellow and orange melons are high in beta-carotene; watermelons have almost no beta-carotene.

   When the melon is ripe, it smells sweet and the stem end is soft; the stronger the fragrance, the sweeter the melon. Melons should be vine-ripened as they will not get sweeter after they are picked. Store ripe melons and cut melons in the refrigerator.

Calories	%Fat	Fat (g)	Saturated Fat (g)	Cholesterol (mg)	Sodium (mg)	Carbohydrate (g)	Protein (g)	Fiber (g)
229	5	1	0.0	0	43	52	4	3

Exchanges: Fruit 3-1/2

Vegetable Salads

Beet
Cabbage
Celery
Corn
Jicama
Onion
Potato
Tomato
Spinach
Squash
Mixed Vegetable

Grain & Legume Salads

Wheat
Wild Rice
Dried Beans

Pasta Salads

Seafood Salads

Cod
Marlin
Scallop
Crab
Lobster
Shrimp

Chicken Salads

Fruit Salads

Apple
Pear
Strawberry

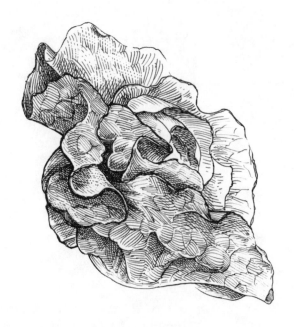

Salads

# **F**resh Beet Salad

2 bunches red beets, unpeeled, washed, and trimmed (about 6 medium beets)
2 T water
1/4 C white wine vinegar
2 tsp caraway seeds
1 tsp sugar
2 T minced red onion
1 tsp horseradish
1/4 tsp ground cloves
1/4 tsp black pepper

Cook beets in water to cover until tender. Peel and slice. Combine remaining ingredients and pour over beets. Let beets marinate for several hours before serving, stirring occasionally.
Serves 6.

Suggestion
• Season to taste with fresh dill.

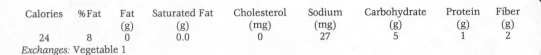

Calories	%Fat	Fat (g)	Saturated Fat (g)	Cholesterol (mg)	Sodium (mg)	Carbohydrate (g)	Protein (g)	Fiber (g)
24	8	0	0.0	0	27	5	1	2

Exchanges: Vegetable 1

Cole Slaw

2 T lemon juice
1/2 C apple cider vinegar
1/2 C cold water
1/2 tsp mustard
2 T frozen unsweetened apple juice concentrate, thawed
1 small green cabbage, finely shredded
4 Granny Smith apples, cored and chopped
1 carrot, grated
2 celery ribs, finely chopped
1 green bell pepper, seeded and chopped
2 T parsley, chopped

Shake lemon juice, vinegar, water, mustard, and apple juice concentrate together in a tightly covered container to make dressing. Combine remaining ingredients in a large mixing bowl. Toss with dressing. Chill thoroughly before serving.
Serves 8.

Calories	%Fat	Fat (g)	Saturated Fat (g)	Cholesterol (mg)	Sodium (mg)	Carbohydrate (g)	Protein (g)	Fiber (g)
82	6	1	0.1	0	35	20	2	4

Exchanges: Vegetable 1, Fruit 1

# **R**ed & Green Cole Slaw

Sauerkraut Salad

Boil 1 C sugar and 1/2 C vinegar; cool completely. Mix 2-1/2 lb low-sodium sauerkraut, 2 C chopped celery, 1 C chopped green pepper, and 1 C chopped onion. Toss with boiled dressing. Marinate in the refrigerator overnight, stirring occasionally.

1/2 C water
2 T sugar
2 tsp safflower oil
1/2 C shredded red cabbage
1-1/2 C shredded green cabbage
1 medium carrot, julienned
1 small red bell pepper, julienned
1/2 C chopped scallions
3 T minced fresh parsley
1/2 C white wine vinegar
1/2 tsp freshly ground pepper

Bring water, sugar, and oil to a boil, stirring well. Pour over cabbage and toss well. Add remaining ingredients, tossing gently to combine. Cover and chill thoroughly before serving.

Serves 6.

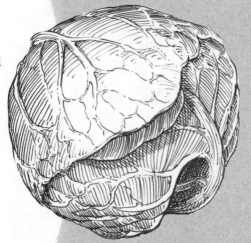

Calories	%Fat	Fat (g)	Saturated Fat (g)	Cholesterol (mg)	Sodium (mg)	Carbohydrate (g)	Protein (g)	Fiber (g)
48	30	2	0.2	0	11	9	1	1

Exchanges: Vegetable 2

Roasted Pepper & Celery Salad with Tomato Vinaigrette

Joyce Goldstein

2 T mild olive oil
1/2 C diced plum tomatoes
2 T tomato purée
1/4 C sherry vinegar
1/4 C raisins or currants, soaked in hot water until plump, drained
Salt and freshly ground black pepper to taste
3 large roasted red peppers, cut in 1/2-inch wide strips
6 ribs celery, strings removed, sliced thin on the diagonal

Mix oil, tomatoes, tomato purée, vinegar, and raisins in a bowl and whisk together. Adjust sweet and sour ratio. If too tart, add a pinch of sugar. You may want a bit more vinegar or a squeeze of lemon juice. Toss the peppers and celery with the vinaigrette.

Serves 6.

Suggestion
• 2 large bulbs fennel, halved, cored, and sliced thin, can be substituted for the celery.

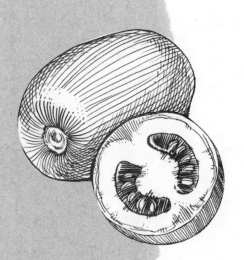

Calories	%Fat	Fat (g)	Saturated Fat (g)	Cholesterol (mg)	Sodium (mg)	Carbohydrate (g)	Protein (g)	Fiber (g)
85	51	5	0.7	0	60	11	1	1

Exchanges: Fruit 1/2, Vegetable 1, Fat 1

Summer Salad of Corn, Chanterelles, & Arugula

Terrance Brennan

2-1/2 C fresh chanterelles
2 tsp olive oil
1 shallot, minced
3 C fresh corn kernels, cooked
Pepper to taste
3 bunches baby arugula, cleaned and washed
6 T aged goat cheese, grated
6 T snipped chives

Vinaigrette
1/2 oz aged balsamic vinegar
1 T minced shallot
Pepper to taste
1 oz extra-virgin olive oil

To make the vinaigrette, mix vinegar, shallot, and pepper in a small mixing bowl. Whisk in olive oil. Set aside.

If chanterelles are large, cut them into fourths. In a medium sauté pan, heat 2 tsp of olive oil over medium heat for 1 minute. Add chanterelles and shallot. Cover and sweat over low heat until tender yet firm, about 10 minutes. If pan

Arugula

Also called *rocket* or *roquette*, arugula has a slightly bitter and robust, herby flavor; it is similar to dandelion. This emerald-green cruciferous vegetable is a member of the cabbage family. Arugula contains vitamins A and C and iron. It should be stored like spinach.

Arugula can be mixed with mild-flavored greens or leaf lettuce and served in hot or cold salads. It is often mixed with radicchio. Balsamic vinegar is a good seasoning for a salad of arugula, red onions, avocado, and wild mushrooms. Arugula can also be added to omelettes, soups, pasta dishes, pizza, and sautéed vegetables.

Chives

Chives have fine, slender leaves and a mild onion flavor. Store them in a plastic bag in the refrigerator for up to two weeks. Snip fresh chives to the desired length. Add them to cooked foods just before serving or their flavor will be harsh. Chives have edible lavender flowers that are very pretty and flavorful in salads.

becomes too dry, add a little water (this should equal 1-1/2 C cooked mushrooms). Let cool. Over high heat, sauté mushrooms and corn in cooking spray for about 2 minutes. Season with pepper to taste. Divide among 6 plates.

Toss arugula with vinaigrette and place on top of corn. Sprinkle goat cheese and chives over salads. Serve immediately.

Serves 6.

Calories	%Fat	Fat (g)	Saturated Fat (g)	Cholesterol (mg)	Sodium (mg)	Carbohydrate (g)	Protein (g)	Fiber (g)
157	46	8	1.9	6	91	20	5	4

Exchanges: Starch 1, Vegetable 1, Fat 1-1/2

Grilled Corn & White Bean Salad

2 C small white beans, soaked overnight and drained
6 ears fresh corn in their husks, soaked in cold water for 20 minutes
1/4 C white wine vinegar
2 tsp Dijon mustard
Freshly ground black pepper to taste
1 T corn oil
1 T chopped fresh thyme
Handful fresh parsley, finely chopped
4 scallions, thinly sliced
1/2 red onion, finely chopped
Pinch of crushed red peppers

Place the beans in a large saucepan with enough water to cover them by several inches. Bring to a boil; reduce heat and simmer gently until tender (begin checking after 25 minutes). Drain and set aside, stirring occasionally.

Light the grill and wait until the coals are ash-colored. Set the corn on the grill and cook, turning often, until they are charred. Set the corn aside until it is cool enough to handle. Remove the husks and silk; cut the kernels from the cobs. Mix corn with the beans.

Shake vinegar, mustard, pepper, and oil in a covered container until well

Boiled Corn

Peel the husks from fresh corn; use a stiff vegetable brush to remove the silk, taking care not to damage the kernels. Bring a large kettle of unsalted water to a boil; add a pinch of sugar. (If salt is added to the cooking water, the corn will be tough.) Drop the corn into the pot and cover tightly. When the water returns to a boil, remove the kettle from the heat. Let stand, still covered, for 5 minutes, then serve the corn immediately. "Seconds" can be kept hot in the covered kettle for up to 20 minutes.

Roasted Corn

Remove any dry husks from corn; leave remaining husks on. Place the corn on the middle rack of the oven and bake at 350° for 10 to 15 minutes. Turn the ears over after the first 5 minutes. Remove the hot, brittle husks and cornsilk, holding the corn with a towel. Serve immediately.

blended. Pour the dressing over the beans and corn. Add the thyme, parsley, spring onions, red onion, and crushed red peppers, tossing lightly. Serve at room temperature.

Serves 10.

Calories	%Fat	Fat (g)	Saturated Fat (g)	Cholesterol (mg)	Sodium (mg)	Carbohydrate (g)	Protein (g)	Fiber (g)
193	11	2	0.4	0	28	36	11	7

Exchanges: Starch 2-1/2

Jicama Salad

3 C peeled and shredded jicama
2 C shredded red cabbage
1 small red onion, finely chopped
4 carrots, grated
1 medium bell pepper, finely chopped
1 T olive oil
1 tsp lime or lemon juice
1 tsp white vinegar
1 tsp water
1 tsp celery seeds
1/2 tsp sugar

Toss jicama, cabbage, onion, carrots, and bell pepper together. Shake remaining ingredients together in a tightly covered container until well blended. Pour over salad and toss lightly.
Serves 8.

Jicama

Also called a *Mexican potato*, the jicama is a very juicy root vegetable. Smaller jicama are juicier than large. It tastes like slightly sweet water chestnuts. It has a tough, thick outer skin that can be peeled easily. The white flesh is crisp like an apple, and it stays crunchy when cooked. It is a fair source of vitamin C and potassium. Store jicama in the refrigerator for seven to ten days.

Jicama is best served raw. It will not turn brown when cut. Jicama is an inexpensive substitute for water chestnuts. It is good in fruit or vegetable salads, or served on a platter with other raw vegetables and dip. It can be used in seasoned marinades, and it is good pickled with onions and herbs. Jicama can also be cooked like sweet potatoes.

Calories	%Fat	Fat (g)	Saturated Fat (g)	Cholesterol (mg)	Sodium (mg)	Carbohydrate (g)	Protein (g)	Fiber (g)
63	29	2	0.3	0	20	11	2	3

Exchanges: Vegetable 2, Fat 1/2

Lettuce, Lacutca satina, ever was, and still continues the principal foundation of the universal tribe of sallets [salads]...it allays heat, bridles choler, extinguishes thirst, excites appetite, kindly nourishes; and above all, represses vapours, conciliates sleep, mitigates pain; besides the effect it has on the morals, temperance, and chastity.

John Evelyn
*Acetaria: a discourse of sallets
1699*

Onion & Romaine Salad

2 T red wine vinegar
1 red onion, very thinly sliced and separated into rings
Freshly ground black pepper, to taste
2 T olive oil
2 T chopped fresh parsley
1 head romaine lettuce, cleaned, trimmed, and torn

Pour the vinegar over the onion rings and season with pepper. Cover and set aside at room temperature for 30 minutes. Toss the onions with oil and parsley. Add the romaine lettuce and toss thoroughly to coat leaves with dressing. Serve immediately.
Serves 4.

Suggestion
• Sprinkle freshly grated Parmesan cheese on each serving.

Calories	%Fat	Fat (g)	Saturated Fat (g)	Cholesterol (mg)	Sodium (mg)	Carbohydrate (g)	Protein (g)	Fiber (g)
87	72	7	1.0	0	9	5	2	2

Exchanges: Vegetable 1, Fat 1-1/2

 # ed Potato Salad

1/2 C plain nonfat yogurt
3 T reduced-fat mayonnaise
1 tsp dried tarragon
1 T tarragon vinegar
1 tsp mustard
4 small stalks celery, thinly sliced
2 hard-boiled egg whites, chopped
1 lb red potatoes, boiled, and cubed

Mix all ingredients except potatoes. Pour dressing over the potatoes and mix until they are evenly coated. Serve warm or cold.

Serves 6.

High-Fiber Peels

To increase the fiber content of your diet, eat fresh fruits and vegetables with their skins. A potato with the skin has twice the fiber of a peeled potato.

Calories	%Fat	Fat (g)	Saturated Fat (g)	Cholesterol (mg)	Sodium (mg)	Carbohydrate (g)	Protein (g)	Fiber (g)
125	17	2	0.4	2	115	22	4	2

Exchanges: Starch 1-1/2, Fat 1/2

Cucumber

Cucumbers have been cultivated for thousands of years. The two varieties include *hothouse* (long, thin, and smooth) and *ridge* (thick and rough-skinned; grown outdoors on raised ridges of soil). English cucumbers are very long, slender, and seedless; they have a very delicate flavor and are called "burpless." Lemon cucumbers are round and pale yellow; they have a very delicate flavor.

Cucumbers need high humidity (grocers often wax them to prevent moisture loss). Store them in the refrigerator for four to five days. They will get softer as they get older, but cucumbers can be recrisped by soaking slices in ice water. Remove the peels if the cucumbers have been waxed.

Red Garden Salad

1/3 C cucumber, peeled, seeded, and chopped
2 T chopped red bell pepper
2 T thinly sliced radishes
1 small red onion, thinly sliced and separated into rings
1/4 tsp dried dill
Black pepper to taste
1/2 C plain nonfat yogurt
2 C cooked and sliced new potatoes, warm

Blend all ingredients except potatoes and heat until warm, stirring frequently; do not boil. Toss warm potatoes in yogurt mixture. Serve immediately.
Serves 4.

Calories	%Fat	Fat (g)	Saturated Fat (g)	Cholesterol (mg)	Sodium (mg)	Carbohydrate (g)	Protein (g)	Fiber (g)
171	1	0	0.1	1	35	38	5	3

Exchanges: Starch 2, Vegetable 1

# Garlic-Crust Mozzarella with Pear Tomato Bread Salad

P. Quint Smith

1 head garlic, cleaned and peeled
Freshly ground black pepper to taste
1 sprig fresh thyme
1/2 C Wondra flour
1 small loaf day-old country-style Italian bread
1 bunch basil
1 T extra-virgin olive oil
1 pt pear tomatoes (mixed red and yellow preferred)
6 fillets of anchovies, chopped
1/4 C pitted green olives (picholine preferred)
1 small jar marinated artichoke hearts, chopped
1/2 lb fresh part-skim mozzarella, room temperature

Mix garlic, pepper, and thyme on a piece of foil about 12 inches square; fold foil to seal garlic in a packet. Bake at 350° for about 30 minutes, or until cloves are very soft and mushy. Transfer garlic to a small bowl and mash with the back of a spoon until smooth. Mix in flour to make a smooth paste. Keep at room temperature.

Remove crust from bread. Cut bread into 1-inch cubes, making 2 to 3 C of

bread cubes. Toast on a cookie sheet at 350° for 5 minutes. The bread should be crusty outside but not dried out inside.

Clean basil and remove leaves. Dry leaves on paper towels and set aside. To make basil oil, place basil stems in a small saucepot with the oil. Simmer for 15 minutes. Cover, remove from heat, and cool.

Clean and split pear tomatoes. Combine bread, tomatoes, basil leaves (chopped if large), anchovies, olives, and artichokes. Moisten with strained basil oil and season with pepper. Place on 6 warm salad plates.

Cut cheese into 6 even slices and coat 1 side with garlic-crust mixture. Cook cheese, crust side down, over medium high heat in a Teflon or nonstick pan for about 3 minutes, or until golden brown. Flip cheese and cook just long enough to warm slightly; remove from pan immediately. Place 1 piece of cheese on each salad plate. Garnish with basil leaves and serve. Drizzle with a little basil oil if desired.

Serves 6.

Calories	%Fat	Fat (g)	Saturated Fat (g)	Cholesterol (mg)	Sodium (mg)	Carbohydrate (g)	Protein (g)	Fiber (g)
246	39	11	4.7	23	488	23	15	2

Exchanges: Starch 1, Vegetable 2, Low-fat protein 1-1/2

Vegetable — 173

# Spinach Salad

1/2 lb raw spinach, washed, stemmed, and torn into bite-size pieces
2 medium oranges, peeled and sectioned, with juice
1 medium red onion, sliced and separated into rings
1/2 small Florida avocado, peeled and diced
Herb vinegar to taste
Freshly ground black pepper

Toss all ingredients together. Serve on chilled salad plates.
Serves 6.

Suggestions
- Lemon juice may be used with or in place of the herb vinegar.
- California avocados may by used, but they are slightly higher in fat than Florida avocados.

Spinach

Spinach originally came from Persia. It is an excellent source of vitamins C and A. It is also a good source of riboflavin, which is concentrated in the leaves. The stems and ribs have more fiber than the leaves. Break up bunches of spinach and place the leaves in loose piles in a plastic bag; store them in the refrigerator.

Spinach can be served raw in salads or cooked in soups, souffles, or quiche. Before cooking, wash the leaves and shake off the excess water; the water that clings to the leaves will be sufficient for cooking. Cook, covered, for about six minutes, or steam lightly; do not overcook. Occasionally lifting the lid during cooking will help keep the spinach bright green. It should not be cooked in iron or aluminum pots, which will give the spinach a metallic flavor. Fresh mint, added during cooking, or nutmeg is a good seasoning for spinach.

Calories	%Fat	Fat (g)	Saturated Fat (g)	Cholesterol (mg)	Sodium (mg)	Carbohydrate (g)	Protein (g)	Fiber (g)
77	48	4	0.7	0	33	10	2	4

Exchanges: Fruit 1/2, Vegetable 1, Fat 1

Acorn Squash Salad

3 lb acorn squash, baked, peeled, seeded, and diced
3 medium Granny Smith apples, cored and diced
2 stalks celery, diced
4 scallions, minced
1/4 C raisins
1 C plain nonfat yogurt
1 T apple cider vinegar
2 tsp honey Dijon mustard
2 T honey
Freshly ground black pepper to taste
1/3 C chopped pecans, toasted

   Toss squash with apples, celery, scallions, and raisins; set aside. Blend yogurt with vinegar, mustard, honey, and black pepper. Pour over squash and
toss until all ingredients are coated evenly. Refrigerate, covered, for at least 2
hours, stirring occasionally. Sprinkle with pecans just before serving.
   Serves 8.

Suggestions
- Add 2 tsp curry powder to yogurt dressing.
- Stir in 1/4 C minced cilantro before serving.

Calories	%Fat	Fat (g)	Saturated Fat (g)	Cholesterol (mg)	Sodium (mg)	Carbohydrate (g)	Protein (g)	Fiber (g)
164	25	5	0.5	1	89	31	4	5

Exchanges: Starch 1, Fruit 1, Fat 1

# Market Vegetable Dinner

Michael Roberts

1/4 C lentils
1 large onion, peeled, halved from tip to stem and slivered
1 red pepper, cut into rounds
1 small zucchini, cut into 1/4-inch thick rounds
1/2 lb large cultivated mushrooms, halved
1/2 C small cauliflower florets
1 ear white corn, kernels removed
1 T Dijon mustard
1/3 C sherry vinegar
1/4 C olive oil
1 C Florida avocado, in large dice, chilled
1 large tomato, in large dice, chilled
1 head butter or Boston lettuce, washed, dried, torn, chilled

Bring a pot of water to a boil and cook the lentils until soft but not mushy, about 15 minutes. Drain and pour into a salad bowl.

Meanwhile, place a wok over high heat on the stove; add cooking spray. Add the onion and quickly spread it across the bottom and sides of the wok. Cook 1-1/2 minutes without stirring. Stir the onions and cook another minute. Scrape into the salad bowl and replace the wok on the stove.

Add cooking spray and when the wok is hot again, add pepper and zucchini. Cook, stirring frequently, about 2 minutes. Add the contents of the wok to the

Where's the cook: is supper ready, the house trimmed, rushes strewed, cobwebs swept?"

Shakespeare
The Taming of the Shrew

Lettuce

The three main varieties of lettuce are *crisphead* (tightly formed, solid heads, like iceberg lettuce), *cos* or romaine (long, coarse leaves), and *butterhead* (loose, coarse leaves that can be very soft or firm). The lettuce family includes arugula, Bibb, Boston, butter, chicory, curly endive, escarole, romaine, iceberg, endive, watercress, green and red leaf lettuce, and radicchio.

Darker-leaved lettuce has more nutrients than lighter leaves. Iceberg lettuce is the least nutritious, being predominantly water. Most other lettuce greens are good sources of vitamin C and beta-carotene and also contain some calcium, folate, and iron.

Store washed lettuce in an airtight container in the coldest part of the refrigerator. To crisp wilted lettuce, rinse it in cold water, shake off the excess water, and refrigerate it in a plastic bag for 12 hours. Wrap leaves in dry paper towels to prevent "rust" from forming. Do not store lettuce near apples, pears, melons, or bananas— they produce ethylene gas, which will cause lettuce to get brown spots.

salad bowl and mix. Replace the wok on the stove.

Add cooking spray and when it is hot again, add the mushrooms. Place a lid on the wok and cook for 30 seconds. Remove lid and cook, stirring frequently, another 1 to 2 minutes. Remove from the heat, add the mushrooms to the salad bowl, and mix. Replace the wok on the stove.

When the wok is hot again, add the corn. Cook 1 minute without stirring, then for another 30 seconds, stirring constantly. Remove from the heat and add the corn to the salad bowl. Mix all ingredients and place the bowl in the refrigerator for 20 minutes.

Combine mustard and vinegar in a small bowl and beat in the oil. Just before serving, add avocado, tomato, and lettuce to the salad bowl. Pour over the vinaigrette and toss everything together.

Serves 4.

Calories	%Fat	Fat (g)	Saturated Fat (g)	Cholesterol (mg)	Sodium (mg)	Carbohydrate (g)	Protein (g)	Fiber (g)
168	35	7	1.0	0	18	25	7	7

Exchanges: Starch 1, Vegetable 2, Fat 1

Cracked Wheat Salad

1/2 C uncooked bulgar wheat
1/4 C chopped tomatoes
1/4 C chopped zucchini
1/4 C chopped yellow squash
1/4 C chopped scallions
1/4 C chopped bell peppers (mixed colors)
1 tsp olive oil
Freshly ground black pepper to taste

Pour boiling water over the bulgar wheat and soak for 30 to 40 minutes, until softened; drain. Toss bulgar with the remaining ingredients. Chill, covered, for several hours before serving.

Serves 4.

Suggestion
• Tuna fish or chicken can be added to this salad.

How to Reduce Risk

Elevated blood pressure and blood fat levels are major cardiovascular disease risk factors that can be modified through diet. The Arizona Heart Institute's 2-gram sodium, low-cholesterol, low-saturated fat, low-refined-carbohydrate diet is designed to help lower cholesterol, blood pressure, and/or triglycerides. It is not a change in eating habits for just today or this month but a change for life.

**Arizona Heart
Institute Foundation**
1–800–345–4278

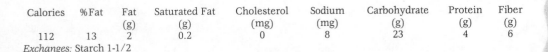

Calories	%Fat	Fat (g)	Saturated Fat (g)	Cholesterol (mg)	Sodium (mg)	Carbohydrate (g)	Protein (g)	Fiber (g)
112	13	2	0.2	0	8	23	4	6

Exchanges: Starch 1-1/2

Wild Rice & Turkey Salad

4 oz wild rice (about 2/3 C), rinsed well
1-1/2 C water
1/3 C brown rice
3/4 lb fresh green beans, cut French style and steamed
3/4 lb cooked turkey breast, cut into 1/2-inch pieces without skin
1/4 lb fresh mushrooms, sliced thin
1 C julienned carrots
1/4 C chopped fresh parsley
Basil-Mustard Vinaigrette (page 470)
6 leaves green leaf lettuce

Bring wild rice and water to a boil. Reduce heat and simmer, covered, for 25 minutes. Add brown rice. Simmer, covered, until water is absorbed, about 20 minutes. Cool for 30 minutes.

Toss rice, beans, turkey, mushrooms, carrots, parsley, and Basil-Mustard Vinaigrette. Serve on lettuce leaves.

Serves 6.

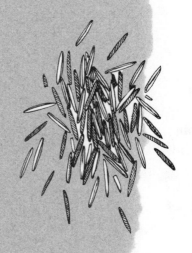

Calories	%Fat	Fat (g)	Saturated Fat (g)	Cholesterol (mg)	Sodium (mg)	Carbohydrate (g)	Protein (g)	Fiber (g)
278	24	8	1.4	44	76	31	23	4

Exchanges: Starch 1-1/2, Vegetable 1, Low-fat protein 2, Fat 1/2

# Lentil, Celery, & Ginger Salad

Hubert Keller

1 large, long carrot, peeled
3 large ripe tomatoes, cored, peeled, seeded
8 to 9 oz green lentils, washed
1 small yellow onion
1 celery stalk, finely chopped
1/2 small red onion, finely chopped
1/4 tsp peeled and finely chopped ginger
1-1/2 T lemon juice
1-1/2 T soy sauce
Salt and freshly ground pepper
1 English cucumber, peeled, seeded, diced
1 tsp sherry vinegar
1/2 tsp Dijon mustard
1 oz onion sprouts

Bring a medium pot of water to a boil. Cut the carrot lengthwise into 8 identical strips at 1/8-inch thick, 3/4-inch wide, and 5 inches long. Blanch the strips in boiling water for 1 minute and then plunge them into cold water. Drain and dry on a cloth or paper towels. Chop the tomatoes very finely. Transfer the tomatoes into a fine sieve over a bowl to eliminate excess water. Cook the lentils and yellow onion gently for about 45 minutes in water; drain and cool. Mix the lentils with celery, red onion, ginger, lemon juice, soy sauce, olive oil, salt, and freshly ground pepper. Taste and adjust seasoning.

Ginger

Ginger is actually the root of a plant that grows in the tropics. It has a sweet but peppery flavor and a spicy aroma. Fresh ginger is widely used in oriental, Indian, and European cooking. It is used in both savory and sweet dishes.

Ginger should be peeled before using. It can be stored in a sealed plastic bag in the refrigerator for a week or so. Grated fresh ginger, packed in a covered container with dry sherry or vinegar water, should keep for weeks or months in the refrigerator; use only enough liquid to cover the ginger so the flavor will keep its intensity. Fresh ginger can also be stored in the freezer, tightly wrapped in plastic or sealed in a plastic bag, and sliced, chopped, or grated as needed.

Crystallized or candied ginger is made by boiling fresh ginger root in a sugar syrup. It is good in desserts and savory dishes.

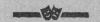

For the cucumber vinaigrette, process the cucumber, sherry vinegar, Dijon mustard, salt, and pepper in a blender with about 5 on-and-off pulses, until the texture is very smooth. Season to taste.

Use 4 round, non-fluted pastry cutters, 3-1/4 inch in diameter and 3/4-inch deep, as molds. Place a mold in the middle of each plate. Curve 2 strips of carrot, end to end, around the interior edge of each mold, trimming them if necessary. Fill the molds with lentil salad, firmly pressing it down with the back of a tablespoon. Garnish the top with a layer of chopped raw tomatoes. Season with salt and pepper and smooth over with a small spatula so that the tomato is level with the top of the mold. Using a paper towel, very carefully soak up any excess liquid which has escaped under the bottom edge of the mold. Meticulously pull off the pastry cutters, leaving a crunchy, refreshing, and vitamin-packed salad in the shape of a small cake. Gently spoon the cucumber vinaigrette around the carrot and lentil cake and garnish attractively with the onion sprouts.

Serves 4.

Suggestion

• A great salad for a great light meal.

Calories	%Fat	Fat (g)	Saturated Fat (g)	Cholesterol (mg)	Sodium (mg)	Carbohydrate (g)	Protein (g)	Fiber (g)
268	5	1	0.2	0	278	50	18	12

Exchanges: Starch 2-1/2, Vegetable 2

# Mediterranean Pasta Salad

4 C cooked tri-colored rotilli pasta, drained and chilled
1/2 C diced red bell pepper
1/2 C thinly sliced scallions
1/2 C finely chopped sun-dried tomatoes
1/4 C crumbled feta cheese
1 T minced fresh garlic
1/4 C red wine vinegar
1/4 C lemon juice
2 T olive oil
Freshly ground black pepper

Toss pasta, bell pepper, scallions, tomatoes, and feta cheese. Mix garlic, vinegar, and lemon juice; while whisking constantly, slowly dribble in the olive oil. Pour vinaigrette over the pasta and toss well. Season with pepper to taste. Chill thoroughly before serving.

Serves 4.

Calories	% Fat	Fat (g)	Saturated Fat (g)	Cholesterol (mg)	Sodium (mg)	Carbohydrate (g)	Protein (g)	Fiber (g)
316	28	10	2.4	8	118	49	9	3

Exchanges: Starch 2-1/2, Vegetable 2, Fat 2

Roasted Bell Peppers

Cut bell peppers (any color) into quarters and remove the cores and seeds.

Lightly coat the skin side of each pepper with cooking spray. Place the peppers on a grill or under the broiler, with skins closest to the source of heat. Cook, without turning, until the skins are blackened. Remove from heat and allow to cool, covered, in a bowl until they can be handled. (Save the juices that collect in the bottom of the bowl to use in cooking.) Peel the skin from the peppers. Use as directed in recipes.

Whole peppers can also be roasted; turn them as they start to char on the side closest to the heat.

Roasted Pepper & Pasta Salad

12 roasted bell peppers (mixed colors), peeled and cut in 1-inch strips, with juices (see margin)
1 clove garlic, crushed
1 heaping tsp Dijon mustard
1/2 C white wine vinegar
2 shallots, minced
3 scallions, thinly sliced
2 T olive oil
1 lb small shell pasta, cooked al dente and drained

Briskly shake pepper juices, garlic, mustard, vinegar, shallots, scallions, and oil in a covered container until well blended. Toss bell peppers, pasta, and dressing thoroughly. Chill, covered tightly, for several hours before serving.
Serves 6.

Calories	%Fat	Fat (g)	Saturated Fat (g)	Cholesterol (mg)	Sodium (mg)	Carbohydrate (g)	Protein (g)	Fiber (g)
383	15	6	0.9	0	18	71	12	4

Exchanges: Starch 4, Vegetable 2, Fat 1

Shrimp & Pasta Salad

2 C cooked tri-colored rotilli pasta
1 C cooked shrimp, peeled and deveined
1/3 C red bell pepper, diced
1/4 C carrots, coarsely grated
1/2 C zucchini, thinly sliced
1 T parsley, chopped
2-1/2 T reduced-fat mayonnaise
2-1/2 T nonfat plain yogurt
2 T vinegar
2 T no-salt-added tomato juice

Lightly toss all ingredients together. Chill for 30 minutes before serving.
Serves 4.

Suggestion
• Tuna fish may be substituted for the shrimp.

Pasta

Pasta includes a wide variety of noodles made of water and flour. It can be made with semolina flour, eggs, spinach (green pasta), beets or tomato paste (red pasta), whole-wheat flour (light-brown pasta), squid ink (black pasta), and other ingredients like quinoa. High-protein pastas include soy flour. Pasta is a good source of complex carbohydrates and B vitamins, and it contains some protein.

Hand-made fresh pasta is more tender than commercial brands or those kneaded with electric machines. Fresh pasta cooks in a few minutes or seconds; it is not suitable for use in cold pasta

Calories	%Fat	Fat (g)	Saturated Fat (g)	Cholesterol (mg)	Sodium (mg)	Carbohydrate (g)	Protein (g)	Fiber (g)
174	19	4	0.6	65	139	24	11	1

Exchanges: Starch 1, Vegetable 1, Low-fat protein 1

salads. Commercial dried pasta requires a longer cooking period (usually at least seven minutes), but it should not be overcooked. Al dente pasta is completely cooked but still firm.

Store dried pasta at room temperature in airtight, moisture-proof containers in the dark for up to 18 months; egg noodles can be kept for up to six months. Freshly made pasta should be kept in the refrigerator and used within two days; it can be frozen and dropped into boiling water without thawing. Cooked pasta covered with sauce can be stored in a covered container in the refrigerator for four days.

Pesto Pasta Salad with Tuna

1 C chopped fresh basil
2 T pine nuts
2 T olive oil
1/4 C freshly grated Parmesan cheese
12 oz tri-color fusilli, cooked al dente and drained
1 can water-packed solid-white tuna, drained and flaked

In a blender or food processor, blend basil, salt, and pine nuts to a smooth paste. While the blender is running, gradually add the oil, then the cheese, and blend until smooth. Pour over warm pasta and toss. Add tuna and toss. Serve warm or chilled.

Serves 6.

Suggestion
• Garlic may be processed with the pesto.

Calories	%Fat	Fat (g)	Saturated Fat (g)	Cholesterol (mg)	Sodium (mg)	Carbohydrate (g)	Protein (g)	Fiber (g)
332	23	9	1.9	8	184	45	18	2

Exchanges: Starch 3, Low-fat protein 1, Fat 1

# Garden Tuna Noodle Salad

1-1/2 C whole-wheat macaroni noodles
1 C diced red bell pepper
1/2 C sliced carrots
1/2 C frozen peas, thawed
1/4 C chopped scallions
1/2 C low-sodium, fat-free Italian dressing
1 can (12 oz) chunk white albacore tuna in water, rinsed and drained

Cook noodles according to package directions, omitting fat and salt. Rinse under cold water; drain. Combine remaining ingredients. Toss with noodles and serve.

Serves 4.

Calories	%Fat	Fat (g)	Saturated Fat (g)	Cholesterol (mg)	Sodium (mg)	Carbohydrate (g)	Protein (g)	Fiber (g)
287	5	2	0.5	16	67	42	29	6

Exchanges: Starch 2-1/2, Vegetable 1, Low-fat protein 3

How to Choose
Fresh Fish

- Look for shiny fish that does not have darkening around the edges or brown or yellowish discoloration.
- Whole fish should have clear, bulging eyes that are shiny and bright.
- The flesh should be firm to the touch, not mushy or dry.
- The scales should lay flat and tight against the skin.
- The gills should be clear red.
- Do not buy fish that has a strong fishy or ammonia odor; fresh fish has a light, briny fragrance.

Caribbean Cod Salad

1/2 lb fresh cod, steamed and flaked
3 tomatoes, chopped
2 medium Bermuda onions, finely chopped
1/2 green bell pepper, diced
1/2 red bell pepper, diced
2 tsp olive oil
Juice of 1 lime
2 tsp Tabasco sauce
2 T minced fresh parsley
Freshly ground black pepper

Mix all ingredients well; cover tightly and refrigerate for 4 hours or overnight. Remove from refrigerator 1 hour before serving. Makes 6 C.
Serves 6.

Suggestions

- Serve over crisp salad greens, on bread as a sandwich, or stuffed in pita pockets.
- For 24 appetizers, make half the recipe; serve with unsalted crackers.

Calories	%Fat	Fat (g)	Saturated Fat (g)	Cholesterol (mg)	Sodium (mg)	Carbohydrate (g)	Protein (g)	Fiber (g)
78	26	2	0.4	20	51	7	8	1

Exchanges: Vegetable 1, Low-fat protein 1

Smoked Teriyaki Marlin & Scallop Salad

Greg Paulson, CEC

1 lb smoked teriyaki marlin
1/2 lb smoked teriyaki scallops
10 large romaine leaves
2 heads radicchio
2 heads manoa lettuce or other greens
1/2 pineapple, peeled, cored
2 papaya, peeled, seeded
2 green onions
2 oz rice sticks (rice flour noodles)

Marinade
1 C low-sodium teriyaki sauce
1/2 C shoyu (soy sauce)
Juice of 3 lemons
1 T ginger, grated
1 tsp minced green onion
2 shallots, chopped
1 head garlic, separated into peeled cloves

- Buy oysters, clams, and mussels that were harvested from certified growing waters.
- Store fish in the coldest part of the refrigerator—on the bottom shelf or in the meat-keeper drawer.
- Refrigerate live seafood immediately in well-ventilated containers—do not cover them tightly or the fish will not be able to breathe.
- Do not eat shellfish that died during storage.
- Use fresh fish within two days or freeze it immediately.
- Cook fish thoroughly, or use frozen fish for raw seafood dishes.
- Scrub scallops, mussels, clams, and oysters in their shells in cold water just before opening.

Warm Ginger Guava Vinaigrette

2 T grated or minced ginger
4 T fresh guava nectar
1 oz minced shallot
2 T rice wine vinegar
1/2 T red wine vinegar
1 tsp sugar
2 T salad oil
2 tsp minced green onion

Combine Marinade ingredients and mix well. Add marlin and scallops and marinate for 12 hours or overnight. Remove from marinade and pat dry (discard marinade). Hot smoke the fish until properly cooked. Remove from smoker and let rest. Slice fillet when ready to serve.

Combine all Warm Ginger Guava Vinaigrette ingredients except oil and mix well. Warm the salad oil and drizzle into the dressing. Keep the dressing warm prior to serving.

Wash and clean romaine, radicchio, and manoa greens. Shred romaine greens and reserve. Slice pineapple and papaya into diamond wedges and reserve. Cook rice sticks and hold.

Arrange greens on plate. Grill pineapple and papaya and place on salad greens. Add sliced marlin and scallops. Top with rice sticks and green onions. Dress with warm vinaigrette.

Serves 6.

Calories	%Fat	Fat (g)	Saturated Fat (g)	Cholesterol (mg)	Sodium (mg)	Carbohydrate (g)	Protein (g)	Fiber (g)
312	24	8	1.4	57	942	32	29	5

Exchanges: Starch 1/2, Fruit 1, Vegetable 2, Low-fat protein 3

Grilled Sea Scallop Salad

1-1/4 lb jumbo sea scallops, cleaned
1 C orange juice, freshly squeezed
4 T fresh basil, chopped
1/2 lb red leaf lettuce, torn
1/4 lb kale, torn
1/4 lb endive, torn
2 medium Roma tomatoes, quartered
16 thin slices cucumber
Lime Vinaigrette (page 477)

Flavorful Salad Greens
Add whole leaves of basil or coriander to salad greens. Sprigs of fresh dill are especially good when the greens will be served with seafood. Some herb flowers, such as chive blossoms, are also very flavorful as well as pretty.

Marinate the sea scallops in orange juice and basil for 1 hour at room temperature; drain. Grill the scallops for 1 to 2 minutes on each side, or until they are just done. Toss the basil with the lettuce, kale, and endive. Arrange the mixed greens on 4 salad plates. Top each serving with grilled scallops, tomatoes, and cucumber. Serve immediately with Lime Vinaigrette on the side.
Serves 4.

Suggestion
• Shrimp or cubed fish or chicken may be substituted for the scallops.

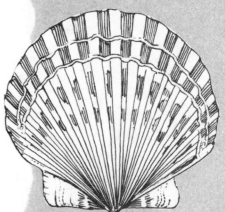

Calories	%Fat	Fat (g)	Saturated Fat (g)	Cholesterol (mg)	Sodium (mg)	Carbohydrate (g)	Protein (g)	Fiber (g)
199	11	2	0.3	45	398	11	34	3

Exchanges: Vegetable 2, Low-fat protein 4

Mustard Greens

The slightly ruffled, jade-green mustard green leaves have a spirited flavor. Mustard greens are an excellent source of beta-carotene and vitamin C; they also contain some calcium and phosphorous—all for only 50 calories per cup. They can be stored in the refrigerator for two to three days.

Use small, tender young leaves raw in salads with other mild greens. Discard tough stems and cook older greens to mellow their flavor. Steam them for 15 to 20 minutes and serve with potatoes and tomatoes. For a Southern dinner, cook mustard greens with collard greens and serve with black-eyed peas and corn bread. Mustard greens are also good in soups and curry. Dill and caraway seeds are good seasonings for mustard greens.

Crab Salad

3/4 lb cooked blue crab meat, shredded
20 medium mustard leaves, washed and torn
1/2 lb cucumbers, peeled, seeded, and finely diced
Juice of 2 limes
2 tsp walnut oil
Freshly ground black pepper to taste
Harvest Dressing (page 475)

Toss all ingredients except dressing; set aside for 5 minutes. Arrange on 4 serving plates. Serve with Harvest Dressing on the side.
Serves 4.

Suggestion
- Other varieties of crab, lobster, shrimp, or cubed chicken can be substituted for the blue crab.

Calories	%Fat	Fat (g)	Saturated Fat (g)	Cholesterol (mg)	Sodium (mg)	Carbohydrate (g)	Protein (g)	Fiber (g)
128	29	4	0.5	85	281	4	19	2

Exchanges: Vegetable 1, Low-fat protein 2

Lobster & Grapefruit Salad

3 lobster tails (8 oz each), cooked, cleaned, and cut in bite-size pieces
1 medium pink grapefruit, peeled and sectioned
1 medium orange, peeled and sectioned
1/2 C plain low-fat yogurt
3 T unsweetened orange juice
1 T fresh lemon juice
1 tsp grated orange rind
1 tsp grated lime rind
1/8 tsp ground white pepper
4 C torn fresh spinach leaves

Mix lobster, grapefruit sections, and orange sections. Blend yogurt, juices, rinds, and pepper. Pour over lobster and toss well. Serve on beds of spinach. Serves 4.

Calories	%Fat	Fat (g)	Saturated Fat (g)	Cholesterol (mg)	Sodium (mg)	Carbohydrate (g)	Protein (g)	Fiber (g)
217	7	2	0.5	104	608	17	33	3

Exchanges: Fruit 1, Low-fat protein 4

Grapefruit

Grapefruit and its juice are excellent sources of vitamin C and potassium. The white variety is good for juicing. Thin-skinned grapefruit are usually juicier; a stem end that comes to a point is usually a sign of thick skin. Pink grapefruit are much sweeter than white; they can be eaten fresh without added sugar. Seedless grapefruit are more convenient, but they may have less flavor than other grapefruit.

Store grapefruit at room temperature for up to a week, or in the warmest part of the refrigerator for 10 to 14 days.

To section a grapefruit or orange, use a sharp paring knife to remove the outer peel and inner white membrane. Working over a bowl, cut out wedges of fruit, leaving behind the membrane that separates the segments. Gently squeeze the juice out of the leftover membrane before discarding it. Remove all seeds.

Radishes

Radishes can be red, black, or white. These cruciferous vegetables are high in vitamin C. To store them, cut off the green tops, wrap them tightly, and keep them in the refrigerator.

The Daikon radish, a Japanese favorite, is a giant white radish shaped like a carrot—it can be 6 to 12 inches long. It has a sweet, fresh flavor and is milder and keeps longer than other radishes. These crisp, juicy radishes are often grated or thinly sliced and served in salads, yogurt dressings, dips, or as a garnish. They can be cooked like turnips or used in soups, stews, and stir-fry.

Horseradish is a very zesty and pungent slender root. Store it tightly wrapped in the refrigerator for a month or more, grating only as needed. Grated fresh horseradish can also be frozen for several months. Use 1/2 to 1 tsp per recipe, or to taste. Horseradish is good with cooked beets, applesauce (to accompany beef or pork), fish sauce, or salad dressing.

Seafood Salad

8 C torn Bibb lettuce
1/2 C thinly sliced radishes
1/4 C sliced scallions
1 C cooked crab meat, chopped
1 C cooked small shrimp
1 C cooked lobster, chopped
2 tomatoes, seeded and diced
1 T lemon juice
1/2 C reduced-fat mayonnaise
3/4 C plain nonfat yogurt
1/4 C skim milk
1 T capers, optional
Freshly ground black pepper to taste

All ingredients should be well chilled. In a large mixing bowl, toss lettuce, radishes, and scallions. Add seafood and tomatoes and mix well. Shake remaining ingredients in a covered container until well blended and pour over salad. Toss lightly until dressing is evenly distributed. Serve immediately.
Serves 8.

Suggestion
• Add herbs of choice to the dressing: dill, fennel seeds, lemon thyme, or parsley.

Calories	%Fat	Fat (g)	Saturated Fat (g)	Cholesterol (mg)	Sodium (mg)	Carbohydrate (g)	Protein (g)	Fiber (g)
106	26	3	0.5	63	234	7	13	1

Exchanges: Vegetable 1, Low-fat protein 2

# Chilled Jumbo Shrimp with Country-Style Vegetables & Truffle Vinaigrette

Sylvain Portay

20 jumbo shrimp tails
3 medium vine-ripe tomatoes
6 oz French string beans (haricots verts), trimmed
12 medium asparagus spears
6 medium artichoke hearts (fresh or canned)
6 oz fava beans
Juice of 2 lemons
2 oz extra-virgin olive oil
2 oz truffle juice (the liquid in a can of truffles)
Pepper to taste
1 bunch parsley, finely chopped
4 parsley sprigs, for garnish

Peel and devein shrimp. Skewer them lengthwise with a toothpick to hold their shape; set aside.

Remove stems from tomatoes and cut into 1/2-inch cubes.

Cook the beans in boiling salted water for about 3 minutes, or until tender. Immediately plunge them into ice water to stop the cooking and to set the color. Drain well; set aside. In the same manner, cook the asparagus for about 4

Moderation

If you want to succeed in changing your diet forever, approach the challenge with a sense of moderation. We cannot emphasize moderation strongly enough. Countless people have tackled change with zeal only to fail in the end. They have spent hours reading labels in the grocery store, denied themselves all their favorite foods, avoided social occasions because they were afraid to spring a dietary trap, and felt guilty if they cheated. More than anything else, they made themselves miserable. Before long, they abandoned their resolve and returned to their bad habits. You are much more likely to be successful if you adapt gradually. If you have a passion for red meat, permit yourself to enjoy it once or twice a week. If you've never had a vegetarian dinner, ease meatless meals into your repertoire gradually. And every once in a while, splurge on your favorite dessert. The idea is not to mourn the permanent loss of chocolate cake but to discover enough delicious, healthy foods that you will miss it less and less.

Diethrich and Cohan
Women and Heart Disease

minutes, the fava beans for about 2 minutes, and the fresh artichoke hearts for about 10 minutes. (Canned artichokes should be sliced about 1/8-inch thick and not cooked.)

To make the vinaigrette, whisk the lemon juice with the oil and truffle juice. Season with pepper to taste. Place all vegetables in a shallow glass casserole and pour half the vinaigrette over them. Marinate in the refrigerator for 1 hour.

Season the shrimp with pepper. Sauté over medium heat until cooked on both sides, about 3 minutes. Drain on paper towels, remove toothpicks, and set in refrigerator.

About 10 minutes before serving, remove shrimp and vegetables from refrigerator. Place equal amounts of vegetables on 4 serving plates. Place 5 shrimps on each bed of vegetables; spoon 1 tsp vinaigrette over each serving. Sprinkle with chopped fresh parsley and garnish with parsley leaves.

Serves 4.

Calories	%Fat	Fat (g)	Saturated Fat (g)	Cholesterol (mg)	Sodium (mg)	Carbohydrate (g)	Protein (g)	Fiber (g)
214	40	10	1.4	102	210	19	17	8

Exchanges: Vegetable 4, Low-fat protein 2, Fat 1

# Chicken Waldorf Salad

1-1/2 C cooked chicken breast, diced
2 large Red Delicious apples, cored and diced
1 C diced celery with leaves
2 T chopped pecans
1/2 C raisins
2 T reduced-fat mayonnaise
2 T plain nonfat yogurt

Toss chicken, apples, celery, pecans, and raisins. Mix mayonnaise with yogurt and pour over salad; lightly toss until all ingredients are evenly coated.
Serves 4.

Sodium

Sodium is a mineral found in a wide variety of foods. Ingesting too much of this mineral can cause fluid retention and/or aggravate high blood pressure. A reasonable guideline is to eat less than 2400 mg of sodium per day. Since the body requires less than 500 mg of sodium per day, this amount is sufficient to meet the average daily requirements.

Americans consume a great deal of sodium chloride—common table salt. One teaspoon of salt contains 2.3 grams of sodium, almost the entire daily allowance. Highly salted foods should be avoided. Almost 80% of our sodium intake comes from processed foods.

**Arizona Heart
Institute Foundation**
1–800–345–4278

Calories	%Fat	Fat (g)	Saturated Fat (g)	Cholesterol (mg)	Sodium (mg)	Carbohydrate (g)	Protein (g)	Fiber (g)
264	25	7	1.3	43	119	34	18	3

Exchanges: Fruit 2, Vegetable 1, Low-fat protein 2, Fat 1/2

Springtime Chicken Salad

1-1/2 lb skinless, boneless chicken breasts, poached and sliced
1 C baby lima beans, cooked
4 medium leeks, cooked
8 scallions, steamed gently
6 small red potatoes, cooked
4 slender carrots, cooked
1/2 head cauliflower, cut into florets, steamed
1/2 lb snow peas, steamed
12 asparagus stalks, steamed
Fresh marjoram or mint for garnish
Dijon Vinaigrette (page 474)

Toss chicken and vegetables gently. Place equal amounts on luncheon plates. Garnish with fresh herb sprigs. Serve Dijon Vinaigrette on the side.
Serves 6.

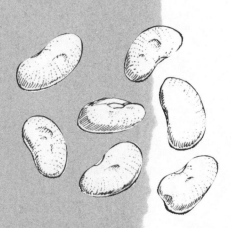

Calories	%Fat	Fat (g)	Saturated Fat (g)	Cholesterol (mg)	Sodium (mg)	Carbohydrate (g)	Protein (g)	Fiber (g)
305	11	4	1.1	62	98	36	33	9

Exchanges: Starch 1-1/2, Vegetable 2, Low-fat protein 3

# Chicken Curry Salad

3 C cooked chicken breast, cut in bite-sized pieces
1 can (15-3/4 oz) unsweetened pineapple chunks, drained
1 C sliced celery
2 T unsalted dry-roasted peanuts
2 T reduced-fat mayonnaise
2 T plain nonfat yogurt
1/2 tsp curry powder
1-1/2 C green seedless grapes

Mix chicken, pineapple, celery, and peanuts. Combine mayonnaise, yogurt, and curry powder; pour over chicken and toss gently. Fold in grapes. Serve on lettuce leaves.
Serves 6.

Calories	%Fat	Fat (g)	Saturated Fat (g)	Cholesterol (mg)	Sodium (mg)	Carbohydrate (g)	Protein (g)	Fiber (g)
229	24	6	1.3	56	102	21	23	2

Exchanges: Fruit 1-1/2, Low-fat protein 3

Grapes

Grapes are harvested ripe—they will not get sweeter after they have been harvested. They contain moderate amounts of fiber, potassium, and vitamin C.

Fresh grapes do not fall off their stems when the clusters are shaken; if they fall, the grapes have been stored too long. Store unwashed grapes in the refrigerator in a plastic bag for up to one week.

- *Almeria:* Pale green. Large; mild, sweet.
- *Cardinal:* Purple-red. Large; slightly tart.
- *Concord:* Blue-black with silvery haze. Mild flavor.
- *Emperor:* Red-black to purplish black. Mild flavor.
- *Flame Seedless:* Deep red. Medium to large; firm and crunchy.
- *Perlette:* Green. Sweet, crisp; seedless.
- *Ribier:* Deep blue-black. Large. Thick skins. Full, mild flavor.
- *Ruby Red Seedless:* Red. Tender skins. Firm; sweet.
- *Thompson Seedless:* Green to light gold.

Now all you have to do is hold the chicken, bring me the toast, give me a check for the chicken salad sandwich—and you haven't broken any rules.

Jack Nicholson
Five Easy Pieces

Crunchy Chicken Salad Pita Pockets

1/3 C reduced-fat mayonnaise
2/3 C lemon nonfat yogurt
4 chicken breasts (4 oz each), cooked and diced
1 small can water chestnuts, drained and julienned
1/3 C chopped celery
1/4 C chopped green pepper
4 Whole-Wheat Pita Breads (page 68)

Blend mayonnaise with yogurt. Toss chicken, water chestnuts, celery, and green pepper with mayonnaise-yogurt dressing. Stuff pitas with chicken salad.
Serves 4.

Suggestions
• Jicama can be substituted for the water chestnuts.
• Serve on whole-wheat toast or as a salad with crisp greens and cherry tomatoes.

Calories	%Fat	Fat (g)	Saturated Fat (g)	Cholesterol (mg)	Sodium (mg)	Carbohydrate (g)	Protein (g)	Fiber (g)
467	20	10	2.0	68	683	56	36	7

Exchanges: Starch 3, Vegetable 1, Dairy 1/2, Low-fat protein 3

Waldorf Salad

1 C diced unpeeled red apple
1/2 C green grapes
1/2 C chopped celery
1 T chopped pecans
1 T unsweetened apple juice
2 T plain nonfat yogurt

Toss apple, grapes, celery, and pecans. Mix apple juice and yogurt until smooth. Toss with apple mixture until all ingredients are coated evenly.
Serves 4.

Calories	%Fat	Fat (g)	Saturated Fat (g)	Cholesterol (mg)	Sodium (mg)	Carbohydrate (g)	Protein (g)	Fiber (g)
51	27	2	0.2	0	19	10	1	1

Exchanges: Fruit 1/2

White Waldorf Salad

2 large Yellow Delicious apples, cored and diced
1 C diced celery with leaves
1 T chopped pecans
1/2 C yellow raisins
2 T reduced-fat mayonnaise
2 T plain nonfat yogurt

Mix all ingredients except mayonnaise and yogurt. Blend mayonnaise with yogurt. Toss with fruit until all ingredients are evenly coated.
Serves 4.

Suggestion
• Use the very pale or white innermost celery hearts.

Calories	%Fat	Fat (g)	Saturated Fat (g)	Cholesterol (mg)	Sodium (mg)	Carbohydrate (g)	Protein (g)	Fiber (g)
163	22	4	0.6	2	81	34	2	3

Exchanges: Fruit 2, Fat 1

Arugula-Poached Pear Salad, Cambazola, & Port Vinaigrette

Stephan Wayne Pyles

2 ripe pears, such as Anjou or Bartlett
2 C dry red wine
1/2 C good quality port
2 whole cloves
1/2 C granulated sugar
2 T raspberry vinegar
1 small shallot
1 small clove roasted garlic
1 T walnut oil
Salt to taste
4 to 6 C arugula, picked and cleaned
4 French bread or sourdough croutons, about 2 inches long
2 oz cambazola cheese
1 oz (about 3 T) walnut halves

Peel, core, and cut in half the 2 pears. In a saucepan just large enough to hold the 4 halves, bring the wine and port to a boil with the cloves and sugar. Reduce heat to low and submerge the pears, cut side down, in the pan. Let simmer for 10 minutes. Remove pears and set aside.

Pour off (or save) all but 1 C of the poaching liquid and reduce it over high heat to 2 T. Place the reduced liquid in a blender and add the 2 T raspberry vinegar, the shallot, and the garlic clove. Blend until smooth and then add the oil in a steady drizzle. Taste dressing and season with salt.

Spread the cambazola evenly on the four croutons and place in a 400° oven just long enough to melt slightly.

Dress the arugula with the vinaigrette and divide between 4 plates. Serve each salad with half a poached pear, a cambazola crouton, and some walnuts.

Serves 4.

Calories	%Fat	Fat (g)	Saturated Fat (g)	Cholesterol (mg)	Sodium (mg)	Carbohydrate (g)	Protein (g)	Fiber (g)
221	49	12	3.7	15	128	23	6	3

Exchanges: Fruit 1, Vegetable 1, Medium-fat protein 1, Fat 1

# Strawberry Salad

2 C sliced fresh strawberries
4 C torn fresh spinach leaves
2 T sliced almonds, lightly toasted
Orange Dressing (page 480)

On individual salad plates, arrange strawberries on a bed of spinach leaves and sprinkle with toasted almonds. Drizzle 2 T Orange Dressing over each salad. Serve immediately.
Serves 6.

Suggestions

- Melba Sauce (page 419) may be substituted for the Orange Dressing.
- Plain or vanilla low-fat yogurt (thinned with a little skim milk and flavored to taste with spices, extract, or fruit) may be substituted for the Orange Dressing.
- Fresh mangoes, blueberries, bananas, oranges, or peaches may be substituted for part or all of the strawberries.
- Fresh mint leaves can be substituted for 1/2 C of the spinach.

On Strawberries
Doubtless God could have made a better berry, but doubtless God never did.

Walton
Compleat Angler

Strawberries

One cup of strawberries has as much vitamin C as one medium navel orange and more vitamin C than eight ounces of grapefruit juice. They are also high in fiber and potassium.

Store strawberries in the refrigerator to keep the color bright red. Small strawberries usually have more flavor than large ones. Strawberries are delicious raw or cooked as preserves or fruit soup.

Calories	% Fat	Fat (g)	Saturated Fat (g)	Cholesterol (mg)	Sodium (mg)	Carbohydrate (g)	Protein (g)	Fiber (g)
44	34	2	0.2	0	30	7	2	2

Exchanges: Fruit 1/2

Vegetables

Steamed Asparagus

2 lb fresh asparagus, cleaned and trimmed
1 C water
2 T lemon juice
Freshly ground black pepper to taste

Arrange asparagus in a microwave-safe 13 × 9-inch baking dish or in a round baking dish. Stems should be nearest the outside edges of the dish, with tips toward the center. In a rectangular dish, place half the asparagus in one direction and the other half in the opposite direction, with the tips in the center of the pan. On a round dish, arrange the asparagus like spokes in a wheel, with the tips meeting in the center.

Add water. Cover tightly and microwave on high for 4 minutes; turn the dish. Continue cooking for another 2 to 4 minutes, until the asparagus is crisp-tender. Do not overcook. Drain. Season with lemon juice and pepper.

Serves 4.

Suggestion
• Serve plain or with Mock Hollandaise (page 459) or use in recipes that call for cooked asparagus.

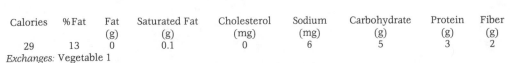

Calories	%Fat	Fat (g)	Saturated Fat (g)	Cholesterol (mg)	Sodium (mg)	Carbohydrate (g)	Protein (g)	Fiber (g)
29	13	0	0.1	0	6	5	3	2

Exchanges: Vegetable 1

Asparagus

Asparagus belongs to the lily family. It is usually green. A white European variety has fat, tender stalks and a delicate flavor. Asparagus is a good source of vitamins A and C, folate, and potassium.

Buy firm, straight spears with closed tips or buds. The stalk should be green for at least two-thirds of its length. Look for round stalks, as ridges mean the asparagus is old. Trim the stem ends before storing. Keep asparagus in the refrigerator standing upright in a container of water (one-inch deep) or store it flat with the stem ends wrapped in wet paper towels and covered with plastic.

Use asparagus as soon as possible—it toughens with age. Cook it standing up in a tied bunch, with the stems in gently boiling water and the tips above water level, for about 12 minutes (invert another saucepan on top as a cover to hold in steam). Asparagus can be served hot or cold. It is also delicious in soup, quiche, or a souffle.

Wild Mushrooms, Asparagus, & White Truffle Oil

Terrance Brennan

3 C cooked mixed wild mushrooms
1/2 T lemon juice
30 asparagus tips (3 inches long)
4 medium Yellow Finn potatoes, cooked and sliced
1 T white truffle oil
2 T snipped chives
2 T chopped Italian parsley
Pepper to taste
2 oz shaved Parmesan cheese (Reggiano)
6 sprigs chervil

Sauté mushrooms in cooking spray over high heat. Add lemon juice. Heat asparagus and potatoes in hot water; drain and add to mushrooms. Remove from heat and add white truffle oil, chives, parsley, and pepper to taste. Divide mixture among 6 plates; garnish with shaved Parmesan and chervil.

Serves 6.

Suggestions

- Use mushrooms in season, such as morels, oyster, shiitake, or black trumpet.
- White truffle oil (available in specialty markets) brings out the flavor of the entire recipe. Garlic oil may be substituted, but the final dish will not taste quite as good.

Calories	%Fat	Fat (g)	Saturated Fat (g)	Cholesterol (mg)	Sodium (mg)	Carbohydrate (g)	Protein (g)	Fiber (g)
130	37	5	2.2	7	182	15	6	2

Exchanges: Starch 1, Fat 1

# Garlic & Green Beans

1 clove garlic, minced
1/2 C celery, thinly sliced
1/4 C julienned red bell pepper
1 pkg (9 oz) frozen green beans, French cut
1 T slivered almonds, toasted

Sauté garlic, celery, and bell pepper until tender. Add beans; cook, covered, until beans are crisp-tender, about 5 minutes. Sprinkle with nuts; serve hot.
Serves 4.

Suggestion

- Remove cores and insides of 8 plum tomatoes; parboil the whole tomato shells. Stuff with Garlic & Green Beans, steam lightly, and serve hot.

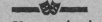
On Vegetarianism

*Then a sentimental passion
of a vegetable fashion
must excite your languid
spleen,
An attachment á la Plato
for a bashful young
potato, or a not too
French French bean!*

W. S. Gilbert

Decorative Toppings for Vegetables

Alfalfa or bean sprouts
Hard-boiled egg white
Chopped parsley
Chopped pimiento
Crumbled cereal
Fresh herb sprigs
Julienned citrus peel
Shredded carrot
Toasted bread crumbs
Wheat germ

Calories	%Fat	Fat (g)	Saturated Fat (g)	Cholesterol (mg)	Sodium (mg)	Carbohydrate (g)	Protein (g)	Fiber (g)
32	32	1	0.1	0	20	5	1	2

Exchanges: Vegetable 1

# Green Beans with Dill

1 pkg (9 oz) frozen French-style green beans
1/4 C finely julienned jicama
1/4 C finely chopped onion
2 T red bell pepper slivers
1 T white wine vinegar
1/2 tsp dill
Freshly ground black pepper to taste

Cook beans over low heat until tender, stirring occasionally. Add remaining ingredients; toss lightly and heat to serving temperature.
Serves 4.

Calories	%Fat	Fat (g)	Saturated Fat (g)	Cholesterol (mg)	Sodium (mg)	Carbohydrate (g)	Protein (g)	Fiber (g)
23	5	0	0.0	0	8	5	1	2

Exchanges: Vegetable 1

Broccoli & Lemon Sauce

6 bunches broccoli, cut into florets with 3-inch stems
1 C reduced-fat mayonnaise
3 C plain nonfat yogurt
1 T grated lemon peel
1/3 C lemon juice
2 tsp white horseradish
2 tsp hot Chinese mustard

Steam broccoli over boiling water until crisp-tender. Immediately plunge broccoli into ice water to stop the cooking and keep its color bright green. Drain well and chill. To make Lemon Sauce, combine remaining ingredients and chill. Serve broccoli on a platter with bowls of Lemon Sauce for dipping.
   Appetizers for 25.

Suggestion
• Broccoli can be steamed in a microwave oven; see manufacturer's instructions for timing broccoli in your particular oven.

Calories	%Fat	Fat (g)	Saturated Fat (g)	Cholesterol (mg)	Sodium (mg)	Carbohydrate (g)	Protein (g)	Fiber (g)
69	38	3	0.5	3	105	8	4	3

Exchanges: Vegetable 1-1/2, Fat 1/2

Broccoli
Broccoli is related to cauliflower. Fresh broccoli is an excellent source of vitamins A and C. It also contains fair amounts of folate, riboflavin, potassium, and some calcium and iron. It is usually green but sometimes has purple highlights on florets. Do not buy broccoli that is yellowing. Younger, tender broccoli has thin stalks; thick stalks are a sign of age. Store broccoli in a plastic bag in the refrigerator for up to a week.

Divide broccoli into three-inch florets for faster cooking; it will also stay greener. Steam it quickly with very little water to keep the color bright and preserve its vitamin C content. If necessary, peel thick skin off the stalks before cooking; the stalks may have to be split lengthwise or cubed so they will cook in the same amount of time as the tops. To cook whole broccoli, stand it upright in a pot and cook it like asparagus.

Stir-Fried Broccoli

1 clove garlic, minced
1-inch cube fresh ginger, peeled and minced
1/8 tsp crushed dried red chili pepper, or to taste
1 large bunch broccoli, divided into small florets (save stems for another use)
3 T water
1 T dry sherry
2 T low-sodium soy sauce

Stir-fry garlic, ginger, and chili pepper over moderately high heat until golden, about 3 minutes. Add broccoli and continue stir-frying until it is bright green, about 2 minutes. Pour in the water, sherry, and soy sauce. Cover and steam for about 5 minutes. Toss before serving.

Serves 4.

Suggestion
• Toss in a spoonful of toasted sesame seeds just before serving.

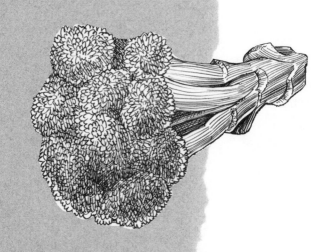

Calories	%Fat	Fat (g)	Saturated Fat (g)	Cholesterol (mg)	Sodium (mg)	Carbohydrate (g)	Protein (g)	Fiber (g)
29	3	0	0.0	0	318	5	3	2

Exchanges: Vegetable 1

# Cackle-berries with Broccoli

1 medium potato, coarsely grated
2 C frozen chopped broccoli, thawed and drained
1/3 C finely chopped onion
1 clove garlic, minced
2 plum tomatoes, peeled and thinly sliced
3 thinly sliced black olives
8 egg whites, lightly beaten
2 whole eggs, lightly beaten
1/4 C grated Parmesan cheese
1 tsp dried parsley
1/4 tsp dried basil
Freshly ground black pepper to taste
6 slices whole-wheat bread, toasted, quartered

   Cook potatoes in cooking spray over medium-low heat in a large oven-proof skillet, stirring often, until tender and golden, about 20 to 25 minutes. Stir in the broccoli, onion, and garlic; cook for 5 minutes, stirring occasionally. Remove pan from heat. Arrange tomato slices on top and sprinkle with black olives.

Cackle-berries

It seems that cowboys are rather sleepy-headed in the morning and it is a part of the cook's job to get them up. The next I knew, Herman had a tin pan on which he was beating a vigorous tattoo, all the time hollering, "We haf cackle-berries und antelope steak for breakfast."...There are times when anticipation is a great deal better than realization. Never having seen a cackle-berry, my imagination pictured them as some very luscious wild fruit, and I was so afraid none would be left that I couldn't wait until the men should eat and be gone. So I surprised them by joining the very earliest about the fire. Herman began serving breakfast. I held out my tin plate and received some of the antelope steak, an egg,

Beat egg whites, whole eggs, Parmesan cheese, parsley, basil, and black pepper. Carefully pour over potatoes in skillet. Bake eggs in the oven-proof skillet at 350° for 10 minutes. When eggs are almost done, broil 6 inches from heat until golden brown and fully set. Serve with toast points.

Serves 6.

Suggestions

- For a thicker final product, bake the eggs in a small, deep pan or Dutch oven.
- Spinach, kale, or other vegetables can be used to replace part or all of the broccoli.

Calories	%Fat	Fat (g)	Saturated Fat (g)	Cholesterol (mg)	Sodium (mg)	Carbohydrate (g)	Protein (g)	Fiber (g)
165	20	4	1.4	74	318	22	13	3

Exchanges: Starch 1, Vegetable 1, Low-fat protein 1

North African Stew

1 medium onion, thinly sliced
1 medium red bell pepper, coarsely chopped
1 tsp cinnamon
2 tsp ground cumin
1/4 tsp cayenne pepper
2 C fresh tomatoes, quartered
1/2 C no-salt-added tomato juice
2 T fresh lime juice
1/4 tsp saffron threads
4 small new potatoes, sliced
2 C broccoli florets
2 C cooked chickpeas, drained

Sauté onion, bell pepper, cinnamon, cumin, and cayenne over medium heat, stirring occasionally, until tender, about 5 minutes. Add tomatoes, tomato juice, lime juice, saffron, potatoes, and 1/2 C of water. Bring to a boil; reduce heat and simmer, covered, until the potatoes are almost tender, about 20 minutes. Stir in the broccoli florets and chickpeas. Increase heat and return to a boil. Reduce heat and simmer, covered, until the potatoes and broccoli are tender, about 10 to 15 minutes.

Serves 4.

Calories	%Fat	Fat (g)	Saturated Fat (g)	Cholesterol (mg)	Sodium (mg)	Carbohydrate (g)	Protein (g)	Fiber (g)
255	10	3	0.3	0	35	50	12	9

Exchanges: Starch 2-1/2, Vegetable 3

Brussels Sprouts

Brussels sprouts are a type of miniature cabbage. They grow on the tall woody stems of the plant and are harvested as small buds. They are rich in vitamin C and folate, and they are a good source of vitamin A and iron.

Buy deep green sprouts. Yellowing is a sign of mishandling and indicates a short storage life. Don't wash them before storing. The sprouts will keep in the refrigerator for about a week. The flavor will become stronger over time.

Brussels sprouts can be eaten raw or lightly cooked— they should not be overcooked. Pull off loose leaves and cut a little cross in the bottom of each stem end. Steam them quickly with very little water to keep their color bright and to preserve their vitamin C. Brussels sprouts are very good seasoned with nutmeg.

Herbed Brussels Sprouts

1 T scallions, sliced in thin rings
1 T lemon juice
1/4 tsp marjoram
1/4 tsp basil
1/4 tsp thyme
2 lb Brussels sprouts, steamed and hot

Warm all ingredients except Brussels sprouts in a skillet. Pour over hot cooked Brussels sprouts, tossing to coat evenly. Serve immediately.
Serves 8.

Calories	%Fat	Fat (g)	Saturated Fat (g)	Cholesterol (mg)	Sodium (mg)	Carbohydrate (g)	Protein (g)	Fiber (g)
47	8	0	0.1	0	26	9	4	5

Exchanges: Vegetable 2

Harvest Pie

2 C shredded green cabbage
1 C sliced fresh mushrooms
1/2 C thinly sliced yellow squash
1/2 C thinly sliced zucchini
3/4 C canned black beans, drained and rinsed
1 tsp chopped fresh basil
1/2 tsp dried thyme
1 small onion, minced
1 clove garlic, minced
1/8 tsp pepper
1 T margarine, melted
1/2 C all-purpose flour
1/2 C skim milk
1/2 C egg substitute
1/4 C (2 oz) shredded farmer's cheese

Sauté cabbage, mushrooms, squash, and zucchini for 5 to 7 minutes, or until tender, stirring frequently. Stir in black beans, basil, thyme, onion, and garlic. Remove from heat and keep warm.

Coat a 9-inch pie plate with cooking spray; brush with melted margarine. Beat flour, milk, and egg substitute; pour into pie plate. Bake at 425° for 15 to

"Rabbit," said Pooh to himself. "I like talking to Rabbit. He talks about sensible things. He doesn't use long, difficult words, like Owl. He uses short easy words, like 'What about lunch?' and 'Help yourself, Pooh!'"

A.A. Milne
The House at Pooh Corner

Cabbage

Cabbage has many forms: it can be round, conical, or flat; the heads can be loose or compact; the leaves can be curly or plain. Store it tightly wrapped in plastic in the refrigerator for up to one week. It is a good source of vitamin C.

Cabbage usually cooks, uncovered, in six to eight minutes; it should be crisptender. Shredded cabbage should be steamed for about 10 minutes. To reduce the strong odor of cooking cabbage, add a whole walnut or two slices of stale bread to the cooking water. To reduce its gassiness, parboil the cabbage for five minutes, rinse it in cold water, and then cook it in fresh water. For a very crunchy salad, cut a cabbage in half and soak it in ice water for an hour before slicing into thin strips or shredding; drain well.

- *Chinese cabbage:* Long shape, pale green; sweeter than other cabbages. Primarily used in stir-frying.
- *Hard whites* (includes Dutch, Danish, and Winter White varieties): Used for cole slaw and sauerkraut. Keeps well.
- *Red cabbage:* Strong flavor. Used raw in salads and slaw; often cooked with apples and spices. Add lemon juice (1 T per 2 C water) or wine (1/4 C per 2 C water) to the cooking water to keep the color bright red. Do not cook red cabbage in iron or aluminum pots.
- *Savoy:* Dark, crinkly leaves; looks like a big, bright green rose. Used for cooking (stuffed cabbage leaves) or raw in salads. Higher in vitamin A than other types of cabbage.

20 minutes, or until the pastry is puffed and browned, rather like a popover. Top with cabbage mixture and sprinkle cheese on top; return to the oven and bake for about 5 minutes, or until cheese melts and is golden. Serve immediately.

Serves 4.

Suggestion
- Omit farmer's cheese; top with low-fat ricotta cheese and sprinkle with chopped fresh basil and freshly ground black pepper.

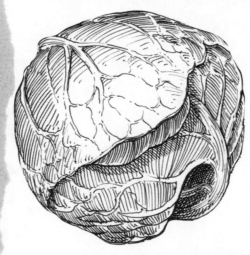

Calories	%Fat	Fat (g)	Saturated Fat (g)	Cholesterol (mg)	Sodium (mg)	Carbohydrate (g)	Protein (g)	Fiber (g)
188	26	6	2.0	7	216	25	10	4

Exchanges: Starch 1, Vegetable 2, Fat 1

Red Cabbage with Caraway Seeds

1 small onion, chopped
1 head red cabbage (1 lb), sliced thin
2 T lemon juice
1/4 C water
1 tsp caraway seeds
Freshly ground black pepper to taste
1/3 C white wine

Sauté onion until soft. Add remaining ingredients except wine and cook, covered, for 20 minutes. Reduce heat, add wine, and cook uncovered for a few minutes, or until cabbage is tender and liquid is absorbed.

Serves 4.

Dietary Guidelines of the American Cancer Society

- Eat less fat.
- Eat more high-fiber foods (fruits, vegetables, whole-grain cereals).
- Eat foods rich in vitamins A and C.
- Eat cruciferous vegetables (cabbage, broccoli, Brussels sprouts, cauliflower, and kohlrabi).
- Drink alcohol only in moderation.
- Eat less salt-cured, smoked, or nitrate-treated food.
- Eat less and stay trim.

Calories	%Fat	Fat (g)	Saturated Fat (g)	Cholesterol (mg)	Sodium (mg)	Carbohydrate (g)	Protein (g)	Fiber (g)
32	8	0	0.0	0	20	7	1	2

Exchanges: Vegetable 1

Carrots

Carrots are an excellent source of fiber and beta-carotene, which produces vitamin A. Young, slender carrots are sweeter than thicker, older carrots. Do not buy carrots that are pale, limp, cracked, soft, or have hairy rootlets.

Cut off and discard the leafy green tops before storing carrots in the refrigerator; they should be loosely wrapped or kept in perforated bags. Keep them away from apples and other foods that produce ethylene gas, as they will cause a chemical reaction that makes carrots taste bitter.

Glazed Carrots

2/3 lb carrots, thinly sliced
1/2 tsp margarine, melted
1 T orange blossom honey

Cook carrots in 1/2 C boiling water, covered, over medium heat for 8 to 12 minutes, or until the carrots are tender; drain. Blend melted margarine and honey; pour over carrots. Cook over low heat, stirring constantly, until carrots are well glazed.
Serves 4.

Suggestion
• Use brown sugar in place of the honey and add a dash of Grand Marnier.

Calories	%Fat	Fat (g)	Saturated Fat (g)	Cholesterol (mg)	Sodium (mg)	Carbohydrate (g)	Protein (g)	Fiber (g)
48	11	1	0.1	0	47	11	1	2

Exchanges: Vegetable 2

Carrots in Beer

4 large carrots, cut into long thin slices
1 C dark beer
1 tsp sugar
1 T chopped parsley
Freshly ground black pepper to taste

    Simmer carrots in beer until tender, stirring frequently. Stir in sugar, parsley, and pepper. Cook for about 2 minutes. Serve hot.
    Serves 4.

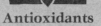

Antioxidants

A diet rich in fruits and vegetables may help lower the risk of a number of major diseases, including heart disease and breast, colon, and lung cancer. Researchers believe that the benefits of these foods are derived from several different nutrients known as *antioxidants*. They include beta-carotene and vitamins C and E.

Together, these vitamins help protect the body against damage by unstable chemicals (free radicals) that can damage cell walls and alter genes. Free radicals are naturally produced by the body as a by-product of cellular metabolism.

Most Americans do not eat enough fruits and vegetables. Only 20% eat one fruit or vegetable each day; only 9% eat two fruits and three vegetables each day.

Calories	%Fat	Fat (g)	Saturated Fat (g)	Cholesterol (mg)	Sodium (mg)	Carbohydrate (g)	Protein (g)	Fiber (g)
74	2	0	0.0	0	70	14	1	3

Exchanges: Vegetable 3

Turnips

Turnips have white skins with purple highlights. Young turnips are sold in bunches with their leaves attached. Turnips are smaller than rutabagas but have a similar flavor and texture; they can be used interchangeably. Turnips can be stored in the refrigerator for one week. The leaves should be removed and wrapped in plastic before storing; they can be used like spinach. Turnips are a good source of vitamin C and potassium.

Turnips can be boiled and mashed (beating in a boiled potato will make them thicker); stir in sherry, instead of butter, just before serving. Nutmeg is also a good seasoning for turnips. For sweeter boiled turnips, leave the skin on during cooking; peel before using. Parboil a strong turnip for about four minutes to mellow the flavor and cook as directed in recipe.

Turnip cubes can be cooked with carrots or in a soup or stew. Whole turnips can be baked for 35 to 40 minutes at 350°.

Carrots & Turnips

3 C diced carrots
3 C peeled, diced turnips
2 T minced fresh parsley
Freshly ground black pepper to taste

Steam turnips and carrots until tender, about 20 minutes. Drain. Season with parsley and pepper. Serve hot.

Serves 8.

Calories	%Fat	Fat (g)	Saturated Fat (g)	Cholesterol (mg)	Sodium (mg)	Carbohydrate (g)	Protein (g)	Fiber (g)
25	4	0	0.0	0	47	6	1	2

Exchanges: Vegetable 1

# Baked Marinated Cauliflower

How to Cook Vegetables

Leave the skin on vegetables and fruits while they cook, use small amounts of water in cooking, avoiding soaking vegetables for any length of time, and whenever possible, save that water and add it to soups and stews.

Diethrich and Cohan
Women and Heart Disease

2 T lemon juice
1/2 C unsweetened orange juice
2 tsp olive oil
2 cloves garlic, minced
1 T mixed fresh herbs, finely chopped
2 tsp sesame seeds
1 C cauliflower florets
1 C fresh button mushroom caps
1/2 C julienned bell pepper
1/2 C zucchini, quartered
8 small new potatoes, quartered and parboiled

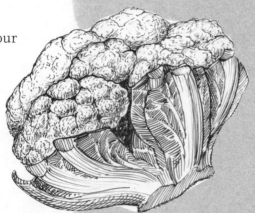

Mix lemon juice, orange juice, oil, garlic, herbs, and sesame seeds. Pour the marinade over the vegetables. Marinate for 1 to 2 hours. Place in a casserole or baking pan just large enough to hold the vegetables. Bake, covered, at 425° for 20 to 30 minutes. Serve hot.

Serves 8.

Suggestion

• Broccoflower can be substituted for the cauliflower.

Calories	%Fat	Fat (g)	Saturated Fat (g)	Cholesterol (mg)	Sodium (mg)	Carbohydrate (g)	Protein (g)	Fiber (g)
99	12	1	0.2	0	8	20	2	2

Exchanges: Starch 1, Vegetable 1

Cauliflower

Cauliflower means "cabbage flower" in Old English. It has a dense, creamy white flower head; the white portion is called the *curd*. It is an excellent source of vitamin C, either cooked or raw. Store it in the refrigerator, wrapped in plastic, for four to seven days.

To cook a whole cauliflower, cut a deep cross at the stem end, so it cooks as fast as the florets. Do not cook it in aluminum, which will discolor the cauliflower. Add lemon peel, lemon juice, or white vinegar to the cooking water to keep cauliflower white. It can also be cooked in a half-milk–half-water mixture, or in pure milk, to preserve its color (save the cooking liquid to use in soups or sauce). Add a slice or two of bread to the water to reduce cooking odors.

Cauliflower Stir-Fry

2 cloves garlic, minced
1/4 C sliced onion
3 C cauliflower florets, steamed and drained
1-1/2 C snow peas, trimmed
1 medium red bell pepper, cut into strips
1 C sliced mushrooms
1 tsp marjoram

Sauté garlic and onion until onion is translucent. Toss in remaining ingredients and stir-fry briefly, until vegetables are hot but still crisp-tender. Heat to serving temperature.

Serves 4.

Suggestion

• Broccoflower can be substituted for the cauliflower.

Calories	%Fat	Fat (g)	Saturated Fat (g)	Cholesterol (mg)	Sodium (mg)	Carbohydrate (g)	Protein (g)	Fiber (g)
58	8	0	0.1	0	20	11	4	3

Exchanges: Vegetable 2

Eggplant Casserole

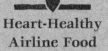

**Heart-Healthy
Airline Food**
Order a low-cholesterol,
low-saturated-fat meal when
you make flight reservations
or at least 24 hours in ad-
vance. Diabetic meals are
usually good heart-healthy
choices. Vegetarian meals—
often a rice-bean dish and
fruit—are another good
choice.

**Arizona Heart
Institute Foundation**
1–800–345–4278

1 medium eggplant, peeled, sliced in 1/2-inch thick rounds
2 egg whites, lightly beaten
1/2 C Italian bread crumbs
1/2 C sliced mushrooms
1/2 C thinly sliced onion
1 C no-salt-added tomato sauce
1/2 tsp oregano
1/2 tsp basil
Freshly ground black pepper to taste
4 oz part-skim milk mozzarella cheese, grated
1 T freshly grated Parmesan cheese

Pound eggplant slices to 1/4-inch thick with a mallet. Brush slices with egg white, then bread crumbs. Sauté in a large nonstick skillet until lightly browned on both sides. Arrange eggplant in a 10-inch square baking dish. Sauté mushrooms and onions in same skillet. Add tomato sauce, herbs, and pepper. Pour over eggplant. Sprinkle cheeses over the top. Bake at 450° for 15 to 20 minutes. Serve immediately.

Serves 6.

Calories	%Fat	Fat (g)	Saturated Fat (g)	Cholesterol (mg)	Sodium (mg)	Carbohydrate (g)	Protein (g)	Fiber (g)
135	26	4	2.2	11	195	17	9	3

Exchanges: Starch 1/2, Vegetable 2, Low-fat protein 1

Eggplant

Eggplants come in a variety of shapes, sizes, and colors, ranging from deep purple to white. Buy smaller eggplants as the larger ones tend to be bitter. Store them wrapped in plastic in the refrigerator. Because they are very perishable, they should be used in two to three days.

Eggplant is always served cooked. It has a bland flavor that is good with other seasonings; it can be stuffed, grilled, steamed, or stir-fried. Pare eggplant with a potato peeler (if cooked with the peels, add lemon or vinegar to the cooking water to preserve the purple color).

- *Casper:* Slender, small, white. Less bitter than purple eggplant.
- *Easter Egg:* Small, round, white.
- *Italian:* Purple and white streaks; miniature; bulbous shape like a standard eggplant.
- *Japanese:* Deep purple, slender; sweeter and milder than regular eggplant.

Ratatouille

2 medium zucchini, sliced
1 small eggplant, cut in cubes
2 medium green peppers, seeded and cut in strips
1 T flour
2 cloves garlic, chopped
1 large onion, sliced
4 tomatoes, peeled and sliced
1 T minced parsley

Place zucchini, eggplant, and green peppers in a plastic bag with the flour; shake to coat vegetables evenly. Set aside. In a large skillet, sauté onion and garlic. Add zucchini, eggplant, and green peppers; simmer, covered, for 1 hour. Add tomatoes and simmer, uncovered, until thick. Gently stir in parsley. Serve hot or at room temperature.

Serves 8.

Suggestion
- Add herbs to taste.

Calories	%Fat	Fat (g)	Saturated Fat (g)	Cholesterol (mg)	Sodium (mg)	Carbohydrate (g)	Protein (g)	Fiber (g)
53	8	0	0.1	0	10	12	2	3

Exchanges: Vegetable 2

Kale with Tomatoes

1 lb kale, stemmed, washed, drained but not dry
1 C coarsely chopped tomatoes
1/2 C diced sweet onion
2 cloves garlic, crushed
1-1/2 tsp olive oil
1/2 tsp freshly ground black pepper
1 tsp chopped fresh basil
1/8 tsp dried whole oregano
1 tsp balsamic vinegar

Place kale in a large Dutch oven (do not add water). Cover and cook over medium heat for 6 to 8 minutes, or until tender. Drain well and squeeze between paper towels until kale is nearly dry. Divide kale among 4 serving plates. Mix remaining ingredients; spoon equal amounts over each serving of kale.
Serves 4.

Kale

Kale, which resembles collards, is a member of the cabbage family. Its blue-green leaves have tightly curled edges. There are several varieties of kale, which have subtle differences in flavor. Ornamental kale has green and violet crinkled leaves—it is not as flavorful as regular kale. Kale is an excellent source of vitamins A, C, and riboflavin, and a good source of calcium and iron. It stores well in the refrigerator without wilting.

Kale is best when cooked. Rinse the leaves and shake off excess water; cook like spinach. It can also be used like collards in soups or stir-fries. The leaves can be stuffed; use them in any recipe for stuffed cabbage.

Calories	%Fat	Fat (g)	Saturated Fat (g)	Cholesterol (mg)	Sodium (mg)	Carbohydrate (g)	Protein (g)	Fiber (g)
58	32	2	0.3	0	18	10	2	3

Exchanges: Vegetable 2, Fat 1/2

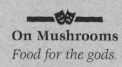

On Mushrooms

Food for the gods.

Emperor Nero

Mushrooms

Mushrooms are edible fungi; they are a good source of potassium and B vitamins. Common mushrooms and enoki are often the only varieties available fresh in American stores. Exotic mushrooms are sold dried or canned, sometimes fresh in specialty stores.

Store fresh mushrooms in a loosely closed paper bag in the refrigerator for four to five days; containers must allow air to circulate so moisture does not collect on the mushrooms. Just before using, wipe them with a damp cloth or, if they are very dirty, rinse them quickly under running water; do not let fresh mushrooms soak.

Store dried mushrooms in airtight plastic bags. Soak them in warm water until soft, about 15 to 20 minutes.

Stuffed Mushrooms

2/3 cup low-fat (1%) cottage cheese
2 oz part skim mozzarella, grated
1 tsp lemon juice
1/4 tsp dill
1 clove garlic, minced
30 medium fresh mushrooms (about 1 lb), cleaned and stemmed
Paprika
Fresh herb sprigs

Mix cheeses, lemon juice, dill, and garlic. Spoon 1 teaspoon cheese mixture into each mushroom cap. Sprinkle lightly with paprika. Bake at 425° until cheese is melted and beginning to brown. Garnish with herb sprigs.

Appetizers for 10.

Calories	%Fat	Fat (g)	Saturated Fat (g)	Cholesterol (mg)	Sodium (mg)	Carbohydrate (g)	Protein (g)	Fiber (g)
37	31	1	0.7	4	92	3	4	1

Exchanges: Vegetable 1/2, Low-fat protein 1/2

Roasted Portobello Mushrooms with Balsamic Tomatoes

Jeff Farnham

6 medium portobello mushrooms
6 diced plum tomatoes
1 clove garlic, chopped
1 shallot, chopped
1/4 C balsamic vinegar
6 oz goat cheese, crumbled
1 C white wine
1 oz chopped fresh sweet basil
Juice of 2 lemons
4 oz virgin olive oil
Mesclun leaves or other leafy greens to garnish

Wash mushrooms well; remove stems and save for another use. Season mushrooms with pepper, brush with a little olive oil or lightly coat with cooking spray, and roast in a moderate oven for 10 minutes, or until tender. Sauté the tomato, garlic, and shallot; add the balsamic vinegar. Top the mushrooms with the tomato mixture and the cheese. Return to oven for about 5 minutes.

To make the dressing, cook the wine, basil, and lemon juice until it is reduced by three-quarters. Process in a blender, slowly pouring in oil so it emul-

I see no objection to stoutness—in moderation.

W.S. Gilbert
Iolanthe

Should You Lose Weight?

Many people who struggle at dieting do not need to lose weight. Consider those who try to fight mother nature (that is, genetics) and, time and time again, fail. If you carry excess weight in your hips and thighs, chances are that neither dieting nor exercise will significantly change your body shape. Constant dieting may be more detrimental to your health than just accepting your genetics. People who are not obese, especially if they do not have hypertension, diabetes, or cardiovascular disease, might actually be better off, from a health standpoint, if they do not diet. ... repeated weight changes (yo-yo dieting) are possibly more damaging than maintaining some constant degree of overweight.

**Arizona Heart
Institute Foundation**
1-800-345-4278

Good Vegetable
Sources of Calcium

Spinach	244
Turnip greens	198
Broccoli	178
Bok choy	158
Collards	148
Mustard greens	104
Kale	94

Milligrams per 1 cup serving, cooked

sifies. Season with ground white pepper. (This makes 2 cups of dressing.)

Arrange mesclun salad leaves around the edge of a 12-inch dinner plate to form a ring. Place mushrooms in the center of the plate. Pour 1 T of dressing per serving over the mushroom and the salad leaves.

Serves 6.

Calories	%Fat	Fat (g)	Saturated Fat (g)	Cholesterol (mg)	Sodium (mg)	Carbohydrate (g)	Protein (g)	Fiber (g)
54	80	5	1.3	5	63	2	1	0

Exchanges: Vegetable 1/2, Fat 1

# Mushroom French Bread Pizza

*If this was adulthood,
the only improvement
she could detect in her
situation was that now she
could eat dessert without
eating her vegetables.*

Lisa Alther
Kinflicks, 1977

1/2 (16 oz) loaf French bread, split
1 can (8 oz) no-salt-added tomato sauce
1-1/2 C shredded part-skim mozzarella cheese
1/2 lb sliced fresh mushrooms, lightly sautéed
1 onion, sliced, sautéed
1/2 green bell pepper, sliced, sautéed
2 tsp dried oregano
1-1/2 T freshly grated Parmesan cheese

Spread tomato sauce evenly over the cut surfaces of the bread. Sprinkle mozzarella cheese on top. Arrange vegetables on the cheese. Sprinkle Parmesan cheese and oregano on top. Bake at 450° for 5 to 6 minutes or until the cheese melts. Serve immediately.

Serves 4.

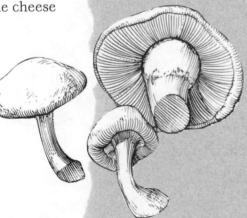

Calories	%Fat	Fat (g)	Saturated Fat (g)	Cholesterol (mg)	Sodium (mg)	Carbohydrate (g)	Protein (g)	Fiber (g)
328	25	9	5.2	25	618	43	20	4

Exchanges: Starch 2, Vegetable 2, Medium-fat protein 1-1/2

Onion Quiche

1 T cornstarch
1/4 C skim milk
1 C plain nonfat yogurt
3/4 C egg substitute
1/4 tsp black pepper
Pinch of nutmeg
1/2 C finely shredded onion
1 C shredded low-fat mozzarella cheese
Basic Pie Crust for 9-inch pie (page 410)

Dissolve the cornstarch in the milk. Mix with yogurt, egg substitute, pepper, and nutmeg, blending well. Spread onion and cheese in the bottom of a quiche pan lined with Basic Pie Crust. Pour liquid over the onions and cheese. Bake at 375° for 30 to 35 minutes, or until nicely browned and the custard is set (a knife tip inserted in the center of the quiche should come out clean). Cool for 10 minutes before cutting and serving.

Serves 6.

Suggestion

- Use spinach leaves, steamed broccoli florets, or other vegetables in addition to or in place of the onions.

Calories	%Fat	Fat (g)	Saturated Fat (g)	Cholesterol (mg)	Sodium (mg)	Carbohydrate (g)	Protein (g)	Fiber (g)
234	37	10	2.7	11	198	23	13	1

Exchanges: Starch 1-1/2, Dairy 1/4, Medium-fat protein 1, Fat 1

# Peas with Broccoli

1-1/2 C fresh broccoli florets
1-1/2 C frozen English peas
1/2 C water
2 T chopped scallions
1/2 tsp dried dill

Bring broccoli, peas, water, and scallions to a boil. Reduce heat and simmer, covered, for 4 to 5 minutes or until crisp-tender. Drain. Season with dill and serve hot.

Serves 4.

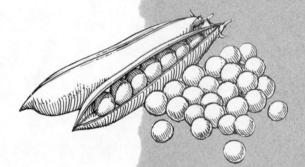

Calories	%Fat	Fat (g)	Saturated Fat (g)	Cholesterol (mg)	Sodium (mg)	Carbohydrate (g)	Protein (g)	Fiber (g)
48	3	0	0.0	0	49	9	4	4

Exchanges: Vegetable 2

Stuffed Green Peppers

8 medium green bell peppers
1 lb ground turkey breast
1/3 C finely chopped onion
1 stalk celery, sliced
1 small zucchini, coarsely grated
1 medium tomato, chopped
1 small clove garlic, minced
2 C cooked brown rice
1/2 tsp dried oregano
1 can (15 oz) low-sodium tomato sauce, divided
1/2 C shredded part-skim mozzarella cheese

Remove the tops, seeds, and membranes of each pepper, leaving the peppers whole. Brown turkey over medium heat; drain well and set aside. Sauté onion, celery, zucchini, tomato, and garlic over medium heat until tender. Combine with rice, turkey, oregano, and 3/4 C of the tomato sauce. Place peppers in over-sized muffin tins or in a 9 × 13-inch baking dish. Fill each pepper with equal amounts of stuffing. Top each pepper with remaining tomato sauce and cheese. Bake at 350° for 10 minutes, or until hot.

Serves 8.

Calories	%Fat	Fat (g)	Saturated Fat (g)	Cholesterol (mg)	Sodium (mg)	Carbohydrate (g)	Protein (g)	Fiber (g)
192	17	4	1.4	37	94	22	18	3

Exchanges: Starch 1, Vegetable 1, Low-fat protein 2

Marinated Potatoes

Sanford D'Amato

1-1/2 C water
1/2 C vinegar
2 Idaho potatoes, peeled and diced small
2 T chopped parsley
2 T oil
1/4 tsp red pepper flakes
20 grinds freshly ground black pepper
2 cloves garlic, finely chopped

Bring water and vinegar to a boil. Add potatoes and cook until tender; drain well and transfer to a bowl. Sprinkle parsley over the potatoes. Heat oil, red pepper, black pepper, and garlic until garlic turns light brown; pour over the potatoes and mix together. Serve warm.
Serves 4.

Calories	%Fat	Fat (g)	Saturated Fat (g)	Cholesterol (mg)	Sodium (mg)	Carbohydrate (g)	Protein (g)	Fiber (g)
103	60	7	0.9	0	4	10	1	1

Exchanges: Starch 1/2, Fat 1

Potatoes

Potatoes are the most popular vegetable in America. Over 80 varieties, including purple, spotted, and striped potatoes, are available. They are generally classified into four groups: *round red* (smooth skins, good for boiling), *round whites* (tan skin, good for boiling), *long whites* (tan skin, oblong shapes, all-purpose), and *russet* or *Idaho* (brown leathery skin, long flattened cylinder, perfect for baking). Potatoes are high in carbohydrates and are a good source of C, vitamin B, potassium, and fiber.

Store potatoes in a dark, cool place with good air circulation. Onions and potatoes both produce different gases that cause each other to spoil; they should not be stored together. Potatoes store well with citrus, however. Raw potatoes should not be stored in a refrigerator. Chilling changes the starch to sugar, altering the flavor.

Green spots on a potato are caused by exposure to sunlight. These spots taste bitter and contain small amounts of a toxic chemical called *solanine;* cooking does not destroy solanine. Discard potatoes that have green spots or sprouting eyes.

- *New potatoes:* Young red potatoes. Red or pink skin; creamy white flesh; tender and delicious. Usually boiled in peels and served with little adornment; also good in cold salads.
- *Purple potatoes:* Dark purple skins and bright purple flesh. Cooking makes the color lighter. Flavor and texture identical to russet potatoes.
- *Red Pontiac:* Thin red skin; very white flesh. Good for boiling.
- *Russet Burbank:* Brown leathery skin; also called *russet* or *Idaho* potatoes. Good for baking, frying, and making chips.
- *Yellow Finn:* Golden skins and creamy yellow flesh; buttery flavor.
- *Yukon Gold:* Yellow skin and flesh; buttery appearance; excellent flavor.

# Potatoes with Rosemary

6 large white potatoes, peeled and cubed
1/2 C chopped onion
1/2 C chopped green pepper
1 medium tomato, peeled, seeded, and chopped
1/4 tsp dried rosemary
Freshly ground black pepper to taste
1/3 C dry white wine

Cover potatoes with water in a saucepan and bring to a boil. Reduce heat and simmer until tender; do not overcook. When potatoes are nearly done, sauté onion and green pepper. Add tomato and sauté until hot, about 1 minute; do not let vegetables become too soft. Stir in rosemary and black pepper; keep warm.

Drain cooked potatoes and mash, using an electric mixer. Beat in wine. Fold in sautéed vegetables. Serve immediately.

Serves 12.

Suggestion
- Low-sodium chicken broth, tomato juice, carrot juice, or skim milk can be substituted for the wine.

Calories	%Fat	Fat (g)	Saturated Fat (g)	Cholesterol (mg)	Sodium (mg)	Carbohydrate (g)	Protein (g)	Fiber (g)
71	2	0	0.0	0	5	15	1	1

Exchanges: Starch 1

Potato-Onion Casserole

4 medium Bermuda onions, very thinly sliced
Freshly ground black pepper to taste
1 tsp honey
4 large unpeeled Idaho or russet potatoes, cooked and cut into thin slices

Sauté the onions and black pepper over low heat for 10 minutes, stirring often, until the onions begin to soften. Add the honey. Continue cooking over low heat for about 10 minutes, stirring occasionally, or until the onions are very soft and are turning golden brown. Spread one-third of the onions in a 10-inch baking dish. Top with half of the potatoes. Continue layering onions and potatoes, finishing with a layer of onions. Bake, covered, at 400° for 30 to 35 minutes or until the potatoes are tender. Remove the cover after the first 20 or 25 minutes to allow for browning.

Serves 8.

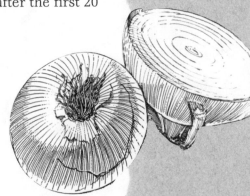

Calories	%Fat	Fat (g)	Saturated Fat (g)	Cholesterol (mg)	Sodium (mg)	Carbohydrate (g)	Protein (g)	Fiber (g)
124	1	0	0.0	0	9	29	3	3

Exchanges: Starch 1-1/2, Vegetable 1

Potatoes & Peppers

1 lb unpeeled potatoes, cut in thick vertical slices
1/2 lb green bell peppers, cut in wide vertical strips
1/2 lb red bell peppers, cut in wide vertical strips
1 large onion, cut in thick vertical slices
1 clove garlic, crushed
1 T olive oil
1 T chopped parsley

Place potatoes, peppers, onion, and garlic in a shallow roasting pan. Drizzle with oil, sprinkle with parsley, and toss to mix well. Bake uncovered, turning vegetables occasionally, until potatoes are tender, about 30 to 35 minutes.
Serves 8.

Suggestion
• Add oregano, rosemary, or other seasonings to vary the flavor.

Calories	%Fat	Fat (g)	Saturated Fat (g)	Cholesterol (mg)	Sodium (mg)	Carbohydrate (g)	Protein (g)	Fiber (g)
99	17	2	0.3	0	6	20	2	2

Exchanges: Starch 1, Vegetable 1

Stuffed Potatoes

1/3 C low-fat (1%) cottage cheese
3 T grated Parmesan cheese
1 T lemon juice
1 T hot Chinese mustard
2 C chopped broccoli, steamed and drained
Freshly ground black pepper to taste
3 hot, freshly baked potatoes, halved
Paprika

Mix cottage cheese, Parmesan cheese, lemon juice, and mustard until smooth. Stir in the broccoli and pepper. Set aside. Lightly break up the potato interiors with a fork, without breaking through the peel. Top each potato half with broccoli-cheese mixture; sprinkle with paprika. Serve hot.
Serves 6.

Suggestions
• A 10-oz package of frozen chopped broccoli can be substituted for the fresh broccoli.
• Kale, spinach, or other greens can be substituted for the broccoli.

How to Bake Potatoes
Use a small skewer or fork to pierce a potato before baking it. This allows moisture to escape during baking, providing a mealy, rather than soggy, texture. It also prevents trapped steam from causing the potato to explode in the oven. Long, slow baking makes a drier, mealier potato.
• *Oven:* Bake at 350° for about 90 minutes, or until tender. For a steamed texture (not dry and mealy), wrap potatoes tightly in foil before baking.
• *Microwave:* Place potatoes on a paper towel in a microwave oven. Bake two 8-oz potatoes for 6 to 8 minutes (or four potatoes for 13 to 15 minutes), turning halfway through the cooking period.

Calories	%Fat	Fat (g)	Saturated Fat (g)	Cholesterol (mg)	Sodium (mg)	Carbohydrate (g)	Protein (g)	Fiber (g)
97	10	1	0.6	3	141	18	5	2

Exchanges: Starch 1, Low-fat protein 1/2

Hashhouse Greek

Dog soup
A glass of water

Belch water
A glass of plain soda water

Moo juice
A glass of milk

Mug of murk
A cup of coffee

Hot cha
Hot chocolate

Hold the hail
Without ice

Adam and Eve on a raft
Two poached eggs on toast

Wreck a pair
Scrambled eggs

A bowl of bird seed
Cereal

Bossy in a bowl
Beef stew

Clean up the kitchen
Hash

Keep off the grass
Without lettuce

Pin a rose on it
With a slice of onion

Warts
Olives

Eve with a lid on
Apple pie

Nervous pudding
Jell-O

Hash-Browned Potatoes

3 medium unpeeled baking potatoes, cooked and coarsely grated
2 T finely chopped onion
Freshly ground black pepper to taste
2 tsp canola oil

Mix potatoes, onion, and pepper in a large bowl. Heat oil in a non-stick skillet over medium-high heat. Spread potatoes across the bottom of the skillet and reduce heat to medium-low. Cook, covered, until potatoes are brown on the bottom. Turn potato cake over and brown the other side. Serve hot.
Serves 4.

Suggestion
• Minced garlic or other seasonings to taste can be mixed in with the grated potatoes before cooking.

Calories	%Fat	Fat (g)	Saturated Fat (g)	Cholesterol (mg)	Sodium (mg)	Carbohydrate (g)	Protein (g)	Fiber (g)
122	18	2	0.2	0	8	24	2	2

Exchanges: Starch 1-1/2, Fat 1/2

# Potato Pancakes

Fad Diets
...crafty diet wizards have appeared all over the country hawking what they claim are the latest dietary methods for nutritional eating. Be wary of them. Fad diets dupe innocent people into thinking, for example, that shedding unwanted pounds is easy, fun, and permanent.... In general, any diet that promises you a miracle is probably a hoax.

Edward B. Diethrich, MD
Heart Test

3 C peeled, grated cooked potatoes
1 medium onion, finely chopped
2 egg whites
1/4 C whole-wheat bread crumbs
White pepper to taste
1 T canola oil

Beat potatoes, onions, and egg whites together. Blend in bread crumbs and pepper. Heat oil in a large skillet over medium-high heat. For each pancake, drop about 1/4 C of potato into hot oil and flatten to about 1/2-inch thick. Repeat with remaining potato mixture, making 12 pancakes. Lightly brown pancakes on both sides. Place pancakes close together on a nonstick baking sheet. Bake at 350° for 10 minutes. Turn and bake for another 10 minutes. Blot each pancake with a paper towel and serve hot.
Serves 12.

Suggestions
• 1/4 C egg substitute can be used in place of the egg whites.
• Leftover mashed potatoes can be substituted for the grated potatoes.

Calories	%Fat	Fat (g)	Saturated Fat (g)	Cholesterol (mg)	Sodium (mg)	Carbohydrate (g)	Protein (g)	Fiber (g)
56	20	1	0.1	0	27	10	2	1

Exchanges: Starch 1/2

 # Gnocchi Verdi

10 oz frozen chopped spinach, cooked and very well drained
8 oz low-fat ricotta cheese
8 oz low-fat cottage cheese
1/4 C egg substitute
1 tsp nutmeg
3 T freshly grated Parmesan cheese
1/4 to 1/3 C flour

Mix spinach with ricotta cheese, cottage cheese, egg substitute, nutmeg, and salt, blending thoroughly. Stir in Parmesan cheese and flour. Drop by teaspoons onto a lightly floured board and shape into balls. Cook until tender in boiling water. Serve hot.

Serves 4.

Suggestion
• Serve with Spaghetti Sauce (page 446), Double Red Sauce (page 447), or Roasted Red Pepper Sauce (page 448).

Calories	%Fat	Fat (g)	Saturated Fat (g)	Cholesterol (mg)	Sodium (mg)	Carbohydrate (g)	Protein (g)	Fiber (g)
123	17	2	1.4	6	388	13	13	1

Exchanges: Starch 1/2, Vegetable 1, Low-fat protein 1-1/2

Stuffed Acorn Squash

1 medium acorn squash, halved lengthwise and seeded
1 C unsweetened applesauce
2 tsp currants
1/4 tsp nutmeg

Place squash cut side down in baking dish. Pour in water to a depth of 1/2 inch. Bake at 350° until tender, about 30 minutes. Remove squash, discard water, and place squash cut side up in the same baking dish. Combine applesauce, currants, and nutmeg; fill squash cavities. Continue baking at 350° for 20 to 30 minutes, or until hot and tender.
Serves 2.

Calories	%Fat	Fat (g)	Saturated Fat (g)	Cholesterol (mg)	Sodium (mg)	Carbohydrate (g)	Protein (g)	Fiber (g)
124	8	1	0.3	0	5	30	2	6

Exchanges: Starch 1, Fruit 1

Winter Squash
Winter squashes are available almost all year round. They are usually large and durable. The hard shell should have a dull finish; a shiny winter squash was picked before it was ripe. Winter squashes are high in vitamin A, and they are good sources of vitamin C, iron, and potassium. Boiling decreases the beta-carotene content as well as dilutes the flavor. Butternut and hubbard squash have more vitamin A than acorn and spaghetti squash.

Any winter squash can be used to replace the pumpkin in pies, muffins, breads. For a delicious dessert, grated winter squash can be substituted for the carrots in a recipe for carrot cake.

- *Acorn:* Dark green with wide ribs; will develop orange highlights the longer it is stored. A little orange is sign of ripeness; if more than half of the squash is orange, the flesh is stringy.
- *Butternut:* Tan skin; bright

orange, sweet flesh; a greenish tint indicates poor flavor. Tender summer crop can be stewed, boiled, or used like pumpkin in pies or sauces. The autumn crop is more firm; it is usually stuffed and baked, like acorn squash. It is good peeled, boiled, mashed, and seasoned with ginger marmalade.

- *Golden Nugget:* Orange with greenish highlights; mildly sweet. Best eaten when immature and tender.
- *Hubbard:* Orange-red skin flecked with dark blue or gray, ridged and bumpy.
- *Pumpkin:* Can be served as a vegetable or a fruit; puréed pumpkin is used in pies, souffles, baked goods, soups, and sauces. Small whole pumpkins can be stuffed and baked like zucchini.
- *Spaghetti squash:* Smooth and yellow. It is cooked unpeeled, and the yellow pulp is scraped into strands that look like spaghetti. It is often served like spaghetti with a tomato or other vegetable sauce.

Pumpkin Souffle

2 C canned pumpkin
2/3 C hot skim milk
1/2 tsp cinnamon
1/4 tsp nutmeg
1/4 tsp ground ginger
1/8 tsp ground cloves
4 egg whites, beaten stiff

Beat pumpkin with milk and spices until fluffy. Gently fold in egg whites. Pour into nonstick casserole. Bake at 400° for 35 minutes. Serve immediately. Serves 8.

Calories	%Fat	Fat (g)	Saturated Fat (g)	Cholesterol (mg)	Sodium (mg)	Carbohydrate (g)	Protein (g)	Fiber (g)
37	6	0	0.1	0	41	6	3	1

Exchanges: Vegetable 1

Steamed Spaghetti Squash with Seasonal Vegetables

Rick Moonen

3-1/4 to 4 lb spaghetti squash, split lengthwise, seeded
4 large vine-ripe tomatoes
Juice of 1 lemon
1 tsp virgin olive oil
Freshly ground black pepper to taste
2 T pignoli nuts (pine nuts)
1/2 C finely diced zucchini
1/2 C finely diced yellow squash
1/2 C sliced mushrooms
1/2 C finely diced red and yellow bell peppers
1/2 C diced asparagus
1/2 C broccoli florets
1/2 C cauliflower florets
1 small clove garlic, minced
2 T coarsely chopped basil

Place the squash halves, cut side down, in a jelly roll pan and add about 1/2 inch water. Bake at 400° for about 25 minutes, or until the flesh yields when pressed firmly with your thumb. Remove the pan from the oven and flip the squash over. When cool enough to handle, scrape the flesh with a fork; the

Pine Nuts

Also called *pignoli* or *piñons*, pine nuts are the kernels from the seeds of stone pine cones. Stone pines grow on the northern coast of the Mediterranean, and the pine nuts are widely used in Mediterranean cooking.

Pine nuts have a very delicate flavor, tasting nutty when cooked. They are seldom eaten raw as they have a faint turpentine taste, which dissipates in cooking. Pine nuts are expensive; blanched almonds are a good substitute when necessary.

Their high oil content makes pine nuts turn rancid easily. Store them in an airtight container in the refrigerator for up to one month or in the freezer for up to six months.

A rich harvest in a hungry land is impressive. The sight of healthy children is impressive. These—not mighty arms—are the achievements which the American nation believes to be impressive.

Lyndon B. Johnson

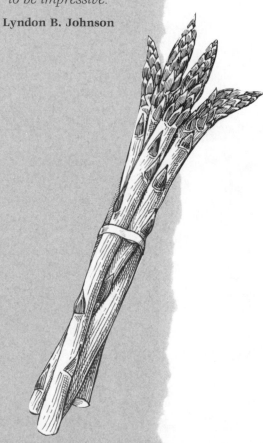

squash will resemble strands of spaghetti. Set aside. There should be 4 to 5 cups of squash.

To prepare the sauce, remove the tomato stems and score an × on the bottom, cutting just through the skin. Plunge the tomatoes into boiling water for 10 seconds. Remove and plunge into ice-cold water to "shock" them. Peel the skins with a small knife. Cut the tomatoes in half and gently squeeze the seeds and pulp into a bowl, being careful not to ruin the tomato meat. Finely dice the meat and place it in a clean bowl. Strain the seeds and pulp to extract all the juice. Squeeze the lemon juice into the tomato juice, season with pepper, and whisk in the oil. Add to the diced tomato meat and set aside.

To prepare the vegetables, heat the pignoli nuts in a large sauté pan with cooking spray until they begin to brown. Add the mushrooms and cook for 20 seconds over medium heat. Add the zucchini, squash, peppers, and asparagus, sautéing quickly for about 1 minute. Season with pepper. Add the broccoli, cauliflower, and garlic; cook for 30 seconds, turning the vegetables with a wooden spoon. Add the basil and toss; remove from heat.

Heat the cooked spaghetti squash in a small pan over medium heat with a few tablespoons of water. The water will steam the squash. Drain well.

To serve, divide the tomato sauce onto 4 heated 12-inch plates. Make nests of spaghetti squash in the center of each plate. Spoon vegetables into each nest. Serve as a main course.

Serves 4.

Suggestion

- 1/4 C of grated imported Parmesan cheese may be sprinkled over the nest of vegetables just before serving.

Calories	%Fat	Fat (g)	Saturated Fat (g)	Cholesterol (mg)	Sodium (mg)	Carbohydrate (g)	Protein (g)	Fiber (g)
236	25	7	1.1	0	35	46	7	15

Exchanges: Starch 2, Vegetable 3, Fat 1

Sautéed Summer Squash

1 C thinly sliced zucchini
1 C thinly sliced yellow crookneck squash
1 C red bell pepper strips
1 C snow peas, trimmed
1 shallot, minced
1/2 tsp dried basil
1/8 tsp pepper

Sauté all ingredients over medium-high heat, stirring constantly, until crisp-tender, about 3 to 4 minutes. Serve hot.

Serves 4.

Summer Squash

Summer squashes have soft skins. Despite their name, they are available all year. Choose summer squashes that have shiny skin. Store them in plastic bags in the refrigerator for four to five days. Summer squashes are good sources of vitamin C and contain some folate. They should be steamed quickly to preserve their vitamin C.

Smaller squashes are more tender; they can be cooked with the peel and seeds. Older, larger squashes might be nicer if peeled and seeded.

- *Pattypan squash:* Also called *custard squash;* floury taste. It can be steamed, boiled, or stuffed and baked when very ripe. These squash are small, two to three inches in diameter, and have scalloped edges.

- *Yellow Crookneck:* Buy yellow squash that is four to six inches long. This

Calories	%Fat	Fat (g)	Saturated Fat (g)	Cholesterol (mg)	Sodium (mg)	Carbohydrate (g)	Protein (g)	Fiber (g)
36	7	0	0.0	0	4	7	2	2

Exchanges: Vegetable 1

squash keeps its bright color when cooked. A straight-necked variety is also available.

- *Zucchini:* Harvested young; buy zucchini that are four to nine inches long. Dark green skins resemble cucumbers; yellowing is a sign of age. Serve zucchini raw in salads, lightly cooked in stir-fry recipes, or stewed (it is an important ingredient in ratatouille, a vegetable stew from Provence). A golden variety of zucchini is available.

Squash Ratatouille

2 large yellow onions, sliced
3 cloves garlic, chopped
6 medium yellow squash, sliced
6 medium zucchini, sliced
1/2 C cilantro, chopped
1/4 to 1/2 tsp red chili powder
Freshly ground black pepper to taste

Sauté the onions and garlic for 6 to 8 minutes, or until the onions are translucent. Add remaining ingredients. Cook, covered, over medium-low heat, stirring frequently, for 30 minutes, or until the ratatouille is the consistency of a thick stew. Season with pepper before serving.
Serves 8.

Calories	%Fat	Fat (g)	Saturated Fat (g)	Cholesterol (mg)	Sodium (mg)	Carbohydrate (g)	Protein (g)	Fiber (g)
89	10	1	0.2	0	10	20	4	6

Exchanges: Vegetable 4

Sweet Potato Stix

4 large sweet potatoes, parboiled, peeled, each cut lengthwise into 6 wedges
Cinnamon to taste

Lightly coat potatoes with cooking spray. Arrange in a single layer on a baking sheet and sprinkle with cinnamon. Bake at 450° until tender, about 20 to 30 minutes.
Serves 6.

Suggestions
- Serve with Ginger Pears (page 418).
- Partially cook potatoes by steaming or microwaving to make them easier to slice.

Sweet Potatoes & Yams

Sweet potatoes belong to the morning glory family and are native to South America. They are not related to potatoes or to yams. Yams are native to Africa and Asia; they are sweeter than sweet potatoes. True yams are rarely available in American stores. American "yams" are a copper-colored variety of sweet potato that is more moist but has less vitamin A and C than regular sweet potatoes.

Sweet potatoes and yams are often used interchangeably. They are high in carbohydrate and are an excellent source of vitamins A and C and potassium. For better nutrition and more fiber, they should be cooked with their skins before peeling.

Sweet potatoes canned in water are less nutritious than cooked fresh potatoes. Canning in sugar syrup adds unnecessary sugar and calories.

Store sweet potatoes in a cool, dark place, but not in

Calories	%Fat	Fat (g)	Saturated Fat (g)	Cholesterol (mg)	Sodium (mg)	Carbohydrate (g)	Protein (g)	Fiber (g)
154	14	2	0.3	0	10	31	3	2

Exchanges: Starch 2, Fat 1/2

the refrigerator; very cold temperatures will make them turn dark.

Prick each raw sweet potato with a fork and bake at 400° for 30 to 35 minutes. To remove stringy fibers from mashed sweet potatoes, beat them with an electric mixer; the strings will be trapped in the beaters.

Sweet potato flour can be made by slicing raw sweet potatoes in thin strips and drying them in the oven at a very low temperature. The dried strips should then be ground into flour in a blender. It can be used to replace part of the white or whole-wheat flour in recipes for muffins or bread.

Orange-Pineapple Yams

1 lb yams, cooked, peeled, and mashed
1–2 T unsweetened frozen orange juice concentrate
1/2 tsp grated orange rind
3/4 C canned unsweetened crushed pineapple
1/2 C unsweetened pineapple juice
Pinch of cinnamon, cloves, and allspice
1-1/2 C miniature marshmallows

Mix yams with all ingredients, except marshmallows, blending well. Lightly pile mixture in a casserole dish. Bake at 350° for 10 to 15 minutes, until hot. Top with marshmallows and broil just until golden brown; do not burn.

Serves 6.

Suggestion
• Sweet potatoes may be substituted for the yams.

Calories	%Fat	Fat (g)	Saturated Fat (g)	Cholesterol (mg)	Sodium (mg)	Carbohydrate (g)	Protein (g)	Fiber (g)
138	1	0	0.0	0	11	34	2	2

Exchanges: Starch 1, Fruit 1

Grilled Sourdough Bread with Tomatoes, Arugula, & Sweet Onions

Louis Spost

1 loaf sourdough bread, sliced
Olive oil cooking spray
4 medium plum tomatoes, diced fine
1 bunch arugula, chopped
1 medium sweet onion, diced fine
1/2 tsp chopped roasted garlic

Mix tomatoes, arugula, onion, and garlic; set aside. Spray sourdough bread slices with olive oil cooking spray. Grill slices of bread. Top bread with the tomato mixture just before serving.

Serves 8.

Suggestion
• Very nice as an appetizer or as an accompaniment to Roasted Monkfish with Porcini Mushrooms (page 262).

Calories	%Fat	Fat (g)	Saturated Fat (g)	Cholesterol (mg)	Sodium (mg)	Carbohydrate (g)	Protein (g)	Fiber (g)
178	4	1	0.1	1	340	36	6	3

Exchanges: Starch 2, Vegetable 1

Onions

Many varieties of onions, differing in shape, color, and flavor, are grown. Their flavor is generally stronger when raw. Store onions in a cool, dry place separate from the potatoes. Whole onions should not be refrigerated because they will affect the flavor of other foods. Raw cut onion can be stored tightly wrapped in the refrigerator for two to three days.

If a stored onion starts to grow green spears, use it immediately or plant it in a pot. The sprouts, which will grow for weeks, can be snipped and used like chives or scallions.

Onions won't make you cry while you're cutting them if you chill them first or cut them under running water. For a more mellow flavor, soak chopped onion in cool water for about an hour.

Whole boiled onions can be stuffed like bell peppers. To keep them firm so they hold their shape when stuffed, drop them in ice water immediately after boiling.

A fragrant, delicious accompaniment for poultry can be made by adding a little honey to sautéing onions. Boiled, puréed onions make a nice thick sauce that can be used plain, in salad dressings, or in making other sauces and gravies.

- *Bermuda:* Brown skin; large, flattened shape; very mild; crisp.
- *Italian:* Red, oblong; mild, sometimes sweet; loses color when cooked. Becomes bitter if cut and exposed to air too long before cooking.
- *Maui:* Light golden brown skin; sweet and mild.
- *Pearl:* White, gold, or red; tiny boiling onions; good with peas, stews.
- *Spanish:* Yellow or white; mild flavor; good cooked or raw; stores well.
- *Vidalia:* Golden brown skin; very sweet and mild—can be eaten raw like an apple.
- *Walla Walla:* Golden brown skin; giant size; sweet; best used raw.
- *Red Torpedo:* Purplish-red skin; long, slender, cylindrical shape.

resh Tomato Pizzas

4 whole-wheat pita breads
4 small tomatoes, thinly sliced
1 green bell pepper, thinly sliced
1/4 pound raw mushrooms, thinly sliced
1/2 tsp oregano
1/2 tsp basil
1-1/3 C part-skim mozzarella cheese, grated

Place pitas on a large baking sheet. Cover each with tomatoes, bell peppers, and mushrooms. Sprinkle with herbs. Top with cheese. Bake at 375° for 15 minutes or until cheese is melted. Serve immediately.
Serves 4.

Suggestion

- Use other sliced vegetables to replace part or all of the bell pepper and mushrooms, such as zucchini, onions, chili peppers, or elephant garlic.

Calories	%Fat	Fat (g)	Saturated Fat (g)	Cholesterol (mg)	Sodium (mg)	Carbohydrate (g)	Protein (g)	Fiber (g)
218	20	5	2.5	11	376	32	12	5

Exchanges: Starch 1-1/2, Vegetable 2, Medium-fat protein 1

# Baked Tomatoes

*If all be well with
belly, feet, and sides,
A king's estate
no greater good provides.*

Horace

4 ripe tomatoes, halved and seeded
2 cloves garlic, minced
1/2 tsp pepper
1-1/2 tsp marjoram
1/2 tsp oregano
1/4 C parsley, minced
2 T Parmesan cheese, grated

Put tomatoes in a baking dish, cut side up. Mix remaining ingredients except parsley and cheese; drizzle equal amounts on top of each tomato half. Sprinkle with parsley and cheese. Bake at 350° until lightly browned, about 20 minutes.
Serves 4.

Calories	%Fat	Fat (g)	Saturated Fat (g)	Cholesterol (mg)	Sodium (mg)	Carbohydrate (g)	Protein (g)	Fiber (g)
46	25	1	0.6	2	61	8	2	2

Exchanges: Vegetable 1

Fish

Cod
Grouper
Haddock
Halibut
Monkfish
Orange Roughy
Redfish
Salmon
Sea Bass
Snapper
Sole
Sturgeon
Swordfish
Tuna
Whitefish

Shellfish

Crawfish
Lobster
Shrimp
Scallops
Oysters

ish & Shellfish

# Codfish with Mussels, Shrimp, Swiss Chard, & Polenta

Maureen Pothier

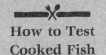
How to Test Cooked Fish

Insert a fork into the fish at a 45° angle and gently twist the fork. If the fish flakes easily and is opaque, white, and tender, it is done. If it is translucent and resists flaking, continue cooking for another minute or two. Do not overcook! Fish that has been cooked too long is dry, mealy, and tasteless.

1-1/4 lb green Swiss chard
1 C white wine (use a fresh, crisp, dry wine)
1/2 C water
2 large shallots, finely minced
3/4 tsp dried thyme
1/4 tsp grated orange peel
16 mussels, beards removed, and washed well
2 lb codfish fillet
12 medium shrimp, peeled and deveined
1/2 C finely diced tomato
1/4 C finely diced leek, washed well
3 T freshly chopped basil
2 T olive oil
Sweet Red Pepper & Black Olive Polenta (page 79)

Wash Swiss chard several times in cold water; shake off excess water. Slice the stems into 1/2-inch pieces and cut large leaves in half (leave small ones whole). Put wine, water, shallot, thyme, and orange peel in a large non-corrosive pot that has a lid.

Thirty minutes before serving, put mussels into the pot with the wine mix-

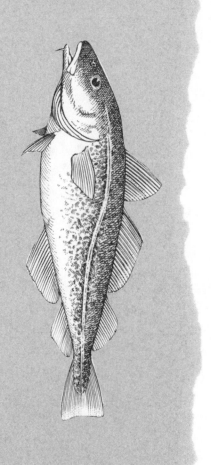

ture. Steam, covered, over medium-high heat until mussels just open, about 5 minutes (they should be slightly undercooked). Remove mussels in their shells immediately. Strain broth through a double thickness of cheesecloth (to eliminate any sand or grit that may have been in the mussels); squeeze all juice out of the shallots and herbs so that all of their flavor remains in the broth.

Broil codfish for about 10 minutes, depending on thickness. While it's cooking, bring strained broth to a boil. Toss the shrimp in the broth until they just loose their transparency and start to turn white, about 5 minutes depending on size (they should be slightly undercooked). Remove shrimp immediately. About 1-1/2 to 2 C of broth should remain in the pot. Add the tomato and leek; simmer for a few minutes to reduce the mixture slightly. Reduce heat to low to keep broth warm. Steam Swiss chard over boiling water until stems are tender, about 5 minutes. When the cod is just about done, add the basil and olive oil to the broth, then return the mussels and shrimp to the broth to warm them.

Place Swiss chard on a warm serving platter. Arrange cod, mussels, and shrimp on top. Pour warm broth over all. Garnish with lemon if desired. Serve with Sweet Red Pepper & Black Olive Polenta.

Serves 4.

Calories	%Fat	Fat (g)	Saturated Fat (g)	Cholesterol (mg)	Sodium (mg)	Carbohydrate (g)	Protein (g)	Fiber (g)
357	26	10	1.6	157	434	11	52	

Exchanges: Vegetable 2, Low-fat protein 7

Grilled Fish in Greek Marinade

Joyce Goldstein

2 T finely minced garlic
2 T oregano
1/3 C olive oil
2 tsp chopped thyme
Grated zest of one lemon
2 T lemon juice
1/4 C ouzo
Salt and freshly ground black pepper
6 fillets (5 oz each) mild white fish, such as cod, swordfish, or sea bass

Warm garlic and oregano in half the olive oil for 2 minutes. Add the rest of the ingredients. Cool the mixture. Marinate 6 pieces of mild fish in this mixture for 3 to 6 hours in the refrigerator. Preheat broiler or make a charcoal fire. Brush fish lightly with olive oil and sprinkle with salt and pepper. Grill fish for 3 to 4 minutes per side.

Serves 6.

Suggestions
- Serve with steamed rice and spinach.
- Add orange zest with the lemon zest.

Interchangeable Fish

Fish that are alike in texture, taste, and fat content can be usually cooked by the same methods and with similar seasonings. The following lists group fish according to these characteristics. Within each group, fish can be used interchangeably in recipes. Substitutions allow the cook to take advantage of the freshest choices available at the market, the best buys, or the weekend angler's good luck.

Thin, delicate, lean
Flounder, small
Sole

Medium-dense, flaky, lean
Bass, freshwater
Cod
Haddock
Flounder, large
Halibut
Pike
Rockfish
Snapper

Medium-dense, flaky, moderately lean
Catfish
Pink salmon
Rainbow trout

Calories	%Fat	Fat (g)	Saturated Fat (g)	Cholesterol (mg)	Sodium (mg)	Carbohydrate (g)	Protein (g)	Fiber (g)
321	19	7	1.2	66	502	35	30	2

Exchanges: Starch 2, Vegetable 1, Low-fat protein 3

*Medium-dense,
extra-firm flakes*

Drum
Grouper
Mahi mahi
Orange roughy
Sea bass

Dense, meaty, lean

Halibut
Grouper
Sea bass
Shark

*Dense, meaty,
moderately lean or oily*

Amberjack
Kingfish
Mackerel
Sturgeon
Swordfish
Tuna, fresh

Baked Cod with Rice & Spinach

1/2 C brown rice
3/4 C water
10-oz pkg frozen spinach, thawed overnight in refrigerator
4 cod fillets (4 oz each)
1 medium red onion, sliced
1 medium tomato, sliced
1 tsp basil

Pour rice and water in the bottom of a nonstick 10 × 6-inch baking pan. Distribute spinach and its liquid evenly over the rice. Place cod on the spinach. Top with onion and tomato; season with basil. Bake, covered, at 350° until rice is tender and fish flakes easily with a fork, about 1 hour.

Serves 4.

Calories	%Fat	Fat (g)	Saturated Fat (g)	Cholesterol (mg)	Sodium (mg)	Carbohydrate (g)	Protein (g)	Fiber (g)
221	9	2	0.5	60	141	25	26	3

Exchanges: Starch 1, Vegetable 2, Low-fat protein 3

Sautéed Grouper Cheeks on Rice Tabbouleh

Sanford D'Amato

24 oz grouper cheeks
Flour (to dust)
Pepper to taste
Rice Tabbouleh (page 86)
Tomato Vinaigrette (page 483)
2 T mixed fresh chopped chives and chiffonade of mint

Season and flour grouper cheeks. Sauté in cooking spray until golden brown. Place on beds of Rice Tabbouleh, spoon the Tomato Vinaigrette over the grouper, and garnish with mint and chives.

Serves 6.

Suggestions
• Serve with zucchini and yellow squash fans.
• Grouper fillets, snapper, or halibut may be substituted for the grouper cheeks.

Calories	%Fat	Fat (g)	Saturated Fat (g)	Cholesterol (mg)	Sodium (mg)	Carbohydrate (g)	Protein (g)	Fiber (g)
187	7	1	0.3	53	82	20	22	1

Exchanges: Starch 1-1/2, Low-fat protein 3

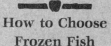

Grilled Grouper Tangerine

1/4 C frozen unsweetened tangerine concentrate, thawed
2 T dry vermouth
1 tsp canola oil
1/2 tsp dried rosemary
1/4 tsp dried thyme
1/4 tsp pepper
1 lb grouper fillets

Combine all ingredients except fish. Pour over the fish and marinate, covered, for 2 hours. Remove fish from marinade and grill the fish until it flakes easily with a fork. Boil the marinade and use for basting during cooking.
Serves 4.

Suggestions

- Orange juice concentrate can be substituted for the tangerine concentrate.
- Fish can be broiled or pan-fried.

Calories	%Fat	Fat (g)	Saturated Fat (g)	Cholesterol (mg)	Sodium (mg)	Carbohydrate (g)	Protein (g)	Fiber (g)
101	21	2	0.4	53	82	0	19	0

Exchanges: Low-fat protein 2-1/2

Braised Haddock with Leeks & Potato-Herb Raviolini

Laura Brennan

1 lb haddock, cut into 4 equal pieces
1 bunch leeks, sliced on diagonal into 1-inch pieces, soaked in warm water to
   clean thoroughly, and sautéed briefly to soften
1 each red, green, yellow peppers, roasted, peeled, and seeded
1/2 pt cherry tomatoes, halved
1/2 C white wine (or white vermouth)
1 to 2 C Lobster Stock (page 486)
1 tsp chopped garlic
1/2 tsp fennel or anise seeds
Pinch hot red pepper flakes
1/2 tsp grated orange rind
24 Potato-Herb Raviolini (page 103), blanched

In a large sauté pan coated with cooking spray, sear the haddock. Remove
fish from pan and drain off any fat in pan. To the pan add the sautéed leeks,
the white wine, lobster stock, garlic, and fennel seed. Simmer for 5 minutes to
combine the flavors. Add the seared fish and the halved cherry tomatoes; simmer for 5 to 7 minutes, until fish is cooked. Add the Potato-Herb Raviolini, the
hot red pepper flakes, and the orange rind. Season with salt and pepper.
   Serves 4.

Calories	%Fat	Fat (g)	Saturated Fat (g)	Cholesterol (mg)	Sodium (mg)	Carbohydrate (g)	Protein (g)	Fiber (g)
336	8	3	0.6	60	140	46	28	5

Exchanges: Starch 1-1/2, Fruit 1/2, Vegetable 3, Low-fat protein 3

*Eat leeks in March
and wild garlic in May
And all year after
physicians may play.*

Old Welsh Rhyme

Leeks

Leeks are not as pungent
as onions or shallots. They
have wide green leaves and
look something like a scallion on steroids. Smaller
leeks may be more tender.
More nutritious than onions
or scallions, leeks contain
some vitamin C, folate, and
potassium.

Store leeks in the refrigerator wrapped in plastic for
up to two weeks. They must
be washed thoroughly to remove the dirt that collects
between the leaves; trim and
slice them lengthwise and
clean under running water.

Leeks are most widely
used fresh in soup, especially
potato soup. They can be
substituted for onions in any
soup or stew. Leeks can also
be served raw in salads or on
sandwiches.

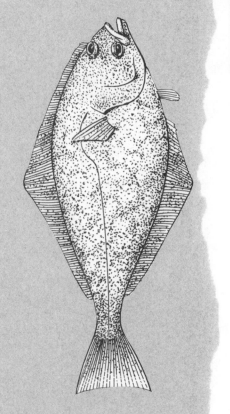

 # Steamed Halibut, Ginger, Leeks, Plum Tomato, & Lemon Thyme

Christopher C. Tobin

8 oz halibut fillet
1 slice (nickel-sized) ginger root, chopped
2 plum tomatoes, sliced
1 leek white, julienned
Fresh thyme or lemon thyme
Dash fresh lemon juice

Place sliced tomato, ginger, and thyme in an oven-proof sauté pan. Place halibut on top and season with pepper and a dash of lemon. Scatter leeks over the top and cover the pan tightly with foil. Bake at 450° for 18 minutes. Remove foil and slide entire ingredients onto a serving plate. Garnish with chopped fresh chives.
Serves 1.

Suggestion
• Sole, fluke, turbot, or flounder may be substituted for the halibut.

Calories	%Fat	Fat (g)	Saturated Fat (g)	Cholesterol (mg)	Sodium (mg)	Carbohydrate (g)	Protein (g)	Fiber (g)
285	11	4	0.8	120	209	17	47	6

Exchanges: Vegetable 3, Low-fat protein 6

Roasted Monkfish with Porcini Mushrooms

Louis Spost

4 monkfish pieces (6 oz each), trimmed
Flour seasoned with curry, coriander, and ground fennel seeds
8 to 10 oz fresh porcini mushrooms, sliced thinly
12 oz orzo pasta
4 oz chicken stock
1 bunch chives
1 beefsteak tomato, sliced in four
24 oz port wine, reduced by 75%
3 tsp sherry vinegar
1 sprig of thyme

Dredge monkfish in seasoned flour. Sear fish in a skillet sprayed with cooking spray and place it in a 325° oven until done (reserve until needed). Heat pasta and porcini mushrooms in chicken stock. In the skillet used for the fish, add reduced port and vinegar. Bring to a boil and reduce until syrupy. Sear tomatoes in a hot skillet. Place a tomato slice in the center of each serving plate. Top with orzo and mushrooms. Cut fish into slices and lay around pasta. Spoon syrup around plate. Sprinkle with chives. Serve with Grilled Sourdough Bread with Tomatoes, Arugula, & Sweet Onions (page 250).

Serves 4.

Calories	%Fat	Fat (g)	Saturated Fat (g)	Cholesterol (mg)	Sodium (mg)	Carbohydrate (g)	Protein (g)	Fiber (g)
659	7	5	0.9	94	186	97	50	7

Exchanges: Starch 5, Vegetable 4, Low-fat protein 5

range Roughy with Tomatoes

2 large onions, sliced
1 medium bell pepper, sliced
1 clove garlic, minced
1 can (1 lb) no-salt-added stewed tomatoes, crushed
1 tsp oregano
1 lb orange roughy, cut into 4 serving-size pieces
1 lemon, sliced
Freshly ground black pepper to taste

   Sauté onions and bell pepper until tender. Stir in garlic, tomatoes, and oregano, cooking for 1 minute. Place fish in a single layer in a nonstick baking dish. Top with lemon slices and pepper; add vegetable mixture. Bake, uncovered, at 350° for 45 minutes. Fish is done when it is opaque and flakes easily with a fork.
   Serves 4.

Calories	%Fat	Fat (g)	Saturated Fat (g)	Cholesterol (mg)	Sodium (mg)	Carbohydrate (g)	Protein (g)	Fiber (g)
290	31	10	1.9	45	143	22	28	4

Exchanges: Starch 1/2, Vegetable 3, Low-fat protein 4

# Poached Redfish with Mushrooms & Thyme

James P. Shannon

3 oz leaf spinach
5 to 6 oz redfish (red drum)
Small pinch salt
3 turns fresh black pepper (from peppermill)
2 to 3 oz stock
3 mushrooms, sliced
1/2 tsp chopped fresh thyme
1/4 tsp sweet butter

Blanch spinach in 1 oz water and keep green and firm; set aside. Season fish with salt and pepper and simmer in stock for about 5 to 6 minutes. Sauté mushrooms and thyme in butter.

Arrange spinach on plate. Top with fish, mushrooms, and thyme. Serve with 1 T natural stock.

Serves 1.

Suggestion

• Salmon may be substituted for the redfish.

Calories	%Fat	Fat (g)	Saturated Fat (g)	Cholesterol (mg)	Sodium (mg)	Carbohydrate (g)	Protein (g)	Fiber (g)
177	16	3	1.1	87	171	4	32	2

Exchanges: Vegetable 1, Low-fat protein 4

**Nondairy Sources
of Calcium**
Sardines, with bones
Salmon, with bones
Tofu
Oysters
Spinach
Broccoli
Artichoke
Pinto beans
Okra
Mustard greens
Navy beans
Kidney beans
Kale
Great Northern beans

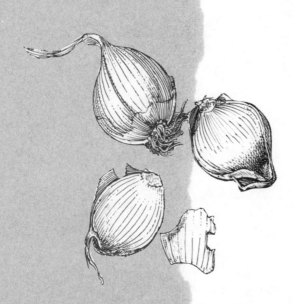

Braised Seasonal Salmon with Shiitake Mushrooms

Sean Kavanaugh

4 salmon fillet (6 oz each)
1 C sliced shiitake mushrooms
2 T chopped shallots
3 oz white wine
1 C fish glace
1 C skim milk
4 scallions
Freshly ground black pepper to taste

Poach salmon with sliced shiitakes and chopped shallots in wine and fish glace. Remove salmon; add skim milk to cooking pan and reduce. Pour over salmon. Garnish with scallions and black pepper.

Serves 4.

Calories	%Fat	Fat (g)	Saturated Fat (g)	Cholesterol (mg)	Sodium (mg)	Carbohydrate (g)	Protein (g)	Fiber (g)
287	33	10	2.0	66	126	6	40	1

Exchanges: Vegetable 1/2, Dairy 1/4, Low-fat protein 5

Roasted Spring Salmon with Lemon Grass Broth

Mark Gould

4 salmon fillets (6 oz each)
2 T minced garlic, sautéed
2 T finely chopped chervil
1 T finely chopped Italian parsley
2 T bread crumbs
8 Oriental spring roll wrappers (6 inch)
4 stalks lemon grass, roughly chopped
1 stalk fennel or celery, finely sliced
1 leek, white part only, sliced
1 lb salmon trimmings and scraps
3 oz dry white wine
3 pt cold water
3 chervil sprigs
3 parsley sprigs
1 tarragon sprig
1 cilantro sprig
1 pinch saffron (optional)
1 star anise
6 white peppercorns, cracked
1/4 C green spring peas, green beans, or asparagus

Fish & Omega-3
Because fish has omega-3 fatty acids, which lower triglycerides and help prevent clotting and coronary artery spasm, even the fattiest varieties such as salmon are thought to be healthful.

Diethrich and Cohan
Women and Heart Disease

1 C mixed mushrooms, browned in cooking spray
2 tomatoes, blanched, peeled, and diced
Fresh chervil sprigs

Season the salmon fillets with ground white pepper. Combine the garlic, chervil, parsley, and bread crumbs. Lightly brush the spring roll wrappers with some water (if your sheets are small, place 2 together so that they overlap by about 1 inch). Sprinkle the moistened sheets with the herb mixture, place the salmon fillets on the sheets, and wrap the dough around the fillets. In a skillet coated with vegetable spray, lightly brown the wrapped fillets on each side and then roast them in a 400° oven for 5 to 7 minutes.

Sweat the lemon grass and vegetables in cooking spray over moderate heat until they are soft but not colored. Add the fish trimmings and cook for a 1 minute; add the wine. Bring the mixture to a boil and continue to boil until reduced by half. Add the cold water and bring back to the boil again. Skim off any impurities. Add the herbs, star anise, and peppercorns. Simmer for 20 minutes, remove from heat, and pass through a fine mesh strainer.

To serve, heat 1-1/2 pt of the lemon grass broth along with the peas to blanch them; add the saffron if desired. When the peas are almost tender, add the tomato and mushrooms, checking the broth's flavor and seasoning with pepper if necessary. Slice the ends from the roasted salmon; discard. Cut each fillet into 3 or 4 pieces. Arrange these in shallow bowls and ladle the broth around the fish, being careful to distribute the vegetables evenly. Garnish each serving with chervil sprigs.

Serves 4.

Calories	%Fat	Fat (g)	Saturated Fat (g)	Cholesterol (mg)	Sodium (mg)	Carbohydrate (g)	Protein (g)	Fiber (g)
623	17	12	2.1	55	114	83	43	6

Exchanges: Starch 5, Vegetable 2, Low-fat protein 4

Poached Salmon Medallion

Steven Allen

3 thin carrots, 5 inches long, julienned
2 leeks, white part only, 5 inches long, julienned
2 thin celery stalks, 5 inches long, julienned
6 oz fish stock
4-1/2 oz shrimp, peeled and deveined
1/2 C spinach leaves, cleaned
White pepper to taste
2 tsp cider vinegar
1 lb, 7 oz skinless, boneless salmon filet
1 oz low-sodium tamari
2 oz sherry vinegar
3/4 C cooked Pritikin whole-wheat spaghetti
6 Savoy cabbage leaves, blanched, folded to form pockets
12 spears cooked asparagus
Herb garnish

Cook the julienned vegetables in fish stock until tender. Remove from stock and keep warm.

Purée shrimp and spinach; season with white pepper and cider vinegar. Place salmon on a cutting board and make a horizontal incision into the thickest part. Spread shrimp purée in salmon pocket and close. Transfer salmon to a sheet of plastic and roll up, jelly-roll fashion, in the plastic (plastic should be

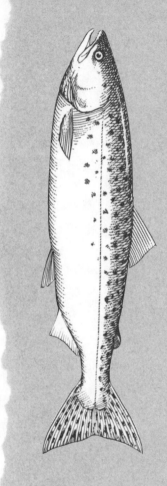

completely outside the roll); tie both ends. Poach in 180° water for about 30 minutes, or until internal temperature reaches 120°. Remove fish from water and keep warm.

Add tamari and sherry vinegar to fish stock and bring to a simmer. Combine warm julienned vegetables with spaghetti and form individual nests; place inside cabbage pockets. Slice the poached salmon roll, on a slight bias, into 6 equal portions; arrange on serving plates. Garnish with cabbage pockets, asparagus, and herbs. Spoon sherry-tamari broth over vegetables and around salmon.

Serves 6.

Suggestion

• Any whole-wheat spaghetti can be substituted for the Pritikin brand.

Calories	%Fat	Fat (g)	Saturated Fat (g)	Cholesterol (mg)	Sodium (mg)	Carbohydrate (g)	Protein (g)	Fiber (g)
244	26	7	1.3	72	296	15	31	4

Exchanges: Starch 1/2, Vegetable 2, Low-fat protein 4

# Escalope of Salmon with Mustard & Cognac

Jimmy Schmidt

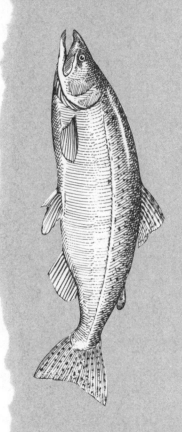

1 C fish fumet
1 C dry white wine (chardonnay)
1 C diced red onion
1/4 C peeled, diced ginger root
1 lb salmon fillet, sliced into 8 escalopes (2 oz each)
3 T Dijon mustard
3 T cracked or grained mustard
1 to 2 T cognac
2 T chopped dill
4 sprigs dill

Bring fish fumet, white wine, onions, and ginger to a simmer over high heat in an acid-resistant saucepan. Cook until reduced by half, about 10 minutes. Transfer to a blender and purée; strain into a saucepan and return to simmer.

Spray grill grate with cooking spray and heat. Lay salmon across preheated grill and cook for 4 minutes. Turn and cook until done, about 4 minutes.

Add mustards, cognac, and dill to sauce. Taste and adjust seasonings. Spoon sauce onto plate and place salmon on top. Garnish with dill sprigs and vegetables. Serve immediately.

Serves 4.

Calories	%Fat	Fat (g)	Saturated Fat (g)	Cholesterol (mg)	Sodium (mg)	Carbohydrate (g)	Protein (g)	Fiber (g)
232	31	8	1.4	43	308	8	27	1

Exchanges: Vegetable 2, Low-fat protein 3

**Great Seasonings
for Seafood**

Basil

Chervil

Cloves

Curry

Dill

Fennel

Ginger

Horseradish

Lemon

Marigold

Nasturtium

Onion

Orange

Oregano

Paprika

Parsley

Saffron

Savory

Tarragon

Thyme

Spicy Hot Grilled Salmon

1/2 C finely chopped onions

1/4 C chopped fresh cilantro

1 T sugar

1/2 C unsweetened pineapple juice

1/2 C lime juice

2 T low-sodium soy sauce

3 serrano chilies

3 cloves garlic, coarsely chopped

4 salmon steaks

Blend all ingredients except salmon in a food processor or blender until smooth. Pour over fish and marinate, covered, in the refrigerator for 6 to 8 hours. Remove salmon from marinade (reserve for basting) and cook it on a grill or under a broiler; the fish is done when it flakes easily with a fork. Baste fish often during cooking with reserved marinade.

Serves 4.

Calories	%Fat	Fat (g)	Saturated Fat (g)	Cholesterol (mg)	Sodium (mg)	Carbohydrate (g)	Protein (g)	Fiber (g)
139	37	6	1.1	37	44	0	21	0

Exchanges: Low-fat protein 3

Salmon — 271

# Salmonburgers

1 can (15-1/2 oz) salmon, drained (reserve 2 T liquid) and flaked
3 slices whole-wheat bread, torn in small pieces
1/3 C chopped onion
1/4 C skim milk
2 egg whites
2 T minced parsley
1 T lemon juice
1/4 tsp dill
Freshly ground black pepper to taste

Combine all ingredients, handling lightly. Shape into 4 patties. Pan-fry in cooking spray until brown, turning once.
Serves 4.

Suggestion

• Serve on buns with crisp lettuce and Cucumber-Dill Sauce (page 458).

Calories	%Fat	Fat (g)	Saturated Fat (g)	Cholesterol (mg)	Sodium (mg)	Carbohydrate (g)	Protein (g)	Fiber (g)
196	28	6	1.5	50	643	13	22	2

Exchanges: Starch 1, Low-fat protein 3

Good & Bad Cholesterol

Some cholesterol is necessary for normal health; however, excess amounts lead to the development of atherosclerosis, an artery-clogging disease that is the major cause of heart attacks and strokes. High-density lipoproteins (HDLs) are a form of cholesterol in the blood that seem to have a protective effect against cardiovascular disease. The most recent evidence shows that the higher the HDL level, the lower the risk of heart disease. Unfortunately, there is no diet or specific food that raises HDL levels. However, HDL levels can be increased by regular aerobic exercise (approved by a doctor) and attaining and maintaining ideal body weight.

Low-density lipoproteins (LDLs) are a form of blood cholesterol that increase the risk of heart disease. A low-fat, low-cholesterol diet can help reduce LDL levels. Therefore, the Arizona Heart Institute & Foundation's approach is to reduce the LDL cholesterol level through diet and to raise HDL cholesterol through exercise (as approved by a doctor) and weight management.

The amount of cholesterol in the blood can usually be reduced by decreasing the cholesterol and saturated fat content of the diet. Cholesterol is found only in animal fat. It is not present in any foods of plant origin. It is important to cut back on items like butter, fatty meats, regular cheese, and whole milk—which will decrease both cholesterol and saturated fat intake. Food labels, however, can be misleading. Products labeled "no cholesterol" may still contain significant amounts of saturated fat.

Arizona Heart
Institute Foundation
1–800–345–4278

 # Sea Bass Poached with Sun-Dried Tomato & Tarragon

Sean Brasel

2 lb sea bass fillet, cut into 4 portions
18 oz clam juice or fish fumet
4 oz julienned sun-dried tomatoes
2 T fresh tarragon
2 carrots, medium dice
4 stalks celery, diced
1 small onion, julienned
6 oz chardonnay wine
2 tsp extra-virgin olive oil
Pepper to taste

Place all ingredients in a medium sauté pan. Simmer, covered, on low heat for 15 minutes. Serve hot.
Serves 4.

Calories	%Fat	Fat (g)	Saturated Fat (g)	Cholesterol (mg)	Sodium (mg)	Carbohydrate (g)	Protein (g)	Fiber (g)
252	18	5	0.9	108	362	10	40	3

Exchanges: Vegetable 2, Low-fat protein 5

Steamed Pacific Snapper with Fennel & Tarragon

Sean Kavanaugh

4 snapper fillets (6 oz each)
1 C julienned fennel
2 oz julienned leeks
1/2 T chopped tarragon
2 C fish stock
2 tsp canola oil

Poach snapper in fish stock with chopped tarragon. Remove snapper when poached. Add julienne of fennel and leeks to the stock. Reduce in canola oil. Pour over snapper and decorate with fennel leaves.
    Serves 4.

How to Use Herbs
Handle fresh herbs as little as possible. Rinse quickly in cool water and pat them dry. Do not chop herbs until just before using. Reserve a little of the herbs to add late in the cooking process; overheating reduces the strength of their flavor and aroma.

Calories	%Fat	Fat (g)	Saturated Fat (g)	Cholesterol (mg)	Sodium (mg)	Carbohydrate (g)	Protein (g)	Fiber (g)
192	21	4	0.7	90	142	4	33	1

Exchanges: Vegetable 1, Low-fat protein 4-1/2

Phyllo Dough

Phyllo is made up of tissue-thin layers of pastry dough; strudel dough is very similar. It is commonly used in Greek and Near Eastern cooking. Fresh or frozen phyllo dough can be purchased in ethnic groceries and specialty shops.

Instead of brushing melted butter between layers of phyllo dough, use a light coating of vegetable oil cooking spray. This substitution can be made with any sweet or savory recipe. If necessary, modify the filling ingredients in traditional recipes for baklava, strudel, and fruit tarts to reduce their fat and sugar content.

Baked Opakapaka in Phyllo

Greg Paulson, CEC

6 opakapaka (pink snapper) fillets (6 oz each)
1 oz macadamia liqueur
Pinch white pepper
8 oz taro leaves or fresh spinach, blanched
10 oz apple banana, small diced
5 oz feta cheese, small diced
18 sheets phyllo dough
3 oz macadamia nuts, crushed
1 pt Mango-Pineapple Chutney (page 463)

Pound out each opakapaka fillet to a 10 × 6-inch rectangle. Brush with macadamia nut liqueur. Season with pepper. Cover fillet with blanched taro leaves, one layer thick. Mix apple banana and feta cheese; place equal amounts down the middle of each fillet. Roll up tightly. Reserve until later.

Lightly coat each layer of phyllo dough with cooking spray and sprinkle lightly with crushed macadamia nuts. Repeat until there are 3 layers, then fold in half (making 6 layers). Place rolled fish in center of phyllo dough and roll up tightly. Trim excess phyllo dough. Bake at 375° for 13 to 14 minutes. Slice into half-inch thick medallions. Serve with Mango-Pineapple Chutney.

Serves 6.

Suggestion

• An ordinary banana may be substituted for the apple banana.

Calories	%Fat	Fat (g)	Saturated Fat (g)	Cholesterol (mg)	Sodium (mg)	Carbohydrate (g)	Protein (g)	Fiber (g)
624	28	20	6.4	111	648	68	43	4

Exchanges: Starch 3, Fruit 1-1/2, Low-fat protein 5, High-fat protein 1

Snapper Soft Tacos with Black Beans & Two Salsas

Karla A. Graves

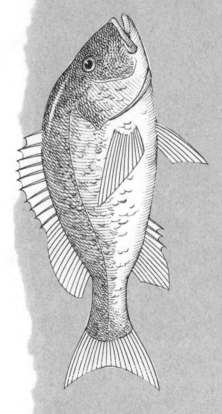

3 lb snapper fillets, bones removed
Pepper to taste
3 C Black Beans (page 94), hot
12 corn tortillas
Tomato Salsa (page 455)
Pineapple Salsa (page 466)
8 oz nonfat sour cream
Shredded cabbage, optional

Place snapper fillets on a broiler or grill and lightly coat with olive oil cooking spray; season with pepper. Cook until fish flakes with a fork. Be careful not to let the fish dry out.

Wrap tortillas in a damp towel and heat them in the oven or a microwave oven.

Cut snapper into 1-inch pieces. Holding a tortilla in your hand, place about 1/4 C Black Beans in the tortilla, followed by 2 to 3 pieces of fish, 1 T of each salsa, and 1 T of sour cream; top with cabbage if desired. Place 2 tortillas on each serving plate; garnish with additional salsas and cilantro.

Serves 6.

Calories	%Fat	Fat (g)	Saturated Fat (g)	Cholesterol (mg)	Sodium (mg)	Carbohydrate (g)	Protein (g)	Fiber (g)
420	10	5	0.9	105	311	45	49	9

Exchanges: Starch 2-1/2, Vegetable 2, Low-fat protein 5

'21' Trim Sole

Michael Lomonaco

2 C fish stock
1/2 C white wine
4 fillets of sole (grey, lemon, or Dover)
4 beefsteak tomatoes, halved, peeled, and pulp scooped out
1 C diced scallions
1/2 C roasted red and yellow bell pepper, julienned
1/4 C chopped fresh herbs (thyme, oregano, tarragon, parsley)

Bring fish stock and white wine to a boil. Set aside.

Cut fish fillets into 2 pieces, following the center bone line. Roll each half into a tight roll, skin side in. Poach fillets in the stock and wine mixture for 8 minutes.

Dry-roast tomato halves in an oven at high heat for 15 minutes. Arrange poached fish fillets on the tomato halves and bake for 3 minutes.

Poach scallions in the stock and wine mixture until completely tender. Add julienned pepper and herbs; cook until liquid is reduced to 1/2 cup.

Serve 2 tomato halves and sole per person. Spoon vegetable fricassee and stock sauce over each serving.

Serves 4.

Calories	%Fat	Fat (g)	Saturated Fat (g)	Cholesterol (mg)	Sodium (mg)	Carbohydrate (g)	Protein (g)	Fiber (g)
127	13	2	0.4	39	103	11	17	3

Exchanges: Vegetable 2, Low-fat protein 2

Fillet of Sole in Parchment

4 sole fillets (4 oz each)
2 tomatoes, chopped
1 small onion, thinly sliced
2 T chopped celery leaves
2 T dry white wine
2 T lemon juice
Freshly ground black pepper to taste
4 thin slices of lemon
1 T sesame seeds
1 tsp minced parsley

Cut 4 pieces of parchment paper twice the size of each fillet; trim into heart shapes. Place 1 fillet on each piece of parchment; top each with equal amounts of tomato, onion, and celery leaves. Mix wine with lemon juice and pour 1 T over each fillet; season with pepper and top with lemon slices, sesame seeds, and parsley. Fold edges of parchment together to make sealed casings. Bake at 400° for 15 to 20 minutes. Serve fish in the parchment casings immediately, before they deflate.

Serves 4.

Calories	%Fat	Fat (g)	Saturated Fat (g)	Cholesterol (mg)	Sodium (mg)	Carbohydrate (g)	Protein (g)	Fiber (g)
133	19	3	0.5	53	93	7	21	2

Exchanges: Vegetable 1, Low-fat protein 3

Cooking in Parchment

Food that is encased in parchment cooks quickly and evenly, while marinating in its own juices. This retains the full flavor and moisture of the food as well as most of the nutrients. Presentation of the balloon-like parchment casings can be dramatic. This is a lovely technique for a special dinner, yet it is simple enough for everyday use.

Parchment paper, although thin, is not fragile. Use 12 × 16-inch rectangles of paper. Fold each in half vertically and cut the edges in a curve; unfolded, the paper will look a little like a heart. Lightly coat one side of the parchment with cooking spray to prevent leaking. Place the food and all seasonings on one half of the unfolded parchment. Do not overfill it; excess paper is needed for folding the casing closed and still allow room for expansion. Fold the other half of the heart over the top of the food.

Fold the edges of the parchment casing securely so that moisture will not escape during cooking. Beginning at the crease near the top of the heart, make short, diagonal, pleat-like folds along the edges, overlapping them as you move around the edge. Each new fold will hold the previous fold in place. At the end, fold the protruding end (the base of the heart) several times to keep it secure.

As the air inside the casing grows hot during cooking, the paper inflates like a balloon and the food gently steams. The paper may brown lightly and prettily. The inflated casings should be transferred to serving plates and served immediately, before they deflate. Guests cut open their own parchment casings to reveal the moist and tender contents. The food can be transferred to the plate or left in the paper.

Cooking in parchment is an easy technique for the busy cook who wants to eliminate last-minute preparation. The parchment casings can be filled and stored in the refrigerator for several hours before cooking. They can also be frozen for several days; thaw for 30 to 60 minutes before placing them in a preheated oven.

Baked Sole Roulades

Karla A. Graves

3 bunches fresh spinach, cleaned, cooked, cooled, chopped
2 oz fresh basil, chopped (about 1 C)
1 oz fresh dill, chopped (about 1/2 C)
3 cloves garlic, minced
1 T olive oil
3 lb fresh sole fillets
4 to 6 roasted red bell peppers (page 183)
Freshly ground black pepper
1 lemon

To make the filling, mix spinach, basil, dill, garlic, and oil; set aside. Lay out fillets, creating six pieces about 3 × 14 inches. You may have to piece the fish together by overlapping. Spread one-sixth of the spinach filling over each piece. Place the bell peppers on the filling, piecing the peppers together as needed. Beginning at the narrow end, roll the fillets gently into a spiral. Set each roll in a baking pan, seam side down. Season with black pepper and lemon juice. Bake at 425° for 10 to 15 minutes. Serve immediately.

Serves 6.

Suggestions
- For a fancier presentation, slice each spiral into 3 pieces and fan them on the serving plate; garnish with a sprig of fresh basil and fresh dill.
- Serve with lemon rice.

Calories	%Fat	Fat (g)	Saturated Fat (g)	Cholesterol (mg)	Sodium (mg)	Carbohydrate (g)	Protein (g)	Fiber (g)
263	18	5	1.0	106	270	12	43	4

Exchanges: Vegetable 2, Low-fat protein 5

Sauté of Northwest Sturgeon & Fresh Vegetable Gazpacho

Mark Gould

For the Sturgeon
4 sturgeon fillets (5-1/2 oz each)
l/2 T fresh thyme, finely chopped
Ground pepper

For the Gazpacho Vegetables
2 T finely diced eggplant, peeled
2 T finely diced zucchini
2 T finely diced yellow squash
2 T finely diced green bell pepper
2 T finely diced red bell pepper
2 T finely diced yellow bell pepper
2 T finely diced red onion
1/4 tsp minced garlic
4 tsp finely chopped sweet herbs (basil, parsley, chives, chervil, tarragon); reserve stems

For the Gazpacho Sauce
1 lb plum tomatoes, stems removed and roughly chopped
2 T shallots, minced
1 tsp garlic, minced
Herb stems (reserved from sweet herbs)

All of the things I really like to do are either immoral, illegal, or fattening.

Alexander Woollcott

To Beer-Bellies

We do not try to get you to change your eating style overnight. We know you have grown accustomed to the way you eat, and so we are happy if a person begins slowly to reduce the harmful foods in his or her diet. We never send a person home telling him or her to "go on a diet." Rather we ask people to adjust their present diets so that they eventually fall closer into line with diets that are safe and sound. For example, if you have been drinking a six-pack of beer each night for the last ten years and are today grossly overweight, our advice is not to stop drinking beer altogether. We will be happy if you reduce your nightly binge to four cans instead of six. Later, we will ask you to drop to three. Our belief is

2 oz white wine
1 C low-sodium tomato juice
Juice of 1 lemon
Ground pepper
1 tsp olive oil

The Sauce: In a saucepan, lightly sauté the shallots until they are translucent. Add the tomatoes and continue to cook until the tomatoes begin to release their juices. Add the white wine, garlic, tomato juice, and herb stems; cook slowly until reduced by half, stirring frequently to avoid scorching.

After the tomato mixture has reduced, remove the herb stems and liquefy the tomatoes in a blender or food processor. Season with pepper and the lemon juice; blend again for 30 seconds. With the machine running, add olive oil until it is all incorporated. Pass the sauce through a fine sieve; taste and adjust the seasoning if necessary.

The Fish: Season the portioned fillets well with the pepper. In a large frying pan over high heat, sauté the fillets skin-side-up for about 60 seconds. Turn over and season with thyme. Continue to sauté on the range or finish cooking in a moderate oven. Drain on paper towels and keep warm.

The Gazpacho Vegetables: In a small frying pan over high heat, cook all of the finely diced vegetables, tossing frequently so as not to scorch the vegetables, about 30 seconds. Add the garlic and sweet herbs; season with pepper to taste. Vegetables should still be crisp and colorful.

To Serve: Ladle 2 oz of the sauce on four warm serving plates (the plates and fish will warm the sauce.) Place the fish in the middle of each plate, thyme-seasoned side up. Spoon 4 piles of the vegetables around the fish and serve.
   Serves 4.

Calories	%Fat	Fat (g)	Saturated Fat (g)	Cholesterol (mg)	Sodium (mg)	Carbohydrate (g)	Protein (g)	Fiber (g)
232	25	6	1.2	81	56	12	31	3

Exchanges: Vegetable 2, Low-fat protein 4

Grilled Swordfish on Rutabaga & Pepper Relish

Sanford D'Amato

4 swordfish fillets (6 oz each; 1-inch thick)
Juice of 3 lemons
2 T olive oil
20 grinds fresh ground pepper
1-1/2 tsp cumin
1/8 tsp cayenne
Rutabaga & Pepper Relish (page 454)
Marinated Potatoes (page 234)

Cilantro Oil
1 bunch cilantro (fresh coriander)
1/2 clove garlic, peeled
2 T olive oil
1/4 C water
10 grinds freshly ground black pepper

Mix lemon juice, oil, pepper, cumin, and cayenne pepper. Add swordfish and marinate for 4 hours, turning periodically.

To make Cilantro Oil, pick leaves from coriander; reserve about one-fourth bunch for garnish. Place remaining leaves in a blender with garlic, oil, water,

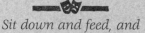

and pepper; purée completely. Store in a plastic squeeze bottle until needed. Shake well before using.

Grill or sauté swordfish in a very hot pan for about 3 to 4 minutes on each side (for a l-inch thick piece). The swordfish should be cooked to medium stage, just warm in the center.

Place swordfish on a bed of Rutabaga & Pepper Relish, garnish with Marinated Potatoes, and squirt Cilantro Oil around the fish. Place cilantro leaves over and around the fish.

Serves 4.

Suggestion

- Use Cilantro Oil in place of regular oil for cooking or salads. Like any oil, it should be used sparingly.

Calories	%Fat	Fat (g)	Saturated Fat (g)	Cholesterol (mg)	Sodium (mg)	Carbohydrate (g)	Protein (g)	Fiber (g)
232	45	12	1.8	80	43	2	29	0

Exchanges: Low-fat protein 4

Seared Rare Peppered Tuna & Vietnamese Dipping Sauce

Patrick O'Connell

8 pieces (1 oz each) tuna, 3/4- to 1-inch thick
Freshly ground black pepper
Vietnamese Dipping Sauce (page 453)

Season the tuna with cracked black pepper. In a hot, smoking skillet, sear the tuna very quickly until it is charred on all sides but is rare in the center (or cooked to your desired preference.) Serve as an appetizer with a fine julienne of peppers, leeks, and carrots and Vietnamese Dipping Sauce.
Serves 4.

Calories	%Fat	Fat (g)	Saturated Fat (g)	Cholesterol (mg)	Sodium (mg)	Carbohydrate (g)	Protein (g)	Fiber (g)
69	26	2	0.4	34	16	0	12	0

Exchanges: Low-fat protein 2

rilled Tuna Sauce Vierge

Michael Hutchings

2 T olive oil
15 twists freshly ground white pepper
1/4 C basil trimmings
3 garlic cloves, crushed
8 tuna steaks (6 oz each), skins removed
Sauce Vierge (page 452)

Mix olive oil, pepper, basil, and garlic. Pour over tuna and marinate for 2 hours or more. Grill the tuna steaks for 2 to 3 minutes on each side, or until firm to the touch. Warm the Sauce Vierge; spoon equal amounts on 8 dinner plates. Top with fish.

Serves 8.

Suggestions
• Garnish with a sprig of basil and straw potatoes.
• If the budget allows, a julienne of first-quality truffles is a wonderful enhancement.

Calories	%Fat	Fat (g)	Saturated Fat (g)	Cholesterol (mg)	Sodium (mg)	Carbohydrate (g)	Protein (g)	Fiber (g)
247	38	11	1.7	89	51	4	33	1

Exchanges: Vegetable 1, Low-fat protein 4

# ennel-Crusted Tuna with Crisp Vegetables

Rick Moonen

4 T fennel seeds
3 tsp coriander seeds
2 T white peppercorns
4 egg whites
8 tuna steaks (6 oz each)
3 C shredded cabbage
1 C sliced snow peas
1/2 C scallions
1/2 C julienned red pepper
1/2 C zig-zag cut carrots
2 T sesame seeds, toasted
Orange, Soy, & Sherry Vinaigrette (page 479)

Grind the fennel, coriander, and peppercorns in a coffee grinder. Spread ground spices on a plate. In a container large enough to hold a tuna steak, lightly beat the egg whites. Dip each tuna steak in egg white and then coat with the spice mix. Sauté the tuna in cooking spray in a hot pan until rare, about 2 minutes on each side. Sauté the vegetables quickly, season with pepper, and toss with sesame seeds.

Types of Fish

- *Ahi:* The Hawaiian name for yellowfin tuna.
- *Cod:* Includes haddock, pollock, hake, whiting, hoki, and scrod. Tender, flaky, white flesh; bland; very lean.
- *Grouper:* See Sea bass.
- *Halibut:* Firm, snow-white meat; mild, sweet; lean.
- *Mahi mahi:* Also called *dorado* or *dolphin* (not related to the mammal called *dolphin*). Tender, firm, moist flesh; sweet; very lean.
- *Monkfish:* Also called *goosefish* or *poor man's lobster;* highly prized in Europe. Firm, chewy flesh similar to lobster; sweet; very lean.
- *Opakapaka:* The Hawaiian name for a pink snapper; pronounced *oh-pock-ah-pock-ah.*
- *Orange roughy:* Tender but firm, pearly white flesh; mild crablike flavor; oily.
- *Pike:* Also called *pickerel.* Flaky; mild; lean.
- *Redfish:* Any of several reddish fishes, usually members of the drum or rockfish families. Tender but firm, moist, flaky flesh; mild; lean.

- *Salmon:* Includes king (Chinook), silver, pink, sockeye, chum, Norwegian, and Nova Scotian. Pink, tender, firm meat; mild but very flavorful; oily.
- *Sea bass:* Includes black sea bass, red and black groupers, and others wrongly labeled as sea bass. Texture varies from flaky to extra firm; mild; lean.
- *Snapper:* True red snapper is scarce; other species often sold as red snapper. Firm, moist, white meat; delicate but distinctive sweet flavor; lean.
- *Sole:* Includes Dover, gray, and lemon sole. Tender but firm, white meat; delicate, sweet or nutlike flavor; very lean.
- *Sturgeon:* Prized for its roe, the source of caviar. Firm, meaty; mild, distinctive flavor; moderately oily.
- *Swordfish:* Firm; mild but rich flavor; oily.
- *Tuna:* Includes albacore, bluefin, yellowfin, and bigeye. Fresh tuna is becoming widely available. Firm and meaty; flavorful but not strong.
- *Whitefish:* Tender, flaky, snow-white flesh; rich, mild; oily.

For each serving, coat a warm plate with Orange, Soy, & Sherry Vinaigrette. Arrange vegetables in the center of the plate. Slice the tuna and place it on top of the vegetables.

Serves 8.

Suggestion

- Garnish with crisp potatoes and chive lengths.

Calories	%Fat	Fat (g)	Saturated Fat (g)	Cholesterol (mg)	Sodium (mg)	Carbohydrate (g)	Protein (g)	Fiber (g)
386	35	15	2.3	89	703	20	39	3

Exchanges: Vegetable 4, Low-fat protein 4-1/2, Fat 1

Grilled Tuna with Herbs & Saffron Onions

Elizabeth Terry

4 medium stuffed olives, minced
1 T capers, drained and minced
3 anchovies, minced
1/4 C fresh chives, minced
1/2 C fresh parsley, minced
1 tsp cumin seeds
2 T olive oil
4 fresh tuna fillets (6 oz each)
1 medium onion, peeled and julienned
1/4 tsp saffron
1 tsp olive oil
2 tomatoes, seeded, julienned
1 cucumber, peeled, seeded, julienned
1 can (15 oz) black beans
3 T dry sherry

Combine the olives, capers, anchovies, chives, parsley, cumin seeds, and 2 T olive oil. Roll the edge of each tuna fillet in this herb-and-olive mixture. The tuna will have a lovely green band of flavor around it. Set the fillets aside, covered, in the refrigerator for 30 minutes (or up to 4 hours) so the tuna will ab-

**Symbolic Meanings
of Herbs & Spices**

Allspice
Compassion

Angelica
Inspiration

Basil
Hatred

Bay Leaf
I change but in death

Camomile
Energy in adversity

Cloves
Dignity

Coriander
Concealed merit

Lavender
Distrust

Liquorice, wild
I declare against you

Marjoram
Blushes

Mint
Virtue

Mustard seed
Indifference

Parsley
Festivity

Peppermint
Warmth of feeling

Rosemary
Remembrance

Saffron, crocus
Mirth

Sage
Domestic virtue

Spearmint
Warmth of sentiment

Sweet basil
Good wishes

Thyme
Activity

Anonymous
The Language of Flowers, 1913

sorb the flavors. Light the grill.

In a small sauté pan, combine 1 tsp olive oil and the saffron. Heat over a low flame. When the saffron begins to perfume the air (about 1 minute), add the onion and shake and stir the pan to cook the onions. The onions will turn a lovely yellow color. Do not brown, just soften the onion (about 4 minutes). Spread the saffron onions on a plate to cool; combine with the tomato and cucumber and set aside. Stir the sherry into the black beans. Set aside. The vegetables will be served at room temperature, although the beans may be heated if desired.

Grill or sauté the tuna for about 3 minutes per side. Spoon black beans into the centers of 4 dinner plates. Ring the beans with the saffron onion mixture. Place a tuna fillet on top of the black beans. Serve.

Serves 4.

Calories	%Fat	Fat (g)	Saturated Fat (g)	Cholesterol (mg)	Sodium (mg)	Carbohydrate (g)	Protein (g)	Fiber (g)
422	32	15	2.4	91	445	29	41	7

Exchanges: Starch 1-1/2, Vegetable 2, Low-fat protein 4-1/2, Fat 1/2

Chargrilled Tuna, Toasted Corn Vinaigrette, & Avocado Salad

Todd English

6 tuna steaks (3 oz each), cubed
Zest of 1 lemon
1 T chopped fresh rosemary
2 T chopped fresh basil
2 cloves garlic, finely chopped
1 tsp finely chopped fresh ginger
3/4 medium avocado
1 lb mesclun greens or mixed lettuces
Toasted Corn Vinaigrette (page 473)

Combine all ingredients except avocado, greens, and vinaigrette and toss until tuna is well coated. Marinate for at least 1 hour.

Season tuna on both sides with pepper. Place tuna on a preheated grill and char on all sides. Remove from heat and keep warm.

Slice avocado into thirds and fan by slicing diagonally across. Place a handful of greens in the center of each serving plate. Top with avocado. Place 2 pieces of tuna on top of each salad. Spoon 1 T of Toasted Corn Vinaigrette over each serving. Garnish with cilantro and serve immediately.

Serves 3.

Calories	%Fat	Fat (g)	Saturated Fat (g)	Cholesterol (mg)	Sodium (mg)	Carbohydrate (g)	Protein (g)	Fiber (g)
359	50	20	3.3	89	65	11	35	5

Exchanges: Vegetable 2, Low-fat protein 4, Fat 2

**Nonfat
Cooking Methods**
Baking
Broiling
Grilling
Poaching
Roasting
Steaming
Stir-frying

How to Pan-Steam Fish

Place the fish steaks in a skillet; sprinkle with pepper. Press a piece of waxed paper directly onto the fish. Cook, tightly covered, over medium heat for 10 minutes, or until the fish is opaque and firm to the touch. Season with lemon or orange, freshly chopped dill, parsley, sage, or other herbs to taste.

Grilled Ahi Tuna

Sean Kavanaugh

12 pieces (2 oz each) ahi tuna
1 zucchini
1 yellow squash
1 small eggplant
1 red bell pepper
1 yellow bell pepper
1 green bell pepper
4 Roma tomatoes
1 T basil
1 tsp each oregano, thyme, chives
1 T garlic
2 T balsamic vinegar
1 T olive oil

Season all vegetables except tomatoes, spray with cooking spray, and grill. Cube all vegetables, including tomatoes. Chop all herbs and toss with balsamic vinegar and olive oil. Drizzle dressing over roasted vegetables.

Place tuna on a hot grill for about 2 minutes on each side (turning tuna to burn in × marks); cook to medium rare to medium. Serve with roasted vegetables, Rosemary Polenta (page 78), and Mesquite-Smoked Tomato Sauce (page 445).

Serves 4.

Calories	%Fat	Fat (g)	Saturated Fat (g)	Cholesterol (mg)	Sodium (mg)	Carbohydrate (g)	Protein (g)	Fiber (g)
293	30	10	1.7	101	55	13	38	3

Exchanges: Vegetable 3, Low-fat protein 5

Grilled Tuna Steak, Roast Hubbard & Oyster Sauce, & Hen of the Woods Mushrooms

P. Quint Smith

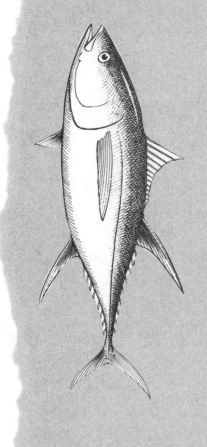

1 lb hen of the woods mushrooms
1 pt Brussels sprouts, blanched
1 lb wax beans, blanched
1 tsp butter
24 shucked oysters, with juice
1 qt Roast Hubbard Squash Sauce (page 449)
6 tuna steaks (6 to 8 oz each)
Whole flat parsley leaves, for garnish

Sauté the mushrooms in olive oil at high heat; do not sweat them (which would release the moisture and its flavor). Thoroughly heat sprouts, beans, mushrooms, butter, and a small amount of water in a sauté pan. Adjust seasoning.

Heat oysters with juice just until oysters begin to plump. Add Roast Hubbard Squash Sauce; quickly bring mixture to a boil and remove from heat. Do not overcook the oysters, or they will shrink to little bits and be chewy.

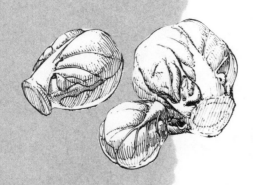

Grill or sauté the tuna steaks to the desired doneness (slightly rare is best). Have all of the above hot and ready to serve at the same time.

Place 4 oysters in the "corners" of each plate (or use a square plate). Pour 1/2 C Roast Hubbard Squash Sauce in the center of each plate and allow it to spread out. Place the vegetables and mushrooms in the center of the plate and top with a tuna steak. Garnish with flat parsley leaves. Serve immediately.

Serves 6.

Suggestion

- Any heavy-stemmed mushroom that can be eaten whole may be substituted for the hen of the woods mushrooms.

Calories	%Fat	Fat (g)	Saturated Fat (g)	Cholesterol (mg)	Sodium (mg)	Carbohydrate (g)	Protein (g)	Fiber (g)
388	25	11	2.8	139	148	29	46	10

Exchanges: Starch 1, Vegetable 3, Low-fat protein 5

Tuna Tacos

1 small red onion, diced
1 to 2 cloves garlic, minced
2 cans (6-1/8 oz) solid white tuna packed in water, rinsed
1/2 C salsa
1 T minced parsley or cilantro
1 tomato, diced
1/2 C grated low-fat cheddar cheese
1/2 C shredded romaine lettuce
6 whole-wheat tortillas

Sauté onions and garlic. Add tuna, salsa, and parsley; cook until warm. Warm tortillas in a nonstick pan until soft, about 15 seconds. Top each tortilla with tuna mixture, tomato, cheese, and lettuce. Fold the tortilla in half to make a soft taco. Serve immediately.
Serves 6.

Suggestion
• Corn tortillas can be substituted for the whole-wheat tortillas.

Calories	%Fat	Fat (g)	Saturated Fat (g)	Cholesterol (mg)	Sodium (mg)	Carbohydrate (g)	Protein (g)	Fiber (g)
295	24	8	1.6	15	330	31	25	4

Exchanges: Starch 2, Low-fat protein 1, Fat 1

Savory Whitefish

1/4 C Jack Daniel's Old No. 7 Mustard
1 T low-sodium soy sauce
1 T grapefruit juice
1/2 C dry white wine
1-1/2 lb whitefish fillets
12 very thin slices of lemon
6 parsley sprigs
2 T sesame seeds, toasted

Combine mustard, soy sauce, grapefruit juice, and wine. Pour over fish and marinate, covered, in the refrigerator for 3 to 4 hours. Arrange fillets on a broiler pan. Broil for about 10 minutes, turning once during cooking. Transfer fish to a serving platter. Garnish with lemon slices, parsley, and sesame seeds.
Serves 6.

Suggestion
• A spicy or mild brown mustard may be substituted for the Jack Daniel's brand.

Calories	%Fat	Fat (g)	Saturated Fat (g)	Cholesterol (mg)	Sodium (mg)	Carbohydrate (g)	Protein (g)	Fiber (g)
162	32	6	1.0	66	133	2	25	1

Exchanges: Low-fat protein 3

# Chilled Whitefish & Pike Dumplings with Sorrel

Michael Roberts

1/2 C finely crushed unsalted crackers
1 lb whitefish
1 lb pike
2 onions
2 carrots
1 egg
2 egg whites
1/2 tsp ground white pepper
4 C fresh or canned low-sodium chicken stock
1 onion, finely diced
1 T minced garlic
3 T malt vinegar
1 C sorrel leaves, tightly packed, center ribs and stems removed
8 small new potatoes
1/2 C plain nonfat yogurt

Grind whitefish, pike, carrots, and 1 onion together in a meat grinder and place in a mixing bowl. Add cracker meal, eggs, half the pepper, and 1/2 C chicken broth. Mix well, cover, and refrigerate for 30 minutes.

Meanwhile, cook the second chopped onion and garlic in cooking spray until

Sorrel

Also called *sour grass*, sorrel has a sharp, sour, lemony taste. It has deep green, arrow-shaped leaves that are rich in vitamin A as well as other vitamins and minerals. Sorrel can be stored in the refrigerator for two or three days, but it is best when used immediately. Remove the stems before using.

Sorrel is used as a vegetable or an herb. It is a good replacement for salt. It is very good with fish, especially salmon and trout. It can be used in place of spinach, although sorrel has a stronger flavor. It is good raw in salads mixed with mild greens; the young, tender sorrel leaves are best. Sorrel also makes a nice addition to poultry stuffing, and it is excellent puréed with soups, sauces, and salad dressings.

Hot & Cold Foods

Serve hot food on hot plates and cold food on chilled plates. Warm dinner and soup plates in the oven on very low heat or in a dishwasher on the dry cycle. Chill salad plates and dessert dishes in the refrigerator.

the onion is soft, about 5 minutes. Add malt vinegar and remaining chicken stock; increase heat to high, bring to a boil, then reduce heat to low. Roughly chop the sorrel leaves and add them to the soup.

Wet your hands with water and form 12 egg-shaped dumplings with the chilled fish mixture. When all the dumplings are formed, carefully drop them into the soup, add the potatoes, replace the cover, and simmer 20 minutes.

Remove the pot from the heat and transfer the dumplings to a large bowl or plastic container. Place yogurt in a small bowl, thin it with 1/2 C of hot soup, and return it to the soup. Pour the soup over the dumplings and chill completely, at least 3 hours.

Just before serving, remove the dumplings from the soup and divide among 4 soup bowls. Spoon the chilled soup around the dumplings and serve.

Serves 4.

Suggestion

• Use unsalted Saltines, Carr's water biscuits, or Matzoh Meal for crushed crackers.

Calories	%Fat	Fat (g)	Saturated Fat (g)	Cholesterol (mg)	Sodium (mg)	Carbohydrate (g)	Protein (g)	Fiber (g)
467	17	9	2.3	181	388	38	57	4

Exchanges: Starch 1-1/2, Vegetable 3, Low-fat protein 7

Louisiana Crawfish with Stir-Fried Vegetables

James P. Shannon

When we're dressing to go to someone's house for dinner, Alice often tries to persuade me that there are ways of showing appreciation to the hostess other than having thirds.

Calvin Trillin
Alice, Let's Eat

4 oz crawfish tails, meat only
1/2 oz turnip, julienned (about 2 T)
1/2 oz carrot, julienned (about 2 T)
1/2 oz red pepper, julienned (about 2 T)
1/2 oz snow peas, julienned (about 2 T)
2 oz crawfish juice or fish stock
1/2 green onion, chopped
Cayenne pepper to taste
4 whole crawfish, boiled

Heat skillet over medium heat. Sauté crawfish tails in cooking spray for about one minute. Add all of the julienned vegetables and sauté for an additional 45 seconds. Add crawfish juice or fish stock and cook until reduced by half. Add green onions and season to taste with cayenne pepper. Serve with whole crawfish.

Serves 1.

Calories	%Fat	Fat (g)	Saturated Fat (g)	Cholesterol (mg)	Sodium (mg)	Carbohydrate (g)	Protein (g)	Fiber (g)
205	10	2	0.4	288	128	4	40	1

Exchanges: Vegetable 1, Low-fat protein 5

Radicchio

Imported from Italy, radicchio looks like tiny purple cabbage. It can be as small as a golf ball or as large as a grapefruit. It has stiff, crisp, reddish-purple and ivory leaves and a pungent, spicy, or bitter flavor. It can be stored in the refrigerator for up to a week.

Radicchio can be mixed with mild greens for salads and seasoned with balsamic vinegar. It can also be grilled like peppers and served with pasta, rice, or warm salad.

Chilled Spiny Lobster Medallions & Papaya

Greg Paulson, CEC

4 oz Hawaiian spiny lobster tail
1/2 pt court bouillon
1 oz radicchio lettuce, small leaves
1/2 papaya, peeled and cut into thin wedges
1 nasturtium flower, for garnish
Ti leaf, cut in diamond shapes for garnish
1 T Lime-Papaya Seed Vinaigrette (page 478)

Poach spiny lobster tails in simmering court bouillon for 10 to 12 minutes, or until slightly undercooked. Chill in stock for 2 hours.

To prepare, remove lobster tail from shell and trim, slice into medallions. Place three small outer leaves of radicchio lettuce on plate. Place lobster medallions on top of lettuce. Arrange papaya wedges between medallions. Pour Lime-Papaya Seed Vinaigrette in center of plate. Garnish plate with an edible nasturtium flower and ti leaf diamonds.

Serves 1.

Calories	%Fat	Fat (g)	Saturated Fat (g)	Cholesterol (mg)	Sodium (mg)	Carbohydrate (g)	Protein (g)	Fiber (g)
130	34	5	1.3	19	110	16	7	4

Exchanges: Fruit 1, Medium-fat protein 1

Chilled Spiny Lobster Medallions & Baby Artichoke

Greg Paulson, CEC

4 oz Hawaiian spiny lobster tail
1 pt court bouillon
2 baby artichokes
1 T Lemon-Thyme Vinaigrette (page 476)
1 lemon, cut into half-circle slices
1 nasturtium flower, to garnish
1 thyme sprig
Zest of 1 lemon

Poach spiny lobster tail in simmering court bouillon for 10 to 12 minutes until slightly undercooked. Remove from stock (discard stock) and chill; cut lobster into medallions. Poach artichoke in boiling water for 12 to 14 minutes. Remove and immediately submerge in ice water; let cool completely.

To prepare, dip each artichoke leaf halfway into Lemon-Thyme Vinaigrette and place on plate. Continue to do this until you complete a circle of artichoke leaves. Place a clean artichoke bottom in the center of the plate. Place lobster medallions on top of the artichoke bottom. Garnish with lemon slices, nasturtium, thyme sprig, and lemon zest.

Serves 1.

Calories	%Fat	Fat (g)	Saturated Fat (g)	Cholesterol (mg)	Sodium (mg)	Carbohydrate (g)	Protein (g)	Fiber (g)
213	35	8	1.3	19	296	29	13	8

Exchanges: Fruit 1/2, Vegetable 4, Low-fat protein 1, Fat 1

Edible Flowers

Flowers are a delightful garnish for drinks, salads, soups, and desserts. Flower salads make a lovely bridal shower or spring luncheon.

Not all flowers are edible. Flowers should not be eaten if they have been treated with pesticides, which includes those from a florist. Serve flowers only if you are certain they are safe. Buy them in a specialty or gourmet market, or grow them in a home garden. Refrigerate the blossoms, tightly wrapped, for up to a week.

- *Chive blossoms:* Mild, sweet onion flavor.
- *Nasturtiums:* Nice peppery flavor.
- *Pansies, violas:* Light grape flavor.
- *Roses:* Sweet.
- *Blossoms:* Almond, apple, chamomile, lavender, lemon, mimosa, orange, peach, plum, squash.
- *Other flowers:* Chrysanthemums, daisies, geraniums, jasmine, lilacs, marigolds.

ineapple-Ginger Shrimp

1/2 C unsweetened pineapple juice
2 T low-sodium soy sauce
1/2 tsp grated fresh ginger
2 tsp cornstarch mixed with 2 T cold water
1 lb shrimp, peeled and deveined
1 C unsweetened pineapple chunks, drained
1 C snow peas, lightly steamed
1/2 C thinly sliced star fruit
2 scallions, chopped
2 C hot cooked brown rice
1 kiwi, peeled and thinly sliced
1 T finely julienned crystallized ginger

Bring pineapple juice, soy sauce, and ginger to a boil; reduce heat. Add cornstarch mixture to pineapple juice and cook, stirring constantly, until thickened and clear. Add shrimp, pineapple, snow peas, star fruit, and scallions. Heat, stirring frequently, for about 5 minutes or until shrimp is opaque. Do not overcook. Serve over rice, garnished with kiwi slices and crystallized ginger.
Serves 4.

Suggestion
• Cubed chicken or mild fish may be substituted for the shrimp.

Calories	%Fat	Fat (g)	Saturated Fat (g)	Cholesterol (mg)	Sodium (mg)	Carbohydrate (g)	Protein (g)	Fiber (g)
252	6	2	0.4	107	431	43	16	4

Exchanges: Starch 2, Fruit 1, Low-fat protein 2

Citrus-Crusted Shrimp with Ginger & Star Fruit

Allen Susser

12 large shrimp
2 lemons, zested, juiced
2 limes, zested, juiced
1 jalapeño pepper, diced
1 T white peppercorns, crushed
2 T brown sugar
1 tsp olive oil
1 tsp sliced fresh ginger
2 star fruit, sliced crosswise
2 oz chardonnay

Peel shrimp and butterfly them by cutting lengthwise, so each shrimp opens like a book and lies almost flat. Don't cut them in half. Combine lime and lemon zest, jalapeño, and peppercorns; set aside. Combine lemon and lime juice with brown sugar in a small saucepan and simmer until 3 T are left. Add the the zest mixture. Cook for 1 more minute and remove from heat. Moisten with olive oil and let cool. Press the mixture onto both sides of the butterflied shrimp, then sear each shrimp in olive oil. Cook for 1 minute; add star fruit and ginger. Add the chardonnay and swirl it around in the pan for a few seconds. Serve immediately.

Serves 4.

Calories	%Fat	Fat (g)	Saturated Fat (g)	Cholesterol (mg)	Sodium (mg)	Carbohydrate (g)	Protein (g)	Fiber (g)
98	16	2	0.2	40	326	15	5	1

Exchanges: Fruit 1, Low-fat protein 1/2

Star Fruit

Also called *carambola*, star fruit is three to five inches long and has five or six prominent ribs. Cutting it in slices crossways yields star-shaped pieces. It is crisp and juicy, with a plum-grape-apple-citrus flavor. When it is fully ripe, star fruit smells flowery and is glossy yellow.

There are 20 varieties of star fruit. It can be sweet or tart, but it is never too tart to be eaten raw. In general, the richer the yellow, the more tart the fruit, and the broader the ribs, the sweeter the fruit.

It is an excellent source of vitamin C, and it is very low in calories (about 50 per 4-inch fruit). It is a refreshing snack following an exercise session.

Store star fruit at room temperature for two to three days. Fully ripe fruit can be refrigerated for seven to ten days. It cannot be frozen successfully. Star fruit does not have to be peeled, but the brown fibers along the tops of ribs should be trimmed. Raw slices don't turn brown.

Use star fruit as a garnish in place of lemon, lime, or orange slices. Lightly sautéed star fruit is a nice garnish for fish or chicken. It is also good in fruit or vegetable salads, sorbets, jams, or jellies.

Grilled Gulf Shrimp with Warm Spinach

James P. Shannon

8 Gulf shrimp, size 16–20
2 tsp Creole seafood seasoning
3 oz spinach leaves, cleaned
1 T water
1 shallot or small onion, minced
1 lemon
1 lime
White pepper to taste
1/2 tsp sweet butter

Thread shrimp on a bamboo or metal skewer; sprinkle with Creole seasoning and set aside. In a small skillet over medium heat, sauté the shallot in cooking spray until clear. Add spinach and water; cook until spinach is done. Season with pepper. Heat a medium skillet or grill until hot; grill the shrimp until cooked on both sides. Remove shrimp from heat; add citrus juices and cook until reduced by half; stir in butter until melted. Season with pepper. Serve shrimp with sauce on the side.

Serves 1.

Calories	%Fat	Fat (g)	Saturated Fat (g)	Cholesterol (mg)	Sodium (mg)	Carbohydrate (g)	Protein (g)	Fiber (g)
164	19	3	1.5	176	237	17	22	5

Exchanges: Fruit 1, Low-fat protein 3

# Shrimp with Black Beans

Shellfish

Because they are high in
omega-3 fatty acids but low
in saturated fat and calories,
shellfish—including shrimp
and lobster, even though
they are relatively high in
cholesterol—are acceptable.

Diethrich and Cohan
Women and Heart Disease

2 lb medium shrimp, peeled and deveined
4 cloves garlic, minced
Red chili powder to taste
4 C cooked black beans, rinsed and drained
2 medium red bell pepper, seeded and finely diced
8 scallions, thinly sliced
4 medium oranges, peeled and sectioned
2 T fresh ginger root, peeled and finely chopped
Citrus Vinaigrette (page 472)

Sauté the shrimp, garlic, and chili powder over medium-high heat for 2 to 3 minutes, or until the shrimp is opaque. Let the shrimp cool for 15 minutes. Toss the shrimp with the black beans, bell pepper, scallions, oranges, and ginger. Serve with Citrus Vinaigrette on the side.

Serves 12.

Suggestion
• Serve over hot rice.

Calories	%Fat	Fat (g)	Saturated Fat (g)	Cholesterol (mg)	Sodium (mg)	Carbohydrate (g)	Protein (g)	Fiber (g)
154	5	1	0.2	71	89	23	14	6

Exchanges: Starch 1, Fruit 1/2, Low-fat protein 2

Types of Shellfish

- *Clams:* Chewy texture; sweet.
- *Crab:* Includes blue, Dungeness, king, and snow. Tender, flaky meat; delicate, sweet.
- *Crawfish:* Also called *crayfish* or *crawdads.* Resemble tiny lobsters. Sweet flavor somewhat like lobster, but not as rich or firm; can be substituted for lobster.
- *Lobster:* Includes large, clawed American or Maine lobsters as well as clawless spiny lobsters (also called *rock lobster* or *langouste*); spiny lobster most commonly sold as frozen rock lobster tails. Tender flesh; sweet, mild.
- *Oysters:* Taste and texture vary—bland and tender ranging to salty and firm.
- *Scallops:* Includes sea, bay or Cape Cod, and calico. Tender but firm texture; mild, sweet.
- *Shrimp:* Most popular shellfish. Cold-water species sold by the pound; warm-water species sold by size. Moderately firm; mild, sweet.
- *Spiny lobster:* See Lobster.

Shrimp Creole

1/2 C chopped red onion
1/3 C chopped green pepper
1 can (28 oz) no-salt-added tomatoes, chopped
1-3/4 C water
1 tsp minced garlic
1/4 tsp rosemary
1/4 tsp paprika
1 bay leaf
1 pkg (6 oz) long-grain and wild rice
1 lb raw shrimp, shelled and deveined
1/4 tsp Tabasco sauce

Sauté onion and green pepper until tender. Add tomatoes and their juice, water, garlic, rosemary, paprika, bay leaf, and rice. Simmer, covered, for 20 minutes. Add shrimp and simmer, covered, for 10 minutes. Stir in Tabasco sauce. Remove bay leaf before serving.

Serves 6.

Calories	%Fat	Fat (g)	Saturated Fat (g)	Cholesterol (mg)	Sodium (mg)	Carbohydrate (g)	Protein (g)	Fiber (g)
127	7	1	0.2	71	103	19	11	2

Exchanges: Starch 1, Vegetable 1, Low-fat protein 1

# Grilled Shrimp with Warm Arugula & Artichoke Salad

Christopher C. Tobin

6 jumbo shrimp
1 slice garlic, chopped
1 scallion, chopped
1 small chili, chopped
1 artichoke, cooked
1 bunch arugula
1 small plum tomato, chopped
2 T balsamic vinegar

Marinate shrimp with garlic, scallion, and chili for at least 1 hour.

Separate leaves from the artichoke and arrange them in a circle on a plate to form a flower. Chop the artichoke heart and sauté it with the arugula and tomato. Place on the artichoke flower and season with balsamic vinegar.

Grill the shrimps until done; arrange them on top of the artichoke flower. Serves 3.

Suggestion

• Grilled scallions are an excellent garnish.

Calories	%Fat	Fat (g)	Saturated Fat (g)	Cholesterol (mg)	Sodium (mg)	Carbohydrate (g)	Protein (g)	Fiber (g)
63	7	1	0.1	41	92	9	7	2

Exchanges: Vegetable 2, Low-fat protein 1/2

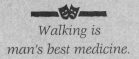

How to Increase Energy Expenditure
Walk more, use the stairs, park in the space farthest from your destination, and do more manual chores around the house. (Decreasing your dependence on automatic devices will help increase your energy expenditure). By following these suggestions and participating in other recreational activities, you can easily increase your general physical activity expenditure by 700 to 2100 calories per week.

Arizona Heart Institute Foundation
1-800-345-4278

Spiced Shrimp

1 lb cooked and cleaned shrimp
1 T olive oil
1 C vinegar
2 T water
1/2 C red onion, sliced paper-thin
1 to 2 whole cloves
1 bay leaf
Dash of Tabasco
1 tsp sugar

Toss shrimp in olive oil. Bring remaining ingredients to a boil and pour over shrimp. Chill for 24 hours before serving.
Serves 4.

Calories	%Fat	Fat (g)	Saturated Fat (g)	Cholesterol (mg)	Sodium (mg)	Carbohydrate (g)	Protein (g)	Fiber (g)
132	29	4	0.7	161	187	6	18	0

Exchanges: Vegetable 1, Low-fat protein 2

Sea Scallops with Pistachio, Flageolet, & Wild Mushroom Couscous

Paul Minnillo

8 sea scallops with muscles removed
1/2 C mushroom stock
1 C couscous, steamed for 18 minutes
1/4 C flageolet beans, rehydrated and cooked
2 T pistachios, toasted
1/4 C wild mushrooms, sautéed
Pepper
1 T chopped mint

Harissa
50 g red chilies with seeds removed (about 2 oz)
2 cloves garlic, chopped
1 tsp caraway
1-1/2 tsp cumin
2 tsp coriander
1 tsp dried mint
2 tsp olive oil

Great Seasonings
for Shellfish
Basil
Celery
Cumin
Curry
Dill
Fennel
Lemon
Mint
Paprika
Parsley
Savory
Tarragon
Thyme

To make the harissa, soak red chilies in water until soft. Combine spices and grind them in a coffee grinder. When chilies are soft, pat them dry with a towel. Put all ingredients in a food processor and blend, adding olive oil to make a thick paste.

Lightly dust scallops with flour. Sauté in hot pan until cooked; set aside. Deglaze the hot pan with mushroom stock. Add couscous, flageolets, pistachios, and mushrooms. Season with harissa and pepper to taste. Arrange couscous and scallops on a serving dish and garnish with mint.

Serves 2.

Suggestion

• To store harissa in the refrigerator, place it in a jar and pour in enough olive oil to cover the surface.

Calories	%Fat	Fat (g)	Saturated Fat (g)	Cholesterol (mg)	Sodium (mg)	Carbohydrate (g)	Protein (g)	Fiber (g)
356	15	6	0.8	19	175	50	26	6

Exchanges: Starch 3, Vegetable 1, Low-fat protein 2

Shrimp & Scallops with Red Bell Pepper Glaze

Franz Peier

1 large red bell pepper, seeded and cut into strips
3 sea scallops
3 large shrimp
1 tsp oil
4 oz spinach leaves, cleaned, rinsed, and dried
1 garlic clove
Hint of nutmeg
Freshly ground black pepper to taste
1-1/2 oz black angel hair pasta (fresh or frozen)

Finely chop bell pepper strips in a food processor; sieve through a colander and place juice in a small saucepan. Cook pepper juice until it is reduced to a glaze. Season scallops and shrimp with lemon juice, pepper, and oil. Sauté until done. Sauté spinach, garlic, and nutmeg for about 30 seconds. Cook pasta in boiling water for 30 seconds. Place spinach in center of plate, forming a well in the center; place pasta in well. Top with scallops and shrimp. Pour red bell pepper glaze around the spinach.

Serves 1.

Calories	%Fat	Fat (g)	Saturated Fat (g)	Cholesterol (mg)	Sodium (mg)	Carbohydrate (g)	Protein (g)	Fiber (g)
311	18	6	0.9	54	215	42	22	3

Exchanges: Starch 2-1/2, Vegetable 1, Low-fat protein 2

How to Boil Shellfish

Shrimp
    1–3 min or until pink
Scallops
    1 min or until opaque
Frozen lobster tails
    3 oz   3–4 min
    6 oz   8 min
    8 oz   11 min
Dungeness crabs
    8 min per pound
Blue crabs
    15 min

Steamed Clams

Place the clams in a bowl, add water to cover, and sprinkle some cornmeal on top; let the clams sit in the refrigerator for 30 minutes. Drain and rinse. Place the clams in a large kettle with two inches of water. Cook, covered, over high heat until the clams have opened. Discard any clams that did not open. Serve immediately.

Boiled Live Lobster

Drop the lobsters into a large kettle of boiling water. Cook 10 minutes per pound. Serve with lemon and pepper; provide nutcrackers and picks.

Scallops Caribbean

2 T sugar
2 T cornstarch
1/2 C unsweetened orange juice
1/3 C white wine vinegar
1/2 C water
1-1/4 lb scallops
2 tsp grated orange rind
1 can sliced water chestnuts, drained
1 can unsweetened pineapple chunks, drained
1/4 lb fresh broccoli, chopped
1/2 C chopped red bell pepper
4 C hot cooked brown rice

Mix sugar and cornstarch in a large skillet. Slowly stir in orange juice, vinegar, and water. Cook over medium heat, stirring constantly, until thickened. Add scallops and cook until done, about 5 to 10 minutes. Stir in orange rind, water chestnuts, pineapple, broccoli, and bell pepper and cook for a few minutes, until hot. Serve over rice.

Serves 6.

Suggestion
• Shrimp or cubed chicken may be substituted for the scallops.

Calories	%Fat	Fat (g)	Saturated Fat (g)	Cholesterol (mg)	Sodium (mg)	Carbohydrate (g)	Protein (g)	Fiber (g)
360	7	3	0.4	30	265	60	26	5

Exchanges: Starch 2, Fruit 1-1/2, Vegetable 1, Low-fat protein 3

# Oysters Rockefeller

1/4 C chopped onion
1 T chopped fresh parsley
1 pkg (10 oz) frozen spinach, thawed and drained
1/4 tsp aniseed
1 T water
1 pt large fresh oysters, drained
1/4 C unsalted whole-wheat cracker crumbs
2 tsp melted margarine

Sauté onion and parsley until tender. Using a blender or food processor, finely chop onion, spinach, aniseed, and water; do not purée. Place 18 oyster shells in a baking dish filled with rock salt. Place 1 oyster in each shell. Top with spinach. Mix crumbs with melted margarine. Sprinkle over oysters. Bake at 450° for 10 minutes. Using tongs, transfer shells to serving dishes, 3 per person. Serve immediately.

Serves 6.

Suggestion

• Oysters may be baked in small ramekins or other individual containers instead of in oyster shells.

Calories	%Fat	Fat (g)	Saturated Fat (g)	Cholesterol (mg)	Sodium (mg)	Carbohydrate (g)	Protein (g)	Fiber (g)
79	40	3	0.8	34	137	7	6	1

Exchanges: Vegetable 1, Low-fat protein 1/2

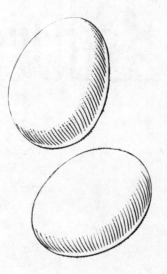

# Chilled Shiitake Mushroom & Chicken Surprise

Fiorenzo Antognini

2 oz boneless, skinless chicken breast, all fat removed
3 fresh shiitake mushrooms, stems removed
Pepper
Low-sodium soy sauce
1/4 C red wine
3 tomatoes, peeled and seeded
1 C plain nonfat yogurt
3 T lemon juice
Curry powder to taste
1 small clove garlic

Pound chicken to form a thin, wide medallion; cut into 3 equal pieces. Season mushrooms with pepper and 1 or 2 drops of soy sauce. Wrap chicken around each mushroom, being careful to completely cover the top of each mushroom and not leaving any part of it exposed. Place in an oven-proof pan and season with pepper and red wine. Poach at 375° for 10 to 12 minutes. Chicken should be cooked but not dry. Remove from oven and chill in its own juices.

...broiled fowl and mushrooms—capital thing!

Charles Dickens
Pickwick Papers

Varieties of Mushrooms

• *Chanterelles:* Wild; buttery texture, faint apricot flavor. Peppery or nutty flavor when cooked. Add near end of cooking time to prevent toughening.

• *Cloud ears:* Mild taste, chewy; often stir-fried with crisp vegetables. Usually sold dried.

• *Enoki:* Crisp, snow-white, long thin stems, tiny caps; neutral flavor. Sold fresh in bunches wrapped in plastic. Do not cook; often used to garnish salads or soup.

• *Morels:* Black or off-white; pointed, pitted caps (like giant raisins); short stems. White morels more delicately flavored; dried morels have woodsy flavor. Use with pasta or grains. Morels are never eaten raw.

• *Porcini:* Also called *cepes* or *Polish* mushrooms. Rust-brown caps, beige stems. Smooth, meaty texture; slightly sweet. Sauté fresh porcini briefly; good plain or with garlic, shallots, parsley, basil, tarragon, lemon, or pepper. Usually sold in dried form.

• *Shiitake:* Sweet, robust, chewy mushroom; tender cap, tough stems. Most widely used mushroom in Oriental cooking. Sold fresh or dried. Fresh shiitake can be two to nine inches in diameter.

• *Truffles:* The most expensive edible fungi (up to $700 a pound), truffles grow underground near the roots of oak, hazelnut, beech, or willow trees. Specially trained pigs are used to sniff out truffles, which cannot be cultivated. Black (Périgord) truffles must be cooked; often sliced very thinly and used as a flavoring ingredient or garnish. White (Piedmontese) truffles most highly prized; mild, raw-garlic flavor; often grated raw into risotto, pasta, or meat dishes.

Blend tomatoes, yogurt, lemon juice, curry powder, and garlic in a food processor. Chill. Spread sauce on a plate, top with chicken, and garnish with cucumber slices and fresh dill.

Serves 1.

Calories	%Fat	Fat (g)	Saturated Fat (g)	Cholesterol (mg)	Sodium (mg)	Carbohydrate (g)	Protein (g)	Fiber (g)
309	10	4	1.0	35	310	43	31	4

Exchanges: Vegetable 5, Dairy 1-1/2, Low-fat protein 2

Broiled Chicken Breasts with Tomato-Balsamic Vinegar Dressing

Arnauld Briand

1 small zucchini, diced
1 small carrot, diced
2 C couscous
2 C warm water
8 plum tomatoes, halved and seeded
3 T balsamic vinegar
1 T olive oil
Pepper
4 skinless, boneless chicken breasts (4 oz each)

Sauté zucchini and carrot. In a separate pan, cook couscous in warm water for about 5 minutes. Add sautéed vegetables. Season to taste. Process tomatoes, balsamic vinegar, and olive oil in a blender. Season to taste.

Grill chicken. Serve with couscous and tomato dressing.

Serves 4.

Safe Handling of Raw Chicken

Wash hands, countertops, cutting boards, knives, and all other surfaces that come into contact with raw chicken in hot soapy water or diluted bleach immediately. Do not cut vegetables or prepare other foods with unwashed equipment that has been used to prepare raw chicken.

Properly cooking chicken will reduce the risk of foodborne illness, but deadly bacteria can be transferred to other foods from the unwashed utensils. Starchy foods and dairy products are most easily contaminated by this means.

Calories	%Fat	Fat (g)	Saturated Fat (g)	Cholesterol (mg)	Sodium (mg)	Carbohydrate (g)	Protein (g)	Fiber (g)
555	12	8	1.5	58	90	84	37	7

Exchanges: Starch 5, Vegetable 2, Low-fat protein 3

Takes a tough man to make a tender chicken.

Robert B. Parker
Crimson Joy

Low-Fat Chicken

For succulent chicken, try browning it under the broiler using no added fat, then complete the cooking by baking at a lower temperature or transferring the chicken to the microwave. Remove the skin before eating.

Diethrich and Cohan
Women and Heart Disease

How to Bake Chicken

Place 1-1/2 lb chicken breasts, skin side up, in a shallow baking pan. Bake at 400°, basting frequently with pan juices, for about 35 minutes or until the meat is cooked. Brush each chicken breast with Cranberry Glaze, Maple-Orange Glaze, or Plum Sauce. Return to oven and bake until the chicken glistens, about 3 minutes. Do not eat the skin.

Chicken & 40 Cloves of Garlic

5-lb roasting chicken
Freshly ground black pepper
40 cloves garlic, unpeeled
Fresh herbs to taste
1 orange or lemon, cut in wedges
1 loaf French bread, sliced

Sprinkle the cavity of the chicken with pepper. Stuff the chicken with herbs and citrus wedges. Place the chicken in an oven-proof casserole and arrange the garlic cloves around the chicken. Bake at 400° until the chicken is tender, about 1-1/2 hours. Allow the chicken to rest for 10 minutes before slicing.

Just before serving the chicken, toast the bread slices under a broiler until golden. Serve with the baked whole garlic cloves, which can be squeezed out of their peels and spread on the toast.

Serves 6.

Suggestion

• 1 tsp dried herbs can be substituted for the fresh herbs.

Calories	%Fat	Fat (g)	Saturated Fat (g)	Cholesterol (mg)	Sodium (mg)	Carbohydrate (g)	Protein (g)	Fiber (g)
477	18	9	2.7	110	549	49	46	2

Exchanges: Starch 3, Low-fat protein 5

Chicken & Red Potatoes

4 small red potatoes, unpeeled, steamed and sliced
1/4 C low-sodium, defatted chicken broth
4 skinless, boneless chicken breast halves (4 oz each)
1-1/2 C chopped, peeled fresh plum tomatoes
3 T chopped red onion
2 T chopped parsley
1 small clove garlic, minced
Freshly ground black pepper, to taste

Place all ingredients in a large skillet or saucepan. Cook, covered, over low heat until chicken is done, about 15 minutes. Serve immediately.
Serves 4.

Suggestion
• Basil, rosemary, or other herbs to taste may be used in addition to or in place of the parsley.

Great Seasonings for Poultry
Almond
Basil
Bay leaf
Cayenne
Celery
Chervil
Cilantro
Curry
Dijon mustard
Dill
Garlic
Lemon
Marjoram
Nutmeg
Onion
Orange
Oregano
Paprika
Parsley
Rosemary
Sage
Savory
Shallots
Tarragon
Thyme

Calories	%Fat	Fat (g)	Saturated Fat (g)	Cholesterol (mg)	Sodium (mg)	Carbohydrate (g)	Protein (g)	Fiber (g)
256	12	4	1.0	62	76	28	28	3

Exchanges: Starch 1-1/2, Vegetable 1, Low-fat protein 3

 # opcorn Chicken

1 egg
2 egg whites
1/4 C nonfat milk
1 C flour
1 C whole-wheat flour
6 boneless, skinless chicken breasts (4 oz each), cleaned and lightly pounded
8 C popped popcorn, finely ground
Roasted Red Pepper Sauce (page 448)

Beat eggs and milk. In a shallow dish, mix the two flours. Dip the chicken breasts in flour, then in the egg wash. Dredge in popcorn to coat each piece evenly. Sauté for 5 minutes each side. Serve with Roasted Red Pepper Sauce.
Serves 6.

Calories	%Fat	Fat (g)	Saturated Fat (g)	Cholesterol (mg)	Sodium (mg)	Carbohydrate (g)	Protein (g)	Fiber (g)
319	12	4	1.1	65	61	39	31	4

Exchanges: Starch 2-1/2, Low-fat protein 3

Red Pepper Chicken with Rice

1/2 C dry red wine
2 bay leaves
6 cloves garlic, minced, divided
3/4 tsp dried rosemary, divided
4 chicken breasts (4 oz each)
6 medium red bell peppers, julienned
1-1/2 C nonfat ricotta cheese
1 tsp freshly ground black pepper
3 C hot cooked brown rice

Mix wine, bay leaves, 2 cloves minced garlic, and 1/4 tsp rosemary. Brush on chicken breasts. Broil chicken for 30 to 35 minutes, basting every 7 to 10 minutes to keep chicken moist. Turn chicken halfway through cooking period. Remove and discard chicken skin and bay leaves.

Lightly sauté remaining garlic and 1/2 tsp rosemary for about 4 minutes; do not brown. Add bell pepper and continue to cook until just tender. Purée half the sautéed red pepper mixture with the ricotta cheese and black pepper in a food processor or blender.

Arrange the chicken on a platter with the sautéed peppers, pepper-cheese sauce, and rice.

Serves 4.

Cooking with Garlic

Do not allow garlic cloves—whether chopped, mashed, or whole—to cook long enough to turn brown. Overcooking will make garlic taste very bitter. A whole clove of garlic may safely be browned in oil (to flavor the oil) only if the clove will be removed before any other ingredients are added.

Calories	%Fat	Fat (g)	Saturated Fat (g)	Cholesterol (mg)	Sodium (mg)	Carbohydrate (g)	Protein (g)	Fiber (g)
348	14	5	1.8	70	413	33	40	3

Exchanges: Starch 1-1/2, Vegetable 2, Low-fat protein 5

# Chicken & Bananas

4 boneless, skinless chicken breasts, 4 oz each
2 T flour
3 tsp curry powder
2 bananas, peeled and halved
2 C hot cooked brown rice, cooked with the juice of 1/2 lime

Drop the chicken, flour, and curry powder into a plastic bag or covered container and shake until the meat is coated; remove from bag and discard excess flour. Brown the chicken on both sides in a skillet; reduce heat and cook, covered, until tender, about 15 minutes. Add the bananas and cook for 5 minutes. Serve over lime rice.

Serves 4.

Suggestion

- *Baked Chicken with Bananas:* Place a layer of sliced sweet potato in a medium casserole dish lightly coated with vegetable spray. Place chicken on top and cover with a second layer of sweet potato. Bake at 375° for 30 to 40 minutes. Gently stir in banana (cut in 1-inch chunks) and return to oven for 5 minutes.

Calories	%Fat	Fat (g)	Saturated Fat (g)	Cholesterol (mg)	Sodium (mg)	Carbohydrate (g)	Protein (g)	Fiber (g)
313	13	5	1.2	62	64	40	28	3

Exchanges: Starch 1-1/2, Fruit 1, Low-fat protein 3

# Chicken Pot Pie with Sweet Potato Crust

6 chicken breasts, 4 oz each, cooked and cubed
6 small onions, peeled and cooked whole
1 T chopped parsley
3 T flour
3 T margarine
3/4 C low-sodium chicken broth
3/4 C skim milk
2 T sherry
2 tsp dried vegetable flakes
3/4 C whole-wheat flour
1 tsp baking powder
1/2 tsp cinnamon
2 C cooked and mashed sweet potato
2 T margarine

Arrange chicken, onion, and parsley in a baking dish. In a small pan, blend 3 T flour and margarine until smooth; slowly whisk in broth and milk. Cook, stirring constantly, until thickened. Add sherry and vegetable flakes; pour over the chicken.

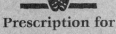

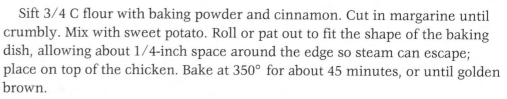

Sift 3/4 C flour with baking powder and cinnamon. Cut in margarine until crumbly. Mix with sweet potato. Roll or pat out to fit the shape of the baking dish, allowing about 1/4-inch space around the edge so steam can escape; place on top of the chicken. Bake at 350° for about 45 minutes, or until golden brown.

Serves 6.

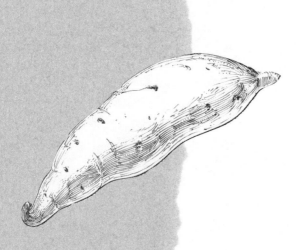

Calories	%Fat	Fat (g)	Saturated Fat (g)	Cholesterol (mg)	Sodium (mg)	Carbohydrate (g)	Protein (g)	Fiber (g)
415	29	13	2.9	63	266	43	31	5

Exchanges: Starch 2-1/2, Vegetable 1, Low-fat protein 3, Fat 1

Breast of Chicken Creole

James P. Shannon

1/8 tsp basil leaves and thyme leaves, freshly chopped
1/2 boneless, skinless chicken breast (4 oz)
1 oz Creole Sauce (page 450)
1-1/2 oz water
2 turns freshly ground pepper (from peppermill)

Place all ingredients in a baking pan. Bake at 380° for 15 minutes. Slice the chicken breast on a bias cut. Top with sauce and serve.

Serves 1.

People Food & Pets

The care and feeding of your pet is something you should discuss with your veterinarian. Pets have very different dietary needs than people, most of which are met through a good brand-name dry pet food. Dr. Bruce Bean, staff veterinarian at the Arizona Humane Society, recommends a strict diet of dry food, as soft food can cause dental problems later in life for both dogs and cats.

Feeding your pet leftovers, failed recipes, milk, cheese, or even egg yolks (when you are only using the whites) is inappropriate and dangerous for your pet. Raw eggs are a health hazard for

Calories	%Fat	Fat (g)	Saturated Fat (g)	Cholesterol (mg)	Sodium (mg)	Carbohydrate (g)	Protein (g)	Fiber (g)
147	23	4	1.0	62	62	2	25	1

Exchanges: Low-fat protein 3

humans because of Salmonella poisoning; the same danger holds true for your pet.

Most "people food" is too rich for dogs and can cause digestive upset. Pets can also suffer from obesity, which can cause impairment of heart, respiratory, and digestive functions. So while you are looking after your own heart and health, keep your pet in mind, too.

Mary Beth Coyle
Arizona Humane Society

Chicken Evangeline

2 medium onions, chopped
1 clove elephant garlic, thinly sliced
1/2 C thinly sliced celery
1 can (8-oz) low-sodium tomato sauce
1/2 C low-sodium chicken broth
1 bay leaf
1/8 tsp cayenne pepper
1 medium red bell pepper, diced
2 whole chicken breasts, cooked and cubed
3 C hot cooked brown rice

Bring onion, garlic, celery, tomato sauce, broth, bay leaf, and cayenne pepper to a boil. Reduce heat and simmer, covered, for 45 to 60 minutes. Add bell pepper and chicken. Simmer, covered, for 10 to 15 minutes. Serve over rice.
Serves 4.

Calories	%Fat	Fat (g)	Saturated Fat (g)	Cholesterol (mg)	Sodium (mg)	Carbohydrate (g)	Protein (g)	Fiber (g)
352	13	5	1.3	66	107	44	32	4

Exchanges: Starch 2-1/2, Vegetable 2, Low-fat protein 4

Chicken Oriental

1/4 C low-sodium soy sauce
1/4 C sugar
1/2 C water
1/2 C white wine
1 lb skinless chicken breast, cut in pieces
2 cloves garlic, sliced
1/2 tsp ground ginger

Boil soy sauce, sugar, and water until sugar is dissolved; add wine. Set aside. Sauté chicken, garlic, and ginger until slightly browned. Pour reserved sauce over chicken and cook over medium heat, covered, until tender. Turn chicken pieces occasionally during cooking. Remove chicken and boil sauce until it is syrupy. Return chicken to pan and stir to coat with glaze.
Serves 4.

Suggestion
• Serve with rice.

Chinese Restaurants

Ask the waiter to omit the MSG, soy sauce, and salt. Start with a clear soup (wonton or other broth) to take the edge off your appetite. Eat plenty of steamed rice—as the Chinese people do. Order chicken, shrimp, and/or vegetable dishes that are steamed or stir-fried. Share an order among two or three people; use chopsticks so you slow down, enjoy the flavors, and leave much of the fatty sauce in the dish.

Avoid fried items such as egg rolls, won tons, fried rice, and Chinese noodles, and dishes that are described as crispy, sautéed, or sweet-and-sour. Diced chicken is usually very fatty; sliced chicken is usually breast meat without the skin.

**Arizona Heart
Institute Foundation**
1–800–345–4278

Calories	%Fat	Fat (g)	Saturated Fat (g)	Cholesterol (mg)	Sodium (mg)	Carbohydrate (g)	Protein (g)	Fiber (g)
175	12	2	0.7	45	644	15	19	0

Exchanges: Fruit 1, Low-fat protein 2-1/2
Note: Occasional use

Sweet & Sour Chicken

1 lb boneless, skinless chicken breast, sliced thin across the grain
1 medium green pepper, chopped
2 medium carrots, thinly sliced
1 red onion, sliced in strips, not rings
1 clove garlic, minced
1-1/4 C water
1/4 C sugar
1/4 C red wine vinegar
1 T low-sodium soy sauce
1 tsp low-sodium chicken bouillon granules
2 T cornstarch
1/4 C cold water
2 C hot cooked brown rice

Stir-fry chicken for about 4 minutes, or until browned. Remove from pan
and drain on paper toweling. In the same pan, sauté green pepper, carrots, onions, and garlic until crisp-tender but not brown. Stir in 1-1/4 C water, sugar,
vinegar, soy sauce, bouillon granules, and chicken. Bring to a boil and boil for
1 minute. Blend cornstarch with cold water and stir into chicken. Cook, stirring constantly, until thickened. Serve immediately over hot rice.
　　Serves 4.

Calories	%Fat	Fat (g)	Saturated Fat (g)	Cholesterol (mg)	Sodium (mg)	Carbohydrate (g)	Protein (g)	Fiber (g)
345	12	4	1.2	62	237	47	28	3

Exchanges: Starch 2-1/2, Vegetable 2, Low-fat protein 3

Stir-Fried Almond Chicken

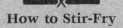
How to Stir-Fry
All ingredients should be cut, measured, and ready to use before beginning to cook. Cut the food to be stir-fried into uniform pieces. Foods that take longer to cook are put in the wok or skillet first; quick-cooking foods are added near the end of cooking. Stir the food constantly with a wide spatula while cooking.

2/3 C low-sodium chicken broth
3 T low-sodium soy sauce
2 T cornstarch
2 T sliced almonds
2 C boneless, skinless chicken breast, cut in 1-inch pieces
6 scallions, sliced
1 C snow peas
2 C sliced fresh mushrooms

Mix broth, soy sauce, and cornstarch; set aside. Stir-fry almonds over high heat for about 1 minute, until browned; remove from pan. Stir-fry chicken for 2 to 3 minutes or until done; remove from pan. Stir-fry scallion and snow peas for 1 minute; remove from pan. Stir-fry mushrooms for 1 minute. Pour broth mixture over mushrooms and cook until bubbly. Return remaining ingredients to pan and cook for 1 minute, or until hot.

Serves 6.

Calories	%Fat	Fat (g)	Saturated Fat (g)	Cholesterol (mg)	Sodium (mg)	Carbohydrate (g)	Protein (g)	Fiber (g)
133	27	4	0.8	36	342	7	17	1

Exchanges: Vegetable 2, Low-fat protein 2

Flavored Skewers

For extra flavor, use long stems of rosemary, thyme, or sage as skewers for cooking vegetable, chicken, and seafood kabobs. Remove the leaves from the stems first. Firm vegetables and meat may need to be punctured with a metal skewer or ice-pick before threading them onto the herb stem.

Grilled Chicken Kabobs

2 T canola oil
1/3 C fresh lemon juice
1 tsp honey
Pinch of tarragon
Pinch of oregano
3 whole boneless, skinless chicken breasts, cut into 2-inch cubes
12 cherry tomatoes
8 oz fresh whole mushrooms
8 small whole onions, peeled
2 medium green peppers, quartered
1/2 fresh pineapple, cut into chunks

Mix oil, lemon juice, honey, tarragon, and oregano; pour over chicken and vegetables. Marinate in the refrigerator for 30 to 60 minutes. Thread chicken, vegetables, and fruit, alternating colors and flavors, on four long metal skewers. Grill or broil 4 to 6 inches from heat for about 25 to 30 minutes or until chicken is cooked, turning frequently and basting often with marinade.

Serves 4.

Suggestion

• Canned unsweetened pineapple chunks can be substituted for the fresh pineapple.

Calories	%Fat	Fat (g)	Saturated Fat (g)	Cholesterol (mg)	Sodium (mg)	Carbohydrate (g)	Protein (g)	Fiber (g)
354	32	13	2.1	99	99	19	42	3

Exchanges: Vegetable 4, Low-fat protein 5

Arroz con Pollo

Joyce Goldstein

12 half-breasts of skinless chicken
3 T finely minced garlic
3 T oregano
4 T sherry vinegar
1/4 C olive oil
2 T freshly ground black pepper
1/4 C dry white wine
1 tsp saffron threads
2 onions, cut into medium dice
2 green peppers, cut into medium dice
2 T finely minced garlic
2 tsp ground cumin
4 tsp paprika
2 C diced canned low-sodium plum tomatoes, drained
2 C Spanish short-grain rice
4-1/2 C defatted chicken stock

Place chicken in a non-aluminum container. Combine garlic, oregano, vinegar, and pepper in a bowl or mortar. Rub to a paste with a spoon or pestle. Whisk in the olive oil. Toss the chicken pieces in this mixture; cover and marinate overnight in the refrigerator. Bring to room temperature for cooking.

are on a diet and with whom you can discuss tempting purchases.

- If you are tempted, ask yourself, "Is this food really necessary?" Make yourself come up with some pretty good reasons for buying an item not on your approved shopping list.

Edward B. Diethrich, MD
Heart Test

Warm the wine in a small pan and add the saffron filaments. Let steep 10 minutes.

Brown the chicken pieces well on all sides over medium-high heat; set aside. Cook the onions and peppers over moderate heat until tender, about 10 minutes. Add the garlic, cumin, paprika, and tomatoes and cook 5 minutes longer. Stir in saffron infusion, rice, and chicken stock. Bring to a boil; reduce heat to a simmer. Cook, covered, over low heat until the rice has absorbed most of the liquid, about 15 minutes. The rice will be a little soupy. Return the chicken to the pan and bake, uncovered, at 350° for about 15 minutes longer. Or you may add the chicken to the pan after 10 minutes of cooking the rice, re-cover the pan, and continue cooking on top of the stove. If the rice seems soupy, let the pan sit off the heat, covered, and most of the liquid will be absorbed. Sprinkle with parsley, optional strips of red pepper or olives, and serve from the pan.

Serves 6.

Calories	%Fat	Fat (g)	Saturated Fat (g)	Cholesterol (mg)	Sodium (mg)	Carbohydrate (g)	Protein (g)	Fiber (g)
692	23	18	3.7	132	185	68	62	4

Exchanges: Starch 3-1/2, Vegetable 2, Low-fat protein 7, Fat 1

# Chicken Quesadillas

2 T lime juice
Freshly ground black pepper to taste
2 whole skinless chicken breasts, cooked and shredded
4 whole-wheat tortillas (7-inch diameter)
1 can (4 oz) green chiles, diced
3/4 C shredded part-skim mozzarella cheese

Sprinkle lime juice and pepper over shredded chicken. Place a tortilla in a shallow pan. Layer with the following: one-third of the chicken, one-fourth of the chiles, and one-fourth of the cheese. Repeat twice. Top with a tortilla and the remaining green chiles and cheese. Bake at 350° for 10 to 15 minutes, or until cheese is melted. Cut quesadilla into wedges and serve immediately.
Serves 4.

Suggestion
• Serve with South-of-the-Border Salsa, Mock Sour Cream, and/or Guacamole.

Calories	%Fat	Fat (g)	Saturated Fat (g)	Cholesterol (mg)	Sodium (mg)	Carbohydrate (g)	Protein (g)	Fiber (g)
383	31	13	3.8	78	417	29	37	3

Exchanges: Starch 2, Fruit 1, Low-fat protein 4-1/2

Chicken Cacciatore

2 C thinly sliced onion
1/2 C chopped green pepper
2 cloves garlic, crushed
8 skinless chicken breast halves
1 can (16 oz) low-sodium tomatoes, drained
1 can (8 oz) low-sodium tomato sauce
4 oz fresh mushrooms, sliced
1/4 tsp oregano

Cook onion, green pepper, and garlic in 1/4 C water over medium heat until tender. Add remaining ingredients and simmer for 40 minutes.
Serves 8.

Suggestion
• Serve with linguini.

Calories	%Fat	Fat (g)	Saturated Fat (g)	Cholesterol (mg)	Sodium (mg)	Carbohydrate (g)	Protein (g)	Fiber (g)
182	18	4	1.0	66	78	9	28	2

Exchanges: Vegetable 2, Low-fat protein 4

Four Turkey Sausages

You've probably been wondering how they figure out just how many calories there are in, say, a four-ounce Italian sausage. I've been wondering the same thing. You may have been wondering about it for the same reason I've been wondering about it: maybe they're wrong. Maybe calculating calories is a science that is about as exact as handicapping horses.

Calvin Trillin

1-1/2 lb ground turkey breast, uncooked
1 egg white

Thoroughly combine turkey, egg white, and seasonings for your choice of sausage (see variations). To test and adjust the seasonings, cook a teaspoon of sausage and taste it; increase the seasonings or add other seasonings to suit your preference (chili peppers, poultry seasoning, Tabasco). Shape the properly seasoned turkey into 12 patties and chill for 1 hour or freeze. Brown sausages in a nonstick skillet over medium-high heat for 5 minutes on each side.
Serves 12.

Seasonings for 4 Variations

Traditional Sausage
1/4 tsp sage
1/4 tsp marjoram
1/4 tsp thyme
1/8 tsp summer savory
1/4 tsp freshly ground black pepper

Garlic Sausage
1 clove garlic, thoroughly mashed
1/4 tsp sage
1/4 tsp freshly ground black pepper
Pinch dry mustard

Apple Sausage
1/4 C grated Granny Smith apple
1 tsp reduced-calorie maple syrup
1/4 tsp freshly ground black pepper

Herb Sausage
1/2 tsp crumbled rosemary
1/4 tsp minced parsley
1/4 tsp freshly ground black pepper

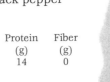

Calories	%Fat	Fat (g)	Saturated Fat (g)	Cholesterol (mg)	Sodium (mg)	Carbohydrate (g)	Protein (g)	Fiber (g)
73	21	2	0.5	34	35	0	14	0

Exchanges: Low-fat protein 2

Turkey Meatballs

1 lb ground turkey breast
1/8 C chopped green pepper
1/8 C chopped yellow onion
1/4 tsp Worcestershire sauce
1/4 tsp garlic powder
1/4 tsp black pepper
1/4 tsp oregano

Mix all ingredients well, handling lightly. Form into 8 balls and place on a cookie sheet. Bake at 325° for 15 to 20 minutes.

Serves 4.

Suggestions

- To make uniform meatballs, shape the meat into a roll of the correct diameter. Cut slices that are as long as the diameter is wide (for example, cut a 1-inch roll into 1-inch slices). Alternatively, pat the meat into a square and then cut it into cubes (for example, cut a 1-inch thick square into 1-inch cubes). Gently roll the pieces between the palms of your hands to make smooth balls.
- Simmer with Spaghetti Sauce or Double Red Sauce and serve over pasta.

Calories	%Fat	Fat (g)	Saturated Fat (g)	Cholesterol (mg)	Sodium (mg)	Carbohydrate (g)	Protein (g)	Fiber (g)
148	21	3	1.0	67	65	1	27	0

Exchanges: Low-fat protein 4

# Grilled Turkey Picatta with Yellow Corn Sauce

Sean Kavanaugh

1 lb turkey breast
4 oz fresh corn kernels, cooked (about 1/2 C)
2 oz green onions, cooked (about 1/2 C)
4 oz green tofu
2 oz glacé de viande
White pepper to taste
2 oz red bell pepper, roasted, peeled, julienned (about 1/2 C)
2 oz green bell pepper, roasted, peeled, julienned (about 1/2 C)
2 oz yellow bell pepper, roasted, peeled, julienned (about 1/2 C)

Cut turkey into four 2- to 3-oz escalopes, flattened to 1/4 inch.

To make the Yellow Corn Sauce, purée the corn, green onions, and green tofu; add the glacé de viande and white pepper and cook for a few minutes.

Sauté the bell peppers; set aside. Grill the turkey very rapidly and transfer to serving plates. Place the peppers on top of each serving of turkey. Serve with Yellow Corn Sauce.

Serves 4.

Calories	%Fat	Fat (g)	Saturated Fat (g)	Cholesterol (mg)	Sodium (mg)	Carbohydrate (g)	Protein (g)	Fiber (g)
204	21	5	1.2	66	127	10	30	2

Exchanges: Vegetable 2, Low-fat protein 4

Stuffed Peppers à la Phoenix

3/4 lb ground turkey breast
1/4 C chopped scallions
1 T chopped cilantro
Freshly ground black pepper to taste
1 C shredded part-skim mozzarella cheese
4 Anaheim or Poblano peppers, seeded and halved
1 T chopped parsley

Cook turkey, scallions, cilantro, and pepper over medium heat until the turkey is no longer pink. Stir in half of the cheese. Spoon mix into the pepper halves. Arrange the peppers in a casserole dish lightly coated with vegetable spray. Bake at 350° for 15 minutes. Sprinkle remaining cheese and parsley over the peppers and bake until cheese is melted, about 10 minutes.
Serves 4.

Suggestion
• Two medium bell peppers can be substituted for the Anaheim or Poblano peppers.

Calories	%Fat	Fat (g)	Saturated Fat (g)	Cholesterol (mg)	Sodium (mg)	Carbohydrate (g)	Protein (g)	Fiber (g)
163	28	5	2.3	58	125	4	24	1

Exchanges: Vegetable 1, Low-fat protein 3

# Grilled Quail with Fennel & Cucumber Salad

Sean Brasel

1 tsp rosemary
1 tsp thyme
1 tsp chopped shallots
1 T olive oil
4 semi-boneless, skinless quail (4 oz each)
1 large bulb fresh fennel (reserve tops), thinly julienned and lightly steamed
2 large English cucumbers, peeled, seeded, thinly sliced
2 Roma tomatoes, julienned
Juice of 2 oranges
2 oz sherry vinegar
1 T extra-virgin olive oil
2 C mixed baby greens

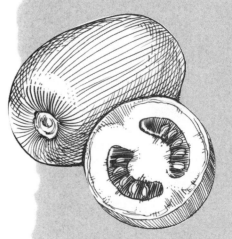

Chop rosemary, thyme, and shallots; mix with 1 T oil and brush over quail. Marinate for 2 hours. Grill quail for 5 to 10 minutes on each side. Mix julienned fennel, cucumber, and tomatoes. Blend orange juice, vinegar, and 1 T chopped fennel. Slowly whisk in 1 T extra-virgin olive oil. Toss the fennel salad with the vinaigrette. Place mixed greens on each serving dish; top with fennel salad. Place a grilled quail on top of each salad and serve.

Serves 4.

Calories	%Fat	Fat (g)	Saturated Fat (g)	Cholesterol (mg)	Sodium (mg)	Carbohydrate (g)	Protein (g)	Fiber (g)
267	42	13	3.0	62	82	16	25	2

Exchanges: Vegetable 3, Low-fat protein 3, Fat 1/2

Meats

Beef
Veal
Lamb
Pork
Goat
Buffalo
Venison

Meats

Beef Burgundy

1 lb lean boneless top round steak, trimmed of fat, cubed
1 pt whole pearl onions, peeled
1 T whole-wheat flour
2 cloves garlic, minced
2 C Burgundy wine
1 C low-sodium beef broth
1 tsp dried thyme
1 bay leaf
8 whole baby carrots, trimmed
1/4 lb fresh mushrooms, sliced
3/4 C peas
Freshly ground black pepper to taste

Sear meat in cooking spray over medium heat. Stir in flour; cook until flour is golden, stirring often, about 4 minutes. Transfer meat to a 2-qt casserole dish. In the same skillet, bring onions, garlic, wine, beef broth, thyme, bay leaf, and carrots to a boil. Pour over meat. Bake, covered, at 350° for 90 minutes. Add mushrooms and bake, covered, for 30 minutes. Stir in peas about 5 minutes before the end of the cooking period. Season with pepper.

Serves 4.

Suggestion
• Serve over parsleyed noodles.

Calories	% Fat	Fat (g)	Saturated Fat (g)	Cholesterol (mg)	Sodium (mg)	Carbohydrate (g)	Protein (g)	Fiber (g)
282	16	5	1.6	73	133	23	32	5

Exchanges: Starch 1, Vegetable 2, Low-fat protein 4

Trim the Fat

When you purchase a cut of meat, cut some more. Specifically, cut off all visible fat before preparing. If you buy the leaner cuts to begin with, you won't have so much to trim. Cooking meat without its fat can sometimes dry it out, but if you keep it covered for a long period of time in a liquid or with a tenderizer it should stay moist and tender.

Edward B. Diethrich, MD
Heart Test

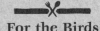

For the Birds

Save fat trimmings in the freezer, adding more as available. Melt it over medium heat and strain out all solids. (Use this fat for making bird food only, not for cooking.) The following recipes make tasty winter treats for wild birds. If you make up your own recipes, be sure to use ingredients that are easily eaten and healthful for the birds that live in your region—ask your local Audubon Society for suggestions.

Winter Bird Food 1

3 C corn meal
1-1/2 C whole-wheat flour
2 C rolled oats
3 to 4 C wild bird seed
1 C melted, strained fat

Winter Bird Food 2

1 C peanut butter
1 C all-purpose flour
4 C cornmeal
1 C melted, strained fat

Mix dry ingredients and add melted fat. Mix by hand to the consistency of putty, adding more grease if needed. Pack into an aluminum pie pan. Store in refrigerator or freezer.

Any product made with melted fat trimmings will spoil if left out for very long in temperatures that are much above freezing. Put the food out in small quantities every few days, not in one large amount that would last for weeks. The pan of bird food may be hung from a tree, or the food may be spread on a tree limb, on a board, or in a small dish.

Pat Beall
Maricopa Audubon Society
Maricopa County, Arizona

Beef Stroganoff

1 clove elephant garlic, minced
1 medium onion, diced
1/2 lb fresh mushrooms, sliced
1 lb beef tenderloin, thinly sliced
1-1/2 C low-sodium beef broth, divided
1 T Worcestershire sauce
1 T minced fresh parsley
1 tsp paprika
3 T all-purpose flour
1 C plain nonfat yogurt
6 C hot cooked noodles, prepared without fat or salt
1 tsp poppy seeds

Lightly sauté garlic, onion, and mushrooms until tender. Add beef and sauté until evenly browned. Stir in 1 C of broth, Worcestershire sauce, and paprika. Bring to a boil; reduce heat and simmer, covered, until beef is tender, about 10 minutes. Mix the remaining 1/2 C of broth and flour; slowly blend into the beef mixture. Bring to a boil, stirring constantly, and boil 1 minute to thicken. Reduce heat and stir in the yogurt—do not boil. Toss hot noodles with poppy seeds. Serve beef over noodles.

Serves 6.

Calories	% Fat	Fat (g)	Saturated Fat (g)	Cholesterol (mg)	Sodium (mg)	Carbohydrate (g)	Protein (g)	Fiber (g)
414	19	9	3.0	58	124	50	33	3

Exchanges: Starch 3-1/2, Low-fat protein 3

# Cottage Pie

1/2 lb ground round steak
1/2 lb ground turkey breast
1 clove garlic, minced
1/2 onion, finely chopped
Freshly ground black pepper to taste
4 small or 2 large tomatoes, peeled and sliced
5 medium potatoes, cooked and mashed
2 oz part-skim cheddar cheese, grated

Brown beef, turkey, garlic, and onion in cooking spray. Season with pepper. Spread one-third of meat into a small casserole dish. Top with a layer of tomatoes. Repeat layers twice, ending with tomatoes. Spread mashed potatoes over the top of the casserole and sprinkle with cheese. Bake at 375° for 30 minutes, or until the potatoes are lightly browned and the cheese is melted.

Serves 4.

Suggestions
- Add herbs or other seasonings to taste to the meat.
- Mash the potatoes with a little skim milk or low-sodium broth; season with Dijon mustard, herbs, or other seasonings to taste.

Calories	%Fat	Fat (g)	Saturated Fat (g)	Cholesterol (mg)	Sodium (mg)	Carbohydrate (g)	Protein (g)	Fiber (g)
305	18	6	2.6	73	276	31	31	3

Exchanges: Starch 1-1/2, Vegetable 1, Low-fat protein 4

Methinks sometimes I have no more wit than a Christian or an ordinary man has; but I am a great eater of beef, and I believe that does harm to my wit.

Shakespeare
Twelfth Night

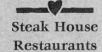

Steak House Restaurants

Order fish or poultry broiled or baked without added fat. If you have red meat, ask the server to limit the portion to 6 ounces or less. Order a lean cut of meat (filet mignon, sirloin, flank, Porterhouse), broiled without butter. Avoid fried items, including French fries and steak fries. A salad, a baked potato or rice, and a vegetable without added fat are essential components of the meal.

Arizona Heart Institute Foundation
1–800–345–4278

Low-Fat Meatloaf
Use ground turkey breast meat to replace part or all of the ground beef in a recipe. Adjust seasonings to taste.

Great Seasonings for Beef

Allspice
Basil
Caraway
Celery
Chili powder
Cumin
Dill
Garlic
Ginger
Horseradish
Marjoram
Nasturtium
Onion
Oregano
Parsley
Rosemary
Savory
Tarragon
Thyme

Spanish Meatloaf

3/4 lb extra-lean ground beef
3/4 lb ground turkey breast
2 slices whole-wheat bread, torn into coarse crumbs
1/3 C finely chopped onion
1/4 C skim milk
2 egg whites, lightly beaten
1-1/2 tsp chili powder
1/2 tsp ground cumin
1/2 tsp dried oregano
1/4 tsp garlic powder
1/4 tsp pepper

Combine all ingredients well, but handling as lightly as possible. Form mixture into a 6 × 4 × 3-inch loaf. Place on a rack in a shallow roasting pan. Bake at 350° for 1 hour, or until a meat thermometer inserted into the thickest part of the meatloaf reads 170°.

Serves 6.

Suggestion
• Serve with South-of-the-Border Salsa (page 457).

Calories	%Fat	Fat (g)	Saturated Fat (g)	Cholesterol (mg)	Sodium (mg)	Carbohydrate (g)	Protein (g)	Fiber (g)
217	35	9	3.0	68	138	7	27	1

Exchanges: Starch 1/2, Low-fat protein 3-1/2

Swiss Steak

1 lb beef top round steak, trimmed of fat
1/4 C whole-wheat flour
Freshly ground black pepper to taste
1/2 C chopped onion
1 can (6 oz) no-salt-added V8 vegetable juice
1 can (16 oz) low-sodium tomatoes, crushed
1/2 C low-sodium beef broth
1-1/2 C carrots, julienned
Parsley sprigs

Coat steak with flour and pepper. To tenderize the meat, pound flour into both sides of the steak with a mallet. Sauté steak on each side until browned. Remove from skillet and set aside. Sauté onions in the same skillet until tender. Return steak to skillet. Add juice, tomatoes, and broth. Cover and simmer for 1 hour. Add carrots and simmer until they are tender, about 30 minutes. Transfer steak to a serving dish. Spoon vegetables and sauce over the meat. Garnish with parsley.
Serves 6.

Suggestions
• Worcestershire sauce to taste may be added.
• Serve with rice or noodles.

Calories	%Fat	Fat (g)	Saturated Fat (g)	Cholesterol (mg)	Sodium (mg)	Carbohydrate (g)	Protein (g)	Fiber (g)
161	19	3	1.1	49	74	12	21	2

Exchanges: Vegetable 2, Low-fat protein 2-1/2

"Don't you know, woman, that I haven't had a bite to eat all day? Do I get fed, or not? Will you put your deft whimsey in a steak?"

"Yes," she said. "Would you like a steak?"

"Will you make these old eyes shine with a chop and a delicate dressing of young onions?"

"Yes," she said. "Yes."

He came over and put his arms about her, his eyes searching hers in a look of love and hunger. "Will you make me one of your sauces that is subtle, searching, and hushed?"

"Yes," she said. "Whatever you like I will make it for you."

"Why will you make it for me?" he asked.

It was like a ritual that both of them knew, and they fastened upon each word and answer because they were so eager to hear it from each other.

"Because I love you. Because I want to feed you

and to love you."

"Will it be good?" he said.

"It will be so good that there will be no words to tell its goodness," she said. "It will be good because I am so good and beautiful, and because I can do everything better than any other woman you will ever know, and because I love you with all my heart and soul, and want to be a part of you."

"Will this great love get into the food you cook for me?"

"It will be in every morsel that you eat. It will feed your hunger as you've never been fed before. It will be like living a miracle, and will make you better and richer as long as you live. You will never forget it. It will be a glory and a triumph."

"Then this will be such food as no one ever ate before," he said.

"Yes," she said. "It will be." And it was so.

Thomas Wolfe
You Can't Go Home Again

 # auerbraten & Gingersnap Gravy

4 lb beef round tip
2 medium onions, thinly sliced
8 peppercorns, slightly crushed
4 whole cloves
1 bay leaf
1 C white vinegar
1/2 C cider vinegar
1 C water
2 C boiling water
10 gingersnaps, crushed
1/2 C plain nonfat yogurt

Marinate the beef in onions, peppercorns, cloves, bay leaf, vinegars, and water in the refrigerator for 1 to 2 days, turning twice each day. Remove the meat from the marinade and pat it dry. Strain the marinade; reserve onions and 1 C of liquid. Brown the meat on all sides. Add boiling water and gingersnaps; simmer, covered, for 1-1/2 hours, turning often. Add reserved onions and marinade; continue cooking until meat is tender, about 2 hours. Remove the meat and keep it warm. Strain the cooking liquid into a saucepan. Mix yogurt with flour and slowly stir into liquid, cooking over medium low heat and stirring constantly, until sauce is thick and smooth. Slice meat and add to the gravy.
Serves 12.

Calories	%Fat	Fat (g)	Saturated Fat (g)	Cholesterol (mg)	Sodium (mg)	Carbohydrate (g)	Protein (g)	Fiber (g)
320	25	9	2.9	127	153	8	49	0

Exchanges: Starch 1/2, Low-fat protein 7

Veal Stew

3 lb boneless veal shoulder, cut in 1-inch cubes
2 T flour
4 medium onions, peeled and quartered
1-1/2 C diced celery
4 carrots, sliced
1 C low-sodium chicken broth
1/2 C water
1/2 C dry white wine
1/8 tsp rosemary
1 lb fresh mushrooms, sliced
1/4 C chopped fresh parsley

Shake the veal and flour together in a plastic bag or covered container until veal is evenly coated; discard excess flour. Brown veal in a large skillet over medium heat. Stir in onions, celery, carrots, chicken stock, water, wine, and rosemary. Bring to a boil; reduce heat and simmer, covered, until veal is tender, about 1 to 1-1/2 hours. Sauté mushrooms and add to the stew. Stir in parsley.

Serves 12.

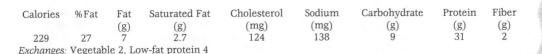

Calories	%Fat	Fat (g)	Saturated Fat (g)	Cholesterol (mg)	Sodium (mg)	Carbohydrate (g)	Protein (g)	Fiber (g)
229	27	7	2.7	124	138	9	31	2

Exchanges: Vegetable 2, Low-fat protein 4

Red Meat

Red meat is not just beef, or meat that's red when raw. Although there is no official definition of the term, nutritionists refer to all muscle meats except poultry as red meat. Pork, veal, venison, and rabbit are all considered red meats, even though some of these cuts may be more lean than beef.

Most red meats have the same amount of cholesterol, but they vary considerably in their fat content. Avoid meats that are highly marbled (streaked with fat) and trim excess visible fat before cooking. Prime meat has the most fat; choice meat is lower in fat; select meat is leanest of all.

Belgian Endive

Escarole and Belgian endive are grown from the same seed. To produce Belgian endive, the plant is kept in total darkness, a natural bleaching method that keeps color from developing in the leaves. This technique is practiced almost exclusively in Belgium.

Belgian endive is tender but crisp, and the hearts have a clean, bitter flavor. The leaves should be tightly wrapped in compact heads; the tips of the leaves can be pale yellow, but any sign of green or brown indicates poor storage. Belgian endive should be stored in a brown paper bag (so it is not exposed to light) in the refrigerator for no more than one or two days.

It is good with mustard vinaigrettes and often appears in salads or on appetizer trays. Braised endive is also popular.

Veal Medallions with Braised Endives

George Haidon

2 veal medallions (2 oz each), pounded thin
2 medium Belgian endives, cut lengthwise
1 large tomato, peeled, seeded, diced
1 T chopped dill and tarragon
1 T chopped shallots
6 balls potato (cut with a melon baller), boiled

Arrange the endives in a skillet lightly coated with vegetable spray. Season with lemon juice and pepper and add a little water. Cover; cook until tender. Keep warm.

Cook veal in a hot pan lightly coated with vegetable spray. Keep warm.

Sauté the tomato and shallots in a hot skillet. Add some of the cooking liquid from the endives. Season. Cook until the tomato sauce is slightly thick. Add the dill and tarragon.

To serve, drain the endives and arrange them on a plate. Place the veal on top. Spoon the sauce over the veal. Arrange the boiled potatoes around the plate.

Serves 1.

Calories	%Fat	Fat (g)	Saturated Fat (g)	Cholesterol (mg)	Sodium (mg)	Carbohydrate (g)	Protein (g)	Fiber (g)
316	23	8	2.8	124	156	26	36	8

Exchanges: Starch 1/2, Vegetable 4, Low-fat protein 4

Roast Lamb with Oranges

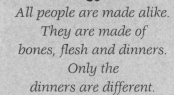
2 lb leg of lamb
1 clove garlic, cut in slivers
1/4 C flour
1/2 C unsweetened orange juice
1 tsp grated orange rind
1/4 tsp rosemary
2 T brown sugar
2 oranges, quartered
Fresh rosemary sprigs

Cut small slits in the lamb and insert slivers of garlic inside the meat. Coat the lamb with flour, brushing off excess. Roast at 350° for 25 to 30 minutes per pound. Mix the orange juice with the grated rind and rosemary. Halfway through cooking, pour 1/4 C orange juice over the lamb. Ten minutes later, pour on the remaining juice and lightly sprinkle the brown sugar over the roast. Serve garnished with oranges and fresh rosemary.

Serves 8.

Calories	%Fat	Fat (g)	Saturated Fat (g)	Cholesterol (mg)	Sodium (mg)	Carbohydrate (g)	Protein (g)	Fiber (g)
259	36	10	3.7	104	82	6	33	0

Exchanges: Fruit 1/2, Low-fat protein 4-1/2

Pork Tenderloin Diable

1 lb pork tenderloin, trimmed of fat
Freshly ground black pepper to taste
1/3 C rice vinegar
1-1/2 T tupelo honey
2 to 3 tsp Jack Daniel's Old No. 7 Mustard

Season tenderloin with pepper. Sear tenderloin on both sides over medium-high heat until browned, about 5 minutes each side. Place pork on a rack in a shallow roasting pan. Combine remaining ingredients and brush over tenderloin, reserving some for basting. Bake at 400° for 30 to 35 minutes, or until a meat thermometer inserted into the thickest part of the tenderloin reads 160°. Baste often during cooking.
Serves 4.

Calories	%Fat	Fat (g)	Saturated Fat (g)	Cholesterol (mg)	Sodium (mg)	Carbohydrate (g)	Protein (g)	Fiber (g)
227	27	7	2.0	105	108	8	33	0

Exchanges: Fruit 1/2, Low-fat protein 4-1/2

Stuffed Leg of Goat

John Novi

1 hind leg of goat
Freshly ground black pepper to taste
Fresh parsley
6 brined black olives, pitted
1 tsp minced garlic
2 T chopped onion
1 T bread crumbs
1 tsp olive oil
1/4 C Swiss chard, centers removed
Plum Red Wine Glaze (page 467)

Debone the leg of goat, leaving about 1 or 2 inches of bone below the bottom joint. Butterfly and fan the meat. Cover with plastic wrap or waxed paper and pound with a wooden mallet, shaping the meat into a square. Season to taste with pepper and parsley. Blend the olives, garlic, onion, bread crumbs, oil, pepper to taste, and Swiss chard in a food processor for 30 seconds. Spread over the square of meat; roll up the meat. Make slices or cuts on the broad side of the meat opposite the skin. Tie it into shape. Season with pepper and chill. Place the meat in a cooking bag and bake at 450° for 20 minutes, or to desired doneness. Serve with Plum Red Wine Glaze.

Serves 3.

Calories	%Fat	Fat (g)	Saturated Fat (g)	Cholesterol (mg)	Sodium (mg)	Carbohydrate (g)	Protein (g)	Fiber (g)
188	25	5	1.1	64	165	11	24	1

Exchanges: Fruit 1/2, Low-fat protein 3

uffalo Pot Roast

3 lb buffalo roast
1 C unsweetened apple juice
2 T sugar
1/4 tsp cinnamon
1/4 tsp ginger
3 whole cloves
1 medium onion, sliced
12 medium dried apricots, plumped
12 medium dried prunes, plumped

In a large pot, brown roast on all sides. Mix apple juice with spices; pour over roast. Add onions. Simmer, covered, for 2 hours. Drain plumped apricots and prunes and place on top of roast. Continue cooking for 30 minutes. Remove cloves. Transfer roast, onions, and fruit to a serving platter.

Serves 12.

Suggestions
- Beef chuck roast may be substituted for the buffalo.
- Defatted pan drippings can be made into gravy.

Calories	%Fat	Fat (g)	Saturated Fat (g)	Cholesterol (mg)	Sodium (mg)	Carbohydrate (g)	Protein (g)	Fiber (g)
171	15	3	1.1	95	47	10	26	1

Exchanges: Fruit 1/2, Low-fat protein 3-1/2

New York State Venison Oriental Style

Walter K. Houlihan

3 C chicken broth
3 T soy sauce
1 tsp sugar
1 tsp freshly ground pepper
1 T hoisin sauce (Peking sauce)
2 T sake
1-1/2 lb venison (loin cut or tenderloin) steaks, 1/2-inch cut
1 tsp oil (corn or safflower)
2 cloves garlic
1/4 lb shiitake mushrooms, stemmed and julienned
2 red bell peppers, seeded and julienned
1 jalapeño (optional, but it adds a nice zing)
4 scallions, cut into 1-inch pieces on the bias
2 T arrowroot or cornstarch mixed with 4 T water
1 crisp apple, peeled, seeded, and small diced

Combine the chicken broth, soy sauce, sugar, pepper, hoisin sauce, and sake in a small saucepan. Bring to a boil and simmer for about 5 minutes.

Turn on the broiler and have all ingredients ready. Season venison steaks generously with salt and pepper. Heat 1 tsp oil in a large sauté pan. Sauté the

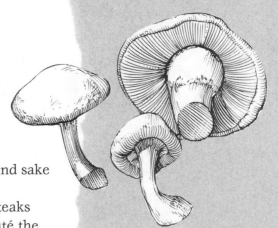

Arrowroot

Arrowroot is a tasteless, fine white powder made from the root of a tropical plant. This starch is used to thicken sauces, glazes, and custards. Its thickening power is about twice that of wheat flour. It should be mixed with cold liquid before it is added to hot foods. Arrowroot is perfectly clear when cooked.

Cornstarch

Cornstarch is a fine white flour made from corn. It is used for thickening sauces and as flour for cake baking. Cornstarch must be mixed with cold water or sugar before it is added to hot foods, or it will form lumps. It loses its thickening power if it is cooked too long or stirred too vigorously; it is usually added at the end of cooking period. Unlike flour, cornstarch makes a clear, not opaque, sauce. One tablespoon of cornstarch is equivalent to two tablespoons of flour or two teaspoons of arrowroot.

garlic until golden brown, without burning, and discard. Add as many steaks to the pan as you can without overcrowding; quickly sear both sides and transfer the meat to an oven-proof platter. Continue this until all steaks are seared.

Add the mushrooms, peppers, jalapeño, and scallions and quickly sauté for another minute (use cooking spray if necessary). Add the heated broth, soy sauce, sugar, pepper, hoisin sauce, and sake and boil for about 1 minute. Slowly add the cornstarch mixture while stirring. This should thicken and give it a nice glazed look. Cook for another minute. Stir in the apples. Season with pepper to taste if desired.

Finish cooking the steaks under a hot broiler. Be careful not to overcook; since venison is naturally low in fat, it will become dry if cooked too long. Slice the steaks on the bias and arrange nicely on a platter or plate over white rice or noodles. Spoon sauce over the meat.

Serves 4 to 6.

Suggestions
- Button mushrooms can be substituted for the shiitake mushrooms.
- Dry sherry may be substituted for the sake.

Calories	%Fat	Fat (g)	Saturated Fat (g)	Cholesterol (mg)	Sodium (mg)	Carbohydrate (g)	Protein (g)	Fiber (g)
189	21	4	1.4	113	68	5	32	1

Exchanges: Vegetable 1, Low-fat protein 4

# **M**edallions of Venison

Rozanne Gold

Moose	1
Buffalo	2
Elk	2
Raccoon	2
Venison	3
Wild duck breast*	4
Wild rabbit	5
Wild duck*	9
Bear	13
Opossum	13

Grams per 3-1/2 ounces
*Without skin

1-1/2 lb boneless venison loin, cut into 12 medallions
1/2 tsp pepper
2 tsp vegetable oil
Sauce Poivrade (page 451)

Pat venison dry and lightly rub each medallion with pepper. Heat a large, nonstick skillet; add 1 tsp oil. Add 6 medallions and cook over high heat for 2 to 3 minutes on each side. Transfer to plate; keep warm. Cook remaining medallions in 1 tsp oil. Serve 2 per person with 2 T Sauce Poivrade spooned over the top.

Serves 6.

Suggestion
• Serve with Barley Pilaf with Sun-Dried Cranberries (page 76). Garnish with bright green watercress, if desired.

Calories	%Fat	Fat (g)	Saturated Fat (g)	Cholesterol (mg)	Sodium (mg)	Carbohydrate (g)	Protein (g)	Fiber (g)
151	25	4	1.3	94	48	0	25	0

Exchanges: Low-fat protein 3-1/2

Fruit & Fruit Desserts

Honey-Ginger Applesauce

1-1/2 lb Granny Smith Apples, peeled, cored, and chopped
1 C water
2 T honey
1 T lemon juice
1-1/2 tsp cinammon
1/2 tsp ground ginger
1/2 C yellow raisins

Cook apples and water in a heavy saucepan for about 10 minutes, or until apples are soft. Add remaining ingredients and continue cooking for another 10 minutes. Stirring occasionally and cooking for a longer time will make the applesauce smoother, darker, and thicker.

Serves 6.

Calories	%Fat	Fat (g)	Saturated Fat (g)	Cholesterol (mg)	Sodium (mg)	Carbohydrate (g)	Protein (g)	Fiber (g)
123	5	1	0.1	0	6	32	1	3

Exchanges: Fruit 2

*Eat an apple
on going to bed,
And you'll keep the doctor
from earning his bread.*

Unknown

Sound Diets

A key element in any sound diet is knowledge. Know what you need, know what a particular diet is going to give you, know what it is going to deprive you of. Too many Americans, in spite of their sincere interest in the subject, are still quite ignorant about what makes a good diet and what makes a bad one. Too easily they are intrigued by the fad diets, the gimmicky food supplements, and the "natural" vitamin wonders on the market that promise a "new" you, but deliver the "old" you in much worse shape than when you began.

Edward B. Diethrich, MD
Heart Test

**Great Seasonings
for Fruit**
Allspice
Almond
Cinnamon
Cloves
Ginger
Mace
Mint
Nutmeg
Vanilla

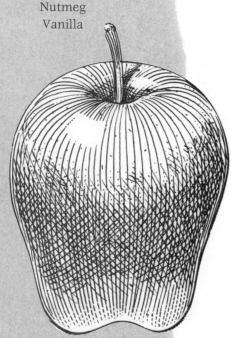

Chunky Cinnamon Applesauce

1/2 C sugar
2 tsp cinnamon
2 C water
12 large cooking apples, peeled, cored, and chopped

Mix all ingredients in a heavy saucepan and bring to a boil. Reduce heat and simmer, uncovered, for 20 to 30 minutes, or until apples are tender. Stir carefully and infrequently during cooking for a chunky texture.
Serves 8.

Suggestions
• Sugar can be omitted during cooking and artificial sweetener to taste stirred in before serving.
• For a festive, rosy-colored applesauce, leave the skins on red apples while cooking. When tender, press the apples through a food mill and discard the peel. Continue with the recipe as directed.

Calories	% Fat	Fat (g)	Saturated Fat (g)	Cholesterol (mg)	Sodium (mg)	Carbohydrate (g)	Protein (g)	Fiber (g)
193	1	0	0.0	0	7	51	1	6

Exchanges: Fruit 3-1/2
Note: Occasional use

Baked Granny Smith Wrapped in Cinnamon & Cocoa Leaves

Allen Susser

2 oz raisins
6 pkg artificial sweetener
2 T cinnamon, divided
2 oz white wine
4 Granny Smith apples, peeled and cored
1 C water
3 sheets of phyllo dough
1 T cocoa

Soak the raisins, 2 pkg sweetener, and 1 T of cinnamon in white wine for 10 minutes. Fill the apples with the mixture. Bake at 325° for 15 minutes in a shallow pan with water. Remove and cool.

Lay out a sheet of phyllo dough. Spray it lightly with butter-flavored cooking spray. Sprinkle it with the cinnamon. Place another sheet of phyllo on top of the first sheet. Spray it lightly with butter-flavored cooking spray. Dust with the cocoa. Place the last sheet of phyllo on top. Spray it lightly with butter-flavored cooking spray and sprinkle with sweetener. Cut the sheets in quarters. Wrap each apple in one of the phyllo pieces, bringing the edges together at the top of the apple. Bake at 375° for 10 minutes, or until the shell is crisp and brown.

Serves 4.

Calories	%Fat	Fat (g)	Saturated Fat (g)	Cholesterol (mg)	Sodium (mg)	Carbohydrate (g)	Protein (g)	Fiber (g)
184	4	1	0.2	0	66	46	2	5

Exchanges: Starch 1, Fruit 2

Apples

Apples have been cultivated since ancient times, with possibly as many as 20,000 varieties. In the early 1900s, nearly 1,000 varieties of apples were sold commercially. Today, only about two dozen types of apples are sold, some in only certain parts of the country. Others are available only in season through local orchards and roadside stands. Apples contain a small amount of vitamin C and fiber.

Apples store well at cool temperatures. They lose their crispness and spoil quickly at room temperature; keep them in the refrigerator. Cut apples turn brown quickly. If they will not be cooked or mixed with dressing immediately, they should be covered with acidulated water; drain before proceeding with the recipe.

Apple Brown Betty

1/2 C sugar
1 tsp cinnamon
1 T grated lemon rind
4 C diced apples
1/2 C brown sugar
4 C cubed cinnamon raisin bread
2 T lemon juice
1/2 C water
1/2 C bread crumbs
1/4 C soft tub margarine, melted

Combine sugar, cinnamon, and lemon rind; set aside. Spread one-third of the apples in a 1-1/2-qt casserole dish. Sprinkle one-third of the brown sugar over the apples. Top with half the bread and sprinkle with half the cinnamon-sugar. Repeat layers of apple, brown sugar, bread cubes, and cinnamon-sugar. Mix lemon juice with water and sprinkle over top. Spread the remaining apples and brown sugar on top; sprinkle with a mixture of the bread crumbs and margarine. Bake, covered, at 350° for 30 minutes. Remove cover and bake for 10 to 15 minutes, or until topping is golden brown. Serve warm.

Serves 8.

Suggestion

• Peaches or apricots may be substituted for the apples.

Calories	%Fat	Fat (g)	Saturated Fat (g)	Cholesterol (mg)	Sodium (mg)	Carbohydrate (g)	Protein (g)	Fiber (g)
253	24	7	1.2	1	185	48	2	3

Exchanges: Starch 1, Fruit 2, Fat 1
Note: Not appropriate for diabetics

Applesnap Cobbler

2 T sugar
1 tsp cinnamon
1-1/2 tsp ginger, divided
1 T + 1 C flour, divided
2 T raisins
5 Granny Smith apples, peeled, cored, and sliced
1/3 C ginger-flavored brandy
1-1/2 tsp baking powder
3 T margarine
2 T chopped pecans
1/3 C finely chopped crystallized ginger
1/3 C skim milk
1 egg white
2 T molasses

   Mix sugar, cinnamon, 1/2 tsp ginger, 1 T flour, and raisins. Sprinkle over apples; add brandy and stir until apples are evenly coated. Spread apples in a 9 × 9-inch cakepan, making an even layer. Mix 1 C flour with 1 tsp ginger and baking powder. Cut in margarine, working until it is the size of rice grains. Stir in pecans and crystallized ginger. Mix milk, egg white, and molasses; stir into flour mixture, making a soft dough. On a lightly floured surface, pat out the dough into a square a little smaller than the pan (slightly raggedy edges will

Varieties of Apples

- *Baldwin:* Red with gray dots; mildly sweet-tart; fairly crisp. All-purpose apple.
- *Braeburn:* Slightly tart; crisp. Good for cooking.
- *Cortland:* Rich red skin, very white flesh; crisp, juicy, sweet. Resists browning. All-purpose apple.
- *Empire:* Large, juicy, sweet; crisp. All-purpose apple.
- *Fameuse:* Red skin, white flesh streaked with red. Small. Good for eating raw.
- *Gala:* Sweet; soft texture. Good for pies and salads.
- *Golden Delicious:* Yellow, sometimes with red blush; lovely texture, aroma, and flavor. Good for eating raw.
- *Granny Smith:* Bright green; crisp, juicy, and distinctive sweet-tart flavor. Good all-purpose apple.
- *Jonathan:* Brilliant red skin; crisp, tender, juicy, and sweet-tart. Develops soft spots easily. Good for eating raw and cooking (but not for baking).
- *Macoun:* Wine-red skin; superior flavor; large, sweet, and juicy. Does not store

well. Superior eating apple.

- *McIntosh:* Bright red; juicy, sweet or slightly tart; soft or medium crisp. Bruises easily. Good for eating raw.
- *Newtown Pippin:* Yellow to yellowish-green skin; slightly tart; crisp, firm texture. Good all-purpose apple.
- *Northern Spy:* Red, pale green, or yellow, with red streaks; fragrant, very juicy, crisp-tender; sweet-tart. Superior all-purpose apple.
- *Red Delicious:* Superior eating apple; large, firm, and sweet; stores well.
- *Rome Beauty:* Deep red; largest apple sold; sweet to bland flavor; tender flesh. Most common baked apple.
- *Roxbury Russet:* Russet skin, yellowish flesh; juicy and flavorful. Stores well.
- *Stayman:* Dull red with green streaks; crisp, juicy, tart. All-purpose apple.
- *Winesap:* Red; tart and juicy; crisp. Stores well. All-purpose apple.
- *York Imperial:* Greenish yellow with red blush; mildly sweet and juicy. Keeps shape well during cooking; excellent for pie or baked.

make a nice homestyle appearance). Place the dough on top of the apples, leaving a narrow (1/4 inch) margin around all edges. Bake at 350° for 45 to 50 minutes, or until the crust is brown and the apples are tender.

Serves 9.

Suggestions

- Two cans of canned sliced apples can be substituted for the fresh apples. The cooking time may be shorter; begin testing apples after 35 to 40 minutes.
- Peaches or plums may be substituted for the apples.
- Change ginger to cinnamon; substitute cinnamon-flavored brandy for the ginger-flavored brandy.

Calories	%Fat	Fat (g)	Saturated Fat (g)	Cholesterol (mg)	Sodium (mg)	Carbohydrate (g)	Protein (g)	Fiber (g)
213	22	5	0.8	0	148	37	3	2

Exchanges: Starch 1-1/2, Fruit 1, Fat 1

# Apple & Dried Fruit Pudding with Orange Sabayon

Steven Allen

3 C boiling water
1 large apple, peeled, quartered, cored
2-1/2 C dried fruit (diced prunes, dates, raisins, currants), packed
3 pkt Pritikin Heart Hot Cereal
1 T orange zest, grated
3 egg whites, slightly beaten
Pinch cinnamon
2 egg whites
3 T orange juice concentrate
Fresh fruit to garnish (such as persimmon or orange wedges, grapes)

Slice the apple in 3/16-inch wedges; simmer in water for about 3 minutes, or until pliable. Remove from water and set aside. In the same water, simmer the dried fruit and cereal, stirring frequently, for about 6 minutes. Pour mixture on a platter to cool. Line sides and bottoms of 6 soup cups with plastic, then with apple slices.

Beat the 3 egg whites and add cooked cereal, cinnamon, and orange zest. Mix until smooth and pour into the cups. In a pan large enough to hold all 6 cups, bring 1 inch of water to a boil. Place the cups in the pan and cover. Bake at 350° for about 45 minutes.

The pet of the harem,
Rose-in-Bloom,
Orders a feast in his favorite
room—
Glittering squares of colored
ice,
Sweetened with syrup,
tinctured with spice,
Creams, and cordials, and
sugared dates,
Syrian apples, Othmanee
quinces,
Limes and citrons and
apricots,
And wines that are known
to Eastern princes.

T.B. Aldrich
When the Sultan
Goes to Ispahan

To make the Orange Sabayon, whip the 2 egg whites with the orange juice concentrate in a bowl over a hot water bath until thick and foamy. Remove from heat.

To serve, pour sabayon onto a dessert plate. Invert the pudding over the plate and unmold; remove plastic. Garnish with fresh fruit.

Serves 6.

Suggestion
• Instant oatmeal may be substituted for the Pritikin Heart Hot Cereal.

Calories	%Fat	Fat (g)	Saturated Fat (g)	Cholesterol (mg)	Sodium (mg)	Carbohydrate (g)	Protein (g)	Fiber (g)
275	5	1	0.2	0	193	66	7	5

Exchanges: Starch 1, Fruit 3-1/2

Apple-Pear Crisp

1-1/2 lb Granny Smith apples, unpeeled, cored, and diced
3/4 lb Bosc pears, unpeeled, cored, and diced
1 tsp cinnamon
1/4 tsp nutmeg
2 T unsweetened orange juice
1/4 C raisins
1/3 C maple syrup
1 C rolled oats
1/3 C whole-wheat flour
2 T canola oil

Toss apples, pears, spices, juice, raisins, and 1 T maple syrup; spread evenly in a 1-1/2 qt baking dish. Mix oatmeal, flour, and oil with a fork until blended. Mix in remaining maple syrup. Sprinkle over fruit mixture. Bake at 350° for 35 minutes, or until topping is lightly browned. Serve warm.

Serves 8.

Suggestion
• Bartlett pears may be substituted if Bosc pears are unavailable.

Calories	%Fat	Fat (g)	Saturated Fat (g)	Cholesterol (mg)	Sodium (mg)	Carbohydrate (g)	Protein (g)	Fiber (g)
197	22	5	0.5	0	4	39	3	4

Exchanges: Starch 1/2, Fruit 2, Fat 1

Fresh-Fruit Ices

Mangoes, papayas, pineapples, kiwis, strawberries, blueberries, mulberries, blackberries, raspberries, cherries, peaches, and apricots make excellent fresh-fruit ices. Peel the fresh fruit and cut it into one-inch pieces (if necessary); freeze until solid. Just before serving, purée the frozen chunks or berries in a blender or food processor.

Use a little vanilla or almond extract, honey, grated orange or lemon peel, or spices for extra flavor if desired. Adding a little skim milk during puréeing will make a fruit sherbet. Adding frozen banana chunks makes a very smooth ice. Mixed-fruit ices are also delicious.

Blueberry Ice

1-1/2 C frozen blueberries
1/4 C skim milk
1/4 C water
1/2 tsp almond extract
2 tsp sugar

Process all ingredients in a blender on low speed until smooth; stop blender to scrape down sides and clear air pockets as necessary. Serve immediately.
Serves 2.

Suggestions
- Artificial sweetener to taste may be substituted for sugar.
- Any type of berry can be substituted for the blueberries.

Calories	%Fat	Fat (g)	Saturated Fat (g)	Cholesterol (mg)	Sodium (mg)	Carbohydrate (g)	Protein (g)	Fiber (g)
124	5	1	0.0	1	26	30	2	2

Exchanges: Fruit 2

Cherry Cobbler

3 cans (16 oz each) sour cherries, drained
1/4 C sugar
2 T flour
3/4 C all-purpose flour
3/4 C rolled oats
3 T brown sugar
1-1/2 tsp baking powder
3 T soft tub margarine
2 egg whites
1/4 C skim milk
1/4 tsp almond extract
1 tsp grated orange peel

Mix cherries with 1/4 C sugar and 2 T flour; adjust sweetness to taste. Spread cherries in a nonstick 8-inch baking dish. Mix 3/4 C flour, rolled oats, brown sugar, and baking powder. Cut in margarine until texture resembles coarse crumbs. Stir in egg whites, milk, extract, and grated orange peel. Spoon over cherries. Bake at 400° for 20 minutes, or until topping is lightly browned. Serve warm.

Serves 8.

Cherries

Cherries can be sweet or sour. The darkest cherries are the sweetest. Cherries contain some vitamin C and A. Eat sweet cherries raw for the most vitamin C. Sour cherries taste better cooked; they are lower in calories and higher in vitamin C than sweet cherries.

Most cherries are picked fully ripe. Cherries that still have their stems are fresher and will last longer. Refrigerate them loosely covered for two to three days. Serve cherries at room temperature for the best flavor.

- *Bing:* Dark red, very sweet; one of the most popular cherries.
- *Montmorency:* Sour cherry; good for pies, cobblers; has six times as much vitamin A as sweet cherries.
- *Queen Anne:* Yellow with red blush; large and sweet. Used to make maraschino cherries.

Calories	%Fat	Fat (g)	Saturated Fat (g)	Cholesterol (mg)	Sodium (mg)	Carbohydrate (g)	Protein (g)	Fiber (g)
308	15	5	0.9	0	153	63	5	4

Exchanges: Starch 1, Fruit 3, Fat 1
Note: Occasional use

Cranberries

A native American berry, the cranberry is very tart. It is rich in vitamin C. Store fresh cranberries in a plastic bag in the refrigerator for up to a month (they will lose their color at room temperature). Cooked cranberries can be kept in the refrigerator, tightly covered, for up to two months. Raw cranberries freeze well.

Boiling makes the water in a cranberry swell, causing it to burst. The creamy yellow interiors and the cooking water will turn red. Add lemon juice and sugar to preserve the color. To add raw cranberries to muffins, cakes, and relishes, chop them coarsely and add a little sweetener; they will be too tart if cooked whole and unsweetened.

Cranberry Clafouti

3 C fresh cranberries
2 C coarsely grated apple
3/4 C unsweetened apple juice
3/4 C + 3 T sugar, divided
2/3 C raisins
2 T cornstarch
1/4 C unsweetened orange juice
1-1/2 C all-purpose flour
1-1/2 tsp baking powder
3 T soft tub margarine
2 egg whites
1/4 C skim milk
1/2 tsp vanilla

Bring cranberries, apples, apple juice, 3/4 C sugar, raisins, and cinnamon to a boil. Cook, covered, until cranberries pop. Mix cornstarch with orange juice; stir into cranberries and cook until the mixture thickens. Pour into an 8-inch cake pan. Mix flour, 3 T sugar, and baking powder. Cut in margarine until the texture resembles rice. Stir in egg whites, milk, and vanilla. Spread over fruit. Bake at 400° for 20 minutes, or until topping is light browned.

Serves 8.

Calories	%Fat	Fat (g)	Saturated Fat (g)	Cholesterol (mg)	Sodium (mg)	Carbohydrate (g)	Protein (g)	Fiber (g)
303	16	5	0.9	0	153	62	4	4

Exchanges: Starch 1, Fruit 3, Fat 1
Note: Occasional use

Figs & Blueberries in Citrus Broth

Hubert Keller

1-1/2 C orange juice, freshly squeezed
1 C grapefruit juice, freshly squeezed
3 T lemon juice, freshly squeezed
2 tsp fresh ginger, finely shredded
2 T honey
1 T rum
16 to 20 ripe black figs
3 T blueberries
1 banana
8 mint leaves for garnish

Mix the 3 citrus juices in a stainless steel or Teflon saucepot. Add ginger, honey, and rum, and bring to a boil. Meanwhile, prick each fig with a fork in a few places. Peel the banana and cut into slices (1/4- inch thick). Plunge the fruits gently in the boiling juices. Turn off the heat, cover, and let cool in juice. Refrigerate for 1 hour. By the end of the chilling time, the blueberries will have released a very attractive reddish color into the citrus broth. Serve in shallow, rimmed soup plates and decorate with fresh mint leaves.

Serves 4.

Calories	%Fat	Fat (g)	Saturated Fat (g)	Cholesterol (mg)	Sodium (mg)	Carbohydrate (g)	Protein (g)	Fiber (g)
305	3	1	0.2	0	7	76	3	8

Exchanges: Fruit 5

Train up a fig-tree in the way it should go, and when you are old sit under the shade of it.

Charles Dickens
Dombey and Son

Figs

Figs are grown primarily in California and the Mediterranean. Fresh figs have very brief shelf-life because they must be picked ripe, and they will spoil within seven to ten days. Fresh figs should be clean and dry, and their thin skins should not be split or torn. Very firm figs won't ripen, and a collapsing fig is overripe. Store fresh figs in the refrigerator and serve promptly.

Figs are an excellent source of fiber. They are also a good source of calcium, iron, and potassium.

Calimyrna and Mission figs are sold fresh or dried. Kadota figs are often canned in a light syrup that should be rinsed off before serving.

Barbados Crumble

1/4 C dark brown sugar
1/2 C unbleached flour
1/4 C whole-wheat flour
1/8 tsp ground nutmeg
1/4 tsp ground cinnamon
1/4 C margarine, cut up and chilled
1 tsp lime juice
1 T rum
2 medium mangoes, peeled and cut in bite-size pieces
5 medium ripe bananas, sliced

For the topping, cut the sugar, flours, nutmeg, cinnamon, and margarine together with a pastry knife until the margarine is the size of small peas. Set aside. Mix lime juice and rum. Beginning and ending with the bananas, layer the fruit in a nonstick baking dish; sprinkle each layer with lime-rum mixture. Sprinkle topping over the fruit, pressing down lightly. Bake at 350° until the topping is lightly browned, about 30 minutes.

Serves 8.

Calories	%Fat	Fat (g)	Saturated Fat (g)	Cholesterol (mg)	Sodium (mg)	Carbohydrate (g)	Protein (g)	Fiber (g)
221	26	6	1.3	0	71	41	2	4

Exchanges: Starch 1/2, Fruit 2, Fat 1

# ot Mango Tart & Candied Lime

Mark Gould

8 mangoes
2 C water
1/2 C sugar
2 oz simple syrup
2 oz white rum
1-1/2 oz soft tub margarine
5 sheets phyllo dough
Candied Lime for garnish (page 414)

For the glaze, peel 4 mangoes and chop their flesh finely. Mix with the sugar and simple syrup in a saucepan and place over a moderate heat. As the mixture warms up, add the water, then bring to a boil and reduce by half. Take the mixture off the heat and add the rum and margarine. Place back on a gentle heat and stir to mix until warmed through again; sieve the mixture while still warm.

For the tarts, layer the 5 sheets of phyllo dough, lightly coating each layer with cooking spray and brushing the top with glaze; cut into four 7-inch circles. Peel the remaining mangoes carefully and cut each lengthwise into 3 lobes; set aside. Trim off all the flesh from around the stones, cut into a small dice, and place into the center of the pastry circles to give it height. Lay each of the reserved mango lobes flat and cut into 1/8-inch slices, half-moon style.

Arrange these half-moons in overlapping fans around the pastry circles, be-

Mangoes can be red, yellow, orange, or green; the smooth satin-finish skin can be a solid color or blushed. The bright orange or yellow-orange flesh is very juicy. Black spots on the skin are common; they are harmless. Mangoes are wonderfully fragrant; they taste peachy sweet. They are rich in vitamins A and C, as well as potassium. They also contain some vitamin E.

Ripen mangoes at room temperature in a paper bag. They are ripe when they yield to slight pressure, like an avocado; when overripe, the skin develops tiny dimples. Ripe mangoes can be refrigerated for up to a week. They can also be frozen in chunks or as a purée for several months.

Peel mangoes over a bowl to catch all juices. The flesh must be sliced off the large, flat seed with a knife, a messy job but worthwhile.

Fresh mango slices are good in fruit, vegetable, and chicken salads. Mangoes make fabulous milkshakes and frozen yogurt. They can replace peaches, papayas, nectarines, or plums in recipes. Green or half-ripe mangoes are used to make relishes and chutneys; they are good with meat, game, and poultry. Used in marinades, mangoes help break down the fibers to tenderize meat. Mangoes also cook well.

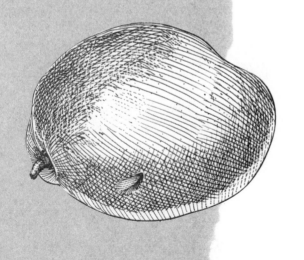

ing careful to leave 1/4-inch edge all around. Save the last few segments to arrange around the space at the center. Lightly sprinkle the whole tart with sugar. Bake at 400° for 8 to 10 minutes. Halfway into the baking and again just before serving, moisten the top of the tarts with the mango glaze.

Place the glazed tarts on warmed serving plates, garnish with Candied Lime, and spoon a little glaze around the plates.

Serves 4.

Suggestions

- Replace puff pastry in your favorite recipes with phyllo dough, as the chef has done with this recipe. His heart-healthy substitution eliminates about 21 grams of fat from this dessert without sacrificing flavor.
- This recipe is not high in fat but has many calories because it contains 7 servings of fruit. We recommend that you have only one-half tart, especially if you are trying to control your weight.

Calories	%Fat	Fat (g)	Saturated Fat (g)	Cholesterol (mg)	Sodium (mg)	Carbohydrate (g)	Protein (g)	Fiber (g)
620	8	6	1.2	0	244	136	6	13

Exchanges: Starch 2, Fruit 7, Fat 1
Note: Not appropriate for diabetics

Dessert Oranges

6 C cut-up fresh oranges, with juice
1 C chopped pitted dates
2 T thinly sliced almonds, lightly toasted

Mix all ingredients. Serve chilled or at room temperature.
Serves 6.

Calories	%Fat	Fat (g)	Saturated Fat (g)	Cholesterol (mg)	Sodium (mg)	Carbohydrate (g)	Protein (g)	Fiber (g)
181	8	2	0.1	0	1	43	3	5

Exchanges: Fruit 3

Oranges

First cultivated by the Chinese, oranges can be sweet (used fresh) or bitter (used in cooking or marmalade). Both varieties can be used as a seasoning in cooked foods. Oranges are rich in vitamin C and potassium, and they are a good source of folate.

Oranges are picked mature and do not become softer or sweeter after harvesting. For maximum juice, choose oranges that are firm and heavy. Grocers often wax citrus; oranges should be scrubbed with soap and water if the rind will be used.

Store at room temperature for several days or in the refrigerator for up to two weeks. Oranges taste best at room temperature.

• *Blood:* Small, slightly rough skin; sweet and juicy; scarlet, reddish-orange, or purple flesh; the juice is dark like burgundy wine. Soft pulp. No bitterness, even in peel. Full-bodied citrus flavor with raspberry aftertaste. Good for juicing or eating fresh. Most are imported from Sicily.

- *Clementine:* Cross between tangerine and orange. Most are imported from North Africa.
- *Hamlin:* Thin skin; good juicing orange.
- *Jaffa:* Very juicy and flavorful. Imported from Israel.
- *Mineola:* Tangerine hybrid. Large, sweet, wine-like juice.
- *Navel:* Characteristic growth at blossom end looks like a belly button; thick skin; easy to peel and segment. Sweet-tart flavor.
- *Pineapple:* Very flavorful; many seeds. Good for juicing or eating fresh.
- *Seville:* Bitter; used in traditional marmalade.
- *Tangelo:* Cross between tangerine and grapefruit.
- *Tangerine:* Small; very flavorful; loose skin peels easily. Good for eating fresh or juicing.
- *Temple:* Cross between tangerine and orange. Very sweet. Loose skin peels easily.
- *Valencia:* Thin skin, few seeds. Good for juicing or eating fresh.

Peach Freeze

2 C peeled and mashed fresh peaches (leave some small chunks)
1 C plain nonfat yogurt
1/2 tsp almond extract
1/4 tsp orange extract
2 T sugar
1 pkg (1/4 oz) unflavored gelatin dissolved in 1/4 C water

Mix peaches, yogurt, extracts, and sugar. Stir in gelatin, blending well. Freeze, covered, for 1 to 2 hours before serving.
Serves 4.

Suggestions

- Artificial sweetener to taste may be substituted for the sugar.
- Apricots, nectarines, or plums may be substituted for the peaches.

Calories	%Fat	Fat (g)	Saturated Fat (g)	Cholesterol (mg)	Sodium (mg)	Carbohydrate (g)	Protein (g)	Fiber (g)
104	2	0	0.1	1	49	21	6	1

Exchanges: Fruit 1, Dairy 1/2

# Peaches Poached in Wine

3/4 cup water
1/4 cup red wine
1 piece of lemon rind
1 cinnamon stick
1 whole clove
4 whole peaches, peeled

Simmer all ingredients gently until peaches are tender. Remove peaches from syrup. Discard lemon rind, cinnamon stick, and clove. Sweeten syrup to taste and pour over fruit. Serve warm or well chilled.
Serves 4.

Peaches

Peaches probably originated in China. More than 2,000 varieties are grown, but they are all generally divided into two groups: *freestone* (pits easy to remove; softer flesh; good for eating fresh, canning, drying) and *clingstone* (pits difficult to remove; firmer, paler flesh; good for canning or poaching). All peaches sold fresh are freestones. Peaches are a good source of vitamin A and potassium, and they contain some vitamin C.

Peaches are golden yellow with a pink or red blush and a slightly fuzzy skin. They do not get sweeter after picking but will become softer and juicier. Peaches that have a green tinge will not ripen, nor will very hard fruit. Mature peaches have a distinct

Calories	% Fat	Fat (g)	Saturated Fat (g)	Cholesterol (mg)	Sodium (mg)	Carbohydrate (g)	Protein (g)	Fiber (g)
51	2	0	0.0	0	1	13	1	2

Exchanges: Fruit 1

"seam" down one side. Buy fruit that is starting to ripen: the seam should yield to gentle pressure, and the peach should smell sweet. Finish ripening peaches at room temperature in a paper bag.

Refrigerate ripe peaches in a plastic bag for three to five days. Cut fruit can be kept in the refrigerator for up to two days. Peaches turn dark after cutting; dip them in acidulated water or use them in salads with citrus fruit.

Poached Pears with Port Sauce & Mascarpone Cheese

Paul Minnillo

4 ripe pears, peeled and cored, preferably with stems still attached
1 bottle port
1 cinnamon stick
1 C granulated sugar
2 T mascarpone cheese
4 T toasted, chopped hazelnuts
Mint leaves

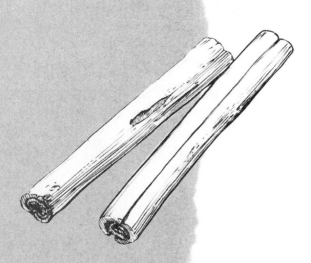

Place pears in a deep saucepan. Pour wine over pears; add cinnamon stick and granulated sugar. If pears are not fully covered by liquid, add enough water to do so. Bring liquid to a boil, then simmer until pears are soft (insert a skewer to test doneness). When pears are done, remove from poaching liquid and cool. Reduce poaching liquid until syrupy, then strain.

Stuff each cooled pear with about 1/2 T mascarpone. Set each pear upright on a plate and drizzle port syrup over the pear. Sprinkle with hazelnuts and mint garnish.

Serves 4.

Suggestion
• Use a good tawny or ruby port.

Calories	%Fat	Fat (g)	Saturated Fat (g)	Cholesterol (mg)	Sodium (mg)	Carbohydrate (g)	Protein (g)	Fiber (g)
357	19	7	2.0	8	62	67	3	3

Exchanges: Fruit 4, Medium-fat protein 1/2, Fat 1
Note: Not appropriate for diabetics

Spicy Mulled Pears

Rozanne Gold

3-1/2 C water
2 C red wine
1 large strip lemon rind
1 large strip orange rind
Juice of 1 lemon
Juice of 1 orange
2 cinnamon sticks
3 bay leaves
20 black peppercorns
8 whole cloves
8 whole allspice
1/3 C sugar
6 pears with stems, peeled

Bring all ingredients except pears to a boil and stir until sugar dissolves. Add pears, making sure all are covered with poaching liquid. Simmer for 60 to 75 minutes, or until pears are cooked through. Remove pears with a slotted spoon and place them in a bowl. Strain the syrup into a small pot. Reduce over high heat to 2-1/2 C. Pour reduced syrup over pears; cool. Refrigerate overnight. Serve 1 pear per person, with syrup. Garnish with a bay leaf or fresh rosemary sprig. Serve as a dessert or, halved, with duck.

Serves 6.

Calories	%Fat	Fat (g)	Saturated Fat (g)	Cholesterol (mg)	Sodium (mg)	Carbohydrate (g)	Protein (g)	Fiber (g)
202	3	1	0.0	0	9	39	1	6

Exchanges: Fruit 2-1/2

Pears

A pear tree can bear fruit for a century or more. With more than 5,000 varieties under cultivation, pears come in many sizes, colors, and textures. They are generally divided into two groups: dessert (juicy white flesh, sweet, strong pleasant scent) or stewing (hard and tasteless, little juice). Pears are a good source of fiber if eaten with the skin. They also contain potassium.

Pears taste best if they are picked mature but unripe, and then ripened at room temperature. Store ripe pears in the refrigerator for three to five days. Do not put them in sealed plastic bags, or the core will turn brown and brown spots will develop under skin. Dried pears can be stored at room temperature for up to six months; after the package is opened, they should be refrigerated in airtight containers.

- *Anjou:* Light green or yellow-green; egg-shaped. Juicy and spicy. Good for cooking or eating raw.

- *Bartlett:* Yellow skin, sometimes with red blush. Smooth flesh; juicy.
- *Bosc:* Russet or cinnamon color. Slender shape; long, tapering neck. Sweet, very juicy, and tender. Holds shape well when cooked or poached.
- *Comice:* Greenish-yellow skin; larger than other pears. Sweet and juicy—best flavor of all pears. Not good for cooking.
- *Firelli:* Freckled blush. Great texture and flavor.
- *Kiefer:* Best used for stewing.
- *Seckel:* Small; spicy flavor.

Prickly Pears

Also called *cactus pears,* prickly pears are the fruit of several varieties of cactus. The skin may be green or purplish red and the flesh yellow or deep gold, with black seeds. Prickly pears taste sweet and smell a little like melons. They can be ripened at room temperature until soft and then stored in the refrigerator for up to a week.

Burgundy-Poached Pears with Prickly Pear Coulis

Gary McCafferty

4 pears, peeled and cored from the bottom
1-1/2 L Burgundy wine
2 T honey
6 prickly pears, peeled
Mint sprigs, for garnish

Place the pears in a 2-qt saucepan with enough wine to cover. Add honey. Place a small, heat-proof plate on top of the pears to keep them submerged. Bring to a boil slowly, over medium-low heat, and then reduce heat slightly. Simmer until the pears are soft but not mushy. Remove from heat and place the pears in a deep bowl. Pour the hot wine over the pears and cover with plastic wrap. Place the hot pears and wine in the refrigerator for 6 to 24 hours (the longer the pears rest in the wine, the deeper their color will be).

For the coulis, purée the peeled prickly pears in a blender and strain through a fine chinois.

To serve, rim the plate with prickly pear coulis. Slice the pear and fan it in the center of the plate. Garnish with mint.

Serves 4.

Calories	%Fat	Fat (g)	Saturated Fat (g)	Cholesterol (mg)	Sodium (mg)	Carbohydrate (g)	Protein (g)	Fiber (g)
130	6	1	0.0	0	2	32	1	7

Exchanges: Fruit 2

# **Pineapple-Strawberry Chiffon**

3/4 C canned unsweetened crushed pineapple, drained
1/4 C sliced fresh strawberries
1 C evaporated skim milk
1 T lemon juice
1 tsp vanilla extract
1 pkg (1/4 oz) unflavored gelatin dissolved in 2 T water
1 tsp grated lemon rind
2 T sugar

   Purée pineapple, strawberries, milk, lemon juice, and extract in blender. Stir in gelatin, lemon rind, and sugar. Pour into 4 dessert dishes and chill until set.
   Serves 4.

Suggestions
- Do not use fresh or frozen pineapple with gelatin; it contains an enzyme that will keep the gelatin from setting.
- Other fruits can be substituted for the pineapple and/or the strawberries.

He had a massive stroke. He died with his tie on. Do you think that could be our generation's equivalent of that old saying about dying with your boots on?

Stephen King
The Stand

Stroke & Potassium
   Fruits and vegetables that are high in potassium may help protect against strokes and the damage to arteries caused by high blood pressure. Bananas, strawberries, potatoes, oranges, grapefruit, tomatoes, and milk are good sources of potassium.

Calories	%Fat	Fat (g)	Saturated Fat (g)	Cholesterol (mg)	Sodium (mg)	Carbohydrate (g)	Protein (g)	Fiber (g)
113	2	0	0.1	2	77	22	7	1

Exchanges: Fruit 1, Dairy 1/2

Plums

More than 100 varieties of plums are grown in America. Dessert plums are juicier and richer-tasting than cooking plums, but both can be eaten raw. They contain some potassium. Buy slightly soft but firm plums. They will not get sweeter after harvesting. Keep firm plums at room temperature to soften. Refrigerate ripe plums in plastic bags for three to five days.

- *Damson:* Very dark skin and flesh; tart; used for making jams and preserves; not good raw.
- *Greengage:* Yellow-green skin and yellow flesh; sweetest and best-flavored variety.
- *Italian:* Navy blue frosted skin, green flesh.
- *Mirabelle:* Golden; small; good stewed or in jam.
- *Nubiana:* Purple-black skin, amber flesh.
- *Santa Rosa:* Purplish-red skin, yellow or red flesh; very tart.
- *Wickson:* Yellow skin and flesh.

Honey Plum Crisp

18 black plums, halved, cored, and thinly sliced
3 T unbleached flour
2 T honey
Grated rind of one-half lemon
1/4 C dark brown sugar
1/2 C unbleached flour
1/4 C whole-wheat flour
1/8 tsp ground nutmeg
1/4 tsp ground cinnamon
1/4 C margarine, cut up and chilled
2 T coarsely chopped pecans
2 T currants

Toss the plums, 3 T flour, honey, and lemon rind. Spread plums in a 2-1/2 qt baking dish.

For the topping, cut the sugar, flours, nutmeg, cinnamon, and margarine together with a pastry knife until the margarine is the size of small peas. Stir in the pecans and currants. Sprinkle topping evenly over the plums. Bake at 400° for 30 minutes, or until the fruit is tender and the topping is crisp and brown.

Serves 6.

Calories	%Fat	Fat (g)	Saturated Fat (g)	Cholesterol (mg)	Sodium (mg)	Carbohydrate (g)	Protein (g)	Fiber (g)
327	30	11	1.8	0	93	58	4	5

Exchanges: Starch 1, Fruit 3, Fat 2

Raspberry Cheese Tart

1 C part-skim ricotta cheese
1 C low-fat cottage cheese
2 egg whites
1 tsp vanilla extract
1/4 tsp almond extract
3 T honey
Graham Cracker Crust (page 411)
1 C fresh raspberries
1/2 C kiwi slices

Blend ricotta cheese, cottage cheese, egg whites, vanilla and almond extracts, and honey in a food processor until smooth. Pour into Graham Cracker Crust and bake at 325° for 30 minutes, or until filling is set. Chill thoroughly. Top with fresh raspberries and kiwis just before serving.

Serves 8.

Suggestions
• Use a 9-inch tart pan for the Graham Cracker Crust.
• Other fresh fruit in season may be used in addition to or instead of the raspberries and kiwis.

Flavorful Fruit

For extra flavor and juice, cook sliced peaches, nectarines, plums, or whole berries over low heat for a few minutes—just until warm. Add a little vanilla or almond extract. Serve plain or as a topping for angel food cake or low-fat frozen yogurt.

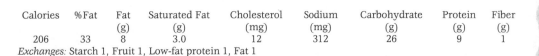

Calories	%Fat	Fat (g)	Saturated Fat (g)	Cholesterol (mg)	Sodium (mg)	Carbohydrate (g)	Protein (g)	Fiber (g)
206	33	8	3.0	12	312	26	9	1

Exchanges: Starch 1, Fruit 1, Low-fat protein 1, Fat 1

Strawberry Clouds

3-oz pkg strawberry gelatin
1-1/2 C boiling water
2 C strawberries, sliced
2 C plain nonfat yogurt

Dissolve gelatin in boiling water. Add strawberries and chill until slightly thickened. Sweeten to taste. Fold in yogurt until completely blended. Spoon into 8 custard cups or dessert dishes. Chill thoroughly.
Serves 8.

Suggestions
• Low-calorie gelatin may be used.
• Black cherry or raspberry gelatin, with matching fresh fruit, may be substituted for the strawberry gelatin and fresh strawberries.

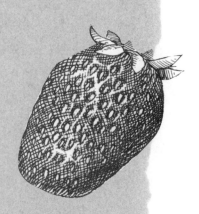

Calories	%Fat	Fat (g)	Saturated Fat (g)	Cholesterol (mg)	Sodium (mg)	Carbohydrate (g)	Protein (g)	Fiber (g)
82	3	0	0.1	1	57	8	13	1

Exchanges: Dairy 1/2

pple Pie Sherbet

1 can (6 oz) frozen unsweetened apple juice concentrate, thawed but cold
2 C skim milk
1/4 tsp cinnamon

   Stir all ingredients together. Add more cinnamon to taste, if desired. Freeze according to preferred method.
   Serves 4.

Suggestion
• Other frozen juice concentrate, with appropriate spices or extracts, may be substituted for the apple juice.

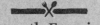

Smooth Freezing
   Smooth frozen desserts depend on small ice crystals. Sugar, egg whites, and gelatin help separate ice crystals so that large, coarse crystals cannot form. The dasher in an ice cream freezer turns the mixture, adding air to keep ice crystals from forming so the texture is smooth. Three general types of ice cream makers are available:

• *Traditional ice cream freezers:* Electric ice cream freezers have generally replaced the old-fashioned freezers that required laborious hand-turning of the dasher. Both manual and electric models require rock salt and water. Some refrigerators have built-in ice cream freezers.

• *Pre-chilled chamber freezer:* These freezers do not require salt or electricity and are virtually mess-free. The ingredients are poured into a pre-frozen cylinder,

Calories	%Fat	Fat (g)	Saturated Fat (g)	Cholesterol (mg)	Sodium (mg)	Carbohydrate (g)	Protein (g)	Fiber (g)
87	3	0	0.2	2	66	17	4	0

Exchanges: Fruit 1/2, Dairy 1/2

and the dasher is turned by hand every four or five minutes for 15 to 30 minutes. Frozen desserts in this cookbook were tested with this type of freezer.

- *Electric ice cream machines:* Self-contained countertop machines have an electric motor that turns the ice-cream canister or the dasher. A variety of sizes and prices are available.

Banana & Passion Fruit Sorbet

Michael Hutchings

1-1/2 lb ripe Java bananas, peeled
1 C simple syrup
1/2 C fresh passion fruit juice
1 C sparkling water

Purée all ingredients in a blender. Pass through a medium-fine sieve. Taste for flavor. Add more simple syrup if needed; if too sweet, add more passion fruit juice. Freeze in an ice cream maker according to the manufacturer's directions. Serve in a chilled wine glass. Makes 1 qt.
Serves 8 (1/2 C each).

Suggestions

- A pleasant sauce can be made by reducing, over heat, passion fruit juice with just enough sugar to cut the acidity. Cool and spoon over the sorbet.
- Ordinary bananas can be substituted for the Java bananas.

Calories	%Fat	Fat (g)	Saturated Fat (g)	Cholesterol (mg)	Sodium (mg)	Carbohydrate (g)	Protein (g)	Fiber (g)
181	1	0	0.1	0	36	47	1	1

Exchanges: Fruit 3
Note: Not appropriate for diabetics

hampagne Sorbet

1 large pink grapefruit, peeled and sectioned
1 C pink grapefruit juice
2 C dry champagne
1/2 C sugar

Purée grapefruit sections, juice, and sugar in an electric blender or food processor. Blend in champagne at low speed. Freeze according to preferred method.
Serves 8.

Suggestions

- Artificial sweetener to taste may be substituted for sugar.
- Alcohol inhibits the freezing process, so allow additional time for sorbet to become firm.
- Serve as an elegant breakfast course, an appetizer, a palate refresher between courses, or a dessert.

Calories	%Fat	Fat (g)	Saturated Fat (g)	Cholesterol (mg)	Sodium (mg)	Carbohydrate (g)	Protein (g)	Fiber (g)
116	1	0	0.0	0	5	20	1	1

Exchanges: Fruit 1-1/2
Note: Not appropriate for diabetics

Cherry Frozen Yogurt

1-1/2 C crushed fresh or frozen pitted dark sweet cherries
1/2 tsp almond extract
2 C plain nonfat yogurt
2 T sugar

Mix all ingredients well. Freeze according to preferred method. Serves 4.

Suggestions
- Artificial sweetener to taste may be substituted for sugar.
- Any fruit may be substituted for the cherries.

Calories	%Fat	Fat (g)	Saturated Fat (g)	Cholesterol (mg)	Sodium (mg)	Carbohydrate (g)	Protein (g)	Fiber (g)
131	5	1	0.3	2	94	25	8	1

Exchanges: Fruit 1, Dairy 1

# Chocolate Sorbet

2 C skim milk
1/3 C sugar
1/4 C unsweetened cocoa powder
1/2 tsp vanilla extract

Mix all ingredients in a blender. Freeze according to preferred method.
Serves 4.

Suggestions

- Artificial sweetener to taste may be substituted for sugar.
- *Chocolate Mint Sorbet:* Replace vanilla extract with peppermint extract.
- *Chocolate Amaretto Sorbet:* Replace vanilla extract with almond extract; stir in sliced almonds before freezing.
- *Mocha Sorbet:* Add powdered instant coffee to taste.
- *Black Forest Sorbet:* Stir in pitted dark cherries before freezing.
- *Double Chocolate Chip Sorbet:* Stir in grated chocolate or miniature chocolate chips before freezing.

Calories	%Fat	Fat (g)	Saturated Fat (g)	Cholesterol (mg)	Sodium (mg)	Carbohydrate (g)	Protein (g)	Fiber (g)
117	7	1	0.6	2	64	25	5	2

Exchanges: Starch 1, Dairy 1/2
Note: Not appropriate for diabetics

I decided long ago never to look at the right hand of the menu or the price tag of clothes—otherwise I would starve, naked.

Helen Hayes

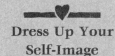

Dress Up Your Self-Image

Pay attention to your physical appearance. Dress as a thin person with a positive image. Overweight people frequently dress in a style that shouts, "I'm fat! Why should I bother to try to look nice?" A defeatist attitude expressed in your clothing is never in style.

Edward B. Diethrich, MD
Heart Test

 # Cranberry Sherbet

2 C fresh cranberries
1-1/4 C water
1/2 C sugar
1 tsp unflavored gelatin dissolved in 1/4 C water
1–2 T orange juice
1-1/4 C skim milk

Cook cranberries in water until skins pop; rub through a sieve. Mix cranberry pulp with sugar and cook over low heat until sugar is dissolved. Remove from heat and stir in gelatin, orange juice, and milk. Freeze according to preferred method.

Serves 4.

Calories	%Fat	Fat (g)	Saturated Fat (g)	Cholesterol (mg)	Sodium (mg)	Carbohydrate (g)	Protein (g)	Fiber (g)
147	1	0	0.1	1	41	34	3	2

Exchanges: Fruit 2, Dairy 1/4
Note: Not appropriate for diabetics

Lemon Sherbet

Easy Ices

Drop the contents of one small can of unsweetened frozen juice concentrate (any flavor) into a blender or food processor. Add one tray of crushed ice cubes. Blend thoroughly, until the ice is very finely grated and smooth. Stop the blender to clear air pockets with a rubber spatula, if necessary. Serve immediately.

1/4 C sugar
1 tsp grated lemon rind
1/3 C fresh lemon juice
2 C skim milk
Yellow food coloring (optional)

Mix sugar, rind, and juice. Add milk slowly, stirring constantly, and stir until sugar is dissolved. Mix in 1 or 2 drops of yellow food coloring if desired. Freeze according to preferred method.

Serves 5.

Suggestion

• Artificial sweetener to taste may be substituted for sugar.

Calories	%Fat	Fat (g)	Saturated Fat (g)	Cholesterol (mg)	Sodium (mg)	Carbohydrate (g)	Protein (g)	Fiber (g)
75	3	0	0.1	2	54	15	3	0

Exchanges: Fruit 1

Diet & Exercise

Diet, exercise, and psychological conditioning can bring your weight into acceptable ranges and at the same time reduce your cholesterol, triglycerides, blood pressure, and sugar levels.

Edward B. Diethrich, MD
Heart Test

Frozen Mocha

1-1/4 C plain nonfat yogurt
1-1/4 C 1% low-fat cottage cheese
3 T sugar
2 tsp instant coffee
2 tsp cocoa powder
2 egg whites
Melba Sauce

Purée yogurt, cottage cheese, and sugar until smooth. Blend in coffee, cocoa, and egg whites until smooth. Freeze according to preferred method. Pour equal amounts of Melba Sauce onto 8 dessert plates. Place a scoop of Frozen Mocha on each plate and garnish as desired.

Serves 8.

Suggestion
- Artificial sweetener to taste may be substituted for sugar.

Calories	%Fat	Fat (g)	Saturated Fat (g)	Cholesterol (mg)	Sodium (mg)	Carbohydrate (g)	Protein (g)	Fiber (g)
70	6	0	0.3	2	187	9	8	0

Exchanges: Dairy 1

Tangerine Sorbet

Franz Peier

2 pieces baked puff pastry, cut in 3-inch strips, 1/4-inch wide
1 tsp + 1 T honey, divided
1-1/2 tangerine with stem and leaves
1 tsp chopped fresh mint
1 T hazelnut flour
1 oz champagne

Brush pastry strips with 1 tsp honey and roll in hazelnut flour. Bake at 400° for 5 to 7 minutes.

Cut off and save the top of the whole tangerine; remove pulp. Purée pulp in a food processor with 1 T honey; sieve through a colander. Whip until smooth. Freeze for about 1 hour. Peel the remaining half tangerine, cut it into thin slices, and mix with chopped mint. Refrigerate until serving time.

Fill a chilled cordial glass with champagne. Place the tangerine shell on a dessert plate. Fill with sliced tangerine and spoon in the sorbet; replace top of tangerine. Serve with puffed pastry strips and champagne on the side.

Serves 1.

Suggestion

• Alcohol-free cider can be substituted for the champagne.

Calories	%Fat	Fat (g)	Saturated Fat (g)	Cholesterol (mg)	Sodium (mg)	Carbohydrate (g)	Protein (g)	Fiber (g)
172	14	3	0.4	0	30	39	1	1

Exchanges: Fruit 3-1/2, Fat 1/2
Note: Not appropriate for diabetics

Desserts

# ngel Food Cake

1 C cake flour, sifted
1 C sugar
1/4 tsp salt
10 egg whites
1 tsp cream of tartar
1/2 tsp vanilla extract
1/4 tsp almond extract

Mix flour with sugar and salt. Set aside. Beat egg whites until foamy; add cream of tartar and continue to beat until stiff but not dry peaks form. Gently fold in flour mixture, vanilla, and almond. Pour batter into an ungreased tube pan. Bake at 375° for about 45 minutes, or until the cake springs back lightly when touched. Invert the pan on a rack. Cool completely in the pan before removing.

Serves 12.

Suggestion

• Serve with fresh raspberries, strawberries, or diced peaches and Melba Sauce (page 419).

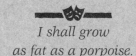

Calories	%Fat	Fat (g)	Saturated Fat (g)	Cholesterol (mg)	Sodium (mg)	Carbohydrate (g)	Protein (g)	Fiber (g)
109	1	0	0.0	0	107	23	4	0

Exchanges: Starch 1-1/2
Note: Occasional use

How to Separate Eggs

To separate an egg, break the shell into two parts (as nearly in half as you can). Holding the egg over a small bowl, pour the yolk from one half of the eggshell to the other and back again, letting the white drip into the bowl.

The shelled egg can also be held in your hand and jiggled slightly so the white drips between your fingers and into the bowl.

Pour the separated white into another bowl before separating the next egg into the first bowl. If a yolk should break, it will contaminate only one egg, and not the entire batch. Even the tiniest bit of egg yolk will prevent the whites from beating to their maximum volume, so remove every speck before proceeding with the recipe.

Toasted Ginger-Cardamom Angel Food Cake

Laura Brennan

12 egg whites (2 C)
1/4 tsp salt
1 tsp cream of tartar
1-1/2 C sugar, sifted
1 C sifted cake flour
1/2 tsp ground ginger
1/3 tsp ground cardamom
Orange Sauce (page 420)
Caramelized Raspberries (page 415)

Mix 1/2 C sugar with cake flour, ginger, and cardamom; set aside. Beat whites until foamy. Add the salt and cream of tartar. Gradually add the cup of sugar, beating constantly until soft peaks form. Sift the flour and sugar mix over the whites and gently fold in. Pour batter into a 10-inch tube cake pan. Bake at 350° for 35 to 45 minutes, or until a straw inserted into the center comes out clean. Invert the pan and cool completely before removing the cake. Cut into 1-inch slices, using a serrated knife. Arrange on a cookie sheet and toast each side briefly under the broiler until brown (be careful they don't burn). Pour 2 T warm Orange Sauce over each slice. Garnish with Caramelized Raspberries.

Serves 10.

Calories	%Fat	Fat (g)	Saturated Fat (g)	Cholesterol (mg)	Sodium (mg)	Carbohydrate (g)	Protein (g)	Fiber (g)
167	1	0	0.0	0	128	38	4	0

Exchanges: Starch 2-1/2
Note: Not appropriate for diabetics

Carrot Cake

1 C all-purpose flour
1 C whole-wheat flour
1/2 C sugar
2 tsp baking soda
1-1/2 tsp ground cinnamon
1-1/2 tsp ground nutmeg
1 C unsweetened applesauce
3 egg whites
3 C coarsely grated carrots

    Mix flour, sugar, baking soda, cinnamon, and nutmeg. Add applesauce and egg whites, stirring until well blended. Stir in carrots. Pour batter into a nonstick 9-inch Bundt or tube pan. Bake at 350° for 70 minutes, or until a toothpick inserted in the center comes out clean. Cool for 5 minutes in the pan; remove from pan and cool completely on wire rack.
    Serves 12.

Suggestions
- Cake can be made in two loaf pans instead of a tube pan.
- Add 1/2 C raisins with carrots.
- Add 1/2 C crushed pineapple, very well drained and dried, with the carrots.

Calories	%Fat	Fat (g)	Saturated Fat (g)	Cholesterol (mg)	Sodium (mg)	Carbohydrate (g)	Protein (g)	Fiber (g)
128	3	0	0.1	0	167	28	4	3

Exchanges: Starch 1, Fruit 1
Note: Occasional use

Sugar

Foods that are high in sugar but low in nutrients are often said to be loaded with "empty calories." Try to choose sweet foods that also offer nutritional value: fruits, whole-grain cookies, and breads. Read labels carefully to find brands that have sugar at the end of the ingredient list.

Sugar has many forms. Avoid prepared foods whose labels list one or more of the following types of sugar among the first few ingredients:

Brown sugar

Corn sweetener

Demerara sugar

Dextrose

Fructose

Fruit juice concentrate

Glucose

High-fructose corn syrup

Honey

Invert sugar

Malt

Maltose

Molasses

Raw sugar

Sucrose

Syrup

Treacle

Cocoa Cake

1 C sifted all-purpose flour
1/2 C whole-wheat flour
3 T cocoa powder
1 tsp baking soda
1 C sugar
1/2 tsp salt
5 T canola oil
1 T vinegar
1 tsp vanilla
1 C cold water

Combine flour, cocoa, baking soda, sugar and salt. Add remaining ingredients and beat with a spoon until smooth. Pour batter into a nonstick 8- or 9-inch square cake pan. Bake at 350° for 35 minutes, or until a toothpick inserted in the center of the cake comes out clean.

Serves 12.

Suggestions

• Decorate the cake with a light dusting of sifted confectioners' sugar.
• Serve with Melba Sauce (page 419) or Cherries Sauce (page 417).

Calories	%Fat	Fat (g)	Saturated Fat (g)	Cholesterol (mg)	Sodium (mg)	Carbohydrate (g)	Protein (g)	Fiber (g)
170	32	6	0.5	0	158	28	2	1

Exchanges: Starch 2, Fat 1
Note: Occasional use

Chocolate Rum Cream Cake

Cake

1/4 C soft margarine
1/2 C plus 3 T sugar, divided
1-1/2 C cake flour, sifted
1-1/2 tsp baking powder
1/4 tsp salt
2/3 C skim milk
1 tsp rum extract
2 egg whites, room temperature

Cream Filling

1/2 C sugar
5 tsp cornstarch
1/8 tsp salt
1-1/2 T unsweetened cocoa
1-1/4 C skim milk
1 egg, lightly beaten
1/2 tsp rum extract

Glaze

2 T sugar
1-1/2 T unsweetened cocoa
3/4 tsp cornstarch
1/3 C skim milk
1/2 tsp rum extract

- *Table sugar or sucrose:* Refined white sugar is made from sugar cane or sugar beets; it has no nutritional value.
- *Brown sugar:* Table sugar that has been mixed with molasses. The darker the sugar, the more molasses it contains.
- *Confectioners' sugar:* Pulverized table sugar, usually mixed with a little cornstarch. Also called *powdered sugar.*
- *Corn syrup:* Liquid sugar processed from cornstarch; half as sweet as sucrose. Sold in light or dark form. Dark corn syrup can be substituted for molasses; either can substitute for honey.
- *Fructose:* The sugar in fruit; a natural by-product of fruits and honey. Fructose is twice as sweet as sucrose but has fewer calories; its sweetness decreases when heated and increases when used with acidic foods.
- *Glucose:* The most common

form of glucose is dextro-glucose (also called *dextrose, corn sugar,* or *grape sugar*). It is made from grape juice, some vegetables, or honey. It is half as sweet as table sugar.

- *Molasses, blackstrap molasses:* A by-product of sugar refining, molasses is made from the liquid removed to make table sugar; contains tiny amounts of some minerals. It has a strong flavor and is primarily used in baking.

- *Raw sugar:* True raw sugar contains impurities and cannot be sold legally in the United States; purification eliminates most of what is thought to be its better nutritive value. Products called raw sugar are often just table sugar mixed with some molasses.

- *Sorghum:* Syrup made from the sorghum plant. It has a lighter color and milder flavor than molasses.

- *Superfine:* Table sugar that is ground very fine; dissolves almost instantly. It is used in baking, frostings, meringue, and cold liquids.

Cake: Cream margarine; slowly add 1/2 C sugar, beating at medium speed with an electric mixer until fluffy, about 5 minutes. Combine flour, baking powder, and salt; beat into creamed mixture in thirds, alternating with the milk. Blend in rum extract. Set aside. Beat egg whites until foamy. Gradually add 3 T sugar and continue to beat to form stiff peaks. Gently fold into batter. Pour into a nonstick 8-inch cake pan. Bake at 350° for 30 to 35 minutes, or until a toothpick inserted in the center comes out clean. Cool slightly before removing from pan; cool completely on a wire rack.

Cream Filling: Mix sugar, cornstarch, salt, and cocoa. Slowly stir in milk until well blended. Bring to a boil over medium heat. Cook 1 minute, stirring constantly; set aside. Very slowly stir one-fourth of the hot milk into the egg. Pour the egg mixture into the remaining hot milk and continue to cook until it thickens, about 3 minutes. Stir in rum extract. Pour the cream filling into a bowl and chill for at least 3 hours

Glaze: Mix sugar, cocoa, and cornstarch. Slowly stir in milk until well blended. Bring to a boil over medium heat. Boil 1 minute, stirring constantly. Mix in rum extract.

Final Assembly: Cut the cake in half horizontally. Spread Cream Filling over the bottom half; cover with top half. Spread Glaze over top cake layer. Refrigerate for 3 hours before serving.

Serves 10.

Suggestion
- Almond, orange, coconut, or vanilla extract can be substituted for the rum extract.

Calories	%Fat	Fat (g)	Saturated Fat (g)	Cholesterol (mg)	Sodium (mg)	Carbohydrate (g)	Protein (g)	Fiber (g)
238	21	5	1.3	22	237	43	5	1

Exchanges: Starch 3, Fat 1
Note: Not appropriate for diabetics

Cheesecake

My tongue is smiling.

Abigail Trillin
Alice, Let's Eat

1 C low-fat (1%) cottage cheese
1 C plain nonfat yogurt
8 oz nonfat cream cheese
1/2 C sugar
2 tsp grated lemon rind
2 tsp vanilla
2 egg whites
Graham Cracker Crust in 8-inch tart pan (page 411)

Blend cottage cheese in a food processor or blender until completely smooth, about 2 minutes. Add yogurt, cream cheese, sugar, lemon peel, vanilla, and egg whites, processing until creamy. Pour into prepared crust. Bake at 350° for 30 minutes. Turn oven off and open the door slightly; leave the cheesecake in the oven for 30 minutes. Refrigerate several hours or overnight before serving.

Serves 10.

Suggestions

- Top with Ginger Pears (page 418), Cherries Sauce (page 417), or Blueberry Topping (page 416).
- Decorate with fresh strawberries, thinly sliced kiwis, raspberries, or other fresh fruit.

Calories	%Fat	Fat (g)	Saturated Fat (g)	Cholesterol (mg)	Sodium (mg)	Carbohydrate (g)	Protein (g)	Fiber (g)
170	22	4	1.2	4	377	24	10	1

Exchanges: Starch 1-1/2, Fat 1
Note: Occasional use

Apple-Spice Cookies

1/4 C soft tub margarine
1/3 C brown sugar
2 egg whites
1 C unbleached white flour
1/2 C whole-wheat flour
1/2 tsp baking soda
1 tsp baking powder
1 tsp cinnamon
1/4 tsp nutmeg
3 T skim milk
1/2 C raisins
1/4 C finely chopped crystallized ginger
2-1/2 C peeled, diced Granny Smith apples

Mix both flours, baking soda, baking powder, cinnamon, and nutmeg. Set aside. Cream margarine and brown sugar. Beat in egg whites. Beat flour mixture into creamed mixture in thirds, alternating with milk. Stir in raisins, ginger, and apples. Drop by teaspoonfuls onto cookie sheets, making 36 cookies. Bake at 400° for 10 to 12 minutes or until golden brown. Place in an airtight container as soon as cookies are cool.

Serves 36.

Calories	%Fat	Fat (g)	Saturated Fat (g)	Cholesterol (mg)	Sodium (mg)	Carbohydrate (g)	Protein (g)	Fiber (g)
53	23	1	0.2	0	60	10	1	1

Exchanges: Starch 1/2

# Apricot Bar Cookies

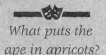
3/4 C all-purpose flour
3/4 C whole-wheat flour
1/2 tsp baking soda
1/2 tsp ground cinnamon
1/4 C packed brown sugar
1/2 C plain nonfat yogurt
1/3 C water
1/4 C canola oil
1/4 C molasses
1 egg white, beaten
1 C rolled oats
3/4 C finely chopped dried apricots
1/2 C golden raisins
3/4 C powdered sugar, sifted
2 T lemon juice

Combine both flours, baking soda, and cinnamon. Mix in sugar, yogurt, water, oil, molasses, and egg white. Stir in oats, apricots, and raisins. Spread in a nonstick 9 × 13-inch baking pan. Bake at 350° for 20 to 25 minutes or until a toothpick inserted in the center comes out clean. Cool in the pan. Mix powdered sugar with lemon juice and drizzle over cooled bars. Cut into 24 pieces.
Serves 24.

Calories	%Fat	Fat (g)	Saturated Fat (g)	Cholesterol (mg)	Sodium (mg)	Carbohydrate (g)	Protein (g)	Fiber (g)
115	21	3	0.2	0	27	22	2	1

Exchanges: Starch 1/2, Fruit 1, Fat 1/2

Apricots

Apricots are native to China. They are pale to golden yellow and have sweet flesh and tender skin. Apricots can be ripened at room temperature after picking, but they tend to be soft and bland; tree-ripened apricots have the best flavor. Canned apricots ripen on the tree longer and often taste better than fresh apricots; their nutritional value is very close to fresh fruit. Apricots are an excellent source of vitamin A and potassium and a good source of vitamin C.

Drying fruit removes the water but not the nutrients; it concentrates the calories, nutrients, sweetness, and flavor. Dried apricots therefore have more iron, fiber, vitamin A, and beta-carotene than an equal amount of fresh apricots.

Honey

Honey is made by bees from the nectar of flowers. Its flavor and sweetness depend on the type of flower—clover, wildflowers, tupelo, sage, thyme, and orange blossoms make very good honey. Darker honeys have a stronger flavor. Honey is rich in enzymes.

Honey can be flavored with herbs or spices. For lavender honey, put chopped lavender flowers into a scalded jar, cover with honey, and seal. Set in a sunny place for five to ten days. Strain; store the honey into a fresh jar.

Honey should not be given to babies. It may contain botulism, the most potent food poison known. Infants under one year of age are very susceptible to this toxin because their digestive tracts are immature.

Honeybee Brownies

1/2 C flour
1/3 C unsweetened cocoa
1/4 tsp salt
2 T margarine
3 T water
1/4 C honey
1/4 C sugar
2 tsp vanilla
2 egg whites

Sift together flour, cocoa, and salt; set aside. Cream margarine, water, honey, sugar, and vanilla. Beat in egg whites, one at a time, blending well after each addition. Gradually beat dry ingredients into creamed mixture. Pour into a nonstick 8-inch square cake pan. Bake at 350° for 25 to 30 minutes. Cut cooled brownies into 2-inch squares.

Serves 16.

Calories	%Fat	Fat (g)	Saturated Fat (g)	Cholesterol (mg)	Sodium (mg)	Carbohydrate (g)	Protein (g)	Fiber (g)
88	41	4	0.9	0	93	13	2	1

Exchanges: Starch 1, Fat 1
Note: Occasional use

Date Layer Bars

1-1/3 C pitted dates, chopped (6-oz pkg)
3/4 C water
1/4 tsp cinnamon
1-1/4 C rolled oats
1/3 C brown sugar
1/4 C whole-wheat flour
3 T margarine, melted

Cook dates, water, and cinnamon over low heat until almost all liquid is absorbed, about 10 minutes, stirring constantly. Remove from heat and set aside. Mix oats, sugar, and flour; stir in margarine until mixture is crumbly. Press two-thirds of oatmeal mixture into the bottom of an 8-inch square cakepan. Bake at 350° for 10 to 15 minutes, until golden brown. Spread date mixture over the baked layer. Sprinkle remaining oatmeal mixture over the dates; press lightly with fingertips. Bake at 350° for 20 minutes. Cool before cutting into 16 squares. Store loosely covered.

Serves 16.

Suggestion

• Figs or other dried fruit may be substituted for part or all of the dates.

Calories	%Fat	Fat (g)	Saturated Fat (g)	Cholesterol (mg)	Sodium (mg)	Carbohydrate (g)	Protein (g)	Fiber (g)
108	22	3	0.5	0	27	21	2	1

Exchanges: Starch 1/2, Fruit 1, Fat 1/2

The American aversion to meals...is not really an aversion to food. As every statistic shows, Americans consume vast quantities of food. They merely parcel their food into things that can be eaten with the hand.

Henry Fairlie

Dates

Dates are a concentrated source of carbohydrates (70% of their total weight is sugar) and fiber. They are a good source of niacin, iron, and magnesium. Dates sold in America are partly dried, so they are still soft; store them tightly wrapped in the refrigerator for several weeks. Like other dried fruits, dates can be chopped more easily if they are refrigerated first.

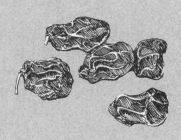

Gingerbread Cookies

3-1/4 C flour
1/3 C margarine
1/2 C sugar
1/3 C molasses
1-1/2 tsp ground cinnamon
1 T ground ginger
3/4 tsp ground cloves
1 tsp baking powder
1/2 tsp vanilla
4 oz plain low-fat yogurt
4 egg whites

With mixer at low speed, beat 1-1/2 C flour and remaining ingredients until well mixed, constantly scraping the bowl with a rubber spatula. Knead in the remaining 1-3/4 C flour to make a soft dough. Wrap the dough in plastic wrap and refrigerate it for 2 hours, or until it is not sticky. Roll out the dough on a lightly floured surface and cut with cookie cutters. Place cookies on a nonstick baking sheet. Bake at 350° for 18 to 20 minutes, or until golden brown.
Serves 26.

Suggestion
• Decorate with raisins, currants, or slivers of crystallized ginger before baking.

Calories	%Fat	Fat (g)	Saturated Fat (g)	Cholesterol (mg)	Sodium (mg)	Carbohydrate (g)	Protein (g)	Fiber (g)
108	21	3	0.5	0	56	19	2	1

Exchanges: Starch 1, Fat 1/2

Oatmeal Raisin Cookies

3/4 C low-calorie margarine
3/4 C sugar
3/4 C brown sugar
1 egg
1 egg white
1 tsp vanilla
1 C all-purpose flour
1/2 C whole-wheat flour
1 tsp baking soda
1 tsp cinnamon
3 C rolled oats
1 C raisins

Cream margarine and sugars until light and fluffy. Beat in eggs and vanilla. Combine flour, soda, and cinnamon; add to creamed mixture, beating well. Stir in oats and raisins. Drop by rounded teaspoonfuls onto ungreased cookie sheets, making 60 cookies. Bake at 375° for 8 to 10 minutes. Store cooled cookies tightly covered or in the freezer.
Serves 60.

Suggestion
• Substitute currants, chopped dried apricots, or chopped dates for the raisins.

Raisins & Currants
Raisins are dried grapes. Golden raisins or sultanas are made from green grapes; they are larger and sweeter than dark raisins. Currants are dried Corinth or Zante grapes; they are not made from fresh currant berries.

Raisins are a concentrated source of carbohydrates. They are an excellent source of potassium and also contain iron, magnesium, and fiber.

Store raisins and currants in a cool, dry place for up to a year; after opening, keep them in an airtight, moisture-proof container. Before baking with raisins or currants, plump them in water, juice, rum, or brandy for at least 15 minutes; otherwise they may be hard and dry.

Calories	%Fat	Fat (g)	Saturated Fat (g)	Cholesterol (mg)	Sodium (mg)	Carbohydrate (g)	Protein (g)	Fiber (g)
65	21	2	0.3	4	45	12	1	1

Exchanges: Starch 1/2, Fruit 1/2

*The proof of the
pudding is in the eating.*

Henry Glapthorne
The Hollander, 1635

Flavored Sugars

- *Lavender:* 2 to 3 sprigs per pound of sugar. Good with carrots, pudding, cakes. Sprinkle over cake or biscuits just after baking.
- *Lemon balm:* 2 to 3 sprigs per pound of sugar. Use in fruit jellies, custards, fruit pies.
- *Orange or lemon:* Pared rind of 2 medium fruits per pound of sugar.
- *Rosemary:* 2 to 3 sprigs per pound of sugar. Use in custard, delicate-flavored ices, sorbets.
- *Vanilla:* 2 vanilla beans per pound of sugar. Replenish used sugar with unflavored sugar; 1 vanilla bean can be used in this way for several years.

Rice Pudding

2 C cooked white rice
1 qt skim milk
1/4 C sugar
1/2 C egg substitute
1/2 tsp vanilla
1/2 C raisins

Combine rice, skim milk, sugar, and egg substitute. Stir in vanilla and raisins. Pour into a nonstick baking dish. Bake at 350° until firm, about 30 minutes.

Serves 8.

Suggestions
- For a creamier pudding, use a short-grain rice.
- Sprinkle with cinnamon before serving.
- Spoon Melba Sauce (page 419) over each serving.
- Use a flavored sugar, such as vanilla, lavender, or lemon.

Calories	%Fat	Fat (g)	Saturated Fat (g)	Cholesterol (mg)	Sodium (mg)	Carbohydrate (g)	Protein (g)	Fiber (g)
168	2	0	0.2	2	96	34	7	1

Exchanges: Starch 1, Fruit 1, Dairy 1/2

Crème Caramel

Rozanne Gold

1/3 C + 3 T sugar
1 egg
2 egg whites
2 C 1% low-fat milk, scalded
1/2 tsp vanilla extract
1/8 tsp almond extract
1/2 tsp freshly grated orange rind

Melt 1/3 C sugar in small pan to caramelize. After 2 to 3 minutes, the sugar will become a dark brown syrup. Pour equal amounts into 6 custard cups.

Beat eggs with 3 T sugar. Add hot milk slowly, whisking constantly. Add vanilla and almond extracts and orange rind. Let sit for 15 minutes. Pour mixture into 6 custard cups. Place cups in a deep pan. Pour boiling water into the pan until it reaches halfway up the sides of the cups. Bake at 350° for 40 minutes. Remove from water bath and refrigerate.

Serves 6.

Calories	%Fat	Fat (g)	Saturated Fat (g)	Cholesterol (mg)	Sodium (mg)	Carbohydrate (g)	Protein (g)	Fiber (g)
117	13	2	0.8	39	70	21	5	0

Exchanges: Starch 1, Dairy 1/2
Note: Not appropriate for diabetics

Eggs

Brown, white, fertile, and non-fertile eggs all have the same nutritional value. Egg whites are a high-protein, low-fat food; they are a good source of riboflavin. The yolks are high in protein, fat, and cholesterol.

Eggs will keep in the refrigerator for four to five weeks; one day at room temperature equals one week in the refrigerator. Do not buy cracked eggs; discard any that crack or break. Store eggs in the original carton, pointed ends down. Do not wash them before storing. Do not keep them in the egg tray in the refrigerator door; this location is too warm and does not protect eggs from air circulation. Keep hard-boiled eggs, including Easter eggs, in the refrigerator.

Eggs should be thoroughly cooked; raw eggs and raw egg products may be contaminated with Salmonella bacteria. Wash your hands and the eggs before cracking them.

Chocolate Mousse

1/2 C boiling water
1 pkg (1/4 oz) unflavored gelatin
1/2 C cold water
3 T skim evaporated milk
1 tsp vanilla extract
3 T sugar
1/4 C powdered nonfat milk
2 T unsweetened cocoa powder
1 C plain nonfat yogurt

Beat hot water and gelatin with an electric mixer for 1 minute. Add cold water and beat for 1 minute. Add evaporated milk and vanilla and beat until frothy. Chill for 45 minutes. Beat in sugar, powdered milk, and cocoa until thick, about two minutes. Gently fold in yogurt until color is uniform. Refrigerate for at least 1 hour before serving.
Serves 4.

Suggestions

- Artificial sweetener to taste may be substituted for the sugar.
- Instant coffee powder, almond extract, grated orange rind, or puréed raspberries to taste may be added with the sugar and cocoa during the final mixing.

Calories	%Fat	Fat (g)	Saturated Fat (g)	Cholesterol (mg)	Sodium (mg)	Carbohydrate (g)	Protein (g)	Fiber (g)
107	4	1	0.3	2	86	19	8	1

Exchanges: Starch 1/2, Dairy 1
Note: Occasional use

Pumpkin Pie

1 C canned pumpkin
1 egg
2 egg whites
1 tsp canola oil
1-1/4 C skim milk
1 T cornstarch
1/3 C honey
1 tsp ground cinnamon
1/8 tsp allspice
1/8 tsp ground ginger
1/8 tsp ground nutmeg
1/8 tsp ground cloves
Graham Cracker Pie Crust (page 411)

The Temptations

Eliminate as many temptations as possible. For example, move the TV out of the kitchen. Put candy dishes away. Don't leave crackers or cookies in plain view. Buy kitchen containers with rural scenes rather than seasonal feasts on them. It's less tempting to look at a haystack than a pumpkin pie.

Edward B. Diethrich, MD
Heart Test

Beat all ingredients with an electric mixer until smooth. Pour into pie crust. Bake at 350° for 1 hour or until filling is set.

Serves 8.

Suggestions
• Cooked and mashed fresh pumpkin can be substituted for the canned pumpkin.
• *Baked Pumpkin Cream:* Substitute evaporated skim milk for the skim milk; bake in a casserole dish without the pie crust.

Calories	%Fat	Fat (g)	Saturated Fat (g)	Cholesterol (mg)	Sodium (mg)	Carbohydrate (g)	Protein (g)	Fiber (g)
162	24	4	1.3	28	185	28	4	1

Exchanges: Starch 2, Fat 1
Note: Occasional use

# Sweet Potato Pie

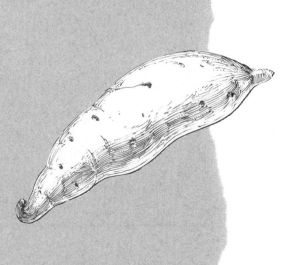

4 egg whites, lightly beaten
1/2 C sugar
1/4 C brown sugar
1 T grated orange rind
1 C unsweetened orange juice
1 tsp cinnamon
1/4 tsp allspice
1/4 tsp nutmeg
2 tsp margarine, melted
2 C cooked, mashed sweet potato
1/2 C skim milk
Basic Pie Crust (page 410)

Beat egg whites with sugars, orange rind, juice, spices, and margarine. Beat in sweet potato; blend in milk. Pour into pie pan lined with Basic Pie Crust. Bake at 350° for 1 hour or until a knife inserted in the center comes out clean.
Serves 8.

Suggestions
- Graham Cracker Crust (page 411) may be substituted for the Basic Pie Crust.
- Grated orange rind or cinnamon can be added to the dry ingredients when making either type of pie crust.

Calories	%Fat	Fat (g)	Saturated Fat (g)	Cholesterol (mg)	Sodium (mg)	Carbohydrate (g)	Protein (g)	Fiber (g)
273	19	6	0.7	0	59	51	5	2

Exchanges: Starch 3, Fruit 1/2, Fat 1

Basic Pie Crust

2 C flour
1 tsp salt
1/3 C safflower oil
3 T cold skim milk

Sift flour and salt together. Mix oil with milk and add to flour mixture. Stir with fork until ingredients are blended and hold together; add more milk, by teaspoons, if necessary. Form dough into two balls. Wrap in plastic and chill slightly. Flatten a ball of dough and place it between two sheets of waxed paper. Roll the dough into a circle large enough to fit in the pie pan. Remove the top sheet of paper and turn the pastry over onto a pie plate; remove the second sheet of paper and ease the crust into the pie pan.

For a single-crust pie, trim off the excess dough and flute the edge with fingers or a fork. For a two-crust pie, add the filling, roll out the second ball of dough, position it on top of the pie, and trim and flute the edges. Use a sharp knife to prick the top of the pie to permit steam to escape while baking.

Yield: Pastry for 2 single-crust 9-inch pies, or for 1 two-crust 9-inch pie.
Serves 8.

Suggestions
- A little sugar, cinnamon, or grated citrus rind can be stirred into the flour.
- A light dusting of sugar or cinnamon-sugar may be sprinkled over the top of a two-crust pie before baking.

Calories	%Fat	Fat (g)	Saturated Fat (g)	Cholesterol (mg)	Sodium (mg)	Carbohydrate (g)	Protein (g)	Fiber (g)
196	43	9	0.9	0	270	24	3	1

Exchanges: Starch 1-1/2, Fat 2

Fat in Packaged Foods
Read package labels carefully to determine the types of fat found in the product. A food labeled "no cholesterol" can still contain saturated fat. Saturated fat is frequently used in commercially prepared products because it does not deteriorate rapidly and it is less expensive than polyunsaturated oils. Imitation nondairy products—such as sour cream, coffee creamer, and whipped topping—usually contain saturated fat in the form of hydrogenated oil or coconut oil.

Arizona Heart Institute Foundation
1–800–345–4278

Graham Cracker Crust

10 graham crackers, finely crushed
2 T margarine, melted

Mix crumbs with margarine. Press into 9-inch pie plate. Bake at 375° for 8 minutes or microwave on high for 2 to 2-1/2 minutes, turning at 1 minute. Cool before filling.

Serves 8.

Suggestion

• Zwieback crackers, vanilla wafers, or ginger snaps (2/3 C crumbs) may be substituted for the graham crackers.

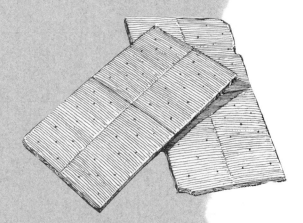

Calories	%Fat	Fat (g)	Saturated Fat (g)	Cholesterol (mg)	Sodium (mg)	Carbohydrate (g)	Protein (g)	Fiber (g)
98	43	5	1.3	1	144	13	1	1

Exchanges: Starch 1, Fat 1

# Meringue Shell

3 egg whites, room temperature
1/2 tsp cream of tartar
1/2 C superfine sugar

Beat egg whites with an electric mixer until frothy. Beat in cream of tartar. Gradually add sugar, continuing to beat until stiff peaks form. Spoon into a 9-inch pie pan lightly coated with cooking spray, spreading gently to cover bottom and sides. Bake at 300° for 1 hour or until crisp and light brown. Cool before filling.
Serves 8.

Suggestion
• Fill with sliced fresh fruit (first macerate the fruit in liqueur if desired). Melt a little low-sugar jelly and brush it over the fruit to glaze it.

How to Beat Egg Whites
Egg whites should be brought to room temperature before beating. Fresher egg whites beat more easily. They will not beat to their maximum volume if they come into contact with any fat. Bowls, beaters, spatulas, and anything else that will touch the egg white must be completely fat- and grease-free. Even the smallest speck of egg yolk (which is high in fat) must be removed from the egg white before beating.

Superfine sugar is better than regular granulated sugar for making meringues. Sifted confectioners' sugar is also acceptable.

Do not beat egg whites in an aluminum bowl; enamel or glass bowls are acceptable. They will reach their highest volume if beaten in a copper bowl because the copper ions will stabilize the foam.

For maximum volume, beat the egg whites slowly at

Calories	%Fat	Fat (g)	Saturated Fat (g)	Cholesterol (mg)	Sodium (mg)	Carbohydrate (g)	Protein (g)	Fiber (g)
53	0	0	0.0	0	33	12	1	0

Exchanges: Starch 1
Note: Not appropriate for diabetics

first, until they are foamy. Add flavorings and cream of tartar (which helps stabilize the foam) when the eggs are half-beaten. The mixing speed can then be increased to medium or high, and the sugar added one tablespoon at a time (do not stop the beaters to add the sugar). The recipe will specify whether the eggs should be beaten to soft or stiff peaks; overbeaten eggs will separate and have to be discarded.

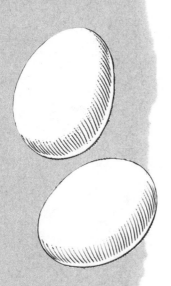

Dessert Pie Crust

3 egg whites, room temperature
3/4 C sugar
1 tsp vanilla extract
1/2 tsp almond extract
16 low-fat, whole-wheat crackers, finely ground
1/2 tsp baking soda
2 T chopped walnuts

Beat egg whites with an electric mixer until frothy. Gradually add sugar, continuing to beat until stiff peaks form. Fold in remaining ingredients. Spoon into a pie pan lightly coated with vegetable spray, spreading gently to cover bottom and sides. Bake at 325° for 45 minutes. Cool before filling.
Serves 8.

Calories	%Fat	Fat (g)	Saturated Fat (g)	Cholesterol (mg)	Sodium (mg)	Carbohydrate (g)	Protein (g)	Fiber (g)
113	18	2	0.4	0	117	22	2	0

Exchanges: Starch 1-1/2
Note: Not appropriate for diabetics

Candied Lime

Mark Gould

4 limes, zest only
8 oz simple syrup
Sugar
Cold water

   Using a zester or a vegetable peeler, remove the outer colored skin of the lime, being careful not to remove the white and bitter pith. The zester will remove thin julienne strips; if you're using a vegetable peeler, you will need to cut these into a julienne.

   Place the zest in a small saucepan and cover with cold water. Bring to a boil and drain the water; repeat this process. This blanching will remove the bitter oils from the skin of the zest.

   After the second blanching, place the drained zest back into the saucepan and cover with the simple syrup. Once the zest boils, remove from heat and let cool in the syrup. When the zest is cool, remove and drain off extra syrup. Place the zest on a plate or tray that is covered with granulated sugar, rolling the zest around to coat it thoroughly and separating it into individual strands. Once separated, leave the now-candied zest on the small plate covered with sugar, cool and dry until needed. Serve with Hot Mango Tart (page 370).

   Makes about 48 candied zests.

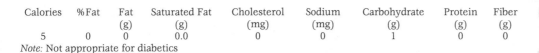

Limes

   Persian limes look like green lemons and are often used interchangeably with lemons. Like lemons, limes are an excellent source of vitamin C. Yellowing is a sign of tartness and aging. Limes can be stored in a plastic bag in the refrigerator for up to six weeks.

   Grocers often wax citrus fruits. Limes should be scrubbed with soap and water if the rind will be grated or zested and used in cooking.

   Key limes grow only in south Florida. These small, round, yellow limes are deliciously tart. They are seldom sold fresh in other parts of the country, but bottled key lime juice is widely available.

Calories	%Fat	Fat (g)	Saturated Fat (g)	Cholesterol (mg)	Sodium (mg)	Carbohydrate (g)	Protein (g)	Fiber (g)
5	0	0	0.0	0	0	1	0	0

Note: Not appropriate for diabetics

Caramelized Raspberries

Laura Brennan

1-1/4 C + 1 T sugar
1 T light corn syrup
1/3 C water
16 raspberries

In a small heavy saucepan, combine the sugar, corn syrup, and water. Cook until the sugars begin to turn brown, or caramelize. Remove pot from heat and, working quickly, skewer raspberries one at a time and dip into the caramel. Place each berry on a lightly oiled pan to harden. Be careful—caramel is very hot and sticky. Serve with Toasted Ginger Cardamom Angel Food Cake (page 393).

Serves 10.

Calories	%Fat	Fat (g)	Saturated Fat (g)	Cholesterol (mg)	Sodium (mg)	Carbohydrate (g)	Protein (g)	Fiber (g)
105	0	0	0.0	0	2	27	0	0

Exchanges: Fruit 2
Note: Not appropriate for diabetics

Blueberry Topping

1 T cornstarch
1/3 C firmly packed brown sugar
2 T lemon juice
1/4 C water
2 C fresh or frozen blueberries

Mix cornstarch with sugar. Stir in lemon juice and water. Add blueberries. Microwave, covered, on HIGH for 5 to 6 minutes, stirring every 2 minutes.
Serves 12.

Suggestions

- Serve warm over pancakes, French toast, crêpes, or frozen yogurt.
- Use as a topping for cheesecake.
- Raspberries, strawberries, blackberries, or mixed berries can be substituted for all or part of the blueberries.
- Cool sauce to room temperature and stir in thinly sliced banana or chopped orange sections.

Calories	%Fat	Fat (g)	Saturated Fat (g)	Cholesterol (mg)	Sodium (mg)	Carbohydrate (g)	Protein (g)	Fiber (g)
39	2	0	0.0	0	4	10	0	0

Exchanges: Fruit 1/2

Cherries Sauce

3/4 C water
3 T sugar
1 C fresh or frozen dark sweet cherries, pitted
2 tsp cornstarch
3 T lemon juice

Bring water, sugar, and cherries to a moderate boil. Boil, uncovered, for 5 minutes, stirring constantly. Blend cornstarch with lemon juice. Stir into cherries and simmer, stirring constantly, until sauce is thickened. Do not overcook.
Serves 6.

Suggestion
• Serve as a topping for cheesecake, pancakes, crêpes, blintzes, or frozen yogurt.

Calories	%Fat	Fat (g)	Saturated Fat (g)	Cholesterol (mg)	Sodium (mg)	Carbohydrate (g)	Protein (g)	Fiber (g)
47	5	0	0.1	0	2	12	0	0

Exchanges: Fruit 1

Ginger Pears

1 lb dried pears, chopped
1/4 lb crystallized ginger, chopped
2-1/2 C water
Juice of 1 medium orange

    Simmer all ingredients, covered, until pears are soft and almost all liquid is absorbed, about 1 hour.
    Serves 8.

Suggestions
- Use as a topping for cheesecake, frozen vanilla yogurt, crêpes, or French toast.
- Serve as a spread for biscuits or Prune Bread (page 45).
- Use as a filling for individual tarts or a pie.
- Dried peaches, apricots, or apples can be substituted for the pears.

Symbolic Meanings of Fruits & Nuts

Almond
Stupidity, indiscretion

Apple
Temptation

Cherry Tree
Good education

Chestnut
Luxury

Citron
Beauty with ill humor

Cranberry
Hardness

Currants
You please all

Fig
Argument

Calories	%Fat	Fat (g)	Saturated Fat (g)	Cholesterol (mg)	Sodium (mg)	Carbohydrate (g)	Protein (g)	Fiber (g)
201	2	0	0.0	0	45	53	1	7

Exchanges: Fruit 3-1/2

Melba Sauce

2 pkg frozen unsweetened raspberries
1/4 C sugar
1 T kirsch

Thaw berries and rub through a sieve to remove seeds. Mix in sugar and kirsch.
Serves 8.

Suggestions
- Artificial sweetener may be substituted for the sugar.
- Fresh berries in season may be used.
- Melba Sauce is best served immediately, but it may be chilled for a short while.
- Serve over strawberries, raspberries, peaches, pears, or citrus.
- Serve over plain cake, angel food cake, rice pudding, frozen low-fat yogurt, crêpes, or French toast.

Calories	%Fat	Fat (g)	Saturated Fat (g)	Cholesterol (mg)	Sodium (mg)	Carbohydrate (g)	Protein (g)	Fiber (g)
63	6	0	0.0	0	0	15	1	2

Exchanges: Fruit 1

Orange Sauce

Laura Brennan

2 C sugar
2 C white wine
Grated rind and juice of 2 oranges

In a nonreactive pot, combine the sugar, white wine, orange juice, and orange rind. Bring to a boil, lower heat, and simmer until reduced to about 3/4 C. It will resemble thin maple syrup. Strain out the orange rind. Serve warm with Toasted Ginger-Cardamom Angel Food Cake (page 393).
Serving size: 1 T.

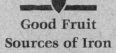

**Good Fruit
Sources of Iron**
Figs, dried
Apricots, dried
Prunes
Raisins
Currants
Cherimoya, raw
Lychees, dried
Mulberries, raw
Jujube, dried
Peaches, dried
Pears, dried

Calories	%Fat	Fat (g)	Saturated Fat (g)	Cholesterol (mg)	Sodium (mg)	Carbohydrate (g)	Protein (g)	Fiber (g)
143	0	0	0.0	0	3	35	0	0

Exchanges: Fruit 2
Note: Not appropriate for diabetics

everages

Cocoa Comfort

1 C nonfat milk
1 T unsweetened cocoa powder
2 tsp sugar
1/4 tsp vanilla extract

Heat the milk in a saucepan or in a microwave oven to serving temperature; do not boil. Add remaining ingredients and stir until dissolved.
Serves 1.

Suggestions

• Artificial sweetener to taste may be substituted for the sugar.
• Beating the cocoa until it is frothy will prevent a skin from forming on the surface.

Calcium

The best way to get calcium is by eating a wide variety of foods from all food groups. The body can use the calcium in milk more easily than the calcium in a supplement. People who can't eat dairy products may be advised to take a supplement.

Among supplements, calcium citrate malate is more soluble than calcium carbonate and is, therefore, more easily used by the body. Because calcium carbonate is poorly absorbed on an empty stomach, it should be taken with a meal, preferably high in carbohydrates (calcium absorption may be reduced by fiber).

Calories	%Fat	Fat (g)	Saturated Fat (g)	Cholesterol (mg)	Sodium (mg)	Carbohydrate (g)	Protein (g)	Fiber (g)
130	8	1	0.7	4	127	23	9	2

Exchanges: Starch 1/2, Dairy 1
Note: Occasional use

Coffee-Almond Milkshake

8 to 12 ice cubes
1 C very cold water
1 C skim milk
1/2 tsp instant coffee (or to taste)
1/4 tsp almond extract
2 tsp sugar

Buzz all ingredients in a blender until smooth. Serve immediately.
Serves 1.

Suggestions

- Artificial sweetener may be substituted for the sugar.
- *Mocha Milkshake:* Omit almond extract and add 1 to 2 tsp unsweetened cocoa powder, or to taste.

Calories	%Fat	Fat (g)	Saturated Fat (g)	Cholesterol (mg)	Sodium (mg)	Carbohydrate (g)	Protein (g)	Fiber (g)
120	3	0	0.3	4	128	21	8	0

Exchanges: Starch 1/2, Dairy 1
Note: Occasional use

# Melonade

1 lemon, cut in 6 or 8 wedges
1 C unsweetened orange juice
1/3 C sugar
6 C diced cantaloupe, puréed
2 C cold water

Bring lemon wedges, orange juice, and sugar to a boil over medium heat, stirring until the sugar is dissolved. Boil gently for about 5 minutes. Strain the syrup into a bowl and let cool; discard lemon. Force cantaloupe purée through a fine sieve into a bowl. Combine syrup, purée, and 2 C of cold water, stirring well. Serve cold or over ice.

Serves 8.

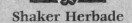
Shaker Herbade

Combine 1/2 cup lemon balm, cut fine, 1/2 cup mint, chopped fine, 1/2 cup regular sugar syrup, and 1/2 cup lemon juice, and let stand 1 hour. Then add 4 quarts of Shaker gingerade or ginger ale. Serves 16.

Canterbury Shaker Village

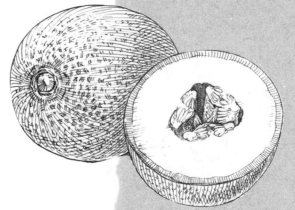

Calories	%Fat	Fat (g)	Saturated Fat (g)	Cholesterol (mg)	Sodium (mg)	Carbohydrate (g)	Protein (g)	Fiber (g)
89	4	0	0.0	0	12	22	1	1

Exchanges: Fruit 1-1/2
Note: Occasional use

Lemons

Lemons are very versatile as they can be used with virtually any type of dish: seafood, poultry, vegetables, fruits, salad dressings, sweet desserts, and beverages.

Very fresh lemons have a greenish tinge; they will keep longer than a completely yellow lemon. Store them in a plastic bag in the refrigerator for up to a month. Lemons are an excellent source of vitamin C.

To get the maximum amount of juice, roll the lemon on a countertop with the palm of your hand before cutting and juicing it. One lemon should yield two to four tablespoons of juice. Freshly squeezed lemon juice can be frozen for up to four months.

Old-Fashioned Lemonade

1 T grated lemon peel
1-1/2 C sugar
1/2 C boiling water
1-1/2 C lemon juice
1 lemon, thinly sliced, optional
Maraschino cherries, with stems, optional

Combine lemon peel, sugar, and water in a jar or covered container; shake until sugar dissolves (if sugar will not dissolve, heat the mixture in a microwave oven for about 2 minutes). Add lemon juice.

By the pitcher: Mix the syrup base with 6 C of cold water in a large pitcher. Pour into ice-filled glasses. Garnish with lemon slices and a stemmed cherry.

By the glass: Syrup base can be stored tightly covered in the refrigerator. For one glass of lemonade, briskly stir 1/4 C of syrup base with 3/4 C of cold water in a tall, ice-filled glass. Garnish with lemon slices and a stemmed cherry.

Serves 8.

Suggestions

- Artificial sweetener to taste may be substituted for the sugar, but do not heat it in the microwave oven.
- *Orange Lemonade:* Substitute orange juice for half the lemon juice.

Calories	%Fat	Fat (g)	Saturated Fat (g)	Cholesterol (mg)	Sodium (mg)	Carbohydrate (g)	Protein (g)	Fiber (g)
149	1	0	0.0	0	10	39	0	0

Exchanges: Fruit 2-1/2
Note: Not appropriate for diabetics

Orange Blossoms

1 can (6 oz) unsweetened frozen orange juice concentrate
2 C skim milk
1 tsp vanilla
10 ice cubes

Buzz all ingredients in a blender until thick and foamy. Serve immediately.
Serves 4.

Calories	% Fat	Fat (g)	Saturated Fat (g)	Cholesterol (mg)	Sodium (mg)	Carbohydrate (g)	Protein (g)	Fiber (g)
111	3	0	0.2	2	64	22	5	0

Exchanges: Fruit 1, Dairy 1/2

*Skim milk does not
come from skinny cows.*

Alba

Milk

Milk is a high-protein food
that contains all the essential
amino acids. It is one of the
best sources of calcium and
phosphorus, and it is rich in
vitamin A and riboflavin. All
milk sold in America is fortified with vitamin D, which
stimulates the absorption of
calcium. Whole milk also
contains vitamin A, which is
removed along with the butterfat to make skim and low-
fat milk; it is then fortified
with vitamin A.

Infants under 12 months
old should never be given
cow's milk. Children aged
one to three years should be
given whole milk, not skim.

- *Whole milk:* 3.5% butterfat.
- *Low-fat milk:* 0.5 to 2.0%
  butterfat.
- *Skim or nonfat milk:* Less
  than 0.5% butterfat.
- *Evaporated milk or skim
  milk:* Not less than 20%

milk solids and not more than 0.5% butterfat. Heating, stabilizing the proteins, and concentrating the product evaporates 60% of the water in milk or skim milk. Evaporated milk can be used straight out of the can in place of cream, or it can be mixed with an equal amount of water and substituted for fresh milk in recipes. Partially frozen evaporated milk can be beaten and used as a low-fat substitute for whipped cream.

- *Dried milk:* Moisture is evaporated by heat, so dried milk has a cooked flavor. It is available in whole, nonfat, or buttermilk versions. Store unopened packages in a cool, dry place. After opening, store it in an airtight, moisture-proof container. Refrigerate reconstituted milk for at least 24 hours before using; store in refrigerator.
- *Raw milk:* Unpasteurized milk. Pasteurization is a method of killing bacteria by heating milk. Raw milk causes many cases of food poisoning each year—it should never be consumed.

Strawberry-Pineapple Shake

1 C unsweetened pineapple juice
1/2 C frozen unsweetened strawberries
1/3 C skim milk powder
1/4 tsp almond extract
1 C cracked ice

Buzz all ingredients in blender until thick and foamy. Serve immediately. Serves 2.

Calories	%Fat	Fat (g)	Saturated Fat (g)	Cholesterol (mg)	Sodium (mg)	Carbohydrate (g)	Protein (g)	Fiber (g)
128	3	0	0.1	2	64	27	5	1

Exchanges: Fruit 1-1/2, Dairy 1/2

# **M**ixed-Fruit Smoothie

1 C unsweetened orange juice
1 banana
3 pineapple rings, unsweetened
1/3 C unsweetened apple juice
1 C crushed ice
1 T honey

Buzz all ingredients in blender until smooth.
Serves 2.

Special Ice Cubes

Use lemon, orange, or other fruit juices instead of water to make ice cubes. Use one or more cubes to flavor a beverage, such as iced tea. Use "matching" ice cubes to chill a drink without diluting it—for example, lemonade ice in a glass of lemonade.

To make decorative ice cubes, fill an ice cube tray half-way with water. Freeze. Arrange one or more fruits, as suggested below, on top of each cube. Carefully pour on just enough water to cover each decoration. Freeze.

Grapes
Cranberries
Orange, lemon, lime slices
Fresh mint leaves
Raspberries
Strawberry slices
Maraschino cherries

Calories	%Fat	Fat (g)	Saturated Fat (g)	Cholesterol (mg)	Sodium (mg)	Carbohydrate (g)	Protein (g)	Fiber (g)
212	2	0	0.1	0	4	54	2	3

Exchanges: Fruit 3-1/2

nacks & Dips

Granola

4 C rolled oats
1/4 C sesame seeds
1 C Grape-Nuts
3 C wheat germ
1/4 C sunflower seeds
1 T cinnamon
1/3 C honey
1 tsp sunflower oil
2 T water
3/4 C raisins
3/4 C chopped dates

Mix oats, sesame seeds, Grape-Nuts, wheat germ, sunflower seeds, and cinnamon. Mix honey, oil, and water; pour over the dry ingredients and stir well. Spread mixture in an even layer in a 9 × 13-inch pan. Bake at 300° for 35 to 40 minutes, or until browned. Stir every 5 to 10 minutes while baking. Allow the granola to cool. Stir in the raisins and dates. Store in a tightly sealed container. Makes 10 C.

Serves 10.

Suggestion
• Dried apricots may be substituted for the dates.

Calories	%Fat	Fat (g)	Saturated Fat (g)	Cholesterol (mg)	Sodium (mg)	Carbohydrate (g)	Protein (g)	Fiber (g)
385	22	9	1.4	0	104	65	16	9

Exchanges: Starch 3, Fruit 1-1/2, Medium-fat protein 1

Bouillon cubes
Catsup
Celery salt
Garlic salt
Horseradish, prepared
Monosodium glutamate
Mustard, prepared
Olives
Onion salt
Oyster sauce
Pickle relishes
Pickles
Popcorn, salted
Potato chips, salted
Pretzels, salted
Sea salt
Self-rising flour
Soups, canned
Soy sauce
Steak sauce
Table salt
Teriyaki sauce
Worcestershire sauce

 **ibbles**

1-1/2 C small unsalted pretzels
1 C bite-sized shredded whole-wheat cereal biscuits
1 C bite-sized crispy rice squares (Chex)
3/4 C bite-sized crispy bran squares (Chex)
4 tsp margarine
1 T low-sodium soy sauce
2 tsp dried oregano
1/2 tsp pepper
2 T grated Parmesan cheese

Toss pretzels and cereals together; set aside. Cook margarine, soy sauce, oregano, and pepper over medium heat until margarine melts, stirring frequently. Pour over dry ingredients; toss well. Add cheese and toss well. Spread in a 9 × 13-inch baking dish. Bake at 275° for 45 minutes or until crisp.

Serves 8 (1/2 C each).

Suggestion
• Add 2 drops of liquid pepper and 1 scant tsp chili pepper with the soy sauce.

Calories	%Fat	Fat (g)	Saturated Fat (g)	Cholesterol (mg)	Sodium (mg)	Carbohydrate (g)	Protein (g)	Fiber (g)
100	25	3	0.7	1	194	17	3	2

Exchanges: Starch 1, Fat 1/2

Dirty Popcorn

4 tsp unsweetened cocoa powder
1 tsp cinnamon
8 tsp sugar
4 C plain air-popped popcorn

   Mix the cocoa, cinnamon, and sugar. Sprinkle over the popcorn and toss lightly until the popcorn is coated evenly.
   Serves 4.

Suggestion
• Artificial sweetener to taste may be substituted for the sugar.

How can I foretell how hungry my guests will be when they sit down to dine?

Alice B. Toklas

Snacks & Serving Size
When you are evaluating products for their calorie and fat content, you should check the serving size. A package of microwave popcorn might have 150 calories per serving but include three servings per bag. If you eat the whole bag of popcorn by yourself, you'll have added 450 calories to your daily intake, not 150.

Arizona Heart Institute Foundation
1–800–345–4278

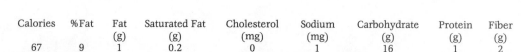

Calories	%Fat	Fat (g)	Saturated Fat (g)	Cholesterol (mg)	Sodium (mg)	Carbohydrate (g)	Protein (g)	Fiber (g)
67	9	1	0.2	0	1	16	1	2

Exchanges: Starch 1
Note: Occasional use

Savory Popcorn

2 tsp margarine, melted and cooled
1/2 tsp ground cumin
1/2 tsp curry powder
1/2 tsp ground cardamom
4 C air-popped corn

Mix margarine with spices. Sprinkle over popcorn and toss well.
Serves 4.

Suggestion

• Substitute herbs or other seasonings to taste.

Calories	%Fat	Fat (g)	Saturated Fat (g)	Cholesterol (mg)	Sodium (mg)	Carbohydrate (g)	Protein (g)	Fiber (g)
41	31	1	0.2	0	12	6	1	1

Exchanges: Starch 1/2

 # **M**icrowave Potato Chips

5 unpeeled Russet potatoes, sliced as thinly as possible
1/4 tsp garlic powder

   Place a single layer of potato slices on a shallow, microwave-safe dish lightly coated with cooking spray (prepare in several batches as necessary). Sprinkle garlic powder or other seasonings over potatoes. Cook, uncovered, on HIGH in a microwave oven for 6 to 7 minutes or until light brown, rotating dish once during cooking. Store cooled potato chips in an airtight container for 2 to 3 weeks.
   Serves 6.

Suggestions
• Slice potatoes only in the amounts that can be cooked at one time.
• Use purple potatoes.

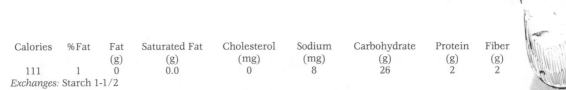

High-Carbohydrate Snacks
Have lots of leftovers around for snacking. As you eat less fat, you are likely to become more hungry frequently. But you will probably find that the less fat you consume the more you can snack on carbohydrates without gaining weight.

Diethrich and Cohan
Women and Heart Disease

Calories	%Fat	Fat (g)	Saturated Fat (g)	Cholesterol (mg)	Sodium (mg)	Carbohydrate (g)	Protein (g)	Fiber (g)
111	1	0	0.0	0	8	26	2	2

Exchanges: Starch 1-1/2

Tortilla Chips

Cut 10 corn tortillas into wedges. Arrange them in a single layer on an ungreased baking dish or cookie sheet. Bake at 350° until crisp, about 15 to 20 minutes. Watch carefully so they don't burn. Serve warm or cold, with salsa or yogurt dip.

Jicama Chips Olé

1 jicama (1-1/2 lb), peeled, quartered, and thinly sliced
1/3 C fresh lemon juice
1/2 tsp chili powder
1/2 tsp ground red pepper

Marinate jicama in lemon juice for 1 hour. Arrange on serving dish and sprinkle with chili powder and red pepper. Serve immediately.
Serves 4.

Calories	%Fat	Fat (g)	Saturated Fat (g)	Cholesterol (mg)	Sodium (mg)	Carbohydrate (g)	Protein (g)	Fiber (g)
66	6	0	0.0	0	13	14	2	3

Exchanges: Starch 1

# Smart Apples

2 C unsweetened apple juice
1 cinnamon stick
2 medium apples, unpeeled, cored, sliced into thin rings (about 20 per apple)

Bring apple juice and cinnamon to a boil. Simmer the apples in the juice for 4 to 5 minutes, or until they are translucent. Remove and pat dry with a paper towel. Spread apple rings in a single layer on a wire rack and bake at 250° until lightly browned, about 30 to 40 minutes. Cool on a wire rack; store in an airtight container.

Serves 8 (5 chips per serving).

How to Resist Temptation

Store your food to minimize temptations. Put the highest calorie and/or the most tempting foods in hard-to-reach places. Use opaque jars and bags for storage. Keep foods that are okay for your diet in front in clear containers.

Edward B. Diethrich, MD
Heart Test

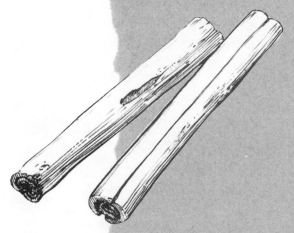

Calories	%Fat	Fat (g)	Saturated Fat (g)	Cholesterol (mg)	Sodium (mg)	Carbohydrate (g)	Protein (g)	Fiber (g)
19	9	0	0.0	0	0	5	0	1

Exchanges: Fruit 1/3

Frozen Banana Pops

3/4 C sugar
1/3 C water
1/2 tsp almond extract
1/3 C + 1 T unsweetened cocoa
1 T canola oil
6 bananas, peeled and cut crosswise in halves
12 ice cream sticks for handles

Combine sugar, water, and almond extract, stirring until sugar is dissolved. Bring to a boil for 1 minute; remove from heat. Stir in cocoa and oil, mixing until well blended and thickened. Cool to room temperature.

Insert a wooden ice cream stick in the cut end of each banana half; freeze for 2 hours. Spread chocolate over each banana, using a knife to coat evenly (chocolate will freeze on contact with banana). Wrap each banana tightly in foil and freeze. Serve frozen.

Serves 12.

Suggestion

• Vanilla, orange, rum, or coconut extract may be substituted for the almond extract.

Calories	%Fat	Fat (g)	Saturated Fat (g)	Cholesterol (mg)	Sodium (mg)	Carbohydrate (g)	Protein (g)	Fiber (g)
115	14	2	0.5	0	1	27	1	2

Exchanges: Fruit 2

Guacamole

1 C plain nonfat yogurt
2 scallions, chopped
1 T lemon juice
1-1/2 C mashed Florida avocado
1 medium tomato, chopped
4 oz can green chilies, chopped
1/2 tsp pepper
1/2 tsp chili powder
1/2 tsp cumin
1/2 tsp garlic

Blend all ingredients; adjust seasonings to taste. Chill before serving. Makes 2 C.

Serving size: 2 T.

Suggestion

• Nonfat cottage cheese can be substituted for the yogurt.

Avocados

Also called *alligator pears,* avocados can have a bright green, thin, smooth skin, or a dark green, purplish, thick, pebbly skin. The yellow flesh has a bright green rim just under the skin. It has a buttery, soft texture and a mild flavor. Avocados contain vitamin E. Avocados are high in fat, but it is mostly monounsaturated fat (like that in olive oil), which has been shown to lower cholesterol. Florida avocados have slightly less fat than California varieties.

Calories	%Fat	Fat (g)	Saturated Fat (g)	Cholesterol (mg)	Sodium (mg)	Carbohydrate (g)	Protein (g)	Fiber (g)
36	57	2	0.4	0	66	3	1	1

Exchanges: Vegetable 1/2, Fat 1/2

Avocado ripens well at room temperature after picking. When ripe, the top of stem end will feel soft. Ripe avocado can be stored in the refrigerator for up to five days.

Puréed avocado can be frozen in an airtight container for three to six months. To keep it from turning dark, stir in one tablespoon of lemon juice for every two avocados. Cut slices should be served immediately or brushed with lemon juice. Burying an avocado pit in guacamole will not help keep it from turning brown; lemon or lime juice must be included in the recipe.

Spicy Avocados

1 clove garlic, coarsely chopped
1 onion, diced
1/2 medium red pepper, cored, seeded, diced
1 /2 medium green pepper, cored, seeded, diced
1 jalapeño pepper, cored, seeded, quartered
1 tomato, peeled, seeded, diced
2 T olive oil
2 T white wine vinegar
1-1/2 C diced Florida avocado

Purée the garlic, onion, red and green peppers, hot pepper, and tomato in a food processor until smooth. Cook the puréed mixture in hot oil, stirring for 2 minutes. Stir in the vinegar and salt; reduce heat and continue cooking for 20 minutes. Cool to room temperature. Gently stir in the avocado.

Serving size: 2 T.

Suggestion
• Serve with unsalted crackers or as a dip for raw vegetables.

Calories	%Fat	Fat (g)	Saturated Fat (g)	Cholesterol (mg)	Sodium (mg)	Carbohydrate (g)	Protein (g)	Fiber (g)
17	78	1	0.2	0	1	1	0	0

Note: 2 T = Free

Almost Guacamole

1 pkg (10 oz) frozen early or baby peas
1/2 C plain nonfat yogurt
1 green chili, seeded and minced
1 T chopped fresh parsley
1 tsp lemon juice
1/2 tsp ground cumin
1/4 tsp salt
Dash of hot sauce
2 T diced red onion
1 C peeled, seeded, and chopped tomato

Cook peas according to package directions, omitting salt. Drain well. Purée peas, yogurt, chili, parsley, juice, cumin, salt, and hot sauce in a food processor or blender until smooth. Stir in onion and tomato. Cover and chill thoroughly. Makes 2 C.
Serving size: 2 T.

Heart-Healthy Snacks

- Skim milk
- Dips made with low-fat cottage cheese or yogurt
- Skim or nonfat yogurt flavored with extract and sweetener
- Shakes made with skim milk, fruit or fruit juices, extract, and sweetener
- Raw vegetables with salsa, low-fat cottage cheese
- Low-sodium V-8 or tomato juice
- Low-sodium pickles
- Fresh or canned juice; fresh, juice-packed, or water-packed canned fruit
- Fruit juice ices
- Dried fruit
- Unsalted popcorn made with acceptable oil or hot-air popped
- Unsalted pretzels
- Rice cakes or grain cakes
- Graham crackers, vanilla wafers, or ginger snaps
- Angel food cake
- Low-calorie gelatin

Arizona Heart Institute Foundation
1–800–345–4278

Calories	%Fat	Fat (g)	Saturated Fat (g)	Cholesterol (mg)	Sodium (mg)	Carbohydrate (g)	Protein (g)	Fiber (g)
42	5	0	0.1	0	109	8	3	2

Exchanges: Vegetable 1-1/2

Yogurt

Yogurt is made from milk that is fermented and coagulated with friendly bacteria. Many companies heat their yogurt, killing the beneficial bacteria. Look for brands that contain live or active yogurt cultures (Acidophilus), which aid digestion. Yogurt is a good source of calcium, protein, riboflavin, phosphorus, and vitamin B_{12}.

Yogurt is very thick and slightly tart. Beating it will make it watery; it should be blended into foods gently. It can be substituted for sour cream and half or more of the mayonnaise or reduced-fat mayonnaise in recipes.

Commercial fruited yogurts can contain large amounts of sugar (up to six teaspoons per eight-ounce container) and other additives. Buy plain nonfat yogurt and add crushed or puréed fresh fruit at home. It can be served chilled or frozen like ice cream.

Spicy Yogurt Dip

1 C plain nonfat yogurt
3-1/2 T chopped onion
1 T white wine vinegar
1/4 tsp dry mustard
1 tsp ground cumin
1/2 tsp ground coriander seed
1/2 tsp fresh ground pepper
2 T freshly chopped coriander leaves

Blend all ingredients well. Store tightly covered in the refrigerator. Makes 1-1/2 C.
Serving size: 2 T.

Suggestions
• Serve cold as a dip with raw vegetables.
• Serve at room temperature as a topping for baked potatoes, steamed cauliflower, or other hot vegetables.

Calories	%Fat	Fat (g)	Saturated Fat (g)	Cholesterol (mg)	Sodium (mg)	Carbohydrate (g)	Protein (g)	Fiber (g)
15	9	0	0.0	0	17	2	1	0

Note: 2 T = Free

Chili-Corn Dip

8 oz low-fat (1%) cottage cheese
1/2 C frozen corn, thawed
2 T picante sauce
1 small clove garlic, minced
2 T canned chopped green chilies, drained
1 T diced sweet red pepper
2 T frozen corn, thawed

   Purée first 4 ingredients in an electric blender until almost smooth. Gently fold in green chilies, sweet red pepper, and 2 T corn. Cover and chill at least 1 hour. Serve with fresh raw vegetables. Makes 1-1/2 C.
   Serving size: 2 T.

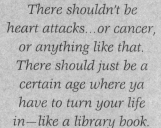

There shouldn't be heart attacks…or cancer, or anything like that. There should just be a certain age where ya have to turn your life in—like a library book. You pack a bag. You go—and that's that.

Betty White
The Golden Girls

Calories	% Fat	Fat (g)	Saturated Fat (g)	Cholesterol (mg)	Sodium (mg)	Carbohydrate (g)	Protein (g)	Fiber (g)
11	8	0	0.1	0	113	2	1	0

Note: 2 T = Free

Sauces, Accompaniments, & Staples

Roasted Tomato-Chipotle Sauce

Rick Bayless

1-1/2 lb ripe tomato
2 to 3 canned *chilies chipotles*
1/2 small onion, chopped
1 large garlic clove, peeled and minced
1 C poultry broth
1/4 C chopped cilantro

Place the tomatoes on a baking sheet and roast 6 inches below a preheated broiler until blackened and blistered, about 6 to 7 minutes. Using a pair of tongs, turn the tomatoes over and roast the other side. Cool. Peel off the skin and remove the cores; scrape all the juice in with the peeled tomatoes.

In a blender or food processor, make a coarse purée from the tomatoes and chilies. Cook the onion in cooking spray over medium heat until it starts to brown, about 7 minutes. Increase the heat to medium-high; add the garlic, and cook for 1 minute. Add the tomato mixture (the pan should be hot enough to sizzle sharply) and cook, stirring constantly, for a few minutes or until sauce is reduced and thickened. Add the broth and simmer until the sauce reaches a medium consistency; season with salt. Remove from heat and stir in chopped cilantro. Serve with Tortas de Lentejas (page 96). Makes 2-1/2 cups.

Serves 6.

Serve with Tortas de Lentejas (page 96).

Chili Peppers

Chili peppers are used as a hot seasoning in Indian curries and in Latin American, Asian, and Arab cooking. The many varieties of chili peppers offer a range of hotness, from mild to incendiary. Small chilies are usually hotter than larger ones.

Fresh chilies can be kept for up to a week in a paper or plastic bag stored in the refrigerator, preferably in the butter compartment; dried chilies will last indefinitely when stored in a dark place.

Calories	%Fat	Fat (g)	Saturated Fat (g)	Cholesterol (mg)	Sodium (mg)	Carbohydrate (g)	Protein (g)	Fiber (g)
34	14	1	0.1	0	216	7	2	2

Exchanges: Vegetable 1

The oils in chili peppers can irritate the skin, so you should wear gloves when handling them and wash your hands well when finished. Don't touch your face or eyes for several hours after handling chili peppers, no matter how well protected or washed your hands are.

Fresh or dried chili peppers should be added in small amounts. It's difficult to predict how hot a particular chili will be until it's been cooked, so taste the cooking food often before adding more chili. Recipes that include tomatoes, vinegar, lemon juice, or other acid ingredients help to cool down the chili pepper's fire. The seeds and veins inside the pepper are the hottest parts; remove them before cooking for a milder flavor. Chilies can also be soaked in cold water or milk before use to help tame their flavor.

All chili peppers are rich in vitamin C; red ones have more vitamin A and other nutrients than green ones.

 # esquite-Smoked Tomato Sauce

Sean Kavanaugh

10 large Roma tomatoes
1 C mirepoix (sautéed diced carrots, onions, celery)
1 T shallots
1 T garlic
1 bay leaf
1 C red wine
1 T basil
1 T sugar

To smoke the tomatoes, place mesquite chips in a pan over high heat until they start to smoke and smolder. Place the tomatoes in a perforated pan on top of the chips, cover, and remove from heat. Let sit for 10 to 12 minutes.

Sauté mirepoix, shallots, garlic, bay leaf, and tomatoes. Add red wine and reduce. Add basil and sugar. Purée and strain through fine chinois.

Serves 4.

Calories	%Fat	Fat (g)	Saturated Fat (g)	Cholesterol (mg)	Sodium (mg)	Carbohydrate (g)	Protein (g)	Fiber (g)
77	7	1	0.1	0	32	16	2	3

Exchanges: Vegetable 3

# Spaghetti Sauce

**How to Use
Canned Tomatoes**

- Cut up canned tomatoes with kitchen shears, right in the can, instead of chopping them with a knife on a cutting board.
- Do not drain canned tomatoes unless the recipe specifically directs it—most recipes include the juice.

1 clove garlic, minced
1 medium onion, chopped
1 large green bell pepper, chopped
1/2 medium carrot, finely grated
8 fresh mushrooms, sliced
1 C dry red wine
3 cans (16 oz each) peeled Italian tomatoes
1 can (8 oz) no-salt-added tomato sauce
1 can (6 oz) no-salt-added tomato paste
1 bay leaf
1 tsp oregano
1/2 tsp basil
1/2 tsp thyme
1/2 tsp black pepper
1 T sugar

Sauté garlic, onion, bell pepper, carrot, and mushrooms. Add remaining ingredients and bring almost to a boil. Reduce heat and simmer, covered, for 60 to 90 minutes or until thick, stirring occasionally and breaking up tomatoes with a spoon or spatula. Adjust seasonings to taste during cooking. Remove bay leaf before serving.

Serves 6.

Calories	% Fat	Fat (g)	Saturated Fat (g)	Cholesterol (mg)	Sodium (mg)	Carbohydrate (g)	Protein (g)	Fiber (g)
130	15	2	0.3	0	67	26	5	5

Exchanges: Vegetable 5

Personalized Diet

At the Arizona Heart Institute we take into account a patient's total lifestyle so that our diet may be personalized to fit that lifestyle for years after the patient leaves the initial program. We believe that proper values and attitudes are as nutritionally healthy for men's and women's total well-being as the food they eat. Most of our patients recognize the wisdom of this, and, because of this personalized approach, we have been very successful in winning the dietary compliance of our patients after they leave the Institute.

Edward B. Diethrich, MD
Heart Test

Double Red Sauce

1 medium onion, chopped
2 medium red bell peppers, seeded and chopped
2 garlic cloves, chopped
1 can (28 oz) no-salt-added Italian plum tomatoes, cut up
7 dried tomatoes, chopped
Freshly ground black pepper to taste

Sauté onion, peppers, and garlic over medium heat until soft, stirring occasionally. Add canned and dried tomatoes. Bring to a boil; reduce heat and simmer 20 to 30 minutes, stirring occasionally, until the sauce is thick. Purée sauce in a food processor or blender, leaving some chunks. Season with pepper. Makes 3 C.

Serves 12.

Suggestion

- Use in preparing Garden Lasagna (page 110) or other dishes that call for tomato sauce, or serve over spaghetti.

Calories	%Fat	Fat (g)	Saturated Fat (g)	Cholesterol (mg)	Sodium (mg)	Carbohydrate (g)	Protein (g)	Fiber (g)
31	9	1	0	0	188	7	1	2

Exchanges: Vegetable 1

Roasted Red Pepper Sauce

I'm not a vegetarian because I love animals. I'm a vegetarian because I hate plants.

A. Whitney Brown

4 red Roasted Bell Peppers (page 183), quartered
2 tomatoes, diced
1/2 white onion, diced
2 jalapeño peppers, finely diced
1 bunch fresh cilantro, chopped
1 T olive oil
1/2 C plain nonfat yogurt

Purée the Roasted Bell Peppers in a food processor, gradually adding the tomatoes, onion, jalapeño, cilantro, and oil. Heat over low heat until warm; stir in yogurt.
Serves 6.

Suggestion
• Serve with Popcorn Chicken (page 319) or over pasta; use in recipes that call for tomato or spaghetti sauce.

Calories	%Fat	Fat (g)	Saturated Fat (g)	Cholesterol (mg)	Sodium (mg)	Carbohydrate (g)	Protein (g)	Fiber (g)
78	33	3	0.4	0	44	12	4	4

Exchanges: Vegetable 2, Fat 1/2

Roast Hubbard Squash Sauce

P. Quint Smith

1 tsp butter
2 T maple syrup
1 small or 1/2 large hubbard squash, cleaned, diced
1 T herbes de Provence
Pepper to taste
1 pt fish stock
1 pt water

Melt butter in a heavy saucepan. Add maple syrup; bring to a boil and reduce mixture slightly. Toss squash, herbs, and pepper; add to maple-butter and toss to coat squash. Roast, covered, at 350° until squash is tender, about 20 minutes. Purée in a food processor until smooth. Bring fish stock and water to a boil. Stir enough boiling liquid into the purée to make a thick sauce. Adjust seasonings.

Serves 15 (1/2 C each).

Calories	%Fat	Fat (g)	Saturated Fat (g)	Cholesterol (mg)	Sodium (mg)	Carbohydrate (g)	Protein (g)	Fiber (g)
33	19	1	0.3	1	10	7	1	1

Exchanges: Starch 1/2

Creole Sauce

James P. Shannon

1 T olive oil
1/2 C chopped onions
2 cloves garlic, chopped
1/2 C chopped celery
1/2 C chopped green onion
1 C green bell peppers, diced
1/2 C red bell peppers, diced
2 C fresh, ripe tomatoes
1/2 bunch fresh thyme, chopped
1/2 tsp Creole Seasoning
1/2 C water

Heat olive oil and sauté all ingredients (except tomatoes, seasonings, and water). Cook for about 5 to 8 minutes, stirring often. Add tomatoes, herbs, and water. Simmer slowly for 5 minutes, then re-season. Makes 3 C. Serve with Breast of Chicken Creole (page 324).

Serving size: 2 T.

Calories	%Fat	Fat (g)	Saturated Fat (g)	Cholesterol (mg)	Sodium (mg)	Carbohydrate (g)	Protein (g)	Fiber (g)
14	43	1	0.1	0	5	2	0	1

Note: 1 serving = Free, 2 servings = 1 Vegetable

Types of Fats

Excessive saturated fat intake tends to increase the level of cholesterol in the blood, even more so than dietary cholesterol intake. The higher the saturated fat content, the more solid the fat will be at room temperature. Saturated fat in the diet can be reduced by avoiding animal fats, such as butter and lard, and by decreasing intake of some vegetable fats, such as coconut, palm, and palm kernel oils (the "tropical oils"). Shortening (which is hydrogenated vegetable oil) and other hardened vegetable oils should be limited as well.

Monounsaturated fats tend to lower the total level of blood cholesterol without affecting the HDLs. Olive, canola, and peanut oils are the best choices. All oils contain about 120 calories per tablespoon, so they should be used sparingly, regardless of the type.

Polyunsaturated fats in small amounts, such as safflower oil, corn oil, and soybean oil, may help to reduce blood cholesterol, but they also tend to lower the HDLs. Polyunsaturated fats may be used in moderation, but the total fat content of the diet should be kept as low as possible.

Total fat intake should be limited to less than 25% of the total daily calories. Saturated fat should contribute no more than 7% of the total calories, with the remainder from polyunsaturated and monounsaturated fat.

Arizona Heart Institute Foundation
1-800-345-4278

# Sauce Poivrade

Rozanne Gold

2 tsp sugar
3 T water
2 C beef broth
1 C full-bodied red wine
3 sprigs fresh rosemary
1/2 tsp crushed black peppercorns
1 T red wine vinegar
1-1/2 tsp cornstarch dissolved in 1-1/2 tsp water

Heat sugar and water in medium saucepan until caramelized, about 5 minutes. Add broth, wine, garlic, rosemary, peppercorns, and vinegar. Cook over low heat and reduce to 1-1/4 C. Strain through a fine-mesh sieve and return liquid to saucepan. Bring to a boil; reduce heat and slowly whisk in cornstarch. Stir constantly until sauce thickens. Serve with Medallions of Venison (page 354). Makes 1 C.
Serving size: 2 T.

Calories	%Fat	Fat (g)	Saturated Fat (g)	Cholesterol (mg)	Sodium (mg)	Carbohydrate (g)	Protein (g)	Fiber (g)
6	9	0	0.0	0	5	1	0	0

Note: 1 T = Free

Sauce Vierge

Michael Hutchings

3 medium vine-ripe tomatoes
2 shallots, finely chopped
2 T julienned basil
1 T extra-virgin olive oil
Juice of 1 lemon
Salt
Freshly ground white pepper to taste

Plunge tomatoes into boiling water for about 30 seconds. Cool in ice bath. Peel, seed, and dice into 1/4-inch cubes. Add the olive oil, basil, lemon juice, and shallots. Adjust seasonings to taste. Serve with Grilled Tuna (page 285).

Serves 8.

Food Logs

Keeping a food and activity record for one week can be extremely helpful, but only if your record is accurate. Be honest! List every item (include quantities) you eat or drink. Also record the time, location, and your emotional state.

The food/activity records will provide you with valuable nutrient, caloric, and physical activity information. They may also suggest patterns: a tendency to overeat in the afternoons or when stressed; high-fat dinners late at night; or an exercise regimen that consists of only a stroll around the block twice a week.

Arizona Heart Institute Foundation
1–800–345–4278

Calories	% Fat	Fat (g)	Saturated Fat (g)	Cholesterol (mg)	Sodium (mg)	Carbohydrate (g)	Protein (g)	Fiber (g)
32	54	2	0.3	0	8	4	1	1

Exchanges: Vegetable 1, Fat 1/2

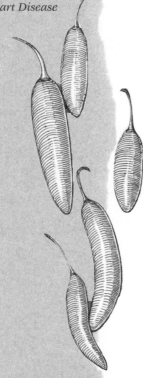

Vietnamese Dipping Sauce

Patrick O'Connell

1 C cold water
3/4 C + 2 T Vietnamese fish sauce
1/4 C sugar
1/4 C minced fresh cilantro
2 T rice wine vinegar
2 T very fine julienne carrot
2 large cloves of garlic, minced
2 jalapeño peppers, finely chopped
Juice of whole lime (unstrained)

Mix all ingredients. Serve with Seared Rare Peppered Tuna (page 284). Serves 10 to 12.

Suggestion

- Vietnamese fish sauce is available in Oriental or specialty stores.

Calories	%Fat	Fat (g)	Saturated Fat (g)	Cholesterol (mg)	Sodium (mg)	Carbohydrate (g)	Protein (g)	Fiber (g)
44	1	0	0.0	0	831	9	2	0

Exchanges: Vegetable 2

Rutabaga & Pepper Relish

Sanford D'Amato

2 lb rutabaga, peeled and diced small
1/2 tsp cumin
Pepper to taste
1 medium red onion, diced small
1 medium red bell pepper, seeded, diced small
1 medium green bell pepper, seeded, diced small
Juice of 1/2 lemon

Sauté rutabaga, 1/4 tsp cumin, and pepper in cooking spray until tender; remove from pan and cool. Sauté onion and both peppers in cooking spray over moderate heat for about 1-1/2 minutes. Add remaining cumin. Sauté for 1 to 2 minutes until crisp-tender. Transfer to a bowl and cool. Mix with rutabaga and season with lemon juice. Serve with Grilled Swordfish (page 282).

Serves 4.

Calories	%Fat	Fat (g)	Saturated Fat (g)	Cholesterol (mg)	Sodium (mg)	Carbohydrate (g)	Protein (g)	Fiber (g)
84	6	1	0.1	0	35	19	3	3

Exchanges: Vegetable 4

Rutabagas

Rutabagas have coarse, dark purple-mahogany skin and dense yellow-orange flesh. They can be used in place of turnips—and rutabagas will provide more vitamin C and beta-carotene. They are also a good source of fiber and calcium. Rutabagas can be stored in the refrigerator, tightly wrapped, for about two weeks. Grocery stores often wax them for longer shelf-life, so they should be peeled before cooking.

Like potatoes, rutabagas can be used in a variety of ways. Thin slices are good sautéed with onions. Chunks of rutabaga can be baked for about one hour at 350°. Parboiled rutabaga can be added to stir-fry dishes. Cubes of rutabaga can be added to stews and soups. They can also be prepared like potato salad. Puréed rutabaga can be used to thicken soup.

Rutabagas are delicious boiled and mashed like potatoes. Stir in sherry, instead of butter, just before serving. They can be savory or sweet; season with brown sugar or honey and yogurt.

Tomato Salsa

Karla A. Graves

3 tomatoes, finely chopped
2 Anaheim chilies, chopped
1/2 jalapeño, seeded and chopped
2 cloves garlic, minced
1 T sugar

Mix all ingredients. Allow flavors to blend for 1 to 2 hours before serving. Serve with Snapper Soft Tacos (page 276).

Serving size: 2 T.

Calories	%Fat	Fat (g)	Saturated Fat (g)	Cholesterol (mg)	Sodium (mg)	Carbohydrate (g)	Protein (g)	Fiber (g)
8	7	0	0.0	0	2	2	0	0

Note: 2 T = Free, 4 T = 1 Vegetable

 oasted Tomato Salsa

1 small head garlic
2 medium red bell peppers
3 medium tomatoes
1 small red onion, diced fine
2 tsp chopped fresh cilantro
1/4 C fresh lime juice
1 tsp hot red pepper sauce
1/2 tsp minced fresh jalapeño pepper
1/2 tsp ground cumin
1/4 tsp ground white pepper

Wrap the garlic in foil and bake at 300° for 40 minutes or until very soft. Squeeze the garlic out of the shells; purée until smooth.

Roast the peppers and tomatoes over an open flame, turning occasionally to blacken evenly. Place the roasted vegetables in a paper bag and let stand for 15 minutes. Rub off the skins with a paper towel. Remove the seeds. Chop into fine dice. Mix with remaining ingredients, including puréed garlic. Let salsa stand for about 1 hour before serving. Makes 2-1/2 C.

Serves 10.

Calories	%Fat	Fat (g)	Saturated Fat (g)	Cholesterol (mg)	Sodium (mg)	Carbohydrate (g)	Protein (g)	Fiber (g)
19	11	0	0.0	0	9	4	1	1

Exchanges: Vegetable 1

South-of-the-Border Salsa

2 C chopped fresh tomatoes
1 can (4 oz) green chilies, diced
2 scallions, chopped
1/2 tsp dried oregano
2 T chopped cilantro
1/4 tsp garlic powder
Dash of Tabasco sauce

Mix all ingredients well. Drain well, squeezing out juice from tomatoes with a spoon or potato masher. Cover and chill overnight to allow flavors to blend.

Serves 12 (1/4 C each).

Calories	%Fat	Fat (g)	Saturated Fat (g)	Cholesterol (mg)	Sodium (mg)	Carbohydrate (g)	Protein (g)	Fiber (g)
11	11	0	0.0	0	139	2	0	0

Note: 1 serving = Free, 1/2 C = 1 Vegetable

Cucumber-Dill Sauce

3/4 C plain nonfat yogurt
1/4 C nonfat mayonnaise
1 tsp chopped fresh parsley
1/2 C diced unpeeled cucumber
1 T minced fresh onion
1/4 tsp dried dill

   Mix all ingredients well. Cover and chill 30 minutes. Stir just before serving.
Makes 1-1/2 C.
   Serving Size: 1 T.

Suggestion
• Serve with baked fish, hot vegetables, or as a salad dressing.

Calories	%Fat	Fat (g)	Saturated Fat (g)	Cholesterol (mg)	Sodium (mg)	Carbohydrate (g)	Protein (g)	Fiber (g)
7	2	0	0.0	0	38	1	0	0

Note: 1 T = Free

Mock Hollandaise

2 T hot water
1/4 C reduced-fat mayonnaise
1/4 C nonfat plain yogurt
1 T fresh lemon juice

Blend hot water, mayonnaise, and yogurt in the top of a double boiler, stirring constantly until heated. Stir in lemon juice. Serve hot.
Serves 10.

Suggestions

- Instead of a double boiler, cook Mock Hollandaise in a microwave oven at 50% power, stirring every 30 seconds until hot. Do not overcook.
- *Red Pepper Hollandaise:* Add 1/4 tsp of chili powder and cayenne pepper to taste.

Calories	%Fat	Fat (g)	Saturated Fat (g)	Cholesterol (mg)	Sodium (mg)	Carbohydrate (g)	Protein (g)	Fiber (g)
21	73	2	0.3	2	40	1	0	0

Exchanges: Fat 1/2

Baked-Garlic Purée

James Peterson

15 heads garlic
2 tsp olive oil

Peel the outside papery skin off the heads, but do not separate the head into cloves or peel the individual cloves. Create 3 or 4 packets of garlic by wrapping 4 or 5 heads together in aluminum foil. Bake the garlic in a 325° oven until the cloves are soft, about 1 hour. Extract the purée from the cloves with a food mill or by pushing the cloves through a strainer with the back of a ladle.

To store the purée in the refrigerator, smooth the top with the back of a spoon and dribble olive oil over it. Cover with plastic wrap or seal in Mason jars. The purée darkens when exposed to air. Makes about 1 C.

Serving size: 1 T.

Suggestion
- Spread the purée on roast chicken, game birds, grilled shrimp, or steamed vegetables.

Calories	%Fat	Fat (g)	Saturated Fat (g)	Cholesterol (mg)	Sodium (mg)	Carbohydrate (g)	Protein (g)	Fiber (g)
30	19	1	0.1	0	3	6	1	0

Exchanges: Vegetable 1

Eat plenty of garlic. This guarantees you twelve hours of sleep—alone—every night, and there's nothing like rest to give you shining orbs (poetic), peepers (colloquial) or lamps (slang). A diet of potatoes and garlic leaves you oodles of time for reading Roget's Thesaurus in Dictionary Form, *too.*

Chris Chase
How To Be a Movie Star, or A Terrible Beauty is Born

Garlic

Garlic grows in heads that contain a cluster of cloves. American garlic is white; Mexican and Italian garlic have purplish husks and a milder flavor.

Garlic should not be stored in the refrigerator, except in very hot, humid climates. Keep it in a cool, dry, well-ventilated place for up to two months. Peeled whole cloves can be stored in oil. Individual cloves of garlic can be planted in small pots.

The sprouts can be snipped like chives to use in salads or as a garnish; they will grow for months.

Garlic is generally used in small amounts, usually one or two cloves at a time. The flavor becomes milder and sweeter when it is cooked for long periods. Garlic can be peeled easily by first crushing the clove with the flat blade of a knife or by trimming the stem ends and cutting the clove in half. Older cloves develop a bitter green or yellow central strip that should be removed and discarded. Chewing fresh parsley can help reduce garlic breath.

Elephant garlic is about the size of an apple or a small grapefruit. It has a mild flavor and does not leave a pungent odor on breath like regular garlic. The cloves are very easy to peel. It can be substituted for ordinary garlic or onion in any recipe; use one clove to replace one onion. Thin slices of raw elephant garlic are delicious in salads.

Basil Pesto

1 tsp chopped fresh garlic
1/4 lb fresh basil
1/4 C pine nuts
1/4 C Parmesan cheese, freshly grated
3/4 C olive oil

Purée all ingredients in a blender or food processor. Store, tightly covered, in the refrigerator for up to 2-1/2 weeks. Makes 2 C.
Serving size: 1 T.

Suggestion
• Serve over pasta with sun-dried tomatoes and shrimp.

Calories	%Fat	Fat (g)	Saturated Fat (g)	Cholesterol (mg)	Sodium (mg)	Carbohydrate (g)	Protein (g)	Fiber (g)
55	96	6	0.9	1	17	0	1	0

Exchanges: Fat 1

Plum Sauce

1 lb fresh black plums, pitted and thinly sliced
1 T vinegar
1/4 tsp grated fresh ginger
2 T unsweetened apple juice
1/4 tsp minced garlic
2 T water

Bring plums, vinegar, ginger, apple juice, garlic, and water to a boil. Reduce heat and simmer, stirring constantly, until plums are tender and mixture is thick. Cool to room temperature.
Serves 4.

Suggestion
• Use as a marinade and/or basting sauce for fish, poultry, or veal.

Stress Reduction Tips
• Learn how to relax.
• Think constructively about the things that bother you.
• Improve your self-talk.
• Be good to yourself.
• Get adequate exercise.
• Get proper nutrition.
• Practice time management skills.

**Arizona Heart
Institute Foundation**
1–800–345–4278

Calories	% Fat	Fat (g)	Saturated Fat (g)	Cholesterol (mg)	Sodium (mg)	Carbohydrate (g)	Protein (g)	Fiber (g)
49	9	1	0.0	0	0	12	1	1

Exchanges: Fruit 1

Chutney

Chutney, a spicy or sweet-and-sour condiment, originated in India. A milder form of chutney has developed from the traditional exotic recipes. Chutney can be mild or hot, chunky or smooth. It is served with meats, fish, meat pies, curries, and cheeses. Sweet chutney is also served with muffins or bread.

Soft, slightly overripe fruit and/or vegetables are cooked to a pulp with sugar, spices, salt, and vinegar (the last three items are preservatives). Dried fruits are sometimes added for sweetness, texture, and color. Whole or ground spices are the most important ingredient in chutney. Because whole spices keep their volatile oils during storage, however, they provide a better flavor.

Mango-Pineapple Chutney

Greg Paulson, CEC

2 mangos, medium diced
1 pineapple, small diced
1 papaya, small diced
1/2 lb brown sugar (about 1-1/8 C packed)
1 oz fresh ginger, grated
1 C orange juice
Juice of 1-1/2 limes
4 oz rice vinegar
1 T chili paste
1/2 T cayenne pepper
1 tsp granulated garlic
1/2 T curry powder
2 oz coconut (about 1 C)
4 oz raisins (about 3/4 C)
1-1/3 oz macadamia nuts, ground (about 15 nuts)
3 oz chopped red bell pepper (about 3/4 C)

Sauté mango, pineapple, and papaya with brown sugar and ginger. Deglaze pan with orange and lime juice. Add rice vinegar, chili paste, cayenne pepper, garlic, and curry powder. Add coconut, raisins, macadamia nuts, and bell pepper. Simmer for 20 minutes. Remove from heat. Serve warm with Baked Opakapaka in Phyllo (page 275). Makes about 12 C.

Serving size: 1/4 C.

Calories	%Fat	Fat (g)	Saturated Fat (g)	Cholesterol (mg)	Sodium (mg)	Carbohydrate (g)	Protein (g)	Fiber (g)
53	19	1	0.5	0	6	11	0	1

Exchanges: Fruit 1

Tropical Fruit Salsa

James Peterson

2 kiwis, peeled
1/4 small pineapple, peeled and cored
1 papaya, peeled and seeded
1 mango, halved, pit removed, fruit cut off skin
1 medium red onion, finely chopped
1 red bell pepper, grilled, skinned, seeded, finely chopped
3 jalapeño chilies, halved lengthwise, seeded, finely chopped
Juice of 2 limes
Leaves from 1 small bunch cilantro, finely chopped
Salt to taste

Combine the fruits in a food processor and pulse them to a semi-liquid consistency. Be sure to leave the fruit chunky. Mix the chopped fruit mixture with the other ingredients in a bowl. Cover with plastic wrap and chill in the refrigerator. Makes about 4 C.

Serving size: 1/2 C.

Suggestions
• This sweet and spicy salsa is delicious served slightly chilled with barbecued foods.
• Tropical Fruit Salsa will keep for up to 3 days in the refrigerator.

Kiwi Fruit

Long known in New Zealand as the *Chinese gooseberry,* kiwi fruit was renamed after the bird for marketing in the United States. These egg-sized oval berries grow in clusters on vines, like grapes. They have brown, fuzzy skin that is easily removed with a vegetable peeler. The dreary exterior conceals a beautiful emerald-green interior that has tiny black seeds; it is often cut in thin slices crossways to make a very attractive garnish. Kiwis can be sweet or sweet-tart, with a flavor like lime, strawberry, melon, and citrus combined. They are very juicy. Kiwis are an excellent source of vitamin C and potassium, as well as a good source of fiber.

A kiwi is ripe when it feels slightly soft when pressed in the palm of hand, like a peach. They can be ripened in a paper bag at room temperature. Unripe fruit can be

Calories	%Fat	Fat (g)	Saturated Fat (g)	Cholesterol (mg)	Sodium (mg)	Carbohydrate (g)	Protein (g)	Fiber (g)
71	6	0	0.1	0	14	17	2	4

Exchanges: Fruit 1

refrigerated and set out later to complete ripening. Ripe kiwis can be kept in the refrigerator for up to a week. Sliced ripe fruit freezes very well for up to six months.

Kiwis can be used like other fruits in salads, muffins, or cooking. Slices make a pretty garnish for fruit or chicken salads, punch, or cheesecake. They cannot be used fresh in gelatin; like pineapples and papayas, kiwis contain an enzyme that prevents gelatin from setting.

Papaya Salsa

1 C diced fresh papaya
1 C diced fresh pineapple
1/3 C diced scallion
2 T fresh lemon juice
2 medium fresh tomatoes, peeled, seeded, diced
3 T chopped cilantro
1 jalapeño pepper, seeded, minced

Combine all ingredients. Cover and let stand at room temperature for 3 hours. Serve with fish or poultry.

Serves 6.

Calories	%Fat	Fat (g)	Saturated Fat (g)	Cholesterol (mg)	Sodium (mg)	Carbohydrate (g)	Protein (g)	Fiber (g)
37	8	0	0.1	0	8	9	1	2

Exchanges: Fruit 1/2

# **P**ineapple Salsa

Karla A. Graves

1 can (16 oz) unsweetened pineapple chunks
1 small red onion
1 clove garlic, diced
1 bunch cilantro leaves, chopped
1/2 jalapeño, seeded, chopped
1/2 tsp oregano
Juice of 1 lime

Mix all ingredients. Allow flavors to blend for 2 hours before serving. Serve with Snapper Soft Tacos (page 276).
Serving size: 2 T.

Suggestion
• Pineapple Salsa is good with any fish dish.

Pineapples

The pineapple is really a cluster of fruits that form one multiple fruit. Ripe pineapple has a sweet fragrance. The center leaves will pull out easily when the pineapple is ripe enough to eat. The color of the shell is not a guide to ripeness; it can be tinted green or yellow. Pineapple will not get sweeter after it is picked. Buy pineapples grown in Hawaii; state standards prohibit harvesting them before they are ripe.

Store ripe pineapple in a plastic bag in the refrigerator for three to five days. Cut pieces last longer than a whole pineapple; they can be refrigerated in an airtight container for a week. Pineapples are a good source of vitamin C and potassium.

To use pineapple as a natural meat tenderizer, simmer it with chicken or meat; boiling will destroy the enzyme that acts as a tenderizer. Fresh or frozen pineapple cannot be used with gelatin because this enzyme will prevent it from setting.

Calories	%Fat	Fat (g)	Saturated Fat (g)	Cholesterol (mg)	Sodium (mg)	Carbohydrate (g)	Protein (g)	Fiber (g)
13	6	0	0.0	0	5	3	0	1

Exchanges: Fruit 1/4

Plum Red Wine Glaze

John Novi

1-1/2 C burgundy red wine
3/4 C sugar
6 overripe small tart Italian plums, pitted
Juice of 2 lemons

Boil wine and sugar to syrup stage. Add plums and again cook to syrup stage. Stir in lemon juice. Serve with Stuffed Leg of Goat (page 350).
Serving size: 2 T.

Calories	%Fat	Fat (g)	Saturated Fat (g)	Cholesterol (mg)	Sodium (mg)	Carbohydrate (g)	Protein (g)	Fiber (g)
33	2	0	0.0	0	2	8	0	0

Exchanges: Fruit 1/2

Cranberry Glaze

1 C jellied cranberry sauce
1/2 C light corn syrup
1 T cider vinegar
Pinch of cinnamon
Pinch of ground cloves

Cook all ingredients in a small, heavy saucepan over very low heat, whisking briskly until the cranberry sauce is melted. Do not boil. Brush the glaze on poultry or ham two or three times during the last 30 minutes of baking. Remove skin before eating. Makes 1-1/2 C.

Serving size: 1 tsp.

Calories	%Fat	Fat (g)	Saturated Fat (g)	Cholesterol (mg)	Sodium (mg)	Carbohydrate (g)	Protein (g)	Fiber (g)
12	0	0	0.0	0	3	3	0	0

Note: 1 tsp = Free

Maple Syrup

Maple syrup is made from the sap of maple trees. It takes 40 gallons of sap to make one gallon of pure maple syrup. It has a high mineral content. Opened bottles of pure maple syrup can be stored in the refrigerator, tightly capped, for up to one year.

Pure maple syrup is expensive, so pancake syrups may actually be 97% corn syrup with only a little maple syrup or artificial flavoring. Read labels carefully if you are looking for pure maple syrup. Reduced-calorie syrup is made by diluting maple-flavored syrup with water and thickening it with cellulose gum. Maple-flavored syrup can be stored at room temperature for four to six months after opening.

Maple sugar is made by boiling maple syrup until enough liquid has evaporated to leave an extremely sweet, soft, granular sugar. It is usually sold in molded pieces, like small candies.

aple-Orange Glaze

1/2 C reduced-calorie maple syrup
1/2 C orange juice
Juice of 1 lemon
1/2 C low-sugar orange marmalade

Cook all ingredients in a small, heavy saucepan over very low heat, whisking briskly until the cranberry sauce is melted. Do not boil. Brush the glaze on poultry or ham 2 or 3 times during the last 30 minutes of baking. Makes 1-1/2 C.
Serving size: 1 T.

Calories	%Fat	Fat (g)	Saturated Fat (g)	Cholesterol (mg)	Sodium (mg)	Carbohydrate (g)	Protein (g)	Fiber (g)
23	0	0	0.0	0	12	6	0	0

Exchanges: Fruit 1/2

Fruit Sauces, Salsas, & Glazes — 469

Basil-Mustard Vinaigrette

2 T olive oil
1/4 C red wine vinegar
1-1/2 tsp Dijon mustard
1/2 tsp leaf basil, crumbled
1 clove garlic, crushed
1/4 tsp pepper

   Shake all ingredients in a covered container until well blended. Makes about 1/3 C.
   Serving size: 1 T.

Italians…seemed never to die. They eat olive oil all day long…and that's what does it.

William Kennedy
Ironweed

The Best Oils

Olive and canola oils (which are high in monounsaturated fatty acids) are the best choices for a heart-healthy diet. Liquid safflower, sunflower seed, walnut, corn, soybean, cottonseed, and sesame seed oils (which are high in polyunsaturated fatty acids) are also acceptable. These oils can be used in many ways as substitutes for saturated fat. However, you should still limit your overall intake of oil in an effort to reduce your total daily intake of fat calories.

Arizona Heart Institute Foundation
1-800-345-4278

Calories	%Fat	Fat (g)	Saturated Fat (g)	Cholesterol (mg)	Sodium (mg)	Carbohydrate (g)	Protein (g)	Fiber (g)
37	95	4	0.5	0	14	1	0	0

Exchanges: Fat 1

Buttermilk

Buttermilk does not contain any butter. Authentic buttermilk is made from whole milk and is a by-product of buttermaking—it is almost impossible to buy today, however. Commercial, cultured buttermilk is artificially soured skim milk. It has a longer shelf-life than whole milk because the fat content is lower. It is good for drinking or baking.

Buttermilk can be substituted for sweet milk in recipes that contain baking powder, with some modification. For each cup of buttermilk, reduce the baking powder by two teaspoons and add one-half teaspoon of baking soda. This will ensure that the proper proportions of acid and alkali needed for leavening will be maintained.

Buttermilk Cucumber Dressing

2/3 C buttermilk
3 T grated cucumber
2 tsp Dijon mustard
1 small scallion, sliced
1 T chopped parsley
Freshly ground black pepper to taste

Mix all ingredients. Refrigerate overnight to allow flavors to blend. Makes 1 C.

Serving size: 1 T.

Calories	%Fat	Fat (g)	Saturated Fat (g)	Cholesterol (mg)	Sodium (mg)	Carbohydrate (g)	Protein (g)	Fiber (g)
5	22	0	0.1	0	19	1	0	0

Note: 1 T = Free

Citrus Vinaigrette

1/4 C unsweetened orange juice
2 T lime juice, freshly squeezed
1 T low-sodium soy sauce
Grated rind of 2 oranges
Grated rind of 1 lime
2 T balsamic vinegar
1/4 C canola oil

Shake all ingredients together in a tightly covered container until well mixed. Makes 1 C.
Serving size: 1 T.

Suggestion
• Serve with seafood.

Saturated Fats

The world seems saturated with fats, especially saturated fats. Here is the long list of them: any solid fat, hardened oils or fats, shortening, lard, suet, butter, cream cheese, bacon fat, meat drippings containing fat, coconut oil, palm oil, cocoa butter, sweet cream, sour or whipped cream.

Edward B. Diethrich, MD
Heart Test

Calories	%Fat	Fat (g)	Saturated Fat (g)	Cholesterol (mg)	Sodium (mg)	Carbohydrate (g)	Protein (g)	Fiber (g)
44	70	3	0.3	0	38	4	0	0

Exchanges: Fat 1

oasted Corn Vinaigrette

Todd English

3 to 4 ears freshly picked corn, shucked and kernels shaved off cob
1 red onion, minced
1 bunch scallions, chopped
1 T finely chopped ginger
1 clove garlic, minced
1 T fresh thyme
2 T fresh basil
1 T fresh cilantro (with sprigs for garnish)
1/2 C balsamic vinegar
1 C olive oil
Juice of 1 orange
Freshly ground black pepper to taste

In a large cast-iron skillet, brown corn kernels in 1 T oil. Add onions and cook until translucent. Add ginger and garlic; cook for 3 to 5 minutes. Add balsamic vinegar and orange juice; remove skillet from heat. Slowly stir in remaining oil and herbs. Add freshly ground black pepper and adjust seasoning to taste. Serve at room temperature with Chargrilled Tuna & Avocado Salad (page 290).

Serving size: 1 T.

Calories	%Fat	Fat (g)	Saturated Fat (g)	Cholesterol (mg)	Sodium (mg)	Carbohydrate (g)	Protein (g)	Fiber (g)
31	85	3	0.4	0	1	1	0	0

Exchanges: Fat 1/2

# Dijon Vinaigrette

1 T Dijon mustard
Freshly ground black pepper to taste
1/4 C lemon juice
2 T water
2 T sherry vinegar
2 T olive oil
1 shallot, minced
1 clove garlic, crushed

   Shake all ingredients briskly in a covered container until well blended. Serve immediately.
   Serving size: 1 T.

Calories	%Fat	Fat (g)	Saturated Fat (g)	Cholesterol (mg)	Sodium (mg)	Carbohydrate (g)	Protein (g)	Fiber (g)
47	90	5	0.6	0	34	2	0	0

Exchanges: Fat 1

Vinegar

   Vinegar is fermented from a distilled alcohol, such as apple cider or wine. It can be stored tightly capped at room temperature for one year, or until sediment settles in the bottom of the bottle.

- *Balsamic vinegar:* From Italy; aged for years in wood barrels. One of the most flavorful vinegars—dark, sweet, woodsy. Good with fresh greens, steamed vegetables, poached fish. Use sparingly.
- *Champagne vinegar:* Made from champagne or chardonnay; a little fruitier than white wine vinegar. Used in salad dressings and sauces.
- *Cider vinegar:* Made from apple juice. Good in marinades for vegetables, salad dressings, and strong-flavored ingredients.
- *Rice vinegar:* Made from rice; less sharp than cider vinegar. Used in Japanese sushi, dipping sauces.
- *Sherry wine vinegar:* Made from sherry; robust, malty. Used in sauces.

- *White or distilled vinegar:* Made from grain alcohol. Strong and acidic. Used in canning and pickling; too strong for salad dressings and cooking.
- *Wine vinegars:* Can be made from red, white, or rose wines. Fruity; good with salad greens and in sauces and dressings. Herb, spice, and fruit vinegars are usually made with white wine vinegar.
- *Flavored vinegars:* One or more herbs or other seasonings bottled with wine vinegar, such as garlic, peppercorns, cinnamon sticks, ginger, coriander seeds, chili peppers, or fruit. Use berry and fruit vinegars with fruit or vegetable salads, poultry, or fish.

# Harvest Dressing

1/2 medium tomato, diced
1/4 cucumber, peeled, seeded and diced
1 T cooked corn
1 T zucchini, finely diced
1 T yellow squash, finely diced
1 T jicama, peeled, finely diced
1/2 T yellow bell pepper, finely diced
2 T fresh cilantro, chopped
1 T champagne vinegar
2 tsp olive oil
2 T no-salt-added V-8 juice
Freshly ground black pepper to taste

Mix all ingredients well. Chill before serving. Makes about 1-1/2 C.
Serving size: 1 T.

Calories	%Fat	Fat (g)	Saturated Fat (g)	Cholesterol (mg)	Sodium (mg)	Carbohydrate (g)	Protein (g)	Fiber (g)
5	68	0	0.1	0	1	0	0	0

Note: 1 T = Free

Lemon-Thyme Vinaigrette

Greg Paulson, CEC

1 oz shallot, minced
1 tsp sugar
1 C rice vinegar
Zest of 2 lemons
Juice of 2 lemons
1 pt salad oil
1 T fresh thyme
Pinch salt
Pinch white pepper

Mix shallot, sugar, vinegar, lemon zest, and juice vigorously. Slowly drizzle in the oil, whisking briskly, to create a temporary emulsion. Season to taste with thyme, salt, and pepper. Makes 2 C.
Serving size: 1 T.

**Lifestyle &
Heart Disease**
...fatty streaks on the artery wall, the first signs of atherosclerosis, can begin to appear by age three. In cultures where coronary-prone behaviors don't exist, these fatty streaks cause no harm. But in industrialized nations, where lifestyle is characterized by such perils as rich diet, emotional stress, and sedentary habits, the fat circulating in the blood is drawn to these streaks, where it begins to wreak havoc.

Diethrich and Cohan
Women and Heart Disease

Calories	%Fat	Fat (g)	Saturated Fat (g)	Cholesterol (mg)	Sodium (mg)	Carbohydrate (g)	Protein (g)	Fiber (g)
68	100	8	1.1	0	1	0	0	0

Exchanges: Fat 1-1/2

Lime Vinaigrette

1/2 T fresh cilantro, minced
1 clove garlic, minced
1 shallot, minced
1 T Chinese mustard
2 T sugar
2 T lime juice, freshly squeezed
2 T rice wine vinegar
1/4 C canola oil

Whisk all ingredients together. Makes about 1-1/2 C.
Serving size: 1 T.

Calories	%Fat	Fat (g)	Saturated Fat (g)	Cholesterol (mg)	Sodium (mg)	Carbohydrate (g)	Protein (g)	Fiber (g)
26	81	2	0.2	0	9	1	0	0

Exchanges: Fat 1/2

Lime-Papaya Seed Vinaigrette

Greg Paulson, CEC

1 tsp finely minced shallot
Finely minced zest of 1 lime and 1 orange
1/4 C mint, chopped fine
4 oz rice vinegar
8 oz cottonseed oil
2 T lime juice concentrate
1 medium papaya, puréed
Seeds from 1 papaya, cleaned, crushed

Combine shallot, lime and orange zest, mint, and rice vinegar. Whisk ingredients briskly. Slowly drizzle in oil while continuing to whisk the mixture (preparing a temporary emulsified dressing.) Fold in lime juice, papaya purée, and papaya seeds. Makes 2 C.

Serving size: 1 T.

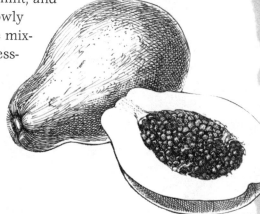

On Papayas
*When you have used it,
you acquire a passion for it.*

William Somerset Maugham

Papayas

Most commercially grown papayas, or pawpaws, come from Hawaii. The thin skin can be pale green, rose-flushed, or butter-yellow. The flesh is soft, silky, and dense. Mildly flavored, papayas taste a little like apricots and ginger. They are sweet and refreshing.

Buy fruit that is at least half yellow and allow it to ripen at room temperature. Papayas are sunny yellow when ripe and feel slightly soft, like an avocado or kiwi. Store ripe fruit in the refrigerator for two to four days. Papaya is rich in vitamins A and C, potassium, and folate.

The pear-shaped papaya contains dark-gray or black shiny edible seeds. Sharp and

Calories	%Fat	Fat (g)	Saturated Fat (g)	Cholesterol (mg)	Sodium (mg)	Carbohydrate (g)	Protein (g)	Fiber (g)
44	94	5	1.2	0	1	1	0	0

Exchanges: Fat 1

peppery, they are often crushed in vinaigrettes or used whole as a garnish. Dried papaya seeds can also be ground like peppercorns.

Good seasonings for papaya include ginger, mace, cinnamon, nutmeg, cardamom, and orange zest. They can be eaten plain with lemon or lime juice, but papayas also make a nice addition to fruit, poultry, or vegetable salads. They can be stuffed and baked like squash or grilled with shish kabobs. Papaya is easily mashed and puréed like a banana for use in soft desserts, puddings, and sauces.

Unripe papayas are often cooked as a vegetable. Papain, an enzyme used as a meat tenderizer, is found in the unripe fruit and leaves. Chunks of green fruit can be cooked with a stewing chicken to tenderize it. Like pineapples and kiwis, papayas cannot be used with gelatin because the papain prevents the gel from setting.

range, Soy, & Sherry Vinaigrette

Rick Moonen

2 C orange juice
1/2 C sherry wine
1/3 C sherry vinegar
2 oz fresh ginger, peeled, sliced
4 shallots, sliced
1/2 C soy sauce
4 cloves garlic
2 C reduced chicken stock
Pepper to taste
1/4 C olive oil
2 sprigs fresh rosemary

In a noncorrosive saucepan, sauté the ginger in cooking spray for 1 minute. Add the shallots and garlic; continue cooking for another minute. Deglaze with vinegar and wine. Add orange juice, soy sauce, and rosemary; cook until liquid is reduced to 3/4 its original volume. Add the chicken stock and cook for 3 minutes. Strain into a blender jar. With the blender on a low setting, slowly add the oil until it is incorporated. Serve warm with Fennel-Crusted Tuna with Crisp Vegetables (page 286).

Serves 8.

Calories	%Fat	Fat (g)	Saturated Fat (g)	Cholesterol (mg)	Sodium (mg)	Carbohydrate (g)	Protein (g)	Fiber (g)
141	46	7	1.0	0	618	14	3	1

Exchanges: Fruit 1/2, Vegetable 1, Fat 1-1/2

Orange Dressing

3/4 C plus 2 T unsweetened orange juice
2-3/4 tsp cornstarch
1 tsp safflower oil
2 tsp honey
1/2 tsp almond extract

Simmer all ingredients until slightly thickened, stirring frequently. Cool to room temperature; cover and chill. Makes 3/4 C.
Serving size: 1 T.

Suggestions

• Serve as a dressing for fruit salad or as a sauce for poached fruit, cake, or frozen yogurt.
• Add finely chopped orange segments.
• Omit almond extract; add a squeeze of lemon juice to taste.
• Omit honey; stir in artificial sweetener to taste before serving.
• Omit almond extract; add Grand Marnier, brandy, bourbon, or rum to taste.
• Omit almond extract; add finely chopped fresh or crystallized ginger and serve over hot cooked carrots.
• Use to marinate or baste chicken or fish (will add flavor but cannot tenderize).

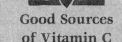

**Good Sources
of Vitamin C**
Oranges or orange juice
Grapefruit or grapefruit juice
Kiwis
Star fruit
Melons
Strawberries
Pineapples
Lemons
Tomatoes
Asparagus
Bell peppers
Broccoli
Brussels sprouts
Cabbage
Cauliflower
Kale
Collards
Turnip greens
Spinach
Swiss chard
Potato
Sweet potato

Calories	%Fat	Fat (g)	Saturated Fat (g)	Cholesterol (mg)	Sodium (mg)	Carbohydrate (g)	Protein (g)	Fiber (g)
18	20	0	0.0	0	0	4	0	0

Note: 1 T = Free, 2 T = 1/2 Fruit

No-Oil Dressing

1/2 C no-salt-added tomato juice
2 T lemon juice
1 T minced red onion
1 tsp chopped parsley
1/4 tsp mustard

Shake all ingredients together in a covered jar until well blended. Makes about 3/4 C.

Serving size: 1 T.

Calories	%Fat	Fat (g)	Saturated Fat (g)	Cholesterol (mg)	Sodium (mg)	Carbohydrate (g)	Protein (g)	Fiber (g)
3	7	0	0.0	0	3	1	0	0

Note: 1 T = Free

# **T**arragon Dressing

3/4 C plain nonfat yogurt
1/2 C tarragon vinegar
1 T olive oil
2 T scallions, finely minced
1/2 tsp tarragon
Pepper to taste

   Put all ingredients in a covered container and shake until blended. Chill for several hours and shake thoroughly before serving. Thin with a little skim milk if desired. Makes 1-1/2 C.
   Serving size: 1 T.

Calories	%Fat	Fat (g)	Saturated Fat (g)	Cholesterol (mg)	Sodium (mg)	Carbohydrate (g)	Protein (g)	Fiber (g)
10	51	1	0.1	0	6	1	0	0

Note: 1 T = Free

Flavored Vinegars
   Vinegars are often bottled with herbs, peppercorns, fruit, or flower petals. Look for examples in specialty and gourmet shops, but save money by making flavored vinegar at home.
- *Herb:* Basil, chervil, dill, fennel, lemon balm, marjoram, mint, oregano, sage, tarragon, or thyme. Steep bruised herb in a good cider or wine vinegar. Keep the bottles in the dark, tightly covered. More herbs can be added later for a stronger flavor, if desired. Garlic cloves, peppercorns, shallots, or grated fresh horseradish can be used alone or with herbs. Use to flavor salads, dressings, sauces.
- *Fruit:* Raspberries, blackberries, black currants, elderberries, or lemon. Use fully ripened soft fruit and a little sugar or honey. Dilute to taste with hot water or soda water for a refreshing drink (two to three tablespoons of fruit vinegar per glass). Use in salad

dressings and in sweet-and-sour dishes.

- *Flower:* Roses, violets, primroses, rosemary or thyme flowers, lavender, carnations, marigolds, elderflowers, or nasturtiums. Use in salad dressings and marinades. Preserved flowers can be used in salads.

Herb Vinegar

Put 1-1/2 C tightly packed herb sprigs in a 1-qt jar. Pour 1 pint of vinegar over the herbs; cover tightly. Store at room temperature for about one week before using.

Raspberry Vinegar

Bruise 1 lb of washed raspberries gently with a wooden spoon to start juices flowing. Add 1 pint of vinegar and cover with a clean cloth. Let stand for one week, stirring daily. Press fruit and strain through muslin or a jelly bag. Measure juice. Add 1 lb of sugar for each pint of juice and cook, stirring constantly, over low heat until sugar is melted. Boil for 10 minutes, or until syrupy, skimming off foam. Cool. Store in tightly sealed sterilized bottles. A dozen or so whole berries may be added to the bottle.

# Tomato Vinaigrette

Sanford D'Amato

3 T rice wine vinegar
8 oz plum tomatoes, peeled, seeded, diced small
1/8 tsp fresh ground black pepper

Mix all ingredients well. Serve with Sautéed Grouper Cheeks on Rice Tabbouleh (page 258). Makes about 1-1/2 C.
Serving size: 1 T.

Calories	%Fat	Fat (g)	Saturated Fat (g)	Cholesterol (mg)	Sodium (mg)	Carbohydrate (g)	Protein (g)	Fiber (g)
12	86	1	0.2	0	1	1	0	0

Note: 1 T = Free

# Vegetable Stock

Michael Lomonaco

4 onions, diced
1 head celery, chopped
2 leeks, cleaned and diced
4 carrots, chopped
1 can (18 oz) plum tomatoes
1 C sliced mushrooms
1/2 C shredded cabbage
2 turnips, diced
1 parsnip, sliced
1 potato, diced
2 cloves garlic
1 small pinch parsley
1 tsp thyme leaves
1 bay leaf
1 whole clove
1/2 tsp black pepper
6 qt water

In a large nonstick soup pot, combine all ingredients except water and cook until the vegetables are wilted, about 15 minutes. Add the water and bring to a boil. Simmer for about 2 hours, until all the flavors have been extracted.

Parsnips

A long, sweetish root, parsnips have a distinctive nutty flavor. They are very popular in Europe. Parsnips are a good source of potassium, and they contain some vitamin C.

Buy parsnips that are about the size of carrots. Larger ones are coarse and woody. Parsnips can be stored in the refrigerator, wrapped in plastic, for up to 10 days. They will get sweeter during storage.

To keep parsnips from turning dark in a stew, blanch or boil them for 15 minutes before adding them to the stew. Cooked parsnips can be puréed and mixed with mashed potatoes or turnips. Parsnip purée can also be used to thicken soup.

Pass the liquid through a sieve, pressing the solids with the back of a spoon to extract all the flavor. The solids have served their purpose, and you now have a flavored stock to cook with. You may, however, take the remaining solids and process them in a food processor into a purée that can be used as a starch-free thickening agent in soups and stews. Both products can be successfully frozen in small batches. Makes 2-1/2 to 3 qt of usable stock.

Lobster Stock

Laura Brennan

5 lb lobster bodies (claws and tails removed)
1/2 head garlic
1 tsp fennel seeds
1-inch piece fresh ginger
2 C Italian plum tomatoes
2 tsp tomato paste
1 orange, cut into 8 pieces
1 tsp dried basil
1 tsp dried oregano
1 tsp dried marjoram
1/2 tsp hot red pepper flakes
1-1/2 C white wine

Combine all ingredients in a small soup/stock pot with water to cover. Bring to a boil, reduce heat, and simmer for 35 minutes. Strain. Makes about 3 C.

Serves 3.

Calories	%Fat	Fat (g)	Saturated Fat (g)	Cholesterol (mg)	Sodium (mg)	Carbohydrate (g)	Protein (g)	Fiber (g)
185	1	0	0.1	0	137	33	3	3

Exchanges: Fruit 1-1/2, Vegetable 3

Eggs

Eat only two to three eggs per week. Remember to count the "hidden" eggs in baked goods and processed foods in addition to the eggs on your breakfast plate.

Eggs contain 5 grams of fat and 75 calories. Substitute two egg whites for each whole egg for cooking and baking. This will eliminate all of the cholesterol and about 43 calories for each whole egg that you replace.

Frozen egg substitutes have no fat and only about 25 calories per "egg."

Egg Substitute

1 egg white
1 tsp canola oil
1 tsp nonfat dry milk powder

Whisk all ingredients until thoroughly blended, but not enough to make the egg frothy. This recipe makes the equivalent of 1 whole egg (1/4 C).
Serves 1.

Suggestions
- This recipe can be multiplied for preparing any number of eggs desired.
- Use a few drops of yellow food coloring if desired. Coloring is unnecessary if the egg substitutes will be mixed with other ingredients (as in muffins or cakes). If the egg will be visible in the final product (as in French toast or omelettes), the food coloring will make the final product look more familiar and more palatable.

Calories	%Fat	Fat (g)	Saturated Fat (g)	Cholesterol (mg)	Sodium (mg)	Carbohydrate (g)	Protein (g)	Fiber (g)
62	66	5	0.3	0	63	1	4	0

Exchanges: Low-fat protein 1

Mock Sour Cream 1

1 C low-fat (1%) cottage cheese
2 T lemon juice

Process cottage cheese and lemon juice in a blender until smooth. Store, tightly covered, in the refrigerator. Use as a topping or to replace sour cream in dishes that will *not* be heated or cooked. Makes 1 C.

Serving size: 1 T.

Suggestions
- If dry curd cottage cheese is used, add 1/4 C skim milk.
- Add chives, parsley, or other herbs to taste.
- Add chopped onion or garlic to taste.
- Add finely chopped dried fruit to taste.

How to Lose a Pound
You can lose one pound of body fat in a month by reducing the amount of fat you eat by 13 grams per day (about one tablespoon). Cutting the fat still further and adding a moderate amount of daily exercise can increase weight loss to one-half pound a week.

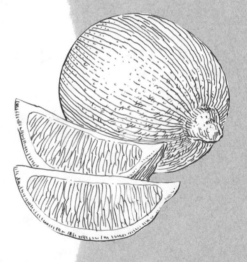

Calories	%Fat	Fat (g)	Saturated Fat (g)	Cholesterol (mg)	Sodium (mg)	Carbohydrate (g)	Protein (g)	Fiber (g)
9	12	0	0.1	1	49	0	1	0

Note: 1 T = Free

Mock Sour Cream 2

1 C low-fat (1%) cottage cheese
1/4 C nonfat buttermilk

Process cottage cheese and buttermilk in a blender until smooth. Store, tightly covered, in the refrigerator. Use to replace sour cream in dishes that will be heated or cooked. Makes 1-1/4 C.

Serving size: 1 T.

Calories	%Fat	Fat (g)	Saturated Fat (g)	Cholesterol (mg)	Sodium (mg)	Carbohydrate (g)	Protein (g)	Fiber (g)
9	14	0	0.1	1	49	0	2	0

Note: 1 T = Free

Yogurt Cheese

32 oz plain nonfat yogurt

Place a large piece of cheesecloth or a yogurt cheese funnel in a large bowl. Pour in the yogurt. If cheesecloth is used, tie the corners of the cloth together. Hang the "bag" of yogurt so the liquid can drain into the bowl; the bag must be suspended so that it is not sitting in a puddle at the bottom of the bowl. If a yogurt cheese funnel is used, follow the manufacturer's directions.

For a soft texture, let the yogurt drain for 1 day; use in place of sour or whipped cream. For a thicker texture, let the yogurt drain for 2 days. Use in place of soft cream cheese.

Store in the refrigerator in an airtight container for up to 1 week. Makes 2 C. Serving size: 1 T.

Suggestion
• Use vanilla nonfat yogurt to make a cream cheese substitute to use in cheesecake and other sweet recipes.

Yogurt Cheese

Plain or vanilla nonfat yogurt can be used to make creamy, low-fat, low-cholesterol alternatives for sour cream and cream cheese. These yogurt products can be used in any recipe. Three cups of yogurt makes one cup of yogurt cheese.

Use nonfat yogurt that does not contain additives for thickening. Modified food starch, vegetable gums, and gelatin will prevent the liquid, or whey, from separating and draining out of the yogurt.

Yogurt cheese funnels are available in specialty shops, department stores, and mail order catalogues. Complete instructions and recipes are included.

Calories	%Fat	Fat (g)	Saturated Fat (g)	Cholesterol (mg)	Sodium (mg)	Carbohydrate (g)	Protein (g)	Fiber (g)
25	3	0	0.1	1	16	5	2	0

Exchanges: Dairy 1/4

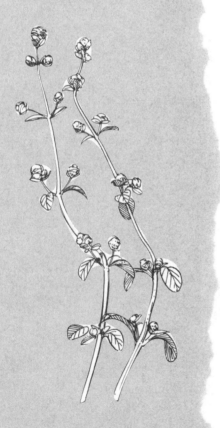

Versatile Cheese Spread

1-1/2 C low-fat (1%) cottage cheese
1 tsp vanilla or almond extract

Blend cottage cheese and extract in a food processor or blender until smooth.
Serves 6 (1/4 C each).

Suggestions

- Serve as a spread for toast, muffins, biscuits, or bread.
- Season with grated citrus rind, mashed or puréed fruit, or fruit salsa. Serve as a topping or spread for fresh fruit salad, muffins, or quick breads.
- Omit extract and season with herbs, minced onion, minced garlic, or salsa. Serve as a topping for baked potatoes or cauliflower, or as a dip with raw vegetables.
- *Blintzes:* Spoon Versatile Cheese Spread onto 6 Dessert Crêpes (page 63) and fold into pocket shapes. Top each serving with Cherries Sauce (page 417), Blueberry Topping (page 416), Ginger Pears (page 418), or other fruit toppings.

Calories	%Fat	Fat (g)	Saturated Fat (g)	Cholesterol (mg)	Sodium (mg)	Carbohydrate (g)	Protein (g)	Fiber (g)
42	12	1	0.4	2	229	2	7	0

Exchanges: Low-fat protein 1

Cinnamon Peanut Butter

1-1/3 C unsalted dry-roasted peanuts
3/4 tsp ground cinnamon

Blend peanuts and cinnamon in a food processor with metal blade for about 5 minutes, or until the desired amount of chunkiness or creaminess is achieved. Makes about 3/4 C of peanut butter.
Serving size: 2 T.

Suggestions
- A touch of honey may be added.
- Almonds, cashews, and other nuts also make interesting, flavorful butters.

Peanuts

Nuts are high in fat and fiber. Peanuts are an excellent source of folate, niacin, thiamin, magnesium, and potassium. They also contain fair amounts of iron, zinc, vitamins B_6 and E, and protein. Store them in a cool, dry, dark place for up to a month, or refrigerate, tightly closed, for three to six months. They will keep longer if they are not removed from the shells. Peanuts can be roasted in their shells at 350° for about 20 minutes.

Plain peanuts are more nutritious than peanut butters that contain salt, sugar, oil, or fat. Natural-style, unsalted peanut butter is best. It should be stored in the refrigerator. If the natural oils rise to the top of the jar, just mix them back into the solids. Occasionally turning the jar upside down will help keep the oil from separating.

Homemade peanut butter can be stored in the refrigerator, tightly covered, for up to 10 days.

Calories	%Fat	Fat (g)	Saturated Fat (g)	Cholesterol (mg)	Sodium (mg)	Carbohydrate (g)	Protein (g)	Fiber (g)
189	76	16	2.2	0	2	6	9	2

Exchanges: High-fat protein 1, Fat 1

# Chefs Offer Healthful Cuisine

Forty of America's best chefs have contributed recipes to this edition of *The Arizona Heart Institute Foundation Cookbook*. Representing every area of the country, these chefs present a broad-based collection of regional ingredients, ethnic influences, and cooking styles. Recipes range from the hearty peasant dishes of Mexico, through the tropical foods of the Hawaiian islands, to the haute cuisine of Europe's finest traditions. All of these recipes are easily incorporated into a low-fat, low-sodium, heart-healthy diet.

America's growing interest in better nutrition is reflected in the menu selections offered at the award-winning restaurants these chefs command. Great emphasis is placed on using the freshest produce and ingredients obtainable. Seasonings are used creatively to reawaken palates long accustomed to salt and butter. Unexpected flavor combinations, as well as new methods of preparing familiar foods, will inspire even the most reluctant to adopt a heart-healthy diet. Eating should be a pleasure, and these chefs make even the most stringent doctor-ordered diet the foundation for an enjoyable meal.

Each of these chefs has earned an impressive reputation for meeting the customer's demands. They now stand at the forefront of a new group of chefs who understand and can satisfy the needs of customers who seek flavorful, pleasurable meals that also promote good health.

Steven Allen

Chef de Cuisine

Golden Mushroom
18100 West Ten Mile Road
Southfield, Michigan 48075
313–559–4230

Steven Allen began an apprenticeship at Reid Ashton's Golden Mushroom when he left high school ten years ago, training under Milos Cihelka, master chef and co-owner of the restaurant. Showing unusual talent and determination, Allen also accepted a six-month externship at Eugenie les Bains in France. When he returned to the Golden Mushroom in 1990, he was promoted to chef de cuisine.

Allen has won four gold medals in national and international competitions and was the grand prize winner of the first Pritikin Culinary Classic. His cooking, which he describes as continental, features game dishes including venison, pheasant, and guinea hen, as well as "luxury staples" such as foie gras, truffles, and caviar. He also uses a wide assortment of wild mushrooms, ordering over 20,000 pounds each year.

The Golden Mushroom has been featured in many publications and is consistently rated among America's top restaurants. The Golden Mushroom, its owners, chefs, and staff have received more culinary awards and acclaim than any other Michigan restaurant.

Two Soup Combination: Carrot & Ginger, Parsnip & Herb, page 122
Poached Salmon Medallion, page 268
Apple & Dried Fruit Pudding with Orange Sabayon, page 362

Being a chef is the most diverse profession I can imagine. A good chef must be an artist, a chemist, a manager of people, a bookkeeper and publicist. A chef must understand good taste, be attuned to the senses, be creative and open to new ideas. But perhaps most importantly, to be a truly great chef, one must be a good teacher, so that the quality of the product served is always consistent and always fantastic.

Steven Allen

iorenzo Antognini

Chef/Owner

Fio's La Fourchette Restaurant
1153 Saint Louis Galleria
St. Louis, Missouri 63117
314–863–6866

Delicious food requires passion, being in love with the art of food. Through creative expression, balance, finesse, and a healthy respect for quality ingredients we bring ourselves to incredible culinary experiences. Increased customer nutritional awareness guarantees the continuous evolution and creativity in cooking styles. Since 1982 we have been offering delicious heart-healthy dishes featuring local ingredients blended with ethnic flavors and personal creations.

Fiorenzo Antognini

Born in Locarno, Switzerland, Fio Antognini has earned an enviable reputation for innovative, imaginative food that combines the best of traditional French haute cuisine and Swiss cuisine with his own personal creations. A health and exercise enthusiast who is well aware of nutrition-conscious diets, he uses only the freshest natural ingredients to create memorable dishes, served in the warmth and intimacy of a French country inn.

Since 1982, Fio's La Fourchette has provided the ultimate in fine dining. The menus change every week, orchestrating seasonal products, market availability, and Antognini's creativity. The restaurant's reputation has come from being customer-oriented: it is able to produce exactly what the guests request, and its trademark is offering something out of the ordinary. Fio's La Fourchette has received outstanding reviews from food critics across the country, as well as top awards from local and national publications.

Antognini has prepared a low-fat, low-calorie gourmet video containing recipes for a healthy lifestyle; it is loaded with tips on heart-healthy food preparation. The easy step-by-step instructions show how to prepare a five-course gourmet meal in your home; the total meal has fewer than 1,000 calories and is low in fat. He produced this 90-minute video in response to the popularity of the five-course "Cuisine of the '90s" featured at the restaurant. The *Cooking Healthy, Cooking Right* video may be ordered by telephone: 314–863–6866.

Chilled Shiitake Mushroom & Chicken Surprise, page 314

Rick Bayless

Chef/Owner

Frontera Grill and Topolobampo
445 N. Clark
Chicago, Illinois 60610
312–661–1434

I cook food with history, food with a time-tested following, food that embraces the wisdom of the ages. Still, it never tastes just right until I make it mine. When I cook a dish with my heart, the flavor resonates with those of all the cooks before me.

Rick Bayless

Born in Oklahoma City, Rick Bayless grew up in his family's restaurant business. After earning a degree in Spanish language/literature and Latin American culture, he returned to the professional kitchen. He has been a cooking instructor and restaurant consultant, owned a catering business, and was host of "Cooking Mexican," a 26-part PBS series aired by 60 stations coast-to-coast. He was named one of "America's 10 Best New Chefs, 1988" by *Food & Wine* magazine and won the James Beard Awards: Best American Chef—Midwest, 1991.

His book *Authentic Mexican: Regional Cooking from the Heart of Mexico* won Second Place, Best International Cookbook, in the 1988 IACP/Seagram's National Cookbook Awards. The result of four years of travel, testing, and writing, this book profiles the best of Mexico's streetfare, marketplace cooking, and dishes from typical regional restaurants.

Bayless is the chef-owner, with wife Deann, of two Chicago restaurants: the casual Frontera Grill and the dressier Topolobampo. The Frontera Grill serves familiar foods, like enchiladas, tacos, and quesadillas for people who love Mexican food. Topolobampo serves more traditional, slow-cooked regional dishes in an elegant setting for people who want to learn more about Mexican food. They have been featured in many newspapers and national magazines, including *Gourmet*, *Food & Wine*, *Bon Appetit*, *Cook's*, *Entrepreneur*, *Esquire*, *Eating Well*, *Self*, *Prevention*, *Glamour*, and *Money*.

Tortas de Lentejas, page 96
Roasted Tomato-Chipotle Sauce, page 444

Food which is simple, based on the finest ingredients, holds an inherent elegance. The use of negative space on a plate is as important as the use of the positive.

Sean Brasel

Sean Brasel

Consulting Chef

Cliff Young's Restaurant
700 E. 17 Avenue
Denver, Colorado 80203
303–831–8900

Sean Brasel has been a consulting chef at Cliff Young's Restaurant for five years. He has studied with Madeleine Kammen, with Jimmy Schmidt, and at the renowned eateries Mondrian and Lafayette, both of which are located in New York City.

Warm, rich, and romantic, Cliff Young's Restaurant has a turn-of-the-century Parisian feel. Housed in a century-old white brick Victorian structure, it incorporates the finest elements of Art Deco, Neoclassical, and Victorian design. The award-winning kitchen at Cliff Young's offers the most current touches applied to a new American cuisine, making the restaurant a popular destination for many celebrities and prominent guests.

Grilled Quail with Fennel & Cucumber Salad, page 338
Sea Bass Poached with Sun-Dried Tomato & Tarragon, page 273

Laura Brennan

Sous Chef

Michela's
One Athenaeum Street
Cambridge, Massachusetts 02142
617–225–2121

*Magra cooking is healthy
Italian food with lots of
flavor without the fat.*

Laura Brennan

    Laura Brennan received a degree in food and nutrition from the University of Rhode Island and her Professional Chef's diploma from Madeleine Kamman's Modern Gourmet Cooking School in 1978.

    Brennan joined Michela's restaurant in August 1990. At Michela's, she has been instrumental in creating "magra" cuisine, which translates simply as Italian lean cuisine—low in fat and high in flavor, made with all-natural, fresh ingredients. Using an abundance of chicken stock, fresh herbs, and citrus oils and zests, Brennan develops robust flavors for vegetable, chicken, and fish dishes that are naturally low in fat, cholesterol, and sodium.

    Michela's regional Italian cuisine has been the focus of critical acclaim, from mass media to specialized culinary publications, including *The New York Times, The Boston Globe, Connoisseur, Gourmet, Town & Country, Travel and Leisure, Metropolitan Home,* and *Vogue.* It has also received *Boston Magazine's* "Best of Boston" awards for its pizza, bread, home-cooked meals, Best Italian Restaurant, and Best Chef.

*Cook with the Seasons!
Use the freshest products
at their peak and prepare
them with respect and
integrity. Combine
ingredients for their taste
and marriage of flavors,
not for presentation's sake.*

Terrance Brennan

Terrance Brennan

Chef

*Prix Fixe
18 West 18th Street
New York, New York 10011
212-675-6777*

Terrance Brennan is one of America's top innovative young chefs and a master of French-inspired New American Cuisine. At the age of 13, he began working at his parent's restaurant in Virginia. After apprenticing at other restaurants and hotels in the Washington, D.C., area, he went to New York to refine his cooking skills at the renowned Le Cirque. He then worked in some of Europe's most highly regarded restaurants, notably Taillevent, Les Crayers, Moulin de Mougin, Geualtiero Marchesi, and Le Gavroche. Returning to New York, he served Montrachet as its sous chef. Other New York credits include executive chef of Annabelles and The Hotel Westbury/Polo Restaurant, both of which received accolades from critics and customers alike.

In 1990, Brennan and his partners opened Prix Fixe, a well-known, popular restaurant which has received national recognition for its concept and culinary expertise. They recently opened Steak Frites, which is earning recognition.

Brennan's guileless cooking style unites tradition with innovation. It combines seasonal, full-flavored ingredients with emphasis on fresh herbs and local organic produce. His menus highlight intense yet light dishes that are visually pleasing and always make culinary sense.

*Summer Salad of Corn, Chanterelles, & Arugula, page 164
Chilled Tomato Bouillon with Tomato & Vodka Granite, page 134
Wild Mushrooms, Asparagus, & White Truffle Oil, page 207
Peach "Consomme" with Summer Berries & Fruit, page 156*

Arnauld Briand

Chef de Cuisine

Caesars Palace Court Restaurant
3570 Las Vegas Blvd., So.
Las Vegas, Nevada 89109
702–731–7731

Born in Paris, Briand is a graduate of the French Culinary Institute. After a year in the French army, he served his apprenticeship in 1976 with the Paris Hilton Hotel. Briand went on to hold various culinary positions at fine restaurants in France and Belgium, then rejoined the Paris Hilton as chef de partie in 1981. In 1982, he relocated to New York City as executive sous chef for Windows on the World in the World Trade Center and was promoted to executive chef for the Windows on the World Cellar in the Sky. Later, he held positions as executive chef for several of New York's better known restaurants.

Briand adds a continental touch to the award-winning cuisine in the Palace Court restaurant at Caesars Palace. As chef de cuisine, he oversees the culinary operation of the resort's most acclaimed restaurant. The Palace Court has received the highest accolades for its dedication to haute cuisine and continental service. The award-winning Palace Court is one of the most elegant gourmet restaurants in America. Housed in a mini-museum setting filled with art treasures of the past, the Palace Court has the atmosphere of a private courtyard. A la carte selections of classical French and American contemporary cuisine offer many sumptuous combinations of hors d'oeuvres, soups, salads, entrees, and desserts.

Broiled Chicken Breasts with Tomato Balsamic Vinegar Dressing, page 316

Even in New York, we had heard of the Palace Court. Its reputation and the Caesars commitment to quality was enough to encourage me to take on a new challenge. ...I have had the opportunity to add some of my own personality to the menu and presentation—a sort of Gallic marriage within this Roman fantasyland. It hasn't been dull so far, and I doubt it ever will.

Arnauld Briand

*Use common sense—
search out the finest raw
products, treat those
products with respect,
and never forget they're
meant to be consumed.*

Sanford D'Amato

Sanford D'Amato

Chef/Owner

Sanford Restaurant
1547 N. Jackson Street
Milwaukee, Wisconsin 53202
414–276–9608

Sanford D'Amato, a Milwaukee native, started cooking in his teens. After graduating from the Culinary Institute of America in 1974, he served a one-year fellowship in the Escoffier Room and then worked in various New York City restaurants. In 1980, he returned to Milwaukee as chef of John Byrons Restaurant, where he received national attention in 1985 *Food & Wine* magazine as one of the top 25 Hot New Chefs and was proclaimed "one of the finest seafood chefs in the country" by *Bon Appetit*. In 1988, he was selected as one of 12 national finalists in the American Culinary Gold Cup, Bocuse D'Or. He also competed in the 1988 and 1989 American Seafood Challenge, earning one of two gold medals awarded in 1989 and taking third place overall.

In 1989, D'Amato and his wife, Angela, opened Sanford Restaurant in the former site of his father and grandfather's grocery store. It has since earned accolades in *Food & Wine, Bon Appetit, Wine Spectator, Milwaukee Magazine, The Chicago Tribune,* and *Esquire.* D'Amato was a 1991 and 1992 James Beard Foundation nominee for Best Midwest Chef. He was one of 12 chefs chosen by Julia Child to prepare her 80th birthday celebration in Boston.

Sauteed Grouper Cheeks on Rice Tabbouleh with Tomato Vinaigrette, page 258
Rice Tabbouleh, page 86
Tomato Vinaigrette, page 483
Grilled Swordfish on Rutabaga & Pepper Relish, page 282
Rutabaga & Pepper Relish, page 454
Marinated Potatoes, page 234

Todd English

Chef/Owner

Olives
10 City Square
Charlestown, Massachusetts 02129
617–242–1999

Todd English began his professional cooking career at the age of 15. At 20, he entered the Culinary Institute of America and graduated with honors. He continued to hone his craft with Jean Jacques Rachous at New York's La Cote Basque. In Italy, he apprenticed at such fine restaurants as Dal Pescatore in Canto Ull O'lio and Paraccuchi in Locand d'Angello. It was in Italy that English developed his unique style and approach to food and cooking. He returned to the United States at 25 to open the award-winning Northern Italian restaurant Michela's. He served as executive chef for three years to high praise from both the press and the public.

English is currently the chef-owner of Olives and Figs, both in Charlestown, Massachusetts. Olives began as a 50-seat store-front restaurant run by English and his wife Olivia; his interpretive European cooking drew national and international attention. The restaurant now occupies a larger dining room and has been voted one of the Top Ten Restaurants by *Esquire Magazine* and Best New Restaurant by *Boston Magazine*. Figs Pizzeria, his latest venture, serves a local crowd a variety of traditional and not-so-traditional pizzas and pastas. English has caught the culinary world's eye by being named the National Rising Star by the James Beard Foundation, as well as one of the Top Ten Hot New Chefs by *Food & Wine* magazine.

Chargrilled Tuna, Toasted Corn Vinaigrette, & Avocado Salad, page 290
Toasted Corn Vinaigrette, page 473

Combining the freshest ingredients and a variety of different culinary influences gives me exciting, beautiful food.

Jeff Farnham

Jeff Farnham

Executive Chef/Co-owner

Amadeus
201 Summer Street
Stamford, Connecticut 06901
203–348–7775

Jeff Farnham hails from Adelaide, Australia, where he began his career as a chef's apprentice at the age of 15. During his apprenticeship, he earned numerous competition awards and certificates and spent a season as sous chef at the internationally acclaimed Breathtaker Alpine Ski Resort. He left Australia in 1985 to further his culinary studies abroad, working in the United States, Great Britain, and throughout Europe. While head pastry chef at the four-star Hotel Alte Post, in St. Anton, Austria, he was offered a position on the Queen Elizabeth 2, the luxury flagship of the Cunard Line fleet; he quickly rose to sous chef. He became executive chef at the Negril Inn, an intimate luxury resort in Jamaica. He returned to Cunard in 1989 as chef de cuisine, and in 1990, at the age of 26, he was promoted to executive chef, a challenging position that involved the management of over 160 kitchen personnel.

Farnham is now co-owner, with Rudolf Sodamin and George Welser, of Amadeus, newly founded in Stamford, Connecticut. The restaurant's successful opening is a tribute to his eclectic menu, which is continental with a Viennese flair. Only the freshest ingredients are used. The burgundy and peach decor sets off Old World art, never-ending mirrors, and cozy banquettes. The exquisite cosmopolitan cuisine and impeccable service at Amadeus set the standard for fine dining in Fairfield County.

Roasted Portobello Mushrooms with Balsamic Marinated Tomatoes, page 228

Rozanne Gold

Culinary Director

Joseph Baum & Michael Whiteman Company
186 Fifth Avenue
New York, New York 10010
212–206–7110
212–632–5100 for dinner reservations, Rainbow Room, 30 Rockefeller Plaza, New York

Learning how to substitute flavor for fat was a learning experience of a lifetime. Feeding people gives me great pleasure. Feeding people healthfully gives me great pride.

Rozanne Gold

As culinary director of the world-famous restaurant consulting firm, The Joseph Baum & Whiteman Company, Rozanne Gold is one of New York's most influential food consultants. She has created menus for the spectacular Rainbow Room and developed a fitness cuisine for the Rockefeller Center Club.

At the age of 23, Gold was the first chef to the Mayor of New York, Ed Koch. A year later, she became the youngest female executive chef in the country for Lord & Taylor, responsible for the creation and financial success of 35 restaurants. She has also created concepts for other very successful restaurants and hotels in New York, Australia, and Spain. She is past president of Les Dames d'Escoffier, the most prestigious group of women in food in New York. She has been featured in *Business Week, Mirabella,* and *Savvy.*

Gold is a food trends expert who appears regularly on national television and writes feature articles on food for national magazines. She is the author of *Little Meals,* her first cookbook, published by Villard in June 1993. *Little Meals* provides an easy, elegant new way to eat and cook...lighter, smaller, simpler.

Barley Pilaf with Sun-Dried Cranberries, page 76
Aromatic Couscous, page 82
Medallions of Venison, page 354
Sauce Poivrade, page 451
Spicy Mulled Pears, page 376
Crème Caramel, page 406

Square One is a restaurant run by people who really love to cook for people who love to eat.

Gourmet Magazine

Joyce Goldstein

Chef/Owner

Square One Restaurant
190 Pacific Avenue at Front Street
San Francisco, California 94111
415-788-1110

Joyce Goldstein taught cooking and the technique and history of cuisines for nearly 20 years. She was the founder/director of the California Street Cooking School and the chef/manager of Chez Panisse Café in Berkeley. Goldstein is the author of *The Mediterranean Kitchen* and *Back to Square One: Old World Food in a New World Kitchen*. She was named Chef of the Year in 1992 by *San Francisco Focus Magazine* and received the 1985 *Cook's Magazine* award for the top 25 chefs.

The name Square One was chosen to imply fresh beginnings every day. The multi-ethnic menu changes daily, emphasizing the robust and sensual foods of the Mediterranean: Italy, Spain, France, Greece, Portugal, Turkey, and North Africa. Square One serves foods that are in season and uses local produce whenever possible. All foods are prepared daily on the premises, including breads, pasta, soups, pastries, ice creams and sorbets, chutney, and preserves. Low-cholesterol items are featured daily.

Cold Lithuanian Beet Borscht, page 116
Roasted Pepper & Celery Salad with Tomato Vinaigrette, page 163
Grilled Fish in Greek Marinade, page 256
Arroz con Pollo, page 330

 **ark Gould**

Executive Chef

Atwater's Restaurant & Lounge
U.S. Bancorp Tower, 30th floor
111 Southwest Fifth Avenue
Portland, Oregon 97204
503–275–3600

Mark Gould began cooking as a child, baking apple pies for family reunions at the age of seven. He is a graduate of Johnson and Wales College in Rhode Island. Gould came to Atwater's from Chicago's prestigious The 95th, where he held the position of executive sous chef. In addition to three years at The 95th, Gould worked at Le Gourmandin in Lyon, France; Hotel Uplandia in Uppsala, Sweden; and Chefs de France in Florida's Epcot Center. He recently attended the exclusive School for American Chefs at Beringer Vineyards in California's Napa Valley, an intensive two-week training program.

Products in their seasonal prime highlight the menu at Atwater's. Gould compares Portland's abundance of fresh local products to that of France and Sweden, where local farmers bring in fresh products to sell to the restaurant and the chef then designs a special meal highlighting those products. In 1990, Gault Millaut, the restaurant review service, named Atwater's one of the Top 40 Places to Dine in the U.S. Atwater's and The 95th are owned and operated by ARA Services.

Roasted Spring Salmon with Lemon Grass Broth, page 266
Sauté of Northwest Sturgeon & Fresh Vegetable Gazpacho, page 280
Hot Mango Tart & Candied Lime, page 370
Candied Lime, page 414

Food is very sensuous;
I have a physical
relationship with it. When
I'm designing a meal, I
want to involve all my
senses. I also concentrate
on maintaining the integrity
of the base product—the
preparation of the meal,
as well as the seasonings
and sauces used, should
enhance the product's taste,
not cover it up or dilute it.

Mark Gould

Karla A. Graves

Chef/Owner

Upstairs Downtown
Howard & Main—Bennet Block
Spokane, Washington 99201
509–747–9830

Karla Graves defines her "rustic cuisine" as "fine food brought back to basics." Her natural ability to combine the freshest ingredients into an array of simple yet elegant foods is inherited from her Italian mother and grandmother. Karla's passion for food began as a child reading cookbooks on the floor of the city library. This resulted in numerous childhood food awards. In spite of a successful business career, she pursued her passion for food and developed her culinary skills by working through cookbooks to become a self-taught chef.

In 1991, Graves left her position as vice president of a national temporary help service to achieve her goal, becoming chef/owner of her own restaurant, Upstairs Downtown. Upstairs Downtown features international country cuisine. The menu has been described as unique and adventurous. Only the most simple and freshest ingredients find their way into her imaginative "back to basics" recipes.

...there's nothing rough or unsophisticated about this absolute gem of a restaurant....The atmosphere is as serene and romantic as anyplace you'll find in Spokane. The food is creative, well-thought-out and beautifully executed.

Jim Kershner
The Spokesman Review

 **Vincent Guerithault**

Chef/Owner

Vincent Guerithault on Camelback
3930 East Camelback Road
Phoenix, Arizona 85018
602–224–0225

Vincent Guerithault, a native of France, combines the finesse and elegance of classic French cuisine with the rustic ingredients of the American Southwest, such as cactus, jicama, cilantro, and chilies, to create a fresh culinary heritage, cited as one of the most exciting styles in the food industry today.

He began his career at age 16 at L'Oustau de Baumanière in Les Baux de Provence, served an apprenticeship at Maxim's in Paris, and became a chef at Fauchone, a famous gourmet shop in Paris. Guerithault came to America in 1976, and in 1986, he opened the popular Vincent Guerithault on Camelback.

Guerithault is the first chef to receive a Citation of Excellence from the International Food & Wine Society. His restaurant consistently receives high ratings from such sources as *America's Best Restaurants*, *Zagat Southwest Restaurant Survey*, *Playboy*, *Condé Nast Traveler*, *The New York Times*, *Gourmet*, *Bon Appetit*, *Travel & Leisure*, *Metropolitan Home*, *GQ*, and *Family Circle*. The restaurant has also received the DiRoNa (Distinguished Restaurants of North America) Award and the Travel Holiday Good Value Dining Award. It was inducted into Nation's Restaurant News Fine Dining Hall of Fame in 1991.

Black Bean Relish, page 33
Papaya Grapefruit Salad with Honey-Lime Vinaigrette, page 32
Grilled Salmon with Jalapeño Honey Glaze, page 34
Pears Poached in Red Wine Sauce, page 35

> *The best and classiest restaurant in town...is thriving thanks to Guerithault's French touch, and his imaginative use of local ingredients.*
>
> **Travel & Leisure Magazine**

Cooking simply and lightly in order to keep the original flavor of the ingredient.

George Haidon

George Haidon

Executive Chef

Maisonette
114 East Sixth Street
Cincinnati, Ohio 45202
513–721-2260

George Haidon is a native of Liège, Belgium. He graduated with "Honors of Great Distinction" after three years at the École Hôtelière de Liège (culinary school). Haidon continued his training in various prominent restaurants in Belgium and then served as chef on Belgium liners of the Compagnie Maritime Belge. Following this, he worked as chef for the Belgium Sabena Airlines in Brussels and in the former Belgian Congo. After working with Monsieur Jean Boujard, a pupil of the great chef Alexander Dumaine, of Saulieu, France, Haidon went to New York. In 1966, he joined the Maisonette Restaurant under the late Pierre Adrian. Haidon was named executive chef in 1971.

Oyster & Scallop Stew with Vegetables, page 151
Veal Medallions with Braised Endives, page 347

 **alter K. Houlihan**

Chef

Ambassador Grill
U.N. Plaza–Park Hyatt
One United Nations Plaza
New York, New York 10017
212–702–5014

The menu reflects the Ambassador Grill's concept to offer creative American cuisine with a twist—at a traditional American value.

Walter Houlihan

As chef of the Ambassador Grill at the U.N. Plaza-Park Hyatt, Walter Houlihan has directed development of the restaurant's successful American-grill menu. Featuring a variety of poultry, seafood, and game, Houlihan emphasizes fresh domestic products prepared with imaginative international influences.

Schooled at the Culinary Institute of America, Houlihan first cooked at the Ambassador Grill in the late 1980s, working with renowned French chefs Roger Dufour, Bernard Ramouneda, and Maurice Coscuella, who created the restaurant's former Gascony menu. Houlihan honed his skills at a number of diverse restaurants and corporations, including Trumpets Restaurant at the Grand Hyatt in New York and Tree Tops in Yonkers. He most recently served as corporate chef for Precision Valve Corporation in the Bahamas. He has cooked for former President Richard Nixon and was the private chef to Prince Abdul Rhaman of Saudi Arabia.

Away from the kitchen, Houlihan feeds his passion for food with an ever-expanding collection of cookbooks, which occupies an entire room in the New Jersey home he shares with his family.

New York State Venison Oriental Style, page 352

Michael's Waterside comes through as a tranquil retreat where traditions are observed but tempered subtly by innovation. It is the kind of warm, gracious place people turn to when they celebrate a special occasion, observe a family rite of passage, or hold a festive holiday dinner.

Gourmet Magazine

Michael Hutchings

Chef/Proprietor

Michael's Waterside
50 Los Patos Way
Santa Barbara, California 93108
805-969-0307

Michael Hutchings' professional career began at Disneyland, where he worked his way up to the position of executive chef at Club 33, the private dining club for the exhibitors and their special guests. The pleasure he found in the creation of fine food led him on to a series of jobs in the best local restaurants. He subsequently trained in the classic European tradition at the world-famous three-star restaurant, Le Gavroche, in England. In 1981, Hutchings became executive chef of the Olive Mill Bistro in Montecito, where food critics and restaurant reviewers proclaimed him a chef of elegance and creativity.

In 1984, he opened Michael's Waterside, housed in a 112-year-old Victorian home in Santa Barbara. The cuisine reflects the tradition of Escoffier updated and tempered by his exceptional talents in utilizing the best and freshest of American ingredients. He grows his own herbs on the grounds of the restaurant and harvests his own wild mushrooms as time permits. He works closely with local purveyors and has developed a special relationship with the abalone growers. Signature dishes at The Waterside created to celebrate native products have won wide acclaim.

Sweet Pea & Fennel Soup, page 129
Watercress Soup, page 137
Grilled Tuna Sauce Vierge, page 285
Sauce Vierge, page 452
Banana & Passion Fruit Sorbet, page 383

Sean Kavanaugh

Executive Chef

The Ritz-Carlton
2401 E. Camelback Road
Phoenix, Arizona 85016
602–468–0700

   Sean Kavanaugh brings to his position as executive chef of The Ritz-Carlton, Phoenix, a diverse background in the culinary field. He joined the hotel's staff in 1988 as chef of The Restaurant and was later promoted to executive sous chef, a position he held until his promotion to executive chef. He oversees the hotel's entire culinary operation, including developing menus for the hotel's two restaurants and supervising a kitchen staff of twenty-five.

   Kavanaugh joined The Ritz-Carlton Hotel Company in 1985 and served as saucier and, later, lead banquet cook at The Ritz-Carlton in Naples, Florida. Prior to that, he held positions as executive chef at Le Mesquite in Ft. Lauderdale, Florida, and as saucier at the Turnberry Isle Yacht and Racket Club in North Miami Beach, Florida.

Grilled Ahi Tuna, page 291
Rosemary Polenta, page 78
Mesquite-Smoked Tomato Sauce, page 445
Braised Seasonal Salmon with Shiitake Mushrooms, page 265
Steamed Pacific Snapper with Fennel & Tarragon, page 274
Grilled Turkey Picatta with Yellow Corn Sauce, page 336

Sean Kavanaugh is doing a terrific job as executive chef at The Ritz-Carlton in Phoenix. I think it is important that we recognize some of the talented hotel restaurant chefs around the country, many of whom are often overlooked because hotel restaurants don't have the reputation of producing outstanding food. Sean is among those who are helping to change the image of the hotel restaurant.

Jacques Pepin

Hubert is more than a master of his trade... passionately devoted to his métier.

Caroline Bates
Gourmet Magazine

Hubert Keller

Chef/Owner

Fleur de Lys
777 Sutter Street
San Francisco, California 94109
415-673-7779

Hubert Keller, who trained with three-star chefs in France, was one of the first to ban the use of butter and cream. He depends on creative blends of broths and vegetable purées to provide texture and flavor. The stunning presentations and combinations he prepares are rich in flavor and pleasing to the eye. Although Fleur de Lys is unmistakably a French restaurant, the menu reflects a variety of regional American influences. Fleur de Lys also offers an outstanding five-course vegetarian menu, for which Keller magically transforms mundane ingredients into edible works of art. Michael Bauer of *The San Francisco Chronicle* has called Fleur de Lys the prettiest, most romantic restaurant in the city. The intimate, warm atmosphere of the dining room is very appealing.

Lentil, Celery, & Ginger Salad, page 180
Figs & Blueberries in Citrus Broth, page 368

# Michael Lomonaco

Executive Chef

The '21' Club
21 West 52 Street
New York, New York 10019
212–582–7200

The use of the freshest and best seasonal ingredients, treated with respect, will ultimately produce the finest food.

Michael Lomonaco

After an eight-year career as an actor trained in the theatre, Michael Lomonaco began studies at New York City Technical College's Department of Hotel and Restaurant Management. Since earning his degree, he has worked in some of New York's most prestigious restaurant and club kitchens, including Le Cirque and Maxwell's Plum.

As executive chef of The '21' Club, Lomonaco has earned a reputation as one of New York's Great Chefs, as proclaimed by the James Beard Foundation. His cooking style has revitalized The '21' Club, allowing it to blossom as a contemporary restaurant. He has been praised for his efforts in *New York Magazine*, *Gourmet*, and *The New York Times*. Appearances at demonstrations across the country, at food and wine events, and participation in charitable causes (Meals-on-Wheels, Share Our Strength, The March of Dimes, and City Harvest) are of particular pride to him. He has made dozens of network, cable, and PBS television appearances, including *The David Letterman Show* and *The Today Show*.

Lomonaco's primary concern is the care and comfort of each guest. His approach to modern American cooking focuses on the use of the world's market basket, the ingredients and tastes that comprise our multi-ethnic society. His work is characterized by a comfortable and confident visual style.

My style of cooking is one that blends the finest ingredients and flavors into a positively provocative pleasure. I feel that in order to create something wonderful, you need to bring out the fullest of flavors, making sure that all the flavors on one plate are compatible with each other.

Gary McCafferty

Gary McCafferty

Pastry Chef

Cliff Young's Restaurant
700 E. 17 Avenue
Denver, Colorado 80203
303-831-8900

Gary McCafferty became interested in cooking when he was just a child and picked up various tricks along the way. When he attended the Culinary Institute of America, he learned to refine these tricks into skills. After graduation, his next big influence was The Rattlesnake Club, where he learned that food could be an art. He then moved on to Cliff Young's Restaurant, where he has honed his skills and gained the confidence needed to create his own style and philosophy.

Cliff Young's Restaurant was nominated for the prestigious Ivy Award, won AAA's Four Diamond Award two years in a row, and won the Holiday Award four years straight. It was selected for DiRoNa (Distinguished Restaurants of North America) and regularly receives a five-star rating from Denver's press.

Burgundy-Poached Pears with Prickly Pear Coulis, page 377

 **aul Minnillo**

Chef/Owner

The Baricelli Inn
2203 Cornell Road
Cleveland, Ohio 44106
216–791–6500

Paul Minnillo began cooking as a young teenager in the kitchen of his father's restaurant. He represents the third generation in a family tradition for restaurant excellence. Upon graduating from Ohio's Miami University with a degree in business administration, he returned to the business and developed relationships with regional purveyors, American and European wine producers, and restaurateurs everywhere.

Minnillo went on to expand his culinary talents, training in New York and London's Dorchester Hotel. He was instrumental in opening the family's crowning endeavor, The Baricelli Inn, where he presides as chef/owner. Located in Cleveland's cultural hub, the elegant brownstone mansion reveals Minnillo's love for the continental dining experience. He travels this country and Europe as often as he can. From his larder he creates a seasonal menu reflecting European traditions, but the ingredients and style are uniquely American.

Sea Scallops with Pistachio, Flageolet, & Wild Mushroom Couscous, page 308
Poached Pears with a Port Sauce & Mascarpone Cheese, page 375

Rick Moonen

Executive Chef

The Water Club
500 East 30th Street
New York, New York 10016
212–683–3333

*The French-trained chef,
Richard Moonen, turns out
eclectic and imaginative
fare that is always well
rooted in common sense.*

Bryan Miller
The New York Times

As a child, Rick Moonen had a curious spirit and an excessive amount of energy; to keep him out of trouble, his mom kept him busy in the kitchen stirring puddings and making bread. The only other thing that could keep him in one spot for a reasonable period of time was Graham Kerr's *Galloping Gourmet* television show. Moonen entered college intending to become a dietitian but fell in love with the intense demands and passions of the kitchen. A graduate of the Culinary Institute of America, he began his career at the Escoffier Room and L'Hostellerie Bressane and became saucier at La Côte Basque and then Le Cirque. He has held executive chef positions at a number of New York's finest restaurants: Le Relais, Century Cafe, Chelsea Central, and The Water Club. Thanks to his career choice, Moonen's circle of friends and supporters happily includes his boyhood idol, Graham Kerr.

Moonen is the founder of the Chef's Coalition for the Pure Food Campaign. Through this organization, over 2,000 of America's top chefs take a strong stand against the release of genetically engineered food products without mandatory labeling and FDA-approved pre-market safety testing. They are committed to preserving the health and well-being of their customers and to ensuring a safe food supply. Moonen serves fresh, clean foods assembled in understandable combinations and offering a balance of textures, flavors, and colors.

Steamed Spaghetti Squash with Seasonal Vegetables, page 244
Fennel-Crusted Tuna with Crisp Vegetables, page 286
Orange, Soy, & Sherry Vinaigrette, page 479

John Novi

Chef/Owner

Depuy Canal House
Route 213
High Falls, New York 12440
914-687-7700

John Novi has been called the "Father of Nouvelle Cuisine" by *Time* magazine. He is the owner, restorer, designer, steward, proprietor, and head chef of Depuy Canal House, a two-story stone tavern built in 1797. It now houses a four-star restaurant; a museum of Colonial American antiques; a cooking school and culinary source; and a banquet, meeting, and multi-arts facility. Novi served apprenticeships at various hotels and restaurants in Europe. He also toured Europe on culinary review with five other chefs, including Craig Claibourne and Pierre Franey.

Novi is developing new food items that use products that can be grown in the Northeast and the Catskills, such as amaranth, quinoa, and other grains. Mock Caviar Spread, the first of these items, looks and tastes like black sturgeon caviar but is made with amaranth grain. He has directed and produced a 22-minute video on specialty farming in the Hudson Valley. He recently conducted a food tasting of goat meat at the Culinary Institute of America, showcasing the first goat meat company in the Catskills. Novi also founded the American Revival Consulting Firm, which restores structures of historical significance to usable condition. Goals include the revitalization of small towns in the Catskills and other historically significant areas.

Roasted Garlic Soup with Swiss Chard Timbale, page 126
Stuffed Leg of Goat, page 350
Plum Red Wine Glaze, page 467

Patrick O'Connell

Owner/Chef

Inn at Little Washington
Middle & Main Streets
Washington, Virginia 22747
703-675-3800

Romance is the Inn's stock-in-trade. Some 25 small weddings have taken place there, and several sets of honeymooners check in every week. There is also plenty of bended-knee activity, with engagement rings buried in bowls of cherries or hidden in tea cozies.

People

A native of Washington, D.C., Patrick O'Connell began his restaurant career at the age of 15, quite by accident, working in a neighborhood restaurant after school. As a student of speech and drama at Catholic University of America, he financed his education working as a waiter. After a year spent traveling in Europe, he began to find the "living theatre" of the restaurant business more compelling than a career as an actor.

The mountains of Virginia proved to be a good antidote to the pressures of the restaurant world. In 1972, together with his partner Reinhardt Lynch, O'Connell began a catering enterprise there which ultimately evolved into The Inn at Little Washington, located at the corner of Main and Middle Streets, in a village of 150 souls. A member of the Paris-based Relais & Chateaux Association, The Inn at Little Washington in 1989 became the first and only establishment in America to achieve Five Stars from the Mobil Travel Guide, Five Diamonds from the American Automobile Association, and the Top National Rating in the Zagat Hotel Survey with the first "perfect" score for its cuisine in the history of the Zagat rating system.

O'Connell is an original member of Who's Who in Food in America and was voted best chef in the Mid-Atlantic Region by The James Beard Foundation in 1992.

Seared Rare Peppered Tuna & Vietnamese Dipping Sauce, page 284
Vietnamese Dipping Sauce, page 453

Greg Paulson, CEC

Executive Chef

John Dominis Restaurant
43 Ahui Street
Honolulu, Hawaii 96813
808–523–0955

I like to use traditional European methods and integrate them with contemporary American and Pacific Rim products. Being in Hawaii, I love to work with the local seafood, fruits, and nuts. At John Dominis, we believe in offering our patrons a full range of flavors, and we feature the finest Hawaiian seafood available.

Greg Paulson, CEC

Greg Paulson, CEC, became executive chef at John Dominis Restaurant in 1988. Under his direction, the seafood restaurant has won numerous awards. Paulson received his formal training at the Culinary Institute of America in Hyde Park, New York. He has earned many national and regional culinary awards. He received his "Certified Executive Chef" honors from the American Culinary Federation's Chef de Cuisine Association in 1990 and is now president of the state chapter. Paulson was named Chef of the Year for Oahu in 1992. He is a Chef Instructor at Kapiolani Community College and Honolulu's Hotel and Restaurant Industry Educational Training and Trust.

John Dominis Restaurant has a breathtaking location on the water's edge, with a spectacular view of the Waikiki skyline to the famed profile of Diamond Head. The decor is unique, beautiful, and comfortable, featuring Hawaiian Koa wood, lava rock, exotic flora, and gentle waterfalls flowing into salt-water pools filled with lobster and tropical fish. The menu is designed with Hawaii's people in mind, using only the best of local and imported seafood.

Smoked Teriyaki Marlin & Scallop Salad, page 188
Chilled Spiny Lobster Medallions & Papaya, page 299
Chilled Spiny Lobster Medallions & Baby Artichoke, page 300
Baked Opakapaka in Phyllo, page 275
Mango-Pineapple Chutney, page 463
Lime-Papaya Seed Vinaigrette, page 478
Lemon-Thyme Vinaigrette, page 476

*There is nothing
new under the sun.
It is just how you prepare it.*

Franz Peier

ranz Peier

Chef/Co-owner

Columbia's
1201 Main Street
Columbia, South Carolina 29201
803–779–1989

Born in Graz, Austria, Franz Peier began his culinary career at the age of 15 in Bad Gleichenberg, one of Austria's most famous culinary schools. He dedicated three years to learning fine culinary arts and then set out to obtain hands-on experience in various quality kitchens, including the luxurious Southhampton Princess Hotel in Bermuda; the Operahallaren, one of the most famous Scandinavian restaurants in the world; and the Restaurant Gourmet and the Restaurant Coq Roti in Stockholm.

As chef-proprietor of the Bia Gasen in Stockholm, Peier was able to explore his own creativity and gain first-hand experience in restaurant management. Through his hard work and inventiveness, the Bia Gasen became one of the city's most popular restaurants. The compliments and awards he received were many.

After his marriage to Miss Peggy Sills of Charleston, Peier emigrated to South Carolina, where his culinary knowledge and innovative ideas directed the fine cuisine at Robert's of Charleston. He is now the chef/co-owner of the popular Columbia's restaurant, where he proudly serves his lean and spontaneous cuisine.

Shrimp & Scallops with Red Bell Pepper Glaze, page 310
Tangerine Sorbet, page 390

James Peterson

Chef Instructor

Peter Kump's New York Cooking School
307 E. 92 Street
New York, New York 10128
212–410–4601

New-York based James Peterson teaches French cooking at Peter Kump's acclaimed New York Cooking School in Manhattan. Former chef-owner of the prestigious New York restaurant Le Petit Robert, he studied at Le Cordon Bleu in Paris and apprenticed at two illustrious French restaurants. Peterson has translated many sophisticated culinary books, including the four-volume Professional French Pastry Series.

A two-time winner of the James Beard Foundation Book Award, Peterson is the author of the award-winning book *Sauces: Classical and Contemporary Sauce Making.* This book not only explains the most fundamental rules for sauce-making and offers explanations for how techniques and ingredients work together, but it also provides sophisticated, yet easy-to-follow recipes for everything from a simple Hollandaise to a spicy salsa to an elegant sauce for a holiday feast.

Tropical Fruit Salsa, page 464
Baked-Garlic Purée, page 460

Every few decades a book is written that says all there is to say on a subject, or has all the information and passion that sets the standard for professionals and amateurs alike. Sauces is one of the best culinary books of this century.

Jeremiah Tower
Executive Chef Stars Restaurant
San Francisco, California

Keep it simple and never mix too many flavors. Season with authority and please...don't forget the olive oil!

Sylvain Portay

Sylvain Portay

Executive Chef

Le Cirque
58 E. 65 Street
New York, New York 10021
212-794-9292

A native of France, Sylvain Portay began his career as an apprentice under Chef Jean-Louise Palladin at La Table des Cordeliers and at the Watergate in Washington, D.C. He later joined the kitchen of Jacques Maximin at Le Chantecler Restaurant at the Hotel Negresco in Nice, France, establishing a reputation as an exceptional, disciplined, professional cook with a great future. He gained further culinary experience under French chefs Alain Ducasse and Jean Delaveyne and also worked in Italy, where he learned the art of Italian cuisine and the authentic techniques of pasta making.

Wishing to return to the United States, he accepted an appointment as chef de cuisine at Antoine Restaurant in Newport Beach, quickly making it one of the top-rated restaurants in California. He then moved back to France as chef de cuisine of the Grill Restaurant in the Hotel de Paris, Principality of Monaco, entrusted with the task of making the Grill a "must" on the Riviera. His success there led to an appointment as chef de cuisine at the Restaurant Louis XV in the Hotel de Paris, at the age of 27. In just two year's time, the Louis XV was elevated to a three-star Michelin restaurant, the highest award given. He is currently the executive chef at Le Cirque in New York.

Chilled Jumbo Shrimp with Country-Style Vegetables & Truffle Vinaigrette, page 194

Maureen Pothier

Executive Chef

Bluepoint Oyster Bar & Restaurant
99 North Main Street
Providence, Rhode Island 02903
401–272–6145

The seventh of nine children, Maureen Pothier was born and raised in Rhode Island. Cooking was her hobby when she was growing up. She studied at the Rhode Island School of Design's Culinary Program. She started as a prep-cook at the Bluepoint Oyster Bar in 1980 and became head chef in 1981. She attended internationally acclaimed Madeleine Kamman's chef and teaching program in 1983. She returned to the Bluepoint as executive chef immediately following graduation. She also attended the prestigious School for American Chefs at Beringer Vineyards, taught by Madeleine Kamman. Pothier currently teaches seafood classes at various schools.

Bluepoint Oyster Bar & Restaurant opened in 1978 under the ownership of Pothier's husband, Paul Inveen. Its bistro style and daily changing menu emphasizing fresh native ingredients were new to the city and became an instant hit. Pothier and Inveen collaborate on the daily operations of the restaurant; she oversees the menu and he maintains the wine list. The menu is always exciting and inventive, and it uses only the finest quality fish, shellfish, meats, and produce. The restaurant and its wine list have earned a number of awards. Bluepoint continues its tradition of low-key style and attention to detail, constantly striving to offer its audience the best of food and wine.

Sweet Red Pepper & Black Olive Polenta, page 79
Codfish with Mussels, Shrimp, Swiss Chard, & Polenta, page 254

Bluepoint is a wonderfully evocative place where you will find some of the best seafood on the Atlantic coast.

John Mariani
Esquire Magazine

Stephan Wayne Pyles

Chef/Owner

Star Canyon
The Centrum
3102 Oak Lawn
Dallas, Texas 75219

He has been praised from one coast to the other— all that praise was not by any means undeserved adulation; Pyles raises Southwestern Cuisine to the level of art. He is an absolute genius in the kitchen.

Craig Claiborne
The New York Times

Recognized as one of the founding fathers of Southwestern Cuisine, Steven Wayne Pyles has been credited by *Bon Appetit* with "almost single-handedly changing the cooking scene in Texas." He was the chef and co-owner of the renowned Routh Street Cafe and the more casual spin-off, Baby Routh. In its first year, *USA Today*, *GQ*, and *Esquire* all named Routh Street Cafe one of the best new restaurants in the country. It was featured or mentioned in virtually every major publication in the country and won many awards during its nine years of operation. His new restaurant, Star Canyon, hosts a rustic yet sophisticated Texas ambience (open January 1994).

Pyles has earned numerous awards and honors. He has prepared state dinners for such dignitaries as Mikhail Gorbachev and Queen Elizabeth. He is the author of a comprehensive overview of culinary styles in Texas, *The New Texas Cuisine*. Pyles also serves on the National Advisory Board of S.O.S., a network of creative food professionals fighting hunger and homelessness in America and overseas. He chairs the Dallas Hunger Link, a perishable food program linking restaurants and shelters. He is also active in charity fundraising in many major cities.

Pumpkin-White Bean Chowder, page 132
Arugula-Poached Pear Salad with Cambazola & Port Vinaigrette, page 202

 **ichael Roberts**

Executive Chef

Twin Palms Pasadena
Green & Delacey Streets
Pasadena, California
Open Fall, 1993

One of the least predictable and most consistently interesting chefs in Los Angeles in the last decade.

Gourmet

Michael Roberts was granted a Certificat d'Aptitude Professionelle by the French Ministry of Education after completing his culinary studies at Centre de Formations Technologiques Ferrandi in 1977. He also holds a degree in music from New York University. Roberts has received numerous honors in the twelve years since he helped pioneer California cuisine at Trumps. He was voted a charter member of *Cook's Magazine*'s 50 Who's Who of Cooking in America and was cited as Great Regional Chef in 1991. He was listed in *Food & Wine* magazine's first Honor Roll of American Chefs and was voted Chef of the Year by the Southern California Restaurant Writers' Assocation. Roberts is a past chair of the Los Angeles chapter of the American Institute of Wine and Food. As a participant of that group's groundbreaking project "Resetting the American Table: Creating an Alliance of Taste and Health," he and Julia Child addressed groups around the country.

Roberts is the author of two best-selling cookbooks: *Secret Ingredients: The Magical Process of Combining Flavors* and *Fresh From the Freezer* (recently reissued as *The Make Ahead Gourmet*). His newest book is *What's for Dinner?* He's penned articles for such diverse publications as *Details Magazine*, *The Advocate*, and the *Los Angeles Times Magazine.* In addition, he's a monthly contributor to the *Los Angeles Times* Syndicated Food Pages and was guest chef on Prodigy network.

Market Vegetable Dinner, page 176
Chilled Whitefish & Pike Dumplings with Sorrel, page 296

Jimmy Schmidt

Chef/Owner

The Rattlesnake Club
300 River Place
Detroit, Michigan 48207
313-567-4400

Novel taste combinations and a preference for regional ingredients have made Jimmy Schmidt one of the brightest stars of American Cuisines.

William Rice

A native Midwesterner, Jimmy Schmidt received the French Classic and Provincial Culinary Arts Diploma from Luberon College, Avignon, France, and the French Institute Technique du Vin Diploma from the Maison du Vin in Avignon. He also earned a Professional Chef's Diploma magna cum laude, graduating first in his class, from Madeleine Kamman's Modern Gourmet. In 1977, he became executive chef and executive general manager of the London Chop House in Detroit, Michigan. With a partner, he opened restaurants in Denver, Detroit, and Washington, D.C. In 1989, he became sole proprietor of Detroit Rattlesnake Club. He has since opened four restaurants with a new partner: Tres Vite, in the historic Fox Theater building in downtown Detroit; Cocina del Sol, in Southfield, Michigan; Buster's Bay, in Orchard Lake, Michigan; and the brand-new Stelline, at Somerset in Troy, Michigan.

Schmidt has earned numerous awards: *Food & Wine*'s Honor Roll of American Chefs in 1983; *Cook's Magazine*'s Who's Who in American Cooking in 1984; *Restaurants & Institutions Magazine* Top Ten Innovators and Trend Setters in 1987; and an Ivy Award in 1988. He is on the national board of directors of Share Our Strength and the board of directors of the Detroit Chapter of City-meals-on-Wheels. He is the author of *Cooking for All Seasons*, writes a weekly column for *The Detroit Free Press*, and has written six articles for *Bon Appetit*.

Escalope of Salmon with Mustard & Cognac, page 527

James P. Shannon

Executive Chef

Commander's Palace Restaurant
1403 Washington Avenue
New Orleans, Louisiana 70130
504–899–8231

That's the Commander's atmosphere—like a well-run party given by old friends. Flowers, conviviality, and most important, splendid food and wines! What could be more fun?

As executive chef at Commander's Palace Restaurant, James P. Shannon uses lessons he learned as a child. His great-grandparents emigrated from Eastern Europe, bringing old ways of growing and preparing food: they cultivated their own vegetables and herbs, raised chickens and hogs, and smoked homemade sausage. From them, Shannon learned self-sufficiency and cooking "from scratch." Growing up in Sea Isle, New Jersey, where commercial fishing is important, Shannon also learned to appreciate the freshest seafood.

Shannon studied at the Culinary Institute of America and then worked at Trump Towers Hotel and Casino. He later joined Commander's as a saucier, rising to become executive chef. His early knowledge of fresh seafood and produce, coupled with the culinary skills he has acquired over the years, have made the Commander's kitchen self-sufficient. It even makes its own Worcestershire sauce, cheeses, and sausages.

Commander's is located in the middle of the Garden District. The Victorian building has been a New Orleans landmark since 1880. The award-winning cuisine reflects the best of the city—its Creole heritage as well as dishes of Commander's own creation. Everything is as fresh as it can possibly be.

Quint Smith

Chef de Cuisine
The Shelby Restaurant
No. 967 Lexington Avenue
New York, New York 10021
212–988–4624

I take what's freshest, using my ideas as well as those of others to which I have been exposed, and I add to that some childhood sensations to create original and tasteful plates.

P. Quint Smith

A native of Oklahoma City, P. Quint Smith has been cooking professionally since he was 13, when he became an assistant chef for a private caterer. After graduating from the Culinary Institute of America in 1983, he worked in New York City as a pastry chef and cook at the Water Club, Monsignor's, and Cafe Destinn. He opened Bowden Square in Southampton, Long Island, was the founding chef of the American Diner in Princeton, New Jersey, and was sous chef at the Village Green Restaurant in Greenwich Village.

The Shelby serves ambitious American cuisine with a Southern touch, emphasizing high-quality food simply prepared and served in a casual but efficient manner. The decor is a blend of many design styles woven together to create an atmosphere of the "New American Bistro." A rotating exhibition of contemporary American art is shown in a traditional setting.

Grilled Tuna Steak, Roast Hubbard & Oyster Sauce, & Hen of the Woods Mushrooms, page 292
Roast Hubbard Squash Sauce, page 449
Garlic-Crusted Mozzarella with Pear Tomato Bread Salad, page 172

Louis Spost

Executive Chef

The Hilton at Short Hills
41 John F. Kennedy Parkway
Short Hills, New Jersey 07078
201–379–0100

Louis Spost is an all-American chef, born in suburban New York. After graduating from the Culinary Institute of America in Hyde Park, he criss-crossed the country, serving as chef in various Hilton Hotels and winning numerous awards in culinary salon competitions along the way. Spost is a member of the American Culinary Federation and the American Institute of Wine and Food.

Since 1987, he has overseen the kitchens of The Hilton at Short Hills, which received *New Jersey Monthly*'s Readers Choice award for Best Hotel Restaurant and Best Sunday Brunch and, for a third year in a row, the prestigious AAA Five Diamond award. Other awards have included the *Wine Spectator*'s Award of Excellence and an Excellent rating from *The New York Times*. Spost has recently worked with a number of guest chefs, including Jean-Louis Palladin, Jacque Cagna, Andre Daguin, and Martin Yan.

A rare blend of luxury and location, The Hilton at Short Hills offers the perfect setting for meetings, conferences, and banquets in northern New Jersey. Luxury has been the rule in creating this unique structure, the first truly deluxe modern hotel in the state. Its distinctive glass and brick facade and its richly appointed interiors mark The Hilton at Short Hills as a special place for special occasions. The Dining Room is known for outstanding gourmet delicacies; fine contemporary American cuisine is augmented by an unparalleled wine list. The Terrace Restaurant features a health-conscious spa menu.

Roasted Monkfish with Porcini Mushrooms, Orzo, & Port Syrup, page 262
Grilled Sourdough Bread with Tomatoes, Arugula, & Sweet Onions, page 250

Since our opening in 1988, we have featured healthy heart menu items. I worked closely with our nutritionist to adjust our recipes. I have always felt that as chefs we have the responsibility to cook with health in mind by using the freshest ingredients, cooking with passion and an understanding of healthy cooking.

Louis Spost

llen Susser

Chef/Owner

Chef Allen's Restaurant
19088 N.E. 29 Avenue
Aventura, Florida 33180
305-935-2900

I love to cook;
I make food my hobby, my
profession, and my charity.

Allen Susser

Allen Susser was born in New York on December 25, 1956, into the celebration and warmth of food. Susser set his career goals early. By 1976, he had cooked his way through New York City Technical College Restaurant Management School at the top of his class, receiving the Ward Arbury Award. He spent the following years absorbing classic French cooking and discipline at Le Bristol Hotel in Paris and at Le Cirque in New York.

Susser was drawn to the warmth of Miami and the adventure of undeveloped territory. While working at Turnberry Isle Resort, he began combining fresh local fish and tropical fruits. In 1986, he opened Chef Allen's Restaurant. He recognized the need to adjust his cooking techniques to the architecture of the sea and landscape—crisp, satisfying, and refreshing. As one of the principle chefs in the area, he continues to develop a "new world cuisine" that is not limited regionally but draws its strengths from the influences of the Caribbean, Latin America, and modern America. Some of his favorite ingredients include mango, star fruit, and mamey; fresh fishes such as cobia, wahoo, and pompano; and the flavors of scotch bonnets, saffron, vanilla, and rum. Chef Allen's Restaurant has won many accolades from local and national food writers. *The New York Times* has called him "the Ponce De Leon of New Floridian cooking."

As chairman of S.O.S. Taste of the Nation and Meals On Wheels–Miami, Susser works to feed the homeless and hungry, as well as the homebound elderly.

Citrus-Crusted Shrimp with Ginger & Starfruit, page 302
Baked Granny Smith Wrapped in Cinnamon & Cocoa Leaves, page 358

Elizabeth Terry

Chef/Owner

Elizabeth on 37th
105 East 37th Street
Savannah, Georgia 31401
912–236–5547

Southern food is very
nuturing and that's how I
cook. I cooked first as a wife
and mother and then as a
chef, and I feel it's
important that you cook
with other people in mind.

Elizabeth Terry

Elizabeth Terry was graduated from Lake Erie College for Women in 1966 with a degree in psychology. She worked in the wine and cheese business in Atlanta, Georgia, and in 1979 opened Thyme for You, a small soup and sandwich shop.

Terry and her husband/wine steward, Michael, opened Elizabeth on 37th in 1981. The simple elegance of their turn-of-the-century Southern mansion sets the perfect tone for her subtle and stunning new regional cooking, based on wonderful old Southern recipes. Her devotion to classic Southern cooking is such that she has extensively researched Savannah cooking of the 18th and 19th centuries. Inhabitants of this cosmopolitan port town have always eaten well, and her creations ensure that this will continue.

Terry's reputation as an innovator and leader in the cuisine of the new South is well established. In 1985, *Food & Wine* magazine named her one of the country's hot new chefs, *Town & Country* recognized her as one of the top ten women chefs in America, and she was profiled by *Time* magazine. Craig Claibourne also acknowledged her talent and creativity, in 1987 naming her as one of the new breed of Southern chefs. In 1988, she was named as one of the top women chefs in America by *USA Today.* Elizabeth on 37th was recently listed in *Food & Wine* magazine's Top 25 Restaurants in America. The James Beard Foundation has twice honored Terry.

Grilled Tuna with Herbs & Saffron Onions, page 288

hristopher C. Tobin

Chef

Busby's American Cafe
45 E. 92nd Street
New York, New York 10128
212–360–7373

People are dining out with many concerns and needs in reference to their diet. A restaurant that is willing to meet these requirements is what we need in this day and age. These are things I feel strongly about and have based our policies on and practice at Busby's.

Christopher C. Tobin

Christopher Tobin grew up in a family that loved traditional home cooking and baking. Following a four-year prep course in high school, he attended the Culinary Institute of America in Hyde Park, New York. He has since held many chef and sous chef positions in various styles and sizes of restaurants and hotels.

He opened Busby's as co-chef in 1989 and in time became head chef. Busby's has been written up in *Gourmet* magazine and was the site of a benefit dinner for the James Beard Foundation.

In his spare time, Tobin is teaching his children and their classmates about nature's food wonders, such as how maple sugar and syrup are made, including demonstrations on collecting the sap and making these products with the children to sample on their favorite foods. Tobin and his wife Susan, a pastry chef who trained at the Culinary Institute of America, are firm believers in letting kids help out in the kitchen.

Steamed Halibut with Ginger, Leeks, Plum Tomato, & Lemon Thyme, page 261
Grilled Shrimp with Warm Arugula & Artichoke Salad, page 306

One way to eat well is to have respect for simple ingredients, but to enhance their natural flavor with contrasting seasoning.

Evan Jones

Culinary Herbs & Spices

Allspice: Dried berries of the allspice tree—not a combination of several spices, although it tastes like a mixture of nutmeg, cinnamon, and cloves. Used with game, poultry stuffing, stews, sauces, gravies, pudding, cake, fruit desserts. A common seasoning used throughout the world.

Anise: Also called *aniseed.* Greenish brown seeds with a sweet, licorice flavor. Used in cookies, cake, bread, and dried figs, as well as savory dishes, including fish. Popular seasoning in European, Mediterranean, and Southeast Asian cooking.

Basil: Also called *sweet basil.* A savory herb with a pungent flavor, somewhat like a combination of licorice and cloves. Many varieties are available, offering a wide range of flavors, including lemon and cinnamon basil; the leaves can be green or purple. For best flavor, tear the leaves with your fingers instead of chopping them with a knife. Good with garlic, tomatoes, seafood (especially mullet), chicken, eggplant, summer squash, zucchini, bell peppers, corn, and meat. Used in French, Spanish, Italian, Greek, and Portuguese cooking.

Bay leaf: Also called *laurel leaf, bay laurel, sweet bay,* or *sweet laurel.* Slender, aromatic leaves; usually sold whole. Imported bay leaves, especially those from Mexico, are milder than California bay leaves. Used to flavor marinade, soup, stew, vegetables, tomato-based spaghetti sauce, poultry, fish, and venison; remove before serving—do not eat bay leaves. Add to the cooking water for cooking pasta or poaching fish. Boil with milk to add flavor to rice pudding. Use sparingly; too much will cause bitterness. Bay leaves are natural insect repellents. Place one in a container of food that is attractive to insects, like flour or dried fruit. Store with rice to give it a pleasant flavor.

Capers: Dried and pickled immature flower buds of a Mediterranean shrub; they should be rinsed to remove salt before using. Extremely flavorful; lemony tang. Use in very small amounts. Size varies; the petite nonpareil capers from southern France are considered the best. Very good with fish. Use in sauces, condiments, or as a garnish.

Caraway: Dark seeds; pungent nutty, anise flavor. Used in bread, cabbage, sauerkraut, potatoes, pork, mustard greens, cakes. Widely used in German and Austrian cooking.

Cardamom: Related to ginger. Spicy-sweet; powerful aroma; orange-like flavor. Cardamom pods are the size of a cranberry and hold 17 to 20 tiny seeds. Dried seeds are sold whole or ground (ground cardamom loses its flavoring power very quickly). Cardamom is an expensive spice; low-priced brands probably are inferior substitutes for real cardamom. Used in curry, breads, pastries, cakes, sausage, desserts. Use one whole pod of cardamom seeds to flavor a pot of coffee. Lightly crush the shell of a pod and add it, with the seeds, to stew or curry; the shell will dissolve during cooking. Widely used in Scandinavian and northern European cakes and pastries. Popular in Arab, Indian, and Pakistani cooking.

Cayenne pepper: Also called *red pepper.* Hot and spicy powder ground from chili peppers.

Celery seed: Seeds of a plant called *lovage,* a wild celery. Tastes like strong celery; use in small amounts because it can be bitter. Good in salads, soups, stews.

Chervil: Related to parsley and tarragon. Delicate flavor; best fresh and uncooked. Add near the end of cooking; do not boil. Often used in combination with tarragon. Good with poultry, veal, shellfish, salmon, salad greens, vinaigrettes, soup.

Chili powder: A mixture of ground dried chili peppers, cumin, oregano, garlic, and other spices. Can range from mild to fiercely hot.

Commercial blends vary from one manufacturer to another.

Chives: Fine, narrow, grasslike, hollow leaves. Mild onion flavor. Rinse lightly just before using. Add to foods just before serving or flavor will be harsh. Long, bright green stems can be used for decoration. Chive blossoms are used in salads or as a garnish. Good with eggs, tomatoes, potato salad, beets, shrimp, fish; add to biscuit dough or potato pancakes.

Cilantro: Also called *Chinese parsley.* The parsley-like leaves of the coriander plant. Strong flavor and fragrance; best fresh. Good with black bean or lentil soup, or rice and beans. Used in Asian cooking, Mexican salsa and other tomato dishes, and highly seasoned food.

Cinnamon: Dried inner bark of the cinnamon tree; sweet, warm flavor. Sold ground or in sticks. Ceylon cinnamon is yellowish-brown and has a mildly sweet flavor. A Ceylon cinnamon stick is formed into a single tight roll. Most cinnamon sold in America is actually from cassia trees, whose bark is similar to cinnamon but inferior; it is stronger and darker than Ceylon cinnamon. Cassia sticks are rolled from both edges, like a double scroll meeting in the middle. Ground cinnamon is used in apple and fruit desserts, sweets, cakes, cookies. Cinnamon sticks are used to flavor syrups, hot punch, or wine and removed before serving.

Cloves: Dried, unopened flower buds of the tropical clove tree; sold ground or whole (nail-shaped). Very pungent; hot, spicy flavor; use sparingly. Used in spice cakes, gingerbread,

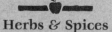

Herbs & Spices

Herbs, the aromatic leaves and soft stems of certain plants, are used for relatively delicate flavoring. They can be savory or sweet, and they may have a light or a pungent aroma. Strong herbs (like sage and oregano) can be cooked for long periods. Delicate herbs (such as chervil and basil) should be cooked briefly, if at all—add them near the end of the cooking time, or use raw.

Fresh herbs are more flavorful than dried. Store fresh herbs like cut flowers, standing up in a container of water in the refrigerator and with the leaves loosely wrapped in plastic. They will last for up to one week; change the water daily. Basil, sage, and some other herb leaves can be layered in a jar, covered with olive oil, and stored in the refrigerator for several months; use a paper towel to pat off as much oil as possible before using the herbs in cooking.

Dried herbs are good when fresh are not in season

or are unavailable. They are more concentrated than fresh, generally three times as strong. Adjust quantities in recipes if substituting one form for another. Dried herbs usually do not keep their flavor for more than six months to a year. Exposure to heat, light, moisture, and air makes them lose their freshness more quickly; store dried herbs in airtight, light-proof containers in a cool, dry place.

The dried bark, roots, flowers, or seeds of some plants are potent aromatics called *spices*. Most spices are best bought whole. Ground spices stay fresh only about half as long as whole seasonings. Because spices are very expensive, some manufacturers mix ground spices with less-expensive, less-aromatic substitutes; an inexpensive brand may not be pure spice. Grate or grind whole spices at home, using a blender, coffee grinder, or other small appliance specifically designed for spices.

puddings, apples, pork, ham, curry.

Coriander: Seeds of the plant whose leaves are called *cilantro*. Mild, delicate fragrance and vague orange or citrus flavor, or a combination of lemon, sage, and caraway. Often used in cake, gingerbread, apple desserts, curry; common in hot dogs. Popular in Arab, Mexican, Indonesian, Chinese, and Japanese cooking.

Cumin: Seeds that look somewhat like caraway; sold ground or whole. Earthy, pronounced fragrance; nutty flavor; amber, white, black (more peppery than other colors). Use sparingly—can easily overpower. Add a little ground cumin to commercial no-salt-added catsup. Used in chili powder, curry, dried beans. Popular in Mexican, North African, Mid-Eastern, Far-Eastern, and Indian cooking.

Curry powder: A pulverized blend of any number of spices, including turmeric, coriander, black and red peppers, cumin, ginger, cinnamon, dried chili, cloves, cardamom, mace or nutmeg, mustard seed, poppy seeds. Can be mild to hot. Pre-mixed blends vary widely from one manufacturer to another—experiment with different brands to determine which one to use in a specific recipe. For the true flavors of Indian curry, roast, grind, and blend the spices at home. In India, commercial curry powder is seldom used; each home cook blends different proportions of freshly ground spices for different dishes.

Dill: Also called *dillweed*. Sold as fresh, feathery leaves, or as dried seeds or leaves. Add several sprigs of fresh dill to cooking water for shrimp

or lobster. Remove fronds from stems and use fresh in potato salad, beets, carrots, cucumbers, zucchini, spinach, mustard greens, salad dressing, green salads, macaroni or tuna salads, fish, yogurt-based sauces; add to horseradish sauce and serve with cold salmon. Good flavor replacement when dill pickles are restricted. Popular in Scandinavia, Germany, Russia, Turkey, the Balkans, and Rumania.

Fennel: Anise or licorice-flavored seeds. The stalks and bulb of the plant are used as a vegetable or as a seasoning for fish, salad dressings, vinaigrettes, salads, and soups. Popular in Italian and Mediterranean French cooking.

Fines herbes: A mixture or three or more delicate herbs, usually parsley, tarragon, chervil, and chives. Most often used in omelettes. Popular in French cooking.

Ginger: The knobby root of the ginger plant. Pinkish brown skin; pale yellow flesh. Fresh ginger is zestier and more flavorful than ground ginger. Dried ground ginger is a poor, sometimes unacceptable substitute for fresh (when a substitution cannot be avoided, though, use 1/4 tsp ground ginger for each tablespoon of grated fresh ginger). Use chunks of fresh ginger to flavor soups, stews, curries, and cooking liquids; remove before serving. Good with onions and garlic. Dried ground ginger is used in muffins, gingerbread, spice cake, fruit desserts, and pumpkin pie. In European cooking, ginger is most often used in sweet foods; in Asian cooking, it is commonly used with meat, fish, and shellfish.

Horseradish: Slender root with brown skin. Very

zesty; loses its pungency when cooked; best used raw. Store tightly wrapped in refrigerator for a month or more. Grated fresh horseradish can be refrigerated or frozen in airtight containers for several months. Mix grated horseradish with vinegar and store in dark containers away from the light. Used with beets, chicken, fish or fish sauce, or salad dressing. Popular in England and northern Europe.

Lavender: Fresh, clean fragrance; pretty violet flowers. Closely related to rosemary. Used in beef stew, roast pork or lamb, roast chicken, salad dressings, fruit or vegetable salads, desserts; to add flavor to sugar, honey, vinegar, and wine; to make herb tea; and as a garnish for punch or salads. Lavender jelly is good with cold lamb.

Lemon balm: Leaves of a perennial plant native to southern Europe. Lemony fragrance; adds subtle lemon flavor. Use freshly chopped leaves in salads, fruit cups, cookies, pudding, sauerkraut, soup, or stew. Use whole leaves as a garnish for meat or vegetables or iced drinks (or frozen in ice cubes). Fresh or dried leaves can be steeped for tea.

Lemon grass: A tropical grass with aromatic oils that taste and smell strongly of lemon. The leaves are used to flavor soup or tea, and the stalks can be chopped for stir-fry dishes. When necessary, lemon peel or lemon verbena can be substituted for lemon grass. Widely used in dishes from Ceylon, Vietnam, and Southeast Asia.

Mace: The scarlet lacy hull that covers the nutmeg seed. Dried blades of mace look like yellow-brown seaweed. Flavor is very similar to nutmeg, but nutmeg is nuttier. Mace is much more expensive than nutmeg. Hard to grind; best to buy in ground form. Use anywhere nutmeg can be used: cakes, puddings, fish and shellfish, soups and stews, cauliflower, carrots.

Marjoram: Similar to oregano, but milder and sweeter. Add near end of cooking, or use in dishes that cook quickly. Especially good with lamb. Widely used in European cooking.

Mint: Sweet flavor, cool aftertaste. Hundreds of varieties available, with wide range of flavors, including spearmint, peppermint, orange, chocolate, and lavender. Add chopped fresh leaves to beets, carrots, cauliflower, peas, potatoes, spinach, cucumbers, tomatoes, eggplant, zucchini, cole slaw, beans, lentils, melon, fruit salads, fruit drinks, salad dressings, marinades, cottage cheese, pie crust pastry. Use sprigs to garnish fruit drinks, iced tea, or any dish, especially fish and lamb. Mint jelly or mint sauce is commonly served with lamb. Steep crushed stems in boiling water for tea. Chew fresh leaves to sweeten breath. Popular in England, Spain, Italy, the Mid-East, and India.

Nasturtium: Flowers, leaves, and seed pods are edible. Young leaves and stems have a subtle peppery, cress-like flavor. Use in salads, sandwiches, soups, and as a substitute for watercress. Flowers are used as a garnish or in salads. Seeds and immature flower buds can be pickled and used as an inexpensive substitute for capers.

"I thought they were called nasturtiums," said Piglet timidly, as he went on jumping.

"No," said Pooh. "Not these. These are called mastershalums."

A.A. Milne
The House at Pooh Corner

Of all the garden herbs none is of greater virtue than sage.

Thomas Cogan

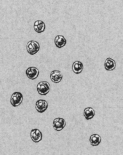

Nutmeg: Large, hard seed; sold whole or ground. Best freshly grated as it quickly loses its best flavor when grated. Sweet flavor; delicate and aromatic. Used in desserts, cakes, and sweet dishes, or with beef, cheese, spinach, Brussels sprouts, turnips, winter squash, sweet potatoes, onion sauce.

Oregano: Robust, spicy herb. Good with tomatoes, cheese, beans, eggplant, zucchini, fish, meat. Generously used in Italian and Mexican cooking.

Paprika: Ground red pepper; mild sweet flavor. Hungarian paprika is hotter than American. Adds color and flavor. Widely used in Hungarian, French, and Spanish cooking.

Parsley: Best fresh. Curly parsley often used as a garnish. To some palates, flat-leaved parsley is more flavorful and preferred in cooking. The flavor is concentrated in the stems, which should be minced with the leaves or used to flavor soup stocks and sauces. Parsley combines well with most herbs. Add sprigs to mixed greens for salad. Chop a whole bunch of fresh parley and freeze for later use. Chew fresh parsley to freshen breath. Widely used in European cooking.

Peppercorns: Dried berries of the pepper vine *Piper nigrum;* sold whole, crushed, or ground (fine or coarse). Freshly ground peppercorns have the best flavor. Whole peppercorns can be stored for three to four years. Most widely used spice in the world.

Poppy seeds: Tiny black seeds of the opium poppy flower (the seeds do not have any narcotic properties). Nutty flavor. Used in cakes, muffins, bread, and curry. Used in European, Mid-Eastern, and Indian cooking.

Rosemary: Tastes like a blend of sage and lavender with a little ginger. Best fresh. Use large sprigs in cooking soup or stew and remove before serving. Dried rosemary can be brittle, like the pine needles on an old Christmas tree; they should be strained out before serving. Good with chicken, fish, lamb, game meat, potatoes, lima beans, Swiss chard, rice, sauces and salad dressings, cold drinks. Rosemary-flavored sugar is good in delicate ices and sherbets. Rosemary blossoms can be used to flavor honey, white wine, or vinegar.

Saffron: Dried stigmas of the crocus flower. Crimson-gold threads used to add color and flavor. Use sparingly—a little goes a long way. World's most expensive spice—takes 75,000 hand-harvested stigma to produce one pound of saffron. Inexpensive brands may have been adulterated with safflower petals or other substitutes. Used in rice dishes, soup, fish stew, paella, sometimes baking. Popular in Italian, French, and Spanish cooking.

Sage: Pungent; use sparingly. Good in poultry stuffing, sausage, onions, cooked tomatoes, string beans, and other vegetables.

Sesame seeds: Also called *benne.* Small, flat, pale seeds of a tropical Asian plant; important source of oil. Sweet, nutty flavor. Scattered on bread before baking; good with rice, pasta dishes, seafood.

Sorrel: Refreshing sour-lemon flavor. Cook only briefly to preserve fresh flavor. Used in soup, turnip greens, spinach, tossed salads, hot potato salad, cornbread stuffing for fish, and sauces for fish; can be substituted for spinach. Good with nutmeg. Popular in French, English, and Dutch cooking.

Star anise: Star-shaped seed of an evergreen tree belonging to the magnolia family; sold dried. Strong licorice flavor; similar to anise but more bitter and pungent. Use whole as a garnish or crushed to flavor poultry and sauces. An expensive spice imported from China. Popular in Chinese recipes for pork and duck.

Tarragon: Light anise flavor; bittersweet. French tarragon is best. Mainly used in delicate dishes; good with sole, chicken, veal, eggs, tomatoes, green beans, carrots, salads, salad dressings, light soups, poultry stuffing. Add finely chopped tarragon to spicy brown mustard.

Thyme: Related to oregano and sweet marjoram. Many varieties available: outdoorsy, minty, caraway, lemon, orange, or clove-like flavor or aroma. Holds up well in long-cooking dishes like stocks and stews. Good with meat, seafood, pork, poultry, chowder, mushrooms, mashed potatoes, tomatoes, eggplant, bread, salad dressing. Often used in European and Creole cooking.

Turmeric: Powdered rootstock of an Indian plant. Adds scarlet-orange color to foods (including hot dog mustard and piccalilli). Mild flavor; use in small quantities to avoid bitterness. Generally used in blends with other spices; good with cumin, dried mustard, coriander, cardamom, ginger, garlic. Widely used in India to add color to sweet dishes.

Vanilla bean: The cured pod of an orchid. Dark brown, tough, long and slender. Vanilla extract is made by soaking crushed pods in alcohol; imitation vanilla extract lacks the depth and flavor of pure vanilla extract.

How to Make Herb Tea
Chamomile, lemon balm, mint, and other herbs make comforting teas. Use herbs alone or in combination with ordinary black tea. Pour boiling water over 1 T fresh herb leaves per serving. Steep for 3 to 5 minutes; discard leaves. Sweeten with honey, or add lemon or orange peel.

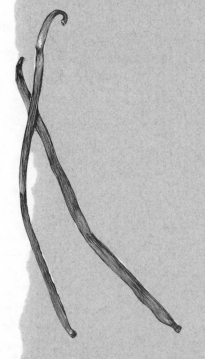

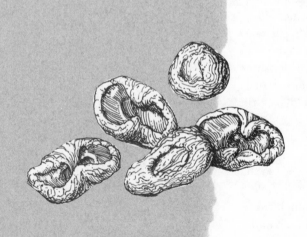

# Culinary Glossary

Acidulated water: A bath of water and an acid ingredient (lemon juice or vinegar), used to prevent cut fruits and vegetables from turning brown. Use 1 T lemon juice for each cup of water, or 2 T vinegar per quart of water.

Adjust: To taste before cooking or serving and add herbs, sweeteners, or other ingredients to satisfy individual preference.

Al dente: Pasta that is fully cooked but not soft or mushy. The phrase is an Italian expression that translates as "to the tooth," meaning that the food offers a slight resistance when bitten.

Baste: To spoon liquids (marinade, pan drippings) over food as it bakes to add flavor and color; keeps food from becoming dry.

Blanch: To plunge raw fruit or vegetables into boiling water briefly and then into cold water. This firms the flesh, loosens skins for easier peeling, and preserves the color and flavor.

Boil: To heat a liquid until bubbles break the surface (212° F at sea level), or to cook food in boiling liquid. Water has a lower boiling point at higher altitudes. The boiling point drops about 2° for every thousand feet above sea level. At 10,000 feet, water boils at 194°. Food must be boiled longer at higher altitudes to cook it fully.

Borscht: Fresh beet soup; can be served hot or cold. Originally from Russia and Poland.

Bouillon: Broth made by cooking vegetables, poultry, meat, or fish in water with herbs and other seasonings, then straining out the solids. Low-sodium bouillon cubes and granules are available. See *Court bouillon.*

Bouquet garni: A "bouquet for garnish," made by tying a bundle of leafy herbs (classically three stalks of parsley, a small sprig of thyme, and a small bay leaf) together with a string or wrapping them in a cheesecloth bag and cooking in a stew or casserole. Dried orange or lemon peel, garlic, marjoram, or other herbs or spices can also be added to the bouquet garni. The bouquet garni is easily removed from the food before serving.

Braise: To brown food first, then finish cooking slowly over low heat, in a small amount of liquid, tightly covered. Long, slow cooking develops flavor and tenderizes the food.

Broth: See *Bouillon.*

Brown: To cook food quickly over high heat, so the surface turns brown but the inside stays moist. Adds color and flavor.

Bruise: To partially crush an ingredient, such as a peppercorn or garlic clove, to release the flavor.

Caramelize: To heat sugar until it liquefies and becomes a clear golden or dark brown syrup. Also called *burnt sugar.*

Casserole: A deep, round, oven-proof baking dish with handles and a lid, or the food it contains.

Cheesecloth: A fine or coarsely woven lightweight, natural cotton cloth. Used to strain liquids, make bouquet garni, or line molds.

Chiffonade: Thin strips or threads of vegetables. The word is a French expression that means "made of rags."

Chinois: A conical sieve that has a very fine mesh; a spoon must be used to press the food through it.

Chop: To cut food into bite-sized pieces with a knife or cleaver.

Chutney: A spicy condiment made of fruit, vinegar, sugar, and spices. Can be mild or hot, smooth or chunky. Good with curries or spread on bread.

Clafouti: Fresh fruit topped with a layer of batter, baked, and served hot; the baked topping may be like a biscuit or a pudding.

Clingstone: Fruit whose pit is strongly attached ("clings") to the flesh. See *Freestone.*

Condiment: A savory, spicy, or salty accompaniment to food; mustard, catsup, chutney, salsa, and pickle relish are popular condiments.

Cooking spray: A product that can be sprayed on utensils and cooking surfaces to keep foods from sticking; foods should be sautéed in cooking spray, rather than butter or oil. Contains oil (olive, corn, or other), lecithin (an emulsifier), alcohol (prevents the sprayer from clogging), and a propellant.

Core: To remove the seeds or tough woody parts in the center of a fruit or vegetable.

Coulis: A thick purée or sauce.

Court bouillon: Broth made of vegetables and herbs (usually onion, cloves, celery, carrots, and bouquet garni), simmered for about 30 minutes, cooled, and then strained. Generally used to poach fish, seafood, or vegetables.

Cover: To add enough liquid to a container so that its contents are completely immersed.

Crab boil: Also called *shrimp boil.* A pre-packaged mixture of herbs and spices added to the water used for cooking crab, shrimp, or lobster. Usually contains mustard seeds, peppercorns, bay leaves, whole allspice, whole cloves, dried ginger pieces, and red chilies.

Cream: To beat one or more ingredients (usually including a fat) until the mixture is soft, smooth, and completely homogenized, so that individual ingredients are indistinguishable.

Crimp: Also called *flute.* To press or pinch two pastry edges together to seal the dough and make a decorative edge. Fingers, a fork, or other utensils can be used.

On the way home I drew up my plan. I would stick to my rigid diet for the first week— no exceptions no matter what; then I would eat all weekend at the parties and family get-together; and during the final week I would go back to the diet and recoup my losses. The first week was no problem. Did I want some ice cream, my mother wanted to know? No, I can't have ice cream. Everything was resisted unless it was part of the program. I was so good I

Crisp: To restore crispness to limp or wilting vegetables by soaking them in ice water.

Croutons: Small cubes of toasted bread used to garnish soup or salad.

Cruciferous: Shaped like a cross or crucifix. Refers to a family of vegetables whose flowers have four petals that look something like a cross. Broccoli, Brussels sprouts, cabbage, cauliflower, and kale are a few of the cruciferous vegetables. They are thought to have a protective effect against cancer.

Crudités: Raw seasonal vegetables served as a party platter, usually with a dip.

Crystallized ginger: Also called *candied ginger*. Fresh ginger that has been boiled in sugar syrup and, after drying, dipped in granulated sugar. Use as a garnish or as an ingredient in cooking. Store in an airtight container in a cool, dry place.

Curry: Any of a number of East Indian–inspired spicy, hot, gravy-based dishes.

Cut in: To mix a solid fat (such as margarine) with flour and/or other dry ingredients with a pastry blender, food processor, or two knives used in scissor fashion until the mixture is reduced to small crumbly particles.

Dash: A tiny amount of seasoning, generally between 1/16 and 1/8 teaspoon.

Deglaze: After food is sautéed and removed from the pan, to heat a small amount of broth, wine, or other liquid in the pan, stirring to dissolve the residue and loosen the cooked-on browned bits. The liquid is used to make a sauce.

Dredge: To lightly coat uncooked food with flour or bread crumbs; helps brown food during cooking.

Dust: To very lightly coat food with a powdery substance, such as confectioners' sugar or flour.

Dutch oven: A large oven-proof pot or kettle with a tight-fitting lid. Used for moist cooking, such as stew.

Egg substitute: No-cholesterol imitation eggs, made with egg white, food starch, oil, skim-milk powder, food coloring, and other additives. 1/4 C equals 1 whole egg. They can be used in most baking and cooking recipes that call for whole eggs. In many recipes, two egg whites can be substituted for one whole egg. In some recipes, or when eggs are used in large quantities, a commercial or homemade egg substitute may be necessary.

Escalope: Also called *scallop*. A very thin, flattened slice of meat or fish, which cooks very quickly.

Fish glace: Fish stock that has been reduced to a syrupy consistency.

Fold: To gently combine a light, airy mixture with a heavier mixture so that the light mixture does not lose its volume. The lighter mixture is placed on top of the heavier mixture; a rubber spatula is used to cut down through the center of the mixture, across the bottom of the bowl, and up the side. The bowl is turned one-quarter turn and the cutting motion is repeated until the two mixtures are as fully combined as specified in recipe (some do not require complete mixing).

Freestone: A fruit whose stone does not adhere to

the pulp. See *Clingstone*.

Fumet: A concentrated stock made from poultry or fish; used to make sauces.

Gazpacho: Uncooked vegetable soup, usually a chunky purée made with tomatoes, bell peppers, onions, celery, garlic, olive oil, and vinegar; served cold. A summer soup from Spain.

Glacé de viande: Meat glaze used to add flavor and color to sauces, made by reducing meat juices to a thick syrup by boiling.

Granite: See *Sorbet*.

Harissa: An extremely hot sauce from Tunisia, made with chili peppers, garlic, cumin, coriander. Traditionally served with couscous, but also used in soup and stew.

Herbes de Provence: A blend of dried herbs commonly used in southern France to season meat, poultry, or vegetables. Available ready-mixed in supermarkets or gourmet shops, it usually contains basil, fennel seed, lavender, marjoram, rosemary, sage, and thyme.

Hoisin sauce: Also called *Peking sauce*. A sweet, spicy, thick, reddish brown sauce used as a condiment or flavoring agent; made of soybeans, garlic, chili peppers, and other spices. It should be stored in the refrigerator in a glass or plastic container.

Hors d'oeuvres: Appetizers.

Ice: See *Sorbet*.

Macerate: To soak fruit in a marinade. The term for soaking meat or vegetables in this manner is *marinate*.

Marinade: A seasoned liquid used to soak meat, chicken, fish, or vegetables. Herbs, spices, and other seasonings add flavor to the marinated food; acid ingredients, such as vinegar, wine, or lemon juice, help break down the proteins and tenderize it.

Marinate: To soak meat, chicken, fish, or vegetables in a marinade. Food should be marinated in a covered glass, ceramic, or stainless steel container in the refrigerator. The term for soaking fruit in this manner is *macerate*.

Medallion: A small, coin-shaped piece of meat.

Miso: Also called *bean paste*. A high-protein, high-salt paste made from fermented soybeans and rice or barley. Thick like peanut butter, it dissolves easily in hot liquids; add it at the end of the cooking period and do not let it boil. Extensively used in Japanese cooking, usually to flavor broth or dipping sauce; it also adds flavor to marinades for fish, poultry, meat, and vegetables. Available in a wide variety of colors, flavors, and aromas. Contains vitamin B_{12} (which is almost never found in non-meat foods) and beneficial bacteria. Store, tightly covered, in the refrigerator.

Nonpareil: French for "without equal." Usually refers to tiny capers from Provence.

Nuoc-nam: Vietnamese name for a sauce called *nam pla* in Thailand and *shottsuru* in Japan. Salty, fermented fish sauce used as a condiment or flavoring agent. Served over rice, or in a small dish for dipping fish or meat at the table.

Ouzo: An anise-flavored liqueur from Greece.

Parboil: To partially cook food by briefly boiling in water. Dense foods (carrots, turnips) are often parboiled before they are added to quick-cooking foods so that all ingredients finish

No mild compound of hashed vegetables, sugar, and imported spices is the Southwestern chile sauce. You start with three or four whole, dried, red chile peppers. They go in a pan, preferably enamel or earthenware, with a clove of garlic and a quart of water. When the mixture has boiled until the chiles are pulpy, put it through a sieve to remove the seeds and membranes of the peppers. The sauce can be thickened a little with flour, and it can be salted, but purists object to this tampering with Nature's experiment in spontaneous combustion. They eat it as is, and they eat it on everything. Often chile seems to replace salt in the Southwestern diet.

Alice Marriott
The Valley Below

cooking at the same time.

Pastry knife or *pastry blender:* A utensil made of several wire strands that are used to cut through solid fats and flour (or other dry ingredients) until the mixture is cut into very small particles.

Phyllo: Tissue-thin layers of dough commonly used in Greek and Near Eastern cooking; similar to strudel.

Pinch: The amount of seasoning that can be held between the tips of the thumb and the forefinger, about 1/16 teaspoon.

Plump: To soak dried fruit in a liquid (such as water, fruit juice, sherry, brandy) until it has softened and, depending on the type of liquid, absorbed flavors.

Poach: To cook food in liquid that is just below the boiling point.

Poivrade: With pepper.

Polenta: A coarsely ground cornmeal used to make mush; popular in Italy.

Potage: A slightly thick soup, usually puréed.

Purée: To mash or grind a fruit or vegetable until it is smooth and thick. A blender or food processor is commonly used to purée foods.

Reconstitute: To restore a dehydrated food to its original state by soaking in liquid, usually water.

Reduce: To simmer or boil a liquid until the volume is reduced by evaporation; produces a thicker consistency and a stronger flavor.

Ricer: A perforated utensil used to press cooked food into small pieces (something like a giant garlic press). Cooked food pushed through the ricer looks something like rice or small squiggles. A ricer can be used to make mashed potatoes, to form spaetzle noodles, or to purée cooked vegetables or fruit for making baby food.

Salsa: Mexican term for "sauce." Vegetable or fruit sauces that are cooked or raw. Can be mild or hot.

Sauté: To cook food quickly in a skillet over direct heat. For low-fat cooking, lightly coat the inside of a nonstick pan with cooking spray and omit butter, margarine, or oil.

Savory: Food that is piquant and full of flavor; not sweet.

Scald: To heat a liquid to just below the boiling point.

Sear: To brown meat quickly at very high heat in a skillet, broiler, or oven.

Season: To add flavor to foods to strengthen or improve their taste. Common seasonings include herbs, spices, condiments, and vinegar. In general, seasonings should be added sparingly; more seasonings to suit the cook's taste should be incorporated as needed, tasting after each addition.

Section: Also called *segment.* To cut the individual pieces or segments in a citrus fruit out of their membranes, making wedges of bright, juicy fruit.

Shoyu: The Japanese term for soy sauce.

Shrimp boil: See *Crab boil.*

Shuck: To remove the husk from an ear of corn, or the shell from a shellfish.

Simmer: To boil very gently, so the liquid barely bubbles.

Simple syrup: Also called *sugar syrup.* A solution

of sugar and water cooked over low heat until clear; the ratio of water to sugar can be varied to make thin (3 parts water to 1 part sugar), medium (2 parts water to 1 part sugar), or heavy (equal parts water and sugar) syrups.

Sorbet: A frozen dessert or palate refresher served between courses. French term for sherbet. Unlike sherbet, a sorbet does not contain milk. It can be sweet or savory. Also called *ice* or *granite,* both of which are usually more granular in texture.

Soufflé: An airy mixture that is lightened by stiffly beaten egg whites; can be baked, chilled, or frozen. They can be sweet or savory, served as a dessert or main course. A baked soufflé should be served immediately; it will fall or deflate easily because the hot air it contains will begin to escape when it is removed from the oven. A soufflé must be made in a special dish that has straight sides.

Spring roll wrapper: Also called *won ton skins* or *egg roll skins.* Round or square paper-thin sheets of dough widely used in Chinese cooking to wrap foods, as for won ton or egg rolls.

Steam: To cook food on a rack or special basket placed over boiling or simmering water in a covered pan. Retains more flavor, texture, and nutrients than boiling or poaching.

Steep: To soak in liquid to extract flavors, as in brewing tea.

Stir-fry: To quickly cook small pieces of food over very high heat, stirring constantly. Food stays crisp-tender. For low-fat stir-frying, coat the inside of the pan with cooking spray and omit oil.

Stock: The broth from boiled chicken, beef, or fish; used to make soup, gravy, and sauces.

Sweat: To cook mushrooms, onions, or other high-water-content foods over low heat until they begin to release their moisture.

Tabasco sauce: A fiery sauce made from vinegar and red peppers. Use sparingly.

Tahini: A thick, creamy paste made of finely ground sesame seeds. Popular in Greece, Cyprus, Lebanon, Jordan, and Syria. Used as the basis for salad dressings and as a condiment.

Tamari: A very dark brown natural soy sauce. More intense but mellower flavor and thicker than soy sauce; can be used in place of soy sauce in any recipe. Keeps at room temperature indefinitely.

Ti leaves: Used in Polynesia to wrap foods before cooking. The leaves are not eaten. Soak dried ti leaves (available in ethnic or specialty stores) before using.

Worcestershire sauce: A hot and zesty seasoning from India made with soy sauce, vinegar, molasses, chilies, tropical fruits, and spices.

Zest: The colored portion of the citrus peel, containing aromatic oils that add flavor to foods. The white pith just under the zest is very bitter and should not be used. The zest can be removed with a special utensil called a *citrus zester* or with a vegetable peeler.

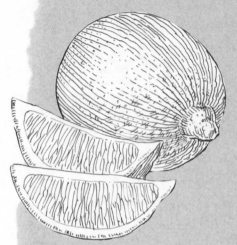

Health Glossary

Alcohol: An ingredient in many beverages, including beer, wine, and liqueurs; contains about 7 calories per gram. Acts as a depressant to the nervous system when taken in excessive amounts.

Amino acid: An essential component of the protein molecule. The body can manufacture 13 of the 22 amino acids that make up protein; the remaining nine (called *essential amino acids*) are obtained only through the diet.

Antioxidant vitamins: Include beta-carotene and vitamins C and E; by preventing oxidation, they may have a protective effect against heart disease, certain types of cancer, cataracts, and other disorders.

Artery: A blood vessel that carries oxygen-rich blood from the heart to the organs throughout the body.

Atherosclerosis: A disease of the arterial wall in which excess cholesterol deposited on the artery walls eventually calcifies or hardens (also called *hardening of the arteries* or *arteriosclerosis*), forming plaque. Over time, plaque buildup causes the inside diameter of the artery to become smaller, and blood flow through the artery is reduced or stopped. Blocked arteries cannot supply an adequate amount of oxygen-rich blood to the heart and other organs, muscles, and tissues, which may lead to a heart attack or stroke.

Basal metabolism: The energy (calories) required to keep the body functioning while at rest (breathing, heart beat, and so forth).

Calorie: A unit of measurement that expresses the energy value of food.

Carbohydrate: A group of substances that provide the body with one of its main sources of energy. The most familiar carbohydrates are starch and sugar.

Cardiovascular: Referring to the heart and the system of arteries and veins that carry blood throughout the body.

Carotene: Natural yellow pigments the body uses to make vitamin A.

Cholesterol: A fat-like substance produced in the liver that is used to form hormones and cell membranes. It is manufactured in the bodies of all animals and is therefore found in all animal products, including meat and dairy foods; it is not found in foods of plant origin. A high level of cholesterol in the blood increases the risk of heart disease.

Coronary artery: An artery on the surface of the heart that supplies oxygen-rich blood to the heart muscle. Coronary artery disease includes atherosclerosis (fatty buildup), thrombus (blood clot), and spasm (intermittent constriction).

Diabetes: A disease in which the pancreas produces insufficient insulin (sometimes the cells become insensitive to the "signal" to open up and let sugar in), causing the level of glucose in the blood to become abnormally high.

Fat: A group of organic compounds made up of fatty acids and glycerol; includes grease and oil. A diet high in fat increases the risk of heart attack, stroke, and breast and bowel cancer. Food contains a combination of three kinds of fat known as *fatty acids.*

Fiber: The indigestible component of plants.

Gram: A unit of mass and weight in the metric system. One ounce is about 30 grams.

Heart attack: The sudden death of part of the heart muscle (myocardium), which occurs when the flow of oxygen-rich blood to the heart muscle is interrupted; usually accompanied by severe pain. Blood clots (thrombi) are responsible for suddenly blocking the coronary artery in 90% of heart attacks.

High-density lipoprotein (HDL): A complex molecule made of protein, cholesterol, and other lipids believed to help remove cholesterol from the body. Also known as the good cholesterol (think "H" for Happy). A high level of high-density lipoproteins is associated with a decreased risk of heart disease.

Hydrogenation: A process that causes oil to become more saturated. Commonly used to turn liquid oil into solid, spreadable margarine.

Hypertension: Blood pressure is the amount of force necessary to pump blood through the body. High blood pressure (hypertension) may injure the arterial walls, making them prone to atherosclerosis. It also causes the heart to work harder. High blood pressure may damage body organs, causing stroke, heart attack, and heart and kidney failure.

Lipids: The technical name for a group of substances commonly called *fats;* includes saturated and unsaturated fats, cholesterol, and triglycerides.

Lipoprotein: A new molecule formed when a protein wraps the cholesterol molecule in a protective shell. Lipoprotein allows fat to mix with the blood, which carries cholesterol to all parts of the body where it completes tasks necessary for normal biological function.

Low-density lipoprotein (LDL): A type of lipoprotein complex that contains the greatest amounts of cholesterol and may deposit cholesterol in the artery walls. Also known as the bad cholesterol (think "L" for Lousy). High levels of LDLs are associated with an increased risk of heart disease.

Mineral: Substances that are essential to building and repairing body tissue and to controlling

Heart Attack

Symptoms

You may experience any or all of the following symptoms. They may vary in intensity or come and go.

- Uncomfortable pressure, fullness, squeezing, or pain in the chest, usually lasting longer than two minutes.
- Pain radiating to the shoulders, neck, jaw, arms, or back.
- Dizziness, fainting, sweating, nausea, shortness of breath, or weakness.

What to Do

- Recognize the symptoms as warning signs.
- Stop activity and sit or lie down.
- Take one nitroglycerin tablet—up to three at five-minute intervals—as prescribed by your doctor. If the pain is still not relieved, call 911 or your local emergency number immediately.
- If you do not have nitroglycerin and have had symptoms for two minutes or more, call 911 or your

local emergency number immediately.

- If you can get to the hospital faster by car, ask someone to drive you. Do not drive yourself to the hospital!

What to Do for Someone Else

- Call 911 or your local emergency number immediately.
- Drive the person directly to the hospital if you can get there quicker than emergency response.
- While waiting for assistance, make the person comfortable, usually lying down on a flat surface with the head slightly elevated.
- Check for medical alert tags around the neck or wrist.
- Start CPR if necessary (if you have been properly trained), until emergency help arrives.

Do Not Deny the Symptoms of a Heart Attack

New therapies can minimize heart muscle damage and even save your life if treatment is begun within the first few hours after the symptoms start.

the body's functions. Small amounts of minerals are essential; the body cannot manufacture minerals, so they must be obtained through the diet.

Monounsaturated fatty acids (MUFA): Liquid at room temperature; tend to reduce only LDLs ("bad cholesterol"), thereby increasing the ratio of HDLs ("good cholesterol").

Myocardial infarction: See *Heart attack.*

Obesity: Weighing more than 20% above desirable weight.

Omega-3 fatty acids: Eicosapentaenoic (EPA) and decosahexaenoic acid (DHA) are fatty acids found in seafood. They may lower the risk of heart attacks by making the blood cells less "sticky" and therefore less likely to form clots.

Overweight: Weighing more than 10% above desirable weight.

Plaque: Deposits of cholesterol, fats, and calcium on the artery walls. Over time, plaque buildup causes the inside diameter of the artery to become smaller, and blood flow through the artery is reduced or stopped.

Polyunsaturated fatty acids (PUFA): Usually liquid at room temperature; in small amounts they tend to lower blood cholesterol levels of both HDL and LDL.

Protein: A group of compounds made up of amino acids; essential for the growth and repair of animal tissue.

Risk factor: A condition that increases the chance that a person will develop heart disease.

Saturated fatty acids (SFA): Usually solid at room temperature; tend to increase blood cholesterol. SFAs are found mostly in animal products

but are also found in palm and coconut oils.

Sodium: A mineral found in a wide variety of foods; helps regulate the amount of water in the body and maintains normal heart rhythm. Ingesting too much sodium can cause fluid retention and/or aggravate high blood pressure.

Stress: Any physical or emotional stimulus that interferes with a person's healthy mental and physical well-being.

Stroke: An injury to the brain that occurs when the blood supply to a part of the brain is cut off and the cells that do not receive oxygen die. Because different areas of the brain control different functions, the specific effects of a stroke depend on which area of the brain was injured. Brain cells cannot be regenerated. Stroke is the third leading cause of death in the United States.

Thrombus: A blood clot. *Thrombosis* refers to a vessel blocked with a clot. *Coronary thrombosis* refers to the formation of a clot in one of the coronary arteries, usually causing a heart attack.

Triglycerides: The main type of fat found in the body. It is visible in food. Four factors elevate triglyceride levels—excess alcohol in the diet, being overweight, lack of exercise, and excess calories in the form of fat, saturated fat, and simple sugars.

Vein: A blood vessel that returns oxygen-depleted blood to the heart and lungs.

Vitamin: A complex organic substance that occurs naturally in plant and animal tissue; small amounts are essential for control of the body's metabolic processes.

Vitamins

A (retinol)	Healthy cell membranes; good vision in dim light; bone and tooth development; immunity; reproduction; anti-cancer functions	Yellow fruits; yellow, orange, and dark green leafy vegetables; milk; egg yolk; organ meats
B_1 (thiamin)	Metabolism of carbohydrates; normal nerve function	Whole grains, legumes, nuts, lean pork, liver
B_2 (riboflavin)	Release of energy from carbohydrates, proteins and fats; maintenance of mucous membranes; normal nerve function	Dairy products, green leafy vegetables, meat, fish, poultry
B_6 (pyridoxine)	Protein metabolism; red blood cell development	Chicken, fish, organ meats, pork, egg yolk, yeast, bran
B_{12} (cobalamin)	Red blood cell formation; normal metabolism of all cells, especially gastrointestinal tract, bone marrow, and nervous tissue	Meat, poultry, fish, oysters, liver, dairy products, eggs
Biotin	Synthesis and breakdown of fatty acids and amino acids	Legumes, mushrooms, peanuts, corn, milk, bananas, grapefruit, organ meats
C (ascorbic acid)	Wound healing; cell, tissue, tooth, and bone formation; iron absorption; antioxidant properties	Citrus fruits, melons, strawberries, broccoli, potatoes, green leafy vegetables, green pepper
D (calciferol)	Absorption and use of calcium and phosphorus; development of bones and teeth	Fortified milk, oily fish, egg yolk, liver; made by the body with sun exposure
E (tocopherol)	Red blood cell function; antioxidant properties	Vegetable oils, wheat germ, liver, egg yolk, nuts
Folacin (folic acid)	Red blood cell formation; metabolism; development of nerve cells	Green leafy vegetables, wheat, fish, dried beans, eggs, lean meat, broccoli, yeast
K (menaquinone)	Blood clotting	Green leafy vegetables, liver, soybeans, soybean oil, green tea
Niacin (nicotinic acid)	Works with thiamin and riboflavin in energy metabolism; nerve function	Poultry, fish, whole grains, dried beans, peanuts, meat, liver
Pantothenic acid	Metabolism of carbohydrates, fat, and protein	Eggs, organ meats, salmon, yeast, whole grains, legumes

Vitamins & Minerals

Vitamins and minerals are essential for good health. Most vitamins have several important effects on one or more of the body's functions; each is found in many different foods.

Antioxidant vitamins include beta-carotene and vitamins C and E. They may have a protective effect against cancer (lung, colon, breast, cervix, esophagus, oral cavity, stomach, bladder, pancreas, and ovaries), heart disease, and other disorders.

Vitamins and minerals must be obtained through

Note: All good sources of the various vitamins and minerals are listed even though some are high in fat and cholesterol (such as eggs, meat, and oil); these sources should be used in moderate amounts. It is best to choose heart-healthy food sources, however, especially if you are trying to increase consumption of a particular nutrient.

the diet. Healthy people who eat a varied diet of at least 1200 to 1400 calories will meet their vitamin and mineral requirements without needing supplements. Recommended dietary allowances (RDAs) have been established for most vitamins and minerals. Self-prescribing megadoses can be dangerous.

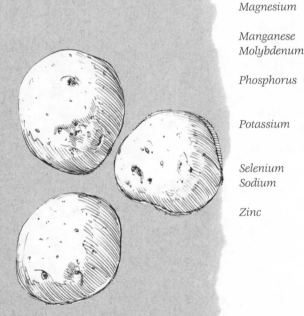

Minerals

Calcium	Development of bones and teeth; proper blood clotting; nerve function; muscle contraction	Dairy products, tofu, oysters, green leafy vegetables, almonds
Chloride	Fluid balance	Table salt, seafoods, milk, meat, eggs
Chromium	Normal glucose metabolism	Yeast, oysters, potatoes, liver, cheese, beef, whole grains
Copper	Component of many enzymes	Peanuts, oysters, whole grains, legumes, nuts, organ meats
Fluoride	Present in bones; beneficial effect on tooth enamel	Fluoridated water; other food varies depending on environment of origin
Iodine	Thyroid hormone function	Seafood, iodized salt
Iron	Transportation of oxygen to the cells	Red meat, egg yolks, whole grains, green leafy vegetables, molasses, shrimp, oysters
Magnesium	Energy production, protein synthesis, muscle contraction, and nerve function	Nuts, legumes, whole grains, dark green vegetables, milk
Manganese	Activator of many enzymes	Fruit, legumes, seeds, nuts, whole grains
Molybdenum	Involved in metabolic processes	Whole grains, legumes, lima beans, organ meats
Phosphorus	Works with calcium in bone and tooth development; energy metabolism	Dairy products, egg yolks, meat, fish, poultry, green leafy vegetables, whole grains, legumes, nuts
Potassium	Fluid balance; acid-base balance	Apricots, potatoes, lima beans, bananas, milk, poultry, avocado, mushrooms, citrus fruits
Selenium	Fat metabolism; antioxidant properties	Cereals, meat, poultry, fish, dairy products
Sodium	Fluid balance; nerve cell conduction; muscle contraction	Table salt, seafood, meats, dairy products
Zinc	Enzyme function, metabolism of proteins	Whole grains, legumes, meat, shellfish, nuts, eggs

Suggested Reading

- American Diabetes Association: *The American Dietetic Association Family Cookbook*. Prentice Hall Press, 1980–1987.
- American Heart Association: *Low-Fat, Low-Cholesterol Cookbook*. Random House, 1989.
- *American Heart Association Kids' Cookbook*. US Times Books, 1993.
- Stan and Jan Berenstain: *The Berenstain Bears and Too Much Junk Food*. Random House, 1985.
- Nancy Clark: *Nancy Clark's Sports Nutrition Guidebook*. Leisure Press, 1990.
- Consumer Guide: *Cholesterol: Your Guide for a Healthy Heart*. Publications International, 1989.
- Edward B. Diethrich and Carol Cohan: *Women and Heart Disease*. Times Books, 1992.
- Marion J. Franz: *Fast-Food Facts: Nutrition and Exchange Values for Fast-Food Restaurants*. DCI Pub., 1990.
- Stanley Gershoff, et al.: *The Tufts University Guide to Total Nutrition*. Harper & Row, 1990.
- Janis Harsila and Evie Hansen: *Light-Hearted Seafood*. National Seafood Educators, 1989.
- Sharon Tyler Herbst: *Food Lover's Companion: Comprehensive Definitions of Over 3000 Food, Wine, and Culinary Terms*. Barron's, 1990.
- Mary Abbott Hess, et al.: *A Healthy Head Start: A Worry Free Guide to Feeding Young Children*. H. Holt, 1990.
- Barbara Kafka: *Microwave Gourmet Healthstyle Cookbook*. William Morrow, 1989.
- Edna Langholz, et al.: *Over 50 and Still Cooking*. Bristol Pub., 1990.
- Jean Mayer and Jeanne P Goldberg: *Dr. Jean Mayer's Diet and Nutrition Guide*. Pharos Books, 1990.
- Harold McGee: *On Food and Cooking: The Science and Lore of the Kitchen*. Charles Scribner's & Sons, McMillan Pub, 1984.
- Dean Ornish: *Dr. Dean Ornish's Program for Reversing Heart Disease: The Only System Scientifically Proven to Reverse Heart Disease Without Drugs or Surgery*. Random House, 1990.
- Jean A.T. Pennington: *Bowes and Church's Food Values of Portions Commonly Used*. Perennial Library, 1989.
- Ellyn Satter: *Child of Mine: Feeding with Love and Good Sense*. Bull Pub., 1986.
- Rodman D. Starke and Mary Winston (eds.): *American Heart Association Low-Salt Cookbook: A Complete Guide to Reducing Sodium and Fat in the Diet*. Times Books, 1990.
- Debra Wasserman and Charles Stahler: *Meatless Meals for Working People: Quick and Easy Vegetarian Recipes*. Vegetarian Resource Group, 1990.

Newsletters

- *Nutrition Action Healthletter*
  Center for Science in the Public Interest
  1501 16th St., NW
  Washington, DC 20036–1499
- *Tufts University Diet and Nutrition Letter*
  P.O. Box 57857
  Boulder, CO 80322–7857

I always choose the plainest food
To mend viscidity of blood.
Hail! water-gruel, healing power,
Of easy access to the poor,...
To thee I fly, by thee dilute—
Through veins my blood doth quicker shoot.

Matthew Green

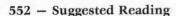

Index